GENERAL GEORGE S. PATTON AND THE ART OF LEADERSHIP

GENERAL GEORGE S. PATTON AND THE ART OF LEADERSHIP

ONE OF AMERICA'S GREATEST EVER GENERALS

WILLIAM NESTER

FRONTLINE
BOOKS

General George S. Patton and the Art of Leadership
One of America's Greatest Ever Generals

First published in Great Britain in 2025 by
Frontline Books
An imprint of Pen & Sword Books Ltd
Yorkshire – Philadelphia

ISBN: 978-1-03612-090-0

Typeset by Lapiz Digital
Printed and bound by CPI UK

The Publisher's authorised representative in the EU for product safety is Authorised Rep Compliance Ltd., Ground Floor, 71 Lower Baggot Street, Dublin D02 P593, Ireland.
www.arccompliance.com

MIX
Paper | Supporting responsible forestry
FSC® C013604

For a complete list of Pen & Sword titles please contact:

PEN & SWORD BOOKS LTD
47 Church Street, Barnsley, South Yorkshire, S70 2AS, UK
E-mail: enquiries@pen-and-sword.co.uk
Website: www.pen-and-sword.co.uk

Or

PEN AND SWORD BOOKS,
1950 Lawrence Road, Havertown, PA 19083, USA
E-mail: uspen-and-sword@casematepublishers.com
Website: www.penandswordbooks.com

CONTENTS

CHARTS

INTRODUCTION

> 'It is as natural for me to be a soldier as it is to breathe.'
>
> 'Genius is an immense capacity for taking pains. Always do more than is required of you. What then of death? Is not the taps of death but the first call to the reveille of eternal life. We live in deeds not years. You can be what you will to be.'
>
> 'Tactics is strategy in miniature and the essence of both is speed.'
>
> 'Leadership … is the thing that wins battles. I have it – but I'll be damned if I can define it. Probably it consists in knowing what you want to do and then doing it and getting mad if anyone steps in the way. Self-confidence and leadership are twin brothers.'
>
> George S. Patton

The art of leadership involves someone with authority over a group getting its members willingly to do what is believed to be necessary to protect or enhance their collective interests. That art is the same for any group's leader from the smallest community to the most powerful nation state, although obviously the challenge swells with the group's numbers, complexity, interests and power versus those of its rivals.

By that measure, George S. Patton excelled at virtually every dimension of leadership, most vitally as a war commander.[1] Patton ranks among America's greatest generals.[2] In that Valhalla he most resembled Thomas 'Stonewall' Jackson and Nathan Bedford Forrest as a fast-moving, hard-hitting general who repeatedly outflanked and devastated enemy forces. As a student of war, he devoured the writings of Julius Caesar and Napolèon for their insights. General John Pershing was his contemporary model and mentor; Patton emulated Pershing's tough, stoic character, and the decisive way he planned and executed strategy, and led troops. 'Leadership,' for Patton,

> is the thing that wins battles. I have it – but I'll be damned if I can define it. Probably it consists in knowing what you want to do and then doing it and getting mad if anyone steps in the way. Self-confidence and leadership are twin brothers.[3]

From his boyhood, Patton aspired to a glorious military career. He explained that: 'It is as natural for me to be a soldier as it is to breathe.'[4] After becoming one, he understood that:

> To be a good soldier, a man must have discipline, self-respect, pride in his unit and in his country, a high sense of duty and obligation to his comrades and to his superiors, and a self-confidence born of demonstrated ability.

At West Point, he defined the leadership and military principles that he later relentlessly asserted in war. One set of maxims shaped everything he attempted:

> Genius is an immense capacity for taking pains. Always do more than is required of you. What then of death? It's not the taps of death but the first call to the reveille of eternal life. We live in deeds not years. You can be what you will to be.

His list of 'Qualities of a Great General' included: 'tactically aggressive (loves a fight); strength of character; steadiness of purpose; acceptance of responsibility; energy; and good health and strength.'[5]

As for waging war, Patton found these essential to strategy:

1. Cut line of communication.
2. Cause enemy to form front to flank.
3. Operate on internal lines.
4. Separate bodies of enemy and fight in Detail.
5. Direct attack.

For cavalry commanders, he identified three qualities:

1. Indomitable courage.
2. Quick perception of right moment to attack.
3. Capacity of inspiring confidence in troops.

As for what to do in battle: 'Tactics is strategy in miniature and the essence of both is speed.' That is as succinct a military maxim for victory as Forrest's 'Get there first with the most.' However, he insisted that 'no set piece of tactics is of any merit in itself, unless it is executed by heroic and disciplined troops who have self-confidence and who have leaders who take care of them.' Victory depended on this key dynamic: 'Battles are won by fire and by movement. The purpose of the movement is to get in a more advantageous place to play on the enemy. This is from the rear or flank.' In any endeavor, flexibility was critical to success: 'successful generals make plans to fit circumstances, but do not try to create circumstances to fit plans.' Among his maxims was 'the best is the enemy of the good,' by which he meant that 'a good plan violently executed now is better than a perfect plan next week. War is a very simple thing, and the determining characteristics are self-confidence, speed, and audacity.'[6]

Implementing plans was as critical as making them and far tougher and longer to realize:

> Commanders must remember that the issuance of an order, or the devising of a plan, is only about five percent of the responsibility of command. The other ninety-five percent is to ensure, by personal observation, or through the interposition of staff officers, that the order is carried out.

Orders should convey ends not means: 'Never tell people how to do things. Tell them what to do and they will surprise you with their ingenuity.'[7]

Technology shapes strategy and tactics which Patton explained as: 'Strategy and tactics do not change, means of applying them differ.'[8] He understood that a nation's style of war reflected its culture:

> The Americans, as a race, are the foremost mechanics in the world. America, as a nation, has the greatest ability for mass production of machines. It therefore behooves us to devise methods of war which exploit our inherent superiority.[9]

Patton was at once a romantic and realist. He loved horses and was a brilliant rider, who naturally sought to be a cavalry commander that led his troops in devastating attacks against the enemy's flanks or deep in its rear like generals Nathan Forrest and Jeb Stuart. To his dismay, World War I's trenches, machine guns and barbed wire rendered cavalry obsolete. Fortunately, it was a short step from horseman to tanker. He explained:

> The Tanks were truly a great opportunity for me ... I am fitted for it as I have imagination and daring and exceptional mechanical ability.

> I believe Tanks will be much more important than aviation and the man on the ground will reap the benefit ... Had I gone in the infantry I would have had one of hundreds of battalions and might have been in reserve on the day of the big fight, spending ... my time like a rat in a trench. In the Tanks one is always in the attacks.[10]

The key tactical question of

> whether infantry or tanks lead in attacking is determined by the character of the ground and of the enemy resistance. Whenever the ground permits tanks to advance rapidly, even with the certainty of loss from mine fields, they should lead. Through dense woods or against prepared positions or unlocated anti-tank guns, infantry leads, followed closely by tanks, which act as supporting artillery.[11]

During the Tunisian campaign, Patton could only partly assert his tank warfare ideas. He was given temporary command of II Corps after its devastating defeat at Kasserine Pass, and for forty-three days tried to rebuild its ranks, supplies and morale, fend off German attacks, then launch counterattacks before being recalled to plan the Sicily campaign. In Sicily, he was free to wage tank warfare on he envisioned it, especially the advance across the island to capture Palermo. Later, he proudly wrote that:

> [F]uture students of the Command and General Staff School will study the campaign of Palermo as a classic example of the use of tanks. I held them back far enough so that the enemy could not tell where they were to be used; then when the infantry had found the hole, the tanks went through and in large numbers and fast. Such methods assure victory and reduce losses.[12]

His Third Army's advances across northern France and central Germany were even swifter, bolder, and sweeping.

Patton was a thoroughly professional soldier and officer whose commanders lauded him in their efficiency reports. For instance, amid the North African campaign General Dwight D. Eisenhower extolled Patton as 'superior' who renders

> willing and generous support to the plans of his superiors regardless of his personal views ... Of the approximately 150 general officers of his grade personally known to me, I would rate General Patton number 5. Additional remarks: This officer is energetic, courageous, well informed, impulsive; definitely a leader type; devoted to the service.[13]

Patton led from the front and tried to inspire his troops by being a model officer that exemplified bravery, problem-solving, tactical innovation and decisiveness. He insisted that 'wars are won by the physical courage, energy, and initiative of junior officers.' He elaborated:

> It may well be that the greatest soldiers have possessed superior intellects, may have been thinkers, but this was not their dominant characteristic ... [They] owed their success to indomitable wills and tremendous energy in execution and achieved their initial hold on the hearts of their troops by acts of demonstrated valor.[14]

At war, Patton was in near constant motion from his headquarters to rear echelon and frontline troops, everywhere exhorting them to greater efforts or acting decisively to overcome challenges, at times enduring shell fire, strafing, mines, snipers and other dangers. He explained his obsession with living up to his own fiery words about leadership: 'I have always talked blood and murder and was looked upon as an advocate of close up fighting. I could never look myself in the face if I was a staff officer and comparatively safe.'[15]

Patton understood the dynamic matrix between 'hard' or physical and 'soft' or psychological power, whereby the latter usually surpasses the former in determining results. He insisted that a strong mind can overcome the toughest matter, explaining:

> I am not a brilliant soldier. So far I have been quite a successful one because I am always fully confident that I can do what I am told to do, and I have my sense developed to the point where I let no personal interests or danger intervene.[16]

War leadership's most vital duty is getting soldiers to do things that emotionally they would rather not do, like risking their lives and limbs and killing and maiming others. That in turn depends on intensely training troops in appropriate skills, discipline and motivation through a virtuous cycle of physical conditioning, technical instruction, teamwork, division of labor and confidence in their ability to do whatever they were ordered to do. He explained the psychological dynamic among pride, discipline, obedience, skill and courage:

> All human beings have an innate resistance to obedience. Discipline removes this resistance and, by constant repetition, makes obedience habitual and subconscious ... No sane man is unafraid in battle, but discipline produces in him a form of vicarious courage which, with his

> manhood, makes for victory. Self-respect grows directly from discipline ... Pride, in turn, stems from self-respect ... Self-confidence, the greatest military virtue, results from the demonstrated ability derived from the acquisition of all the preceding qualities and from exercise in the use of weapons.[17]

Patton was a martinet. He not only pushed his troops relentlessly forward in pursuit or combat against the enemy but insisted that they strictly adhere to rules on dress and daily shaving. Whether more troops hated or admired him is impossible to determine but undoubtedly he provoked more fear than love. In what can be called the 'Patton treatment', he played at once good and bad cop with officers who failed in their duties, castigating and extolling, instructing and inspiring, and threatening and rewarding to provoke fear and evoke pride.

Among the paradoxes that made Patton a great leader was that while he reveled in being the center of adoring attention, he downplayed his own contributions to successes and celebrated those of his colleagues and troops. After a campaign ended and his adrenaline resided, Patton typically felt mingled gratitude, elation, pride, and humility. For instance, after Sicily's conquest, he wrote to his wife Beatrice that:

> I have lived a long time in the last thirty days, but I feel humble. It was the superior ability of the American soldier, the wonderful efficiency of our mechanical transport, the work of Bradley, Keyes, and the Army Staff that did the trick. I just came along for the ride ... I certainly love war.[18]

Eisenhower understood how critical Patton's tough, confident, emotional soft power dimension of leadership was to his victorious campaigns:

> Patton is preeminently a combat commander. Many people fail to realize that the first thing that usually slows up operations is an element of caution, fatigue or doubt on the part of a higher commander. Patton is never affected by these and, consequently, his troops are not affected. Several of his subordinate commanders turned in magnificent performances in the late show, but if they had an example of pessimism, caution, and delay above them, they could not possibly have acted as they did.[19]

Patton had a secret flaw that inflicted him with deep shame and feelings of intellectual inferiority. At West Point, he admitted to his future wife Beatrice that: 'I am either very lazy or very stupid or both for it is beastly hard for me to learn and as a natural result I hate to study.'[20] Dyslexia delayed his ability to read and write, and he remained a dreadful speller. He overcompensated by trying to excel in sports and war. Eventually, he overcame his dyslexia and intellectually bloomed. Gradually, he improved his skills and became a vivid, insightful analyst and storyteller. Over the decades sixteen of his articles appeared in various military publications including *Cavalry Journal* and *Army and Navy Journal*. Although he was an average student at West Point, he was an honor graduate of both Fort Leavenworth's Command and General Staff school and Fort McNair's War College.

Patton's greatest attribute was his drive to be the best at whatever he chose or was ordered to do. He recognized that developing a successful military career depended not just on will and chance but on incessant training and study. One crucial ingredient was to

> read military history in its earliest and hence crudest form and to follow it down in natural sequence permitting the mind to grow with his subject until he can grasp without effort the most abstruce question of the science of war.[21]

Yet he believed that instincts were just as vital as skills in being a successful leader: 'I have a sixth sense in war as I used to have in fencing, and … can put myself in the enemies head and I am also willing to take chances.'[22] His campaign and battle plans often suddenly came to him after pondering the problem for a while. At times, he slept on a command question and reawakened with the solution. He reflected that:

> Whether ideas like this are the result of inspiration or insomnia I don't know, but nearly every tactical idea I have had popped into my head like Minerva and not as historians attempt to describe generals who work things out on paper in a laborious manner.[23]

He thought deeply about and carefully observed an array of subjects and often reached insights. For instance, as a West Point cadet he wrote:

> I have recently evolved a theory which is of great comfort to me. Namely I think that people who are not musical are usually not good at languages because their ear is so constructed that the fine differences of sounds do not affect them hence they cannot pronounce.[24]

He was a good singer and eventually became proficient at French.

As for Patton's personality, actor George C. Scott brilliantly embodied him in the 1970 movie as immaculately uniformed, ramrod stiff and gravel voiced whose words mingled poetry and profanity, wisdom and crudity. Only the voices differed, with Scott's baritone and Patton's tenor.

Patton created and played his own persona as the tough combat officer and eventually general with machismo, boasts, scowls and curses. He called that act putting on his 'war face'. Most officers actually have the opposite personality, of being taciturn, cerebral and polite equally to colleagues and common soldiers. During World War II, he initially welcomed but soon regretted his 'Blood and Guts Patton' image. Countless soldiers retorted to the notion with 'Yea, his guts and our blood.' He admitted that:

> This 'Blood and Gut' stuff is quite distasteful to me. I am a very severe disciplinarian because ... without discipline to send men into battle is to commit murder. This war makes higher demands on courage and discipline than any war of which I have known. But when you see men who have demonstrated discipline and courage, killed and wounded, it naturally raises a lump in your throat and sometimes produces a tear.[25]

Indeed, Patton's eyes frequently teared and his voice choked when he tended severely maimed soldiers on the battlefield or visited them in hospitals. He wept openly when his aide and friend Major Richard Jenson was killed in Tunisia.

Despite his countless addresses to his troops, Patton never mastered the art of public speaking. Journalist George Fisher recalled that:

> He never talked very long and he certainly followed no convention of finished oratory. He would start off rather slowly, and his squeaky, high-pitched voice did not carry very well ... I had the personal feeling that the General regularly got himself punch-drunk with profanity ... The reaction of the troops was somewhat mixed. There were many, of course, to whom roughness of oral intercourse was normal, and it was Patton's habit to act as if this were true of every man in uniform ... Patton was forever preaching a gospel of warfare that was somehow alien and antipathetic to young Americans who had reluctantly and only temporarily suffered themselves to become soldiers.[26]

Patton, of course, would insist that transforming flabby civilians into hardened warriors was his most critical military duty.

Patton's rising fame attracted more attention from journalists and the public, which of course further boosted his image. He loved being the center of attention and often either unwittingly or deliberately uttered controversial remarks that stirred more interest in him.

During World War I, newspaper reports of some controversial statements he made prompted his father to write him this psychologically profound advice:

> I have been worrying for fear that the 'gift of gab' you have developed may get you in trouble – unless restrained such a gift is always dangerous. The temptation to say smart or striking things is hard to resist – and it is only the next day that cold reason condemns. You are now 34 and a Col[onel] and the dignity going with your rank invests what you say with more importance so I hope in your speeches you will be very careful ... Another gift you have developed I really regret ... is ... the ability to write verse upon vulgar & smutty subjects ... The very men to whom you...recite such stuff ... will laugh – and apparently enjoy it – but you have really lowered yourself in their eyes – above all it lacks dignity.[27]

Patton's quick-temper and provocative views often overpowered his self-control. Twice that cost him an army command. During Germany's occupation in August 1945, he casually quipped to several reporters that being a Nazi in Germany was no different from being a Republican or Democrat in the United States. For that Eisenhower relieved him from Third Army's command. Most notoriously, during the Sicily campaign he slapped two soldiers suffering combat fatigue that he accused of malingering. When Eisenhower reprimanded him, he defended himself as trying to restore their sense of self-respect and fighting spirit. Eisenhower penalized Patton by promoting his deputy, General Omar Bradley, over him to command First Army that would invade Normandy.

Patton provoked opposing views. Colonel Redding Perry of 2nd Armored Division recalled that:

> The amazing thing about George was that he was just a bit of everything – brave and timid, tender and harsh, coarse and poetic, sacrilegious and religious – all the opposites mixed up into a really legendary, adorable character.

Journalist and novelist John Marquand, who at times covered Patton, lambasted him as 'a tackles, high-strung, profane officer with a one-cell juvenile mind.'[28] His harshest critic was Omar Bradley, first his deputy then commander, who disparaged Patton's character and had mixed views of his generalship.[29]

Behind the macho mask, Patton harbored deep insecurities and fears about his courage and masculinity. In his sophomore year at West Point, he confessed to his parents that:

> I have lived 19 years and yet it seems that I have wasted them … Even in games I have never been a great success. I am fare in everything but good in nothing … Other boys appear to make successes but though [I] want to I dont [*sic*] succeed. Perhaps … I lack that small fraction of courage, will power, or what ever it is which makes them succeed.[30]

While recovering in a field hospital from his wound during the battle of Meuse-Argonne, Patton penned this poem *Fear* with remarkable lines like:

> I am that dreadful blighting thing …
> Like rust that gnaws the faultless blade,
> Like microbes to the blood.
> I know no mercy and no truth,
> The young I blight the old I slay.
> Regret stalks darkly in my wake.
> And ignominy dogs my way.
> Sometimes in virtuous garb I rove,
> With facile talk of easier way,
> Seducing, where I dare not rape,
> Young manhood from honor's way…
> I bow all heads, and break all hearts.
> All owe me homage – I am FEAR![31]

Patton's dread that he lacked courage spurred him to overcompensate by taking unnecessary risks in sports and war. He explained that:

> The word fearless is a misnomer. All men fear, and some show it less than others, hence when we say that officers must be brave we mean they must show fear less – be more stoical. And this too may be developed.[32]

During his campaigns, he came under rifle, machine gun, shell and bomb fire scores of times. Amidst his 1943 Sicily campaign, he finally mastered normal reactions at danger for self-preservation:

> The first afternoon they shelled us … and some of the fragments would howl overhead. I was disgusted to find that my pulse went up – I timed it – but soon I got my self [*sic*] in hand. Mostly I can have a shell hit or mine go off quite close without winking or ducking. This is a great asset,

> and besides if they are going to get you, they hit you before you hear them. One must be an actor.[33]

As both a daredevil and accident prone, Patton sporadically racked up ever more severe injuries throughout his life. Just from 1905 to 1924, he suffered eighteen broken bones, four lacerations, a dislocated ankle, two concussions, severe burns to his face, gunshot through his hip and five severe head injuries.[34] A horse kick and car wreck inflicted his concussions. Stoically, he lived with chronic and worsening aches and pains. He eventually died not in combat but from an automobile crash that crushed his spine and eventually caused his heart and lungs to collapse.

His personality changed with time, and not for the better. As a boy, he was well mannered and even keeled but as he aged his moods swung more erratically from rage to tears, and from fierce confrontation to abject contrition. His concussions inflicted and harshened a medical condition called 'subdural hematomas' where blood swells with other fluids in his brain.[35] Those concussions may have also aggravated his narcissism or obsession with promoting himself, seeking glory and adulation from others, and trying to surpass and defeat rivals with soaring victories and deeds. However, that narcissism's foundation was genetic exacerbated by his parents spoiling him as a child.[36]

Patton seesawed between elation and despair, rage and compassion. He could chew out a subordinate for some mistake in the morning and comfort him for a similar mistake in the afternoon. Off duty, he was mostly genial and humorous. His humor was deeply felt and observed, although mostly ironic or ribald. That combined with his authoritarian, pragmatic outlook produced quips like this:

> I am personally sorry for Mussolini because I had a great admiration for a man who could do so much with so little, and it was a typically Italian stunt to murder him. I think he should have been properly hanged.[37]

Patton was a devout Episcopalian in practice but not theology. He believed in Providence, that God favored some individuals for special purposes, and he was among them. God had chosen him to be a great military commander and would protect him along that dangerous journey. He penned this revealing passage two nights before his task force invaded Morocco:

> In forty hours I shall be in battle, with little information and on the spur of the moment I will have to make most momentous decisions,

> but I believe one's spirit enlarges with responsibility, and, with God's help, shall make them and make them right. It seems that all my life has been pointed to this moment. When this job is done, I presume I will be pointed to the next step in the ladder of destiny. If I do my full duty, the rest will take care of itself.[38]

Patton was a romantic and mystic. He began composing poems as a youth and penned hundreds during his life. His poems are precocious and deeply felt if rarely profound. He was easily moved to tears. He immersed himself in history and modeled himself on the heroic deeds of great courageous warriors of earlier times. He also communed with war dead whenever he could. During a visit to Gettysburg as a West Point cadet, he strolled alone on Cemetery Hill and

> let the spirits of the dead thousands laid there in ordered rows sink deep in me. Then just as the sun sank ... I walked down to the scene of Pickett's charge ... and ... where ... two of my great uncles died I watched the wonder of the day go out. The sunset painted a dull red the fields over which the terrible advance was made and I could almost see them coming growing fewer and fewer, while around and beyond me stood calmly the very cannon that had so punished them. There were some quail calling in the trees near by ... I think it takes an evening like that to make one understand what men will do in battle.[39]

During World War I's Battle of Meuse-Argonne, he was lying grievously wounded in a shell hole when he had a near spiritual experience:

> I was overwhelmed by a deep feeling of warmth and peace and comfort, and of love. I know profoundly death was related to life ... how everlasting the soul – and the love was all around me, like a subdued light.[40]

After his father died, he twice encountered his ghost, first five days after his death and then at the cemetery where he was buried.[41]

Patton believed in reincarnation and sensed he had been a warrior in many past ages. At times, he glimpsed scenes from what he assumed were former lives. One night as a cadet, a gray man with folded arms and the head of an Egyptian mummy appeared beside his bed and stared down at him and

> was not the least bothered by my sitting up but took his time and finally vanished and left the open door. Strange to say I was not very much

> frightened ... I had not been reading or thinking of Egypt. Perhaps he was me as I was 4000 years ago.[42]

During World War I, Patton had two experiences that bolstered his belief in reincarnation. When he was being driven in the countryside around Langres where his tank corps was based, he identified first an ancient Roman army camp and then a theater before they came into view, and later concluded that he had somehow spent part of a previous life in that area.[43]

Patton captured his belief that he was an avatar warrior with these lines:

> So forever in the future
> Shall I battle as of yore
> Dying to be born a fighter
> But to die again once more.[44]

Patton could confess his weaknesses and fears to those he loved and trusted, like his parents and wife. In his senior year at West Point, he and his long-time sweetheart, Beatrice Banning Ayer, decided to marry. Her father opposed the marriage unless Patton gave up a military career and embarked on a more lucrative, secure profession. In one of his more revealing letters, Patton explained his conundrum to his parents:

> All my life I have done everything I could to become a soldier for I feel it is my job and that war will come ... When however I proposed to Beatrice I did something from instinct and against reason. At least its seems unlogical because she does not like war ... I have no strength of character ... I think of Beat[rice] and straight away stop all sane mental manoevers and fall down and worship her ... Would an embrionic [*sic*] great man have acted as I did or do I show myself a mess?[45]

Patton adored Beatrice. While on campaign in Mexico, he confessed to her father that 'I miss her terribly because the longer I am married to her the more I love her. She is so wonderful and always new.'[46] She was indeed a lovely woman, pretty, charming and bright. She also had the patience to be a military officer's wife and endure hardship posts and long absences of her husband on duties that might kill or maim him. He was unable to share joy with her and their family during numerous birthdays, Christmases, weddings parties and their son's birth; nor was he there when her parents died. She provided Patton an emotional keel that kept him from dead-ending or outright destroying his career with erratic acts or language. He listened carefully to her advice and critiques. She edited his articles and other writings. As a bonus, her inherited wealth supported their lifestyle of horses, servants and dinner parties.

He admitted that 'all I try to do is for the effect it will have on you. In fact my attitude towards you is more that of a lover uncertain of his chances than of a husband. Still it is a good way to be.' They had a loving, passionate relationship. When away, he tried writing to her daily about his activities, hopes, gains and setbacks, along with stories and poetry, at times bawdy. Yet sometimes his barracks humor got the better of him. On campaign in Mexico, he warned her: 'I enclose to [two] disgusting poems I have composed. Tear them up.' The next morning, he wrote: 'On rereading those poems I am sorry I sent them to you, you will think me nasty but at the time I thought them very clever.' One evening from France's frontline, he wrote: 'Here is a nasty joke. You will like it. A wife once woke up in the night and said to her husband, "John if that is your elbow sticking in my back turn over; if it is not I will."'[47]

Most vitally, Patton could confess to Beatrice all the fears, failures and rages that he hid behind his scowling 'war face' or jovial 'man's man face.' For instance, in October 1917 as an overworked staff officer at Pershing's Paris headquarters far from the frontline, he wrote that 'I would give a lot to have you consol me and tell me that I amounted to a lot even when I know I don't.'[48] Yet at times, he vented his deep frustrations and anger against her, provoking her to anger and tears.

Patton was a distant but strict father to his three children, treating them more like miniature recruits to be bullied into conformity rather than children to be lovingly nurtured. Biographer Martin Blumenson revealed how brutal he could be: 'Once when he [was] rehearsing his young daughter for a horse show, he berated her constantly, criticizing and cursing her, finding everything wrong.' Finally, he shouted, 'Get off that Goddamned horse and let me show you how to do it.' As he mounted and 'spurred toward the obstacle, she was heard to say, "Dear God, please let that son of a bitch break his neck."'[49]

Yet, on rare occasions, Patton could be understanding of a child's failure. Amid his preparations to invade Sicily, he learned that his son had flunked math and would have to repeat his year at West Point, just like he had in his freshman year. With mingled concern and humor, Patton wrote:

> I am naturally very distressed about George's failure but apparently he came by his mathematical ability very naturally, and I now feel convinced he will end up as at least a lieutenant general, that is, if he continues to follow so accurately in my footsteps.[50]

When he was an adult, his son gave this appraisal:

> He was a first-class father. He taught me all kinds of things: to shoot, to ride, and we worked on ship models together ... When I was a little boy I was scared to death of him. Then when I got to be about 11, I just decided one day I wasn't going to [be] scared ... of him. He never laid a hand on me, not once. He locked me in my room once. That was the worst thing he ever did.[51]

In England, as Patton prepared his Third Army for deployment in Normandy, he shared these thoughts with his son at West Point that mingled advice and explanation of himself:

> There are two types of successful soldiers. Those who get on by being unobtrusive and those who get on by being obstrusive. I am of the latter type and seem to be rare and unpopular; but it is my method. One has to choose a system and stick to it. People who are not themselves are nobody. To be a successful soldiers [*sic*], you must know history ... You must read biography and especially autobiography ... Soldiers, all men in fact, are hero-worshippers. Officers with a flair for command realize this and emphasize in their conduct, dress, and deportment the qualities they seek to produce in their men.[52]

The most vivid, insightful description of Patton was by Captain Betty South, in charge of twenty-five nurses at a hospital in France during World War II:

> I looked at the great Third Army field commander proposing the toast. His magnificent, tall figure excited my admiration, but I was surprised at the thin, high-pitched voice that so poorly matched his striking looks and impressive bearing. The brick-red face, with his round, receding forehead sparsely framed by silvery-white hair, magnetized me chiefly because of the eyes. For in those blue eyes there was an intensity that burned with white-hot heat. There was arrogance unspeakable there, authority unrelinquished even to his superior officer, the Supreme Allied Commander, whom he was toasting. In the depth of those eyes there was a breath-taking boldness, utter fearlessness, naked daring, headlong defiance, proud contempt. Sparks of haughty aloofness,

> rude scornfulness, indomitable willfulness flew from his eyes to sear all about him in the room. Stark egotism and love of glory leapt out from behind the thin lashes, mixed with the immeasurable assurance and unshaken confidence in his own ability that unceasing hard work, personal fortune, and social position bestowed upon him … Yet … while we were still in the drawing room, I had furtively watched this great general … and I saw a tired, aging man, a sorrowful, solitary man, a lonely man … I sense the … shallow places of his being, as well as the stormy depths … I watched the general's gentle twinkling eyes, full of infectious humor when something amused him, change abruptly to flashing, angry blazes at something else that displeased him … His agility in leaping back and forth between vulgar and shocking profanity and cultured gentlemanly speech bewildered me.[53]

General George S. Patton and the Art of Leadership is his most psychologically penetrating biography that captures the paradoxical character behind his brilliant military feats and often dismaying failures. Throughout Patton explains his values and deeds through hundreds of quotes along with scores of insights from those who knew him – comrades and critics alike.

Chapter 1

BECOMING

> 'I am different from other men my age. All they want to do is live happily and die old. I would be willing to live in torture, die tomorrow if for one day I could be realy [*sic*] great.'
>
> 'Of course I may be a dreamer but … I will do my best to attain what I consider – rightly or wrongly – my destiny.'
>
> George S. Patton

George Smith Patton Jr was born on 11 November 1885, in San Gabriel, California, 10 miles east of Los Angeles. His parents were George Smith Patton Sr and Ruth Wilson. His father was a successful lawyer and businessman, who eventually became a Los Angelos district attorney. His mother was the daughter of Benjamin Wilson, a mountain man who settled in San Gabriel, developed a vast estate called Lake Vineyard Rancho that produced wine, various fruits, cattle, sheep and horses, and served a term as Los Angeles' mayor. Two years after Patton's birth came his sister Anne, called Nita. The Patton household also included his aunt, Nannie, his mother's unmarried sister along with servants.

The Pattons produced numerous soldiers after immigrating to Virginia in the eighteenth century. During the American Civil War, sixteen Pattons fought for the Confederacy and three were killed defending it. His grandfather graduated second in his class at the Virginia Military Institute (VMI) in Lexington, rose through the rebel ranks to command 22nd Virginia at New Market, and was killed at Winchester. Patton's father attended VMI then moved to Los Angeles where he studied law.

'Georgie' as he was known enjoyed a carefree life as a country boy who learned to ride and shoot before he learned how to read and write. He was nice and polite but also high-strung, sensitive and cried easily. He was sickly with bouts of whooping cough, measles and tonsillitis until his tonsils were removed.

His parents, aunt and sister embraced him with affection and indulged his demands. He was loving to his mother, aunt and sister, and adored his father for all his professional feats and manliness. He recalled that: 'When I went to tell Papa and Mama good night I used to kiss Papa many times and Mama only once. This was childish and thoughtless.' He also made this startling confession:

> Occasionally Nita and I would wear each others [*sic*] clothes to dinner. One night when I was wearing her clothes Papa began talking about [Robert E.] Lee and I got all excited and when he told me that since I was dressed as a girl I should not get so bloodthirsty I cried.[54]

His later excessive machismo may have partly been attempts to purge such early transgressions.

He attributes his moderate drinking of alcohol to his father's attitude and behavior similar to southern Europeans: 'We always had white wine for midday dinner on Sunday and Nita and I were always given a little.' His father did not lock his liquor cabinet and told his son he could drink whiskey or any other libation whenever he liked. 'Papa's idea was to make me think drinking common place and so set less store by it. Also he used to impress on me that an ambitious man could not afford to drink.'[55]

Patton was tutored at home until he was 11, when his parents enrolled him at the Classical School for Boys at nearby Pasadena. He studied there from September 1897 to June 1903. Those classical studies reinforced his romantic worship of his ancestor and ancient heroes, and desire to become a modern-day warrior. Yet he underperformed as a student for reasons that perplexed him and his family.

Dyslexia is a complex affliction not understood at the time. The difficulty dyslexics have in reading and writing tends to harm their self-esteem. Patton biographer Carlo D'Este explained that dyslexics tend to suffer 'an inability to concentrate, sharp mood swings, hyperactivity, obsessiveness, impulsiveness, compulsiveness, and feelings of inferiority and stupidity.' Many overcompensate by playing rough sports, taking risks and boasting. D'Este concludes that dyslexia is 'the key not only to understanding the source of Patton's drive to succeed but of the authoritarian, macho, warrior personality he created for himself.'[56] He eventually developed a photographic memory to finesse his dyslexia. From a young age, he memorized and wrote poems.

Aged 17, Patton was attracted to Beatrice Banning Ayer. She was then a sweet, pretty, precocious 16-year-old, the daughter of a wealthy family with a mansion in Boston and country estate Avalon at Pride's Crossing near Salem, Massachusetts, and a distant cousin. She was fluent in French and an accomplished musician who played the piano, mandolin and guitar, and composed songs. Her father Frederic Ayer was president of the American Woolen Company in Lawrence. She and her family joined the Pattons on vacation on Catalina Island in August 1902. After the Ayers returned home, Patton began correspondence with Beatrice that seven years later blossomed into romance.

***

Patton was obsessed with emulating and surpassing his illustrious ancestors and determined to pursue a military career. When he was 18, his father asked Senator Thomas Bard to sponsor him for West Point, explaining that:

> Since his earliest boyhood my son has been possessed by the ambition to enter the army, an instinct that may possibly be accounted for by the hereditary effects of ... blood. He is a well grown athletic manly boy ... he has a good head, a sound heart, and is, I believe, a clean minded gentleman.[57]

Bard expressed his reluctance given Patton's mediocre grades. His father mobilized half a dozen business, lawyer and army officer friends to recommend his son to Bard. The senator finally agreed to reconsider if Patton studied for a year at VMI as preparation for West Point. Patton entered VMI in September 1903. He excelled there, meriting among ninety-three students second place in history and English, sixth in drawing, ninth in mathematics and tenth in Latin. Astonishingly, he earned no demerits and received an overall evaluation of 'excellent'.[58] On 15 February 1904, he took an exam with sixteen boys required by Bard and scored the highest. That won him Bard's recommendation to the army on 4 March 1904. Patton journeyed to Fort McHenry, Baltimore for the physical exam and was ecstatic to receive the army's official appointment, dated 24 May 1904.[59]

Patton entered the United States Military Academy at West Point on 16 June 1904, with a class of 148 cadets. He was then 6 foot and 1 inch tall and a lean, muscular 167 pounds. Given Patton's prevailing image as a scowling, profane martinet and brilliant general, it is hard to realize that he was once a bashful, awkward, insecure youth. A few days after arriving at the academy, he penned this letter:

> Dear Mother,
> West Point is pretty nice and so far I have been treated a lot better than V.M.I. The corps are quite nice and they never touch you or sware. We have to take a bath every night and have but eight minutes to take it. They make us shave every day ... The two fellows who I am in with now are very nice and work hard and try to keep the room and them selves [*sic*] clean but they are not gentlemen in the sense of being refined and using good grammar ... Did Beatrice get the flowers. [*sic*] I was sorry that I did not get a twenty dollar bunch as I had to turn in all my money and so might have just as well have spent it ...
>
> Your loving son.
> Geo. S. Patton.[60]

Despite trying as hard as he could, others surpassed him in mind and body. He tried out for the football team but dislocated his shoulder. He did poorly his first year, flunked mathematics, and was held back to the 1909 class with 155 cadets. The seemingly endless setbacks and disappointments forced him to question destiny and his choice of career. In his sophomore year, he confessed to his father that:

> I have always thought I was a military genius or at least that I was or would be a great general. Well looking over the situation ... I see little in which to base such a belief ... I am neither quicker nor brighter ... than other men nor do they look upon me as a leader.[61]

Yet even then Patton sensed he was a budding warrior and anachronism perhaps destined for greatness, which he conveyed in this letter to his father:

> In fact from what I have seen here and at the Institute I belong to a different class perhaps almost extinct or one which may have never existed yet far removed from these lazy, patriotic, or peace soldiers as heaven is from hell. I know that my ambition is selfish and cold yet it is not a selfish for instead of sparing me, it makes me exert my self to the utter most to attain an end which will do neither me nor any one else any good. Of course I may be a dreamer but ... I will do my best to attain what I consider – rightly or wrongly – my destiny.[62]

Despite his worsening doubts, he saw himself as separate and above the other cadets:

> When you get this letter, it will have been just a little over a year … since I started to learn the profession of killing my brothers … And in this year of contact with the world my respect for man has dwindled instead of increasing. For even among the best and the best I take it are those who devote themselves to the service of Mars, there is not the self sacrificing love of fame or self denying … that I feel and which I expected of others but rather a languid lacitude careless indifferent or hazy uncertainty not becoming in my estimation a soldier or a man. But let this be: the fewer of a species there are the greater is its individual worth. And if my nature prove [*sic*] incapable of the task I have set my self or if the opportunity never comes I can at least die happy in my own vanity knowing that I stood alone and that alone I fell.[63]

Patton gradually improved as a student and athlete. He became skilled at running, winning the 120-yard and 220-yard races during field day in June 1908. He made the football team but was relegated to third string. He received promotions to corporal, sergeant major and adjutant, and earned the grade of expert rifleman. He became a martinet, issuing demerits to underclassmen for minute infractions. Those who loathed him called him 'spooney' or obsessed with appearances and a 'bootslick' or sycophant to his superiors. Most fellow cadets respected rather than liked him, and he had only a few casual and no close friends. The 1909 edition of West Point's yearbook, *The Howitzer*, did generously and accurately note that: 'We believe that George's heart, despite its armored exterior, has a big soft spot inside.'[64]

While Patton's self-doubts diminished, they still haunted him. He feared 'that I am a characterless, lazy, stupid yet ambitious dreamer; who will degenerate into a third rate second lieutenant and never command any thing [*sic*] more than a platoon.'[65]

He recognized that character building was the academy's key contribution to a cadet's development:

> I am sure that the spirit of self-confidence and a sense of duty, which we get at West Point, is the most vital characteristic a soldier can have, and I would deeply regret any changes in our curriculum which would make it easier to learn.[66]

Looking back, he took pride in one key assertion of courage and leadership during his West Point days. He abhorred the cadet practice during meals of 'silence' or standing at attention when an unpopular officer appeared:

> I have always been opposed to such acts, as … it is very close to mutiny … On one occasion, when I happened to be in command of the Battalion and had marched it to lunch, the officer in charge entered, and I immediately saw that a 'Silence' was about to be perpetrated … I therefore called the Corps to attention and marched them home without lunch. The officer … criticized me for my action until I explained why I did it.[67]

Patton's pending graduation and officer's commission infused him with confidence to commit a bold act. He spent his Christmas 1908 leave with Beatrice and her family. Over the preceding seven years, he and Beatrice had exchanged chaste letters and visits. During that time, he dated other girls but none intrigued him as much as Beatrice for her beauty, passion, high spirits, sense of adventure and horse-riding skills. All along he tried to dismiss his attraction to her as 'puppy love' but finally realized that Beatrice 'is the only girl I ever loved.' Now he confessed his love for her and asked her to marry him. She assured him that she shared his feellings. That astounded him because

> my boldness in daring to tell you I loved you strikes me with over powering force. I don't see how I ever did it for I am nothing and have neither prospect nor possibility of becoming some one [*sic*] and … it seems horribly wicked to have caused such a wonderful girl as you to fall in love with a fool … Dreams happy dreams that melt like fog before the sun of reality.[68]

There was just one obstacle. He had to secure her father's approval.

Rather than confront Ayer in his home, Patton waited until he returned to West Point. He wrote to him that 'I have loved Beatrice ever since the summer in in California' and asked him to embrace their marriage.[69] Ayer liked Patton but did not want a soldier for a son-in-law. He gave Patton the tough choice that he could have a military career or Beatrice, but not both, and tried to convince him to quit the army by appealing to his manhood:

> A man in the army must … always feel unsettled – That his location and home life are subject to the dictation … of another whom he may despise or even hate. A man like you should be independent of such control – His own master – Free to act and develop in the open world … Every independent man should choose his own course in life.[70]

Hamlet-like, Patton hesitated to make that cruel choice. In his reply, he suggested that he would abandon his profession yet admitted:

> I am different from other men my age. All they want to do is live happily and die old. I would be willing to live in torture, die tomorrow if for one day I could be realy [*sic*] great ... There is inside me a burning something ... At least I think a man can not [*sic*] do wrong to try.[71]

For now, Patton and Beatrice had to shelve any marriage plan.

***

Patton graduated from West Point ranked 46th of 103 graduates on 11 June 1909. The 1909 army included 84,971 troops, with 4,299 officers and 80,672 enlisted men.[72] Second Lieutenant Patton's first assignment was to 15th Cavalry's K Troop at Fort Sheridan, Illinois on 12 September 1909. In his free time, Patton began writing articles on military affairs for various publications like the *Journal of the United States Cavalry Association*.

Like any good leader, Patton partly progressed through at times embarrassing trials and errors. At Fort Sheridan, he erupted at a private who left a horse untied in the stable. He ordered him to run and tie the horse then run back. When the soldier walked instead, he cursed him and ordered him to run, which he did as his comrades laughed at him. Patton realized that he had humiliated the soldier, assembled the company and apologized. He found that 'one of the hardest things I ever did. I think though I am glad I did it now that it is done.'[73] That was his sole indiscretion. Otherwise, Patton was a model junior officer. In his efficiency report, Captain Francis Marshall described him as

> a young man of especial promise. He is the most enthusiastic soldier of my acquaintance and misses no chance to improve. I am confident that as he develops he will be an especially valuable officer. I ... know him to be efficient, loyal, and capable.[74]

***

Meanwhile, Patton and Beatrice continued to exchange forlorn love letters. Beatrice tried to change her father's mind by locking herself in her room and staging a hunger strike, alleviated each midnight when she lowered by rope a basket that her younger sister filled with food.[75]

Ayer remained adamant until he received in February 1910 a letter from Patton detailing the financial assets his parents gave him and promising to leave the army if he discovered a more appealing career. Ayer finally granted not only approval but explained:

> my custom when my children have married and left our home was to give them a monthly income, and [I] shall do the same for Beatrice … I admire your firmness of purpose in sticking to the army until more strongly tempted by another occupation, and with every good wish for your early and steady advancement.
>
> I am Sincerely, your friend.
> F. Ayer.[76]

Patton promised Beatrice's mother, Ellen,

> to take the best care in the world of her and keep her happy … When I think of marrying Beatrice and her leaving home for me it frightens and surprises me. Frightness, at the thought of the wonder of it and of the vastness of my responsibility.[77]

Patton and Beatrice married at St John's Episcopal Church near the Ayers family mansion Avalon at Beverly Farms, Massachusetts on 26 May 1910. They honeymooned in England for most of June 1910 then moved her most cherished possessions to Patton's quarters at Fort Sheridan. Beatrice was soon pregnant and gave birth to a daughter, they called Beatrice, on 11 March 1911.

Patton experienced not joy but horror at the sight of his newborn child and actually bolted from the room and vomited in the kitchen sink. Biographer Carlo D'Este explained that

> Patton thought he would never again be alone with his bride, and he resented the intrusion … Patton had been the center of his family's attention his entire life, and he was woefully unprepared abruptly to play second fiddle not only to an infant, but an infant girl … Unable to cope with this shattering blow to his outsize ego, Patton grew sullen and would suffer the first of what would be occasional bouts of depression … Patton's disinterest in and jealousy of his daughter lingered.[78]

Patton received orders to transfer to 15th Cavalry's A Troop at Fort Myer, Virginia in autumn 1911; he reported for duty on 3 December. Fort Myer was considered the army's best posting since it was across the Potomac from Washington and the residence for the army's chief of staff. The 15th Cavalry provided escorts for federal parades and funerals for prominent national leaders. To Patton's chagrin, he was assigned the ignominious position of quartermaster. Nonetheless, he fulfilled his duty with such diligence that his commander, Captain Julian Lindsay, rated him 'excellent' and lauded his 'intelligence and judgment', and skill in 'instructing, drilling, and handling enlisted men.'[79]

Off duty, Patton played on the post's polo and steeple-jumping teams. He drank at the Army and Navy Club and was accepted as a member by the exclusive Metropolitan Club. He continued writing articles, with his then most acclaimed 'Principles of Scouting', published in February 1912. He also designed what became the American cavalry's last official saber, the double-edged United States Saber M-1913 with a straight rather than curved blade for thrusting rather than slicing, a deadlier tactic.

At Fort Myers, Patton nurtured one of the most important relationships of his life when he encountered Secretary of War Henry Stimson on his early morning ride. Patton's manly vigor attracted Stimson and thereafter they rode frequently together. Stimson introduced Patton to Army Chief of Staff General Leonard Wood and they also occasionally rode together. Stimson and Wood requisitioned Patton as an aide for special events.

Patton's greatest thrill and challenge during this time came after the Olympic Committee invited him to represent America in the Pentathlon competition during the July 1912 Olympics in Stockholm, Sweden. The Pentathlon included pistol shooting at a target 25 meters away, a 300-meter swim, a 4,000-meter run, a 5,000-meter steeplechase and fencing. Of forty-two contestants, he scored a disappointing twenty-first in firing with a .38 pistol, but seventh in swimming, sixth in fencing, third in the steeplechase and third in the run, earning overall an excellent fifth rank. He was disappointed in his pistol shooting, especially since he scored 197 of 200 points in practice; he attributed his poor performance to nervousness. He overexerted himself so harshly during the run that he fainted at the finish line. His greatest feat was defeating French champion Lieutenant Jean de Mas Latrie in fencing. He reveled in the comradeship among athletes with their 'high spirit of sportsmanship and generosity' that

> speaks volumes for the characters of the officers of present day. There was not a single instance of a protest or any quibbling or fighting for points ... Each man gave his best and took what fortune gave him like a true soldier, and at the end we all felt more like good friends and comrades than rivals in a severe competition.[80]

His wife, sister, and parents had accompanied him to the Olympics. Afterward, the family traveled on the continent for a month. At Saumur, Patton spent several days at France's Cavalry School of Application mostly in an advanced fencing course. Then he and Beatrice journeyed throughout the Loire river valley, Normandy and Brittany. His familiarity with those regions greatly boosted his strategy when his Third Army fought through them during World War II.

Back in Washington, Patton used his connections with Secretary of War Stimson and Army Chief of Staff Wood to return to Saumur in July 1913 for the five-week master of sword course. He became the only American officer to earn a master of the sword degree.

He received orders to transfer to Fort Riley, Kansas where he arrived on 1 October 1913. He took the two-year Mounted Service School's advanced degree, passing the first year's course in May 1914 and second year's in June 1915. During that time, he wrote articles for the Mounted Service School's journal, *The Rasp*, including 'The Diary of the Instructor in Swordsmanship'.

At Fort Riley, during one of his stints as duty officer, a black soldier was accused of raping a white woman from the nearby town, and a mob gathered to lynch him. Although 'opposed to rape,' Patton

> felt it was my duty as an officer to see that a soldier of the United States Army was not lynched. I, therefore, informed the leading citizens that, if any attempt were made, it would be over my dead body. As a result of my stand, the man was not lynched, and, later, was found not guilty.[81]

During this time, he suffered injuries in both a car and a horse accident, including getting kicked in the head by his mount. That head injury may have exacerbated his mood swings. Beatrice gave birth to their second child, Ruth Ellen, on 28 February 1914. Patton accepted this daughter with resignation rather than rejection. Gradually, he had warmed to his first daughter, Beatrice, as she developed a personality and craved attention. In June 1914, Patton received a letter from the American Olympic Committee inviting him to join the team for the 1916 Olympics to be held in Berlin. World War I prevented Patton from attending the canceled event.

For his 1915 evaluation, Patton received an 'excellent' rating from Major Charles Rhodes as a

> most promising young officer of high ideals, devotion to duty, and marked industry. He is somewhat impulsive and intolerant of the

> opinions of others, and needs a period of severe duty away from troops and to round out his efficacy as an all round officer.[82]

***

Meanwhile, a crisis erupted in Europe when a Serbian agent named Gavrilo Princeps shot to death Austrian Archduke Ferdinand and his wife Sophie in Sarajevo, the capital of Austria's province of Bosnia-Herzegovina on 28 June 1914. No terrorist ever provoked worst death and destruction.[83]

Bosnia-Herzegovina's population was linguistically and culturally Slavic, not Germanic. Neighboring Slavic Serbia won independence from the Ottoman Empire in 1878. Serbia's government and people longed to have Bosnia-Herzegovina as their own province. Instead, Vienna beat them to the punch by annexing Bosnia-Herzegovina in 1908. With Austria-Hungary's army ten times stronger than their own, the Serbs could merely protest. A cabal within Serbia's government secretly established the Black Hand terrorist group to undermine Austrian rule. Princeps was a Black Hand agent and part of a conspiracy to murder the archduke that day. Austrian police arrested and interrogated Princeps and other Black Hand members, learning their link with Belgrade. On 23 July, Vienna issued Serbia a ten-point ultimatum with a forty-eight-hour deadline. Two days later, the Serbs accepted every demand except the one that would have let Austrians oversee the investigation and prosecution of anyone in their government responsible for the Black Hand.

Austria declared war against Serbia on 28 July. That set off a diplomatic and military chain reaction. Europe was then split into two alliances, what became known as the Central Powers of Germany and Austria-Hungary, and the Allies of France, Russia and Britain. Slavic and Orthodox Christian Russia and Serbia were also allies. A classic security dilemma caused those alliances. Each great power feared its rivals and so sought allies to deter any attack while expanding its military. All along each side pointed to the other's allies and swelling military to justify its own. Technological revolutions in manufacturing with mass assembly lines; metallurgy and chemicals with high alloy steel and explosives; transportation with railroads and motor vehicles; communication with telegraph, telephone and radio; warships with submarines; and intelligence with airplanes, wiretapping and cutting-edge mathematics for codebreaking made victory more dependent than ever on mobilizing, transporting and launching vast armies against the enemy before the enemy did the same. Each government was on a hair trigger. Railroad trains, tracks and timetables were key elements of military planning. Historian A.J.P. Taylor explained that General Staff plans rendered war 'by timetable unstoppable after a certain point. All were trapped by the ingenuity of their preparations.'[84] Thus did war become a self-fulfilling prophecy.

No government wanted a general war in 1914 or for the foreseeable future. Indeed, the royal families of Britain, Germany and Russia were affectionate cousins with each other. Yet no government asserted diplomacy that might have defused the crisis. As if in a nightmare, all national leaders and their advisors observed what unfolded in horror as they mindlessly fulfilled alliance duties.

St Petersburg reacted to Vienna's war declaration by ordering its army to mobilize on 30 July. That prompted Berlin to demand that Paris and St Petersburg stand down. When Paris ordered mobilization on 1 August 1914, Berlin followed later that day and declared war against Russia. German troops marched into Luxembourg on 2 August 1914. After Berlin declared war against France on 3 August 1914, London began mobilization. Berlin demanded that Brussels permit free passage of the German army through Belgium, which was by international treaty a neutral country with inviolable borders. When Brussels refused on 4 August 1914, Berlin declared war and ordered its army to attack Belgium. Later that day, London declared war against Germany. Austria-Hungary declared war against Russia on 5 August 1914, Serbia war against Germany on 7 August 1914, France war against Austria-Hungary on 10 August 1914 and Britain war against Austria-Hungary on 12 August 1914.

Berlin's plan for swiftly winning the war nearly succeeded. After studying railroad timetables, troops numbers and supplies, the General Staff decided to mass most troops against France, which could mobilize within two weeks, and overwhelm it, then shift most of their troops to overwhelm Russia, which needed five weeks to mobilize. German Chief of Staff Helmuth von Moltke explained that: 'We shall never again strike as well as we do now, with France's and Russia's expansion of their armies incomplete.'[85]

Five German armies, each two hundred men strong, fought swiftly through Belgium against its vastly outgunned army, punched back at Mons a small British Army, and curled south toward the rear of French armies fighting two other German armies eastward. In Paris, General Joseph Gallieni saw an opportunity as the German fight flank passed 20 miles east of Paris. He massed reserves and struck that exposed flank, driving it back in the Battle of the Marne. The French lines stabilized east and north-east where they linked with British and Belgium troops. In eastern Europe, the Germans inflicted devastating defeats on the Russians at the battles of Tannenberg and Masurian Lakes, driving them eastward.

After those initial freewheeling campaigns, the war stalemated because of three relatively recent technologies – barbed wire, machine guns and breech-loading cannons. Two men with a machine gun, one feeding it long belts of ammunition and the other pointing and pulling the trigger while in a bunker protected by barbed wire rolls could slaughter hundreds of attackers entangled before them. Likewise, rapid firing long- and short-range cannons could obliterate advancing masses of troops. That caused each army to halt and burrow trenches and bunkers deep into the earth. The Western Front was a score or so miles wide of opposed trench complexes that extended over 400 miles from the North Sea to the Swiss border. The Eastern Front was more than 600 miles long and less impermeable with troops stretched thinner. In May 1915, when Italy joined the Allies to fight Austria that front soon became densely fortified about 100 miles between the Alps and Adriatic Sea. On any front, the overwhelming advantage for defenders did not prevent generals on each side from ordering their troops 'over the top' in what were all but suicidal charges. 'Victories' were proclaimed for advances of several miles of churned earth that often cost tens of thousands of dead and wounded. Never was war more unimaginatively or murderously fought.

The war was 'world' or 'global' because never before had belligerents included countries from such diverse regions, gathered troops and supplies from such diverse sources, or fought on such diverse fronts. Each alliance side enticed other countries to join, with the Allies embracing Britain's dominions Australia, New Zealand, Canada and South Africa along with Belgium and Japan in 1914, Italy in 1915, Romania and Portugal in 1916, and the United States in 1917; and the Central Powers the Ottoman Empire in 1914 and Bulgaria in 1915. Britain, France and Belgium mobilized their colonial troops for war and conquered German colonies in Africa. Britain launched three expeditions against the Ottoman Empire, one disastrously against the Gallipoli Peninsula on the Bosphorus Straits, and two ultimately successful in the Holy Land and Mesopotamia. Japan captured German colonies in the Far East. German submarines prowled the north Atlantic sinking hundreds of merchant ships and dozens of warships.

President Woodrow Wilson declared America's neutrality on 4 August 1914.[86] He was determined that the United States would stay firmly on the sidelines, but a series of crises challenged that policy.

Berlin announced on 4 February 1915, that its submarines would sink any vessels traversing a designated zone drawn around the British Isles and France. On 7 May 1915, a submarine sank the British passenger ship *Lusitania,* with 128 Americans among the 1,195 dead. Chancellor Theobald von Bethmann Hollweg claimed that was a legitimate act because *Lusitania* carried war supplies and that he had actually warned American Secretary of State William Bryan on 26 April 1915. Wilson initially reacted to enraged congressional and newspaper editor calls for America to join the war against Germany, with the puzzling remark: 'There is such a thing as a man being too proud to fight.' Wilson eventually issued three protests to Berlin.

A German submarine fired a torpedo into the British passenger ship *Sussex* on 24 March 1916, killing around eighty people although the vessel did not sink and no Americans were among the dead. For four weeks, Wilson and his advisors debated how to respond before the president declared on 18 April 1916, that the United States would sever diplomatic relations if Germany did not end unrestricted submarine warfare against all passenger and merchant vessels. Von Bethmann Hollweg issued on 4 May 1916 what became known as the *Sussex* pledge, that henceforth Germany would no longer indiscriminately sink merchant ships, and only do so if they were carrying war supplies and after the crew and passengers evacuated the ship into lifeboats.

Wilson worked with Congress for passage of the National Defense Act in June 1916, that authorized the army's expansion to 11,450 regular officers and 223,800 enlisted men and 17,000 National Guard officers and 440,000 volunteers by 1921. Those men and about 1.5 million more would be needed much sooner. In August 1916, Congress established the Council of National Defense of prominent corporate, academic and labor leaders to study ways to mobilize the nation for war.

Wilson reasoned that the best way to keep America from the war was to help end it. On 5 November 1916, he offered to facilitate negotiations among the belligerents for a face-saving 'peace without victory' settlement. No one expressed interest. A self-destructive dilemma trapped the belligerents. Each had already suffered such horrendous losses that the rulers could only justify more sacrifices from their populations by promising huge financial and territorial spoils from the enemy after victory.

***

Patton was eager to get into that war any possible way. He wrote to Army Chief of Staff Wood for permission to take a year's furlough so he could join the French army for

> I have always wanted to have the actual experience of combat, not as an observer but as a participant because … I can get knowledge which will be of great military value. It is only by doing things others have not done that one can advance.

Wood replied,

> Don't think of attempting anything of the kind, at present … We don't want to waste youngsters of your sort in the service of foreign nations … Stick to the present job … I know how you feel, but there is nothing to be done.[87]

Chapter 2

MEXICO

> '[A]ll three shot at me, one bullet threw gravel on me, I fired back with my pistol five times ... I always expected to be scared [in a fight] but was not nor was I excited.
>
> I was afraid that they would get away.'
>
> George S. Patton

Patton's first war experience was not in France but in Mexico. He received orders on 15 August 1915, to command 8th Cavalry's D Troops at Fort Bliss, near El Paso, Texas. That proved to be a fortuitous posting since Fort Bliss was on the frontline of a worsening war zone that stretched along most of the frontier.

The possibly of war with Mexico was nothing new. America's relations with its southern neighbor had seesawed between violent conflict and peaceful trade for nine decades since Mexico won independence from Spain in 1821. Although America's independence war four decades earlier helped inspire Mexicans to revolt, their leaders formed not a republic but a series of dictatorships. The new regime did open Mexico to trade and immigration. Enterprising American merchants and trappers settled in California and New Mexico, while mostly families migrated to Texas, where they outnumbered Mexicans by ten to one by 1835. That year, the latest dictator, Antonio Lopez de Santa Anna, suspended the 1824 Constitution that guaranteed autonomy for the provinces. That provoked the Texans to revolt. Santa Anna led an army that massacred rebel forces at the Alamo and Goliad, but the Texan army commanded by General Sam Houston destroyed his army and captured him at San Jacinto and forced him to sign two treaties that granted Texas independence. A coup overthrew Santa

Anna and repudiated the treaties. America's annexation of Texas as a state in 1845 and President John Polk's dispatch of an army to the Rio Grande river in 1846 provoked war with Mexico. Over the next two years, American armies overran New Mexico, California and northern Mexico, and an army captured Mexico City. In the 1848 treaty of Guadeloupe Hidalgo, Mexico's government ceded Texas, New Mexico and California to the United States for $18.25 million, then with the 1853 Gadsden Purchase, sold a strip of land in southern New Mexico and Arizona to the United States for $10 million.

Mexico's political instability persisted. The failure of President Benito Jaurez's government to pay Mexico's international debts prompted an 1862 invasion by a French army that captured the capital and imposed a government led by Emperor Maximilian. Jaurez steadily built-up Mexico's army until it recaptured the country and executed Maximilian in 1867.

Political instability again engulfed Mexico after Jaurez died in 1872 and persisted until Porfirio Diaz's presidency from 1877 to 1880 and from 1884 to 1911. Although there were regular elections, they were rigged to keep Diaz in power along with a majority of supporters in Congress so that an increasingly corrupt dictatorship rather than democracy ruled Mexico. Relations between the United States and Mexico were never better during this time as Diaz opened the country to foreign investors who developed railroads, plantations, mines and oil fields.[88] Nearly all the newly created wealth either flowed to American shareholders or into the hands of Mexico's already wealthy elite while most Mexicans remained abysmally poor. Presidents William Taft and Diaz held summits in the sister cities of El Paso, Texas and Jaurez, Mexico in October 1909.

Liberal reformer Franciso Madero challenged Diaz in the 1910 election, but fled to San Antonio, Texas after the regime trumped up criminal charges against him in June. Madero called for a revolt against Diaz's regime to begin on 20 November 1910.[89] Eventually, several regional war lords rebelled against Diaz in hope of taking over Mexico, most prominently Emilio Zapata in the south and Pascual Orozco and Franciso 'Pancho' Villa in the north. Diaz resigned and fled into exile on 25 May 1911. The warlords conveyed Madero to the presidential palace on 7 June 1911, but soon began fighting among themselves along with another aspirant for power, Victoriano Huerta and his followers. Huerta initially backed Madero but had him arrested on 18 February 1913 and murdered the next day. Huerta enriched himself and his cronies by confiscating ever more American-owned mines, plantations and railroads.

That murder appalled newly elected President Woodrow Wilson, who formally took the oath of office on 4 March 1913. He refused to recognize Huerta's regime initially and after it won a rigged election in October 1913, he protested the seizure of American property. Wilson backed the revolt of political leader Venustiano Carranza and his followers, most vitally General Alvaro Obregon known as Constitutionalists against Huerta after he promised to respect American investments. Carranza and Villa formed an alliance that fought Huerta's regime and his Federale forces.

An incident on 9 April 1914, gave Wilson an excuse to wield America's military against Huerta.[90] Federales arrested nine American sailors who landed to buy supplies for the flotilla commanded by Admiral Alexander Mayo anchored at Tampico. Although the local Mexican commander, General Morelos Zaragosa, swiftly released the sailors, Mayo demanded that he order a twenty-one gun salute for the American flag. Wilson backed Mayo's demand. Huerta insisted on mutual twenty-one-gun salutes to each other's flags. Wilson refused and majorities in both houses of Congress on 22 April 1914 authorized him to use military force to force Huerta to yield. Learning of a German arms shipment bound for Veracruz, Wilson had Secretary of War Josephus Daniels send this message to Admiral Frank Fletcher commanding the squadron at Veracruz: 'Take Vera Cruz at once!'[91]

Fighting erupted that led to seventeen Americans dead and sixty-three wounded while they inflicted several hundred casualties on Mexican troops and civilians before capturing the port. The squadron forced that German merchant ship to sail away with its arms cargo. Wilson imposed an arms embargo on all Mexican war lords. General Frederick Funston arrived to lead the occupation army at Veracruz. As American commanders did elsewhere, Funston imposed sweeping sanitation measures that cleaned piles of garbage from the streets and waterways, and improved sewage and drinking water systems. Over the next year those reforms reduced the civilian death rate from disease by 25 per cent and saved countless American military lives.[92]

In early November 1914, Obregon's troops forces occupied the oil fields around Tampico and Carranza informally promised not to nationalize those American investments. Wilson responded by withdrawing American troops from Vera Cruz on 23 November 1914, and a few days later Carranza's troops occupied that port. Meanwhile, fighting erupted between Constitutionalists and Villistas. Obregon inflicted devastating defeats on Villa at Celaya in April 1915 and at Leon in July 1915. He then turned his army against Huerta's regime in Mexico City.

Huerta resigned the presidency on 15 July 1915 and fled into exile. Obregon marched his army into the capital to secure Carranza in power. By autumn 1915, Carranza's Constitutionalists controlled seven eighths of Mexican territory with 13 million of the country's 15 million people. and was endorsed by twenty of twenty-seven state governors.[93] In return for Carranza's promise to protect American investments in Mexico, Wilson recognized his regime on 19 October 1915. That appeared to end the chance of war between the two countries.

***

Meanwhile, Patton enjoyed his duties at Fort Bliss. Shortly after arriving, he described the post:

> The officers [*sic*] quarters are in one long line facing a similar line of barracks across the parade [ground] with the stables behind the barracks. So for a big post it is quite compact. There are no trees at all. We are about a mile from the border but cant [*sic*] see the river as the post is on a mesa which extends back of the stables to the mountains 30 miles away perfect[ly] flat no trees. The town is behind the officers [*sic*] quarters ... There are not twenty houses in the town and one saloon ... We have a three room house and a stable and a garage and so are very comfortable.[94]

The region was still the Wild West. Among the local characters was Dave Allison,

> a very quiet looking old man with a sweet face and white hair. He is the most noted gunman here in Texas and just at present is marshall. He alone killed all of the Orasco outfit (a notorious local bandit gang) five of them about a month ago and he kills several Mexicans each month. He shot Orasco and his four men each in the head at sixty yards. He seemed much taken with me and is going hunting with me.[95]

Brigadier General John 'Black Jack' Pershing took command at Fort Bliss on 23 April 1915. He was then 56 years old with an excellent military record for iron courage and discipline.[96] He entered West Point in 1882 and graduated thirtieth among his seventy-six classmates in 1886. He was first assigned to 6th Cavalry that fought Apaches in Arizona and in 1890 and 1891 against the Sioux in Dakota Territory. In 1892, he was transferred to the 'Colored' 10th Cavalry for several years, a stint for which his colleagues dubbed him 'Black Jack'. He served as

General Nelson Miles aide in 1896 and became a tactical instructor at West Point in 1897. During the war with Spain in 1898, he fought at the battles of El Caney and San Juan Hill, Cuba then served in occupation forces in Cuba, Puerto Rico, Guam and finally the Philippines where he fought guerrillas trying to liberate their country from American rule, before returning stateside to attend the War College in 1903.

Pershing would never have achieved his subsequent rank, duties and fame without the patronage of President Theodore Roosevelt and Senator Francis Warren of Wyoming, his father-in-law and chairman of the Senate Military Affairs Committee. Pershing's courage, professionalism, and iron will dazzled Roosevelt when their regiments, 10th and 1st Volunteer 'Rough Rider' cavalry regiments fought alongside in Cuba. Subsequent reports of Pershing's military prowess in the Philippines swelled Roosevelt's administration. On 20 September 1906, Roosevelt promoted Pershing from captain to brigadier general, leapfrogging him over 832 mostly lackluster seniors who bristled at his promotion.

Pershing served as an observer of the Russo-Japanese War in 1905, and the Balkan War in 1908, and was posted to the Philippines from 1909 to 1913, during which he fought in several campaigns against rebels. He was transferred to the Presidio at San Francisco in 1913. Now a colonel, he left his family there in their comfortable home when he was ordered to command Fort Bliss. He was devastated to learned that on 27 August 1915, his wife and three daughters died during a fire at their home; only his son survived.

Patton soon became Pershing's aide and protegee. He noted the difference between Pershing's professional and personal sides:

> In his office or on his inspections an unnatural severity, most unlike and distasteful to him, seemed of necessity to invest him, but in his quarters ... displacing worry by marvelous control of the will, he laughed and talked of casual, simple things interluding from time to time his conversation by some incisive question of momentous decision.[97]

Patton's sister Nita came for what became a long visit. Nita was a willowy 5 foot and 9 inches tall, with blond hair, 28 years old and unmarried. Patton introduced Nita to Pershing, and they were smitten with each other. Eventually, they would become engaged but never married.

The collapse of Mexico political system into civil war led to worsening violence by criminal gangs across that country and into the

United States where they robbed and murdered American civilians and soldiers. At his San Antonio headquarters, General Funston commanded the scattered undermanned regiments defending the border. He conveyed orders from the White House that troops could repel raiders into the United States but could not chase them or fire at them in Mexico. Pershing protested that policy, arguing that the raids would not end unless the gangs were pursued and destroyed. Funston requested reinforcements, explaining that

> If I do not have an adequate force ready for instant use, a single act of indiscretion by a subordinate commander on either side may start a conflagration that will extend along the entire border, and result in an international crisis.[98]

From Fort Bliss, Lieutenant Patton led ten-man patrols along the frontier and tracked but never caught up to raiders and rustlers. His most important duty was protecting a 30-mile stretch of the railroad east of El Paso. It was rough, exhausting duty. He wrote that: 'It may be fine to die with ones boots on but it is very hard on the feet to sleep with them on which is what I have been doing up to last night.'[99]

Several times, Patton thought they had encountered robbers or raiders but they turned out to be something else. One night, a soldier reported hearing Mexicans on a bridge.

> Patton crept up and called, 'Who is there?' A voice which to me sounded foreign said 'Friend' and at the same moment six heads with rifles stuck over the bank. Strange to say I did not think of running but wondered if I could get one before I was gotten. I called out what are you doing here and to my surprise and delight they answered patrol 13th cav[alry]. They should not have been there as I was covering the bridge.

Another time 'we saw two men on horseback and thinking there were bandits we ambushed them only to find that he was an old rancher and son.' Then there was the time when his

> corporal was a head of me going up a very sharp grade when all at once he simply fell off his horse and grabbed his rifle. I asked him what was the trouble and he said a bullet had just missed him. I went up there and he said there it goes again. This time I heard it and once more – it was an eagle screaming at us.[100]

Patton's most dangerous encounter was a pay day when

> a number of men got drunk. Two were very drunk at the saloon and I tried to get them to camp. One tried to hit me but did not. After I got them to camp I went back … I heard shots and met the two men coming back … one with a pistol. He was crazy drunk and did not recognize me but as I was the only one between him and town … I started to stop him and was pretty close and very scared when the 1st sgt … grabbed him from behind.[101]

The worst scare came in November 1915 when Patton and his patrol received two telegrams from Pershing. One warned that notorious bandit Cico Cano and his 200 desperados were ready to raid across the border. The other ordered Patton to drive back eighty Caranza men who had already crossed. Patton dutifully led his men to the reported crossing spot but found both reports were false rumors. He recalled that: 'We were all disgusted at not finding the Mexicans. It was fine to see how pleased the men were at the prospect of a fight. I think they would have done well.'[102]

***

Mexico's civil war between the Constitutionalists and Villistas persisted. Wilson tried to strengthen Carranza's regime with arms sales and letting him transfer troops by American owned railroads against Villa's army in northern Mexico. The Constitutionalists defeated the Villistas in a series of battles, forcing Villa to withdraw with around 400 troops deep in northern Mexico's Sierra Madre Mountains.

Villa blamed Wilson for his defeats and sought vengeance. He declared that 'I will devote my life to the killing of every Gringo I can get my hands on, and the destruction of all Gringo property.'[103] In December 1915, he ordered all Americans to abandon their businesses and homes in Mexico or die. His troops stopped a train near Santa Isabel in northern Mexico on 10 January 1916, forced eighteen American passengers to disembark and murdered them. Over the next few weeks, he and his men murdered a dozen or so other American ranchers and miners across the region.

Wilson demanded that Carranza crush Villa and if he failed, warned that the American army would do so. Villa then led 484 troops across the border to attack Columbus, New Mexico on 9 March 1916. His men scattered through the town, looting and burning the Commercial

Hotel and other businesses, and murdering ten civilians. Colonel Henry Slocum commanded the 553 troops of 13th Cavalry based at Camp Fulong outside the town. The Americans repulsed Villa's troops, killing sixty-seven, wounding several score, and capturing seven while suffering eight troops killed and fifteen wounded. The seven captured Villistas were tried and found guilty of murder, with six sentenced for execution and one to life in prison.

***

President Wilson responded to the attack by having Secretary of War Newton Baker organize a 'Punitive Expedition' commanded by Pershing to pursue and destroy Villa and his army.[104] He had Secretary of State Robert Lansing inform Carranza of the expedition and the expectation that his government would do everything possible to crush Villa. Pershing organized the campaign at Columbus, and initially included 7th, 10th, 11th and 12th Cavalry regiments with 4,800 troops, 4,175 riding and pack horses, a score of cars and trucks, and eight airplanes; eventually reinforcements swelled the Punitive Expedition to over 10,000 troops.

Patton was crushed to learn that 8th Cavalry would remain at Fort Bliss. He was determined to join the expedition but the only way was to convince Pershing to make him an aide.[105] To that end,

> I got permission to speak to the General and asked him to take me to Mexico in any capacity. He replied, 'Every one [*sic*] wants to go; why should I favor you?' 'Because,' I answered, 'I want to go more than anyone else.' This modest reply failed to get any answer except a curt 'That will do.'... Undiscouraged I then went home and packed my bedding and saddle. At 5 o'clock next morning the telephone rang and on answering it the General's voice inquired, 'Lieut. Patton, how long will it take you to get ready?' When he heard that I was ready he exclaimed 'I'll be G. – D. – You are appointed aide.'[106]

Pershing issued the order detaching Patton from 8th Cavalry to his staff on 13 March 1916.

Pershing split his force into two wings, with one marching south from Columbus and the other from Palomas Ranch 50 miles west on 16 March 1916. Several days later, the wings united 85 miles south at Colonia Dublan a village a few miles from Casas Grandes. For the next eleven months, Colonia Dublan was the Punitive Expedition's central operations base from which Pershing dispatched patrols and regiments in different directions that mostly sought vainly to catch up to the enemy. The closest they came to eliminating Villa was at Guerrero on 29 March 1916, when Colonel George Dodd and 370 troops of his 7th Cavalry routed several hundred Villistas on 29 March 1916 and killed around thirty of them; a bullet wounded Villa's leg but he escaped. On 4 May 1916, Colonel Robert Howze's 11th Cavalry attacked around 120 Villistas at Cusihuiriachi, killed 61 of them and scattered the rest. Thereafter, there were sporadic skirmishes and killings but no significant battles with the Villistas. Pershing hired four Japanese cooks who had worked for Villa to dose his coffee with poison. They succeeded in doing so on 8 July 1916, but the dose was not powerful enough to kill him.

***

Meanwhile, Pershing sought to avoid fighting Carranza's army. Wilson authorized generals Funston and Hugh Scott to meet with Obregon at Jaurez to coordinate a joint campaign against Villa, but they failed to agree. Obregon claimed that Villa was dead and urged them to withdraw their expedition. The Americans explained that they would remain in Mexico until they eliminated any threat to the United States. Fighting broke out between 300 Carrancistas troops led by General Felix Gomez and 2 companies of combined 83 10th Cavalry troops led by captains Louis Morey and Charles Boyd at Carrizal on 20 June 1916. The Mexicans repelled an American charge, killed twelve and captured twenty-three, while suffering around thirty dead including Gomez and a couple score wounded. Negotiations between the Wilson and Carranza governments resulted in the release of the American prisoners as a prelude to a Joint High Commission with three man delegations from each country to negotiate at New London, Connecticut on 6 September 1916. They talked until 15 January 1917 but failed to forge an agreement.

Nonetheless, war between the United States and Mexico did not occur mostly because Carranza's regime was overextended fighting Emilio Zapata's army in southern Mexico and Villa's reconstituted army in northern Mexico. Villa's troops captured Chihuahua on 15 September 1916 and held it until General Jacinto Trevino massed enough soldiers to force him to withdraw. Villa briefly recaptured Chihuahua in late November and Torreon on 22 December 1916 before withdrawing.

***

Patton led patrols that

> Searched mountains and all dwellings in area … It got cold sleeted, snowed, hailed and finally rained. We all suffered much … Gen. approved what I had done. Took a big drink and went to bed … Slept well. Awoke at 6 [am] covered with snow.

One day, Patton was nearly crushed when his horse stumbled and rolled over him.

Pershing sent Patton on two dangerous courier missions. In the first, he dictated an order that Patton was to carry to 13th Cavalry. Getting there was perilous:

> To deliver this message, it was necessary to drive for about an hour and a half in a broken-down Ford, using headlights over a roadless country full of Villistas. I then secured a horse and, after riding all night in very bad weather consisting of rain, sleet, hail, and snow, joined the squadron.

The major assembled the squadron and issued instructions to implement Pershing's order by patrolling mountains west of their camp. Patton interrupted him and told him the order meant he should patrol east instead. The major berated Patton, but later when they both joined Pershing, he verified Patton's interpretation. For Patton, correcting the major 'took high moral courage and built up my self-confidence.'[107]

The other adventure also involved carrying a message through enemy territory accompanied by two soldiers. Patton recalled that,

> As I started the General shook me warmly by the hand saying, 'Be careful, there are lots of Villistas.' Then still holding my hand he said, 'But remember, Patton, if you don't deliver that message, don't come back.'

Along the way, Patton and his men encountered a 10th Cavalry patrol that warned him not to proceed because Villistas were likely ahead. Patton proceeded anyway and later excitedly wrote a letter home that:

> I went 26 miles through the mountains at night with two men We expected to be jumped and once hid from … whom thought we thought were Mexicans. I did not know where the troops I was hunting were but I finally found them by the reflection of their [camp] fires on a cloud … I crossed the continental divide at about 8000 feet and its was very cold. But hot by day. I have never been so dirty in my life. The General is fine and a great soldier.

This feat also boosted his confidence.[108]

Patton finally got his baptism of fire, appropriately in a Wild West shootout. On 14 May 1916, Pershing dispatched Patton with ten troops, two guides, and three drivers packed in three cars to buy corn for the expedition. They purchased corn at the villages of Coyote and Rubio. At Rubio, a guide reported a rumor that General Julio Cardenas, one of Villa's closest advisors, was at his nearby ranch. Patton ordered his men to head there.

As they approached the ranch, Patton tersely issued these instructions:

> Three men from each of these cars were to race across the southern face of the ranch. That would leave six of the men in the cars to cover the road, and the northern, western, and southern sides of the house. The other nine would meet on the eastern side and search the place.

As Patton approached the ranch gate 'three armed men dashed out on horseback ... So schooled was I not to shoot that I merely drew my pistol and waited to see what would happen.' He ordered them to halt but they rode on until they saw the other American troops had cut them off, so they turned and galloped back toward Patton and

> all three shot at me, one bullet threw gravel on me, I fired back with my pistol five times ... I always expected to be scared [in a fight] but was not nor was I excited. I was afraid that they would get away ... I kept wondering why they did not hit me. The guns seemed pointed right at me ... Then my men came around the corner and started to shoot ... just as I got around the corner three bullets hit it.[109]

Patton killed two of the three Villistas, including Cardenas.

Worried that other Villistas were inside the ranch house, he had his men place a dead tree against the wall and he climbed up. As he stepped gingerly across the roof it collapsed and he plunged down to his armpits. Fortunately, no one was in the room below to slash or shoot his dangling body. He pulled himself free and descended from the roof. He and his men searched the house but found only Cardenas's terrified wife, mother and baby.

Patton had his men gather any firearms and saddles, strapping each corpse atop a car hood. As they

> were just about to start ... we saw about 40 men coming toward us at a gallop, about 1000 yards away. The men [Patton's men] were a little nervous but stood [their ground] ... and at that time some shots were fired.[110]

Patton and his men raced away and eventually reached the expedition's camp.

Patton's shootout at the Cardenas ranch made him the campaign's hero. Pershing reported the gunfight in his official report to Funston, the first time that Patton is 'mentioned in dispatches', a special army status. Meanwhile, reporters accompanying the expedition finally had a colorful story and they made the most of it. Pershing appreciated the favorable news for a campaign whose purpose and results many congressmen and newspaper editors increasingly questioned. Yet he was skeptical and wary of the fickle press and issued instructions for his officers and soldiers to be circumspect around reporters.

Patton had one more adventure but it was bloodless. He led a cavalry company that for three days chased Villistas leader Pedro Luhan and several of his men 75 miles, and finally caught up to them at a ranch on 15 June 1916. He recalled that:

> I planned the surprise and tried to work up a fight. We surrounded the hacienda and a hill back of it with a dismounted line and the eight of us galloped up to the door but nothing doing. They would not shoot. If they had we would have murdered them. It had all the elements of good tactics but no shooting.[111]

Patton's gun fight, capture, and two courier missions were his campaign's highlights along with being promoted to first lieutenant on 23 May 1916. Tedium followed as the expedition failed to catch up and defeat any large groups of Villistas let alone capture or kill Villa. Patton recalled that Pershing used the campaign as a rigorous training exercise by having each regiment undergo

> a complete course in range and combat firing, marches, maneuvers, entrenching, and combating exercises with … ammunition. Every horse and man was fit; weaklings had gone; baggage was still at the minimum and discipline was perfect … General Pershing knew to the minutest detail each of the subjects in which he demanded practice, and by his physical presence and personal example and explanation, insured himself they were correctly carried out.[112]

Pershing was Patton's outstanding model as an officer and a man. Their friendship deepened although they could not openly express it for fear of provoking jealousy and whispers of favoritism. Pershing advised Patton on an article he wrote entitled *Cavalry Work of the Punitive Expedition* that appeared in the *Cavalry Journal*'s January 1917 issue. Patton explained the role of cavalry in an increasingly mechanized age:

> For open warfare under modern conditions, it is more necessary than ever to have troops that are able to move rapidly from one place to another over any kind of country and arrive at the point of action fit for a fight. In addition to the important functions of reconnoitering and screening and the dashing sphere of mounted combat, the cavalry must know how to fight on foot and expert use of the pistol or saber are determined for successful mounted attack, and training in rife firing and mastery of the principles of fire tactics are equally essential in the disarmament fight.[113]

Then Patton suffered his latest severe accident. On 2 October 1916, his face and right hand were badly burned when he pumped too much gasoline into his lamp and the overflow ignited, the tent caught fire, and he tried to smother the flames. In the field hospital, a high fever worsened his misery and prolonged his recovery. He wrote to Beatrice that she was

> fortunate in not being able to kiss me right now. My face looks like an old after-birth of a Mexican cow on which had been smeared several very decomposed eggs ... And both ears are red and inflamed and I have no hair nor eyebrows nor eye lashes. No I have nothing catching. I simply set myself on fire with the above distressing results.[114]

Pershing granted Patton leave to visit his family. During that time, his father was amidst what would be a lost campaign for one of California's Senate seats in Congress. When reporters asked him what his son thought of the expedition and Washington politics, Patton senior causally shared his critical views of both and they ended up in front page articles. That prompted Pershing to fire off a letter to Patton in which he first conveyed his hope that 'you are rapidly recovering from your accident and your personal appearance has improved. At the same time you are no doubt enjoying the visit with your family.' He then warned Patton to

> not be too insistent on your own personal views. You must remember that when we enter the army we do so with the full knowledge that our first duty is toward our government, entirely regardless of our own views under any given circumstances.[115]

This was the first of numerous offhand remarks by Patton that stirred controversy.

Patton returned to the front resigned and homesick rather than enthused. The harsh conditions and inability to find let alone destroy the enemy discouraged him. In a letter to Beatrice, he complained that: 'This job I now have is not good as I have not enough to do and get lazy.' He recalled that: 'It is just about a year since ... you cried and wished I would resign.' He then confessed that:

> If I could only be sure of the future I would get out. That is if I could be sure that I would never be above the average army officer I would ... If I knew that I would never be famous I would settle down and raise horses and have a good time. It is a great gamble to spoil your and my own happiness in the hope of greatness.[116]

Wilson ordered Pershing on 12 January 1917, to withdraw the Punitive Expedition. By 5 February 1917, Pershing had led '10,690 soldiers, 9,307 horses, more than 300 wagons, trucks, and passenger cars, 2,030 Mexican refugees, 21 Villista prisoners, and 533 Chinese' to Columbus. The expedition's cost was somewhere between $130 million and $340 million. The Americans suffered 65 dead, 67 wounded, 24 captured and released, and 3 missing while inflicting 169 killed, at least 115 wounded, and 19 captured on the Villistas and 82 killed and at least 51 wounded on the Carrancistas.[117] The campaign failed to achieve its core missions to kill or capture Villa, destroy his army, and deter the Mexican gang raids across the border that robbed, raped and murdered. Yet, as an extended eleven-month harsh field condition and sometimes live-fire exercise, it was crucial to help prepare Pershing, Patton and other officers for the command, supply, training and combat challenges they would face in France.

Pershing officially dissolved the Punitive Expedition on 14 February 1917. A heart attack killed Funston on 19 February 1917, and Pershing replaced him as commander of the Southern Department headquartered at San Antonio, Texas. Patton wanted to remain Pershing's aide but received word of his transfer from 8th to 7th Cavalry at Fort Bliss near El Paso, on 1 February 1917, and joined his new regiment as Troop A's commander on 27 February 1917. Patton and Pershing would not be long separated. Six weeks later, the United States entered World War I and new chances to make history arose for them both.

Chapter 3

LORRAINE

'In the report I submitted ... I said, couching the remarks in the euphemistic jargon appropriate to official correspondence, that the Frenchman was crazy and the Tank not worth a damn.'

'The duty of "tanks" and more especially of "light tanks" is analogous to the duty performed by cavalry in normal wars. I am a cavalryman.'

'But the tank corps established its reputation for not giving ground. They only went forward. And they are the only troops in the attack of whom that can be said.'

George S. Patton

President Woodrow Wilson asked Congress to declare war against Germany on 2 April 1917.[118] Until then, he was determined to keep America from the stalemated soaring bloodbath that erupted in Europe in August 1914. But now he believed that the nation had no choice but to fight. Two German policies provoked his decision – one overt, the other covert.

Germany's overt war of unrestricted submarine warfare. Chancellor Theobald von Bethmann Hollweg had Ambassador Johann von Bernstorff informed Secretary of State Robert Lansing on 31 January 1917, that it would begin the following day of 1 February 1917. Each week thereafter Germany would permit one American vessel to steam a designated course through a vast kill zone surrounding the British Isles and France's Atlantic coast with its hull painted with red and white stripes, and carrying documents certifying it conveyed no war goods.

That enraged Wilson but he still wanted to avoid war. In a joint congressional session, he explained that the United States would break diplomatic relations with Germany but war was not inevitable because 'I refuse to believe that it is the intention of the German authorities to do ... as they warned us they would feel at liberty to do.'[119] The Germans soon disabused Wilson of his latest delusion. Submarines sank one American merchant vessel on 6 February 1917, another on 16 February 1917, and three on 18 March 1917. Outrage among Americans swelled with each sinking.

Another provocation was Germany's attempts to entice Mexico to war against the United States. On 16 January 1917, Foreign Minister Arthur Zimmerman sent instructions to Ambassador Heinrich von Eckhardt to offer

> Mexico a proposal of alliance on the following basis: make war together, generous financial support, and an understanding on our part that Mexico is to reconquer the lost territory in Texas, New Mexico, and Arizona.[120]

British naval intelligence intercepted, decoded, and on 24 February 1917, passed that message to American Ambassador Walter Page, who promptly sent it to the White House. Had Berlin made that offer the previous year when General John Pershing's Punitive Expedition was imbedded in northern Mexico, Carranza's regime would likely have embraced it. That would have bogged the United States down in war with its neighbor that forced Wilson to ignore German submarines torpedoing American merchant ships. Instead, Berlin's message incensed Wilson and his cabinet, and when the president publicly revealed it on 1 March 1917, Congress, newspaper editors and most Americans. Wilson requested and received congressional authority to 'employ any instrumentalities or methods that may be necessary and adequate to protect our ships and our people in their legitimate pursuits on the seas.'[121]

In his 2 April 1917 war resolution to Congress, Wilson justified war against Germany not just to protect the nation's immediate geopolitical interests in trading abroad and keeping peace with Mexico, but more vitally as a crusade that realized America's most cherished ideals. He argued that

> right is more precious than peace, and we will fight for the things we have always carried nearest our hearts – for democracy, for the right of those who submit to authority to have a voice in their own Governments, for the rights and liberties of small nations, for the universal dominion of right by such a concert of peoples as shall bring peace and safety to all nations and make the world itself free.[122]

Congress overwhelmingly approved his resolution by 82 to 6 in the Senate on 6 April 1917, and by 373 to 50 on 6 April 1917.

***

Declaring war was easy enough. Mobilizing an army powerful enough to prevail in France and a navy powerful enough to safely convey and supply it across the Atlantic was a Herculean task. America's army numbered only 5,775 officers and 103,224 enlisted men along with 66,594 mobilized National Guardsmen and was mostly deployed on the Mexican border; 101,174 National Guardsmen were unmobilized. The navy numbered around 360 vessels including 151 warships manned or administered by 8,383 officers and 186,354 enlistees. In addition, there were 776 marine officers and 26,973 enlistees; the Marine Corps' ranks would expand five-fold to fight in the trenches alongside the soldiers.

Producing all the needed ships, vehicles, weapons, uniforms, food, equipment, medicines and fuel depended on mobilizing America's economy which, in turn, depended on sustaining the initial overwhelming American public support for the war as the cost in lives and money soared. To those ends, the White House and Congress swiftly worked together to enhance existing or create new institutions. The previously established Council of National Defense and General Munitions Board acquired more powers to coordinate efforts. The War Industries Board selected and coordinated production among over 35,000 manufacturing firms. The Overman Act, signed into law on 20 May 1918, empowered the president for the war's duration and six months thereafter to reorganize, abolish or nationalize any business or organization. Wilson wielded that law in various ways to mobilize the steel, railroad, energy and agribusiness industries.

3.1 Federal Government, War and Navy Budgets, and National Debt, 1914–1920[123]

Year	Federal Budgets ($)	War Department ($)	Navy Department ($)	National Debt ($)
1914	725,525,000	208,349,000	139,682,000	1,188,235,000
1915	746,093,000	202,060,000	141,836,000	1,191,264,000
1916	712,967,000	183,176,000	153,854,000	1,225,146,000
1917	1,953,857,000	377,941,000	239,633,000	2,975,619,000
1918	12,677,359,000	4,869,955,000	1,278,840,000	12,455,225,000
1919	18,492,665,000	9,009,076,000	2,002,311,000	25,484,506,000
1920	6,357,677,000	1,621,953,000	736,021,000	24,299,321,000

Of course, America's taxpayers had to pay for all that and much more. The war eventually cost the United States $35 billion. Wilson, Congress and the Federal Reserve devised a series of measures that paid the bills eventually with 58 per cent from selling bonds, 22 per cent from raising taxes, and 20 per cent from expanding the money supply.[124]

The Committee on Public Information led by George Creel tried to 'sell the war' and boost business, interest group and broad public support with propaganda films, posters and popular songs; 'Liberty Bond' drives led by Hollywood stars; tens of thousands of rousing talks by Four Minute-Men before factory workers, town hall meetings, corporate boards and church congregations; austerity campaigns to free more food for the soldiers and sailors that included wheatless Mondays and Wednesdays, beefless Tuesdays, and porkless Thursdays and Saturdays, and collection drives for scrap metal, rubber and cloth.

The federal government received sweeping counterespionage and counter-revolution powers with the Espionage Act, Trading with the Enemy Act and Sedition Act that Wilson respectively signed into law on 15 June 1917, 6 October 1917 and 16 May 1918. The Department of Justice's War Emergency Division, especially its Alien Enemy Bureau, hunted for German spies and communist agitators. Eventually, 1,200 enemy aliens were arrested and interned for the war's duration. J. Edgar Hoover was among the investigators. The volunteer American Protective League eventually numbered 200,000 members and assisted Washington's counter-intelligence efforts. The Department of Justice worked with local officials to crack down on the revolutionary communist Industrial Workers of the World (IWW) by arresting and prosecuting hundreds of them during their strikes. The Department of Justice shut down a number of socialist newspapers and journals. Socialist Party leader Eugene Debs was the most infamous radical convicted for 'sedition'. The Department of Justice deported several hundred foreign agitators to Russia that the communists had taken over.

The number of regular and guard troops rose from 208,034 in April 1917 to 3,685,458 in November 1918. Although over 650,000 men volunteered, 2,180,290 were draftees and the rest were National Guardsmen. The Selective Service Act that Wilson signed into law on 19 May 1917, required all men from 21 to 31 years old to register by 5 June 1917; an amendment expanded that span to those between 18 and 45 years. The nation was split among 4,648 local draft boards and 155 regional judicial districts. The first draft round came on 20 July 1917, when blindfolded Secretary of War Newton Baker pulled the first capsule with a number from a large glass jar. Of 24,234,021 men who registered, 3,088,000 eventually were drafted, and the rest that were summoned were sent home, 51.4 per cent for physical or psychological defects, 27.4 per cent for reasons of family or religion, and the rest from other disqualifiers. Eventually, 64,693 applied for noncombatant status as 'conscientious objectors' to participate in violence, and around 57,000 won that status; 337,649 dodged the draft.[125]

3.2 Army Personnel, 1914–1920[126]

Year	Total	Officers	Enlisted
1914	98.544	5,033	93,511
1915	106,754	4,948	101,806
1916	108,399	5,175	103,224
1917	421,467	34,224	387.243
1918	2,395,742	130,485	2,265,257
1919	851,624	91,975	759,649
1920	204,292	18,999	185,293

3.3 Navy Personnel, 1914–1920[127]

Year	Total	Officers	Enlisted
1914	56,898	3,406	53,583
1915	57,072	3,593	53,479
1915	60,376	4,022	56,354
1916	194,617	8,383	186,354
1917	448,606	23,623	424,975
1918	272,144	19,397	252,787
1920	121,845	10,642	111,203

Blacks numbered 367,710 soldiers and 5,528 sailors. Black soldiers served in segregated battalions that mostly involved transportation or supply while black sailors mostly cooked or cleaned. Nearly all blacks who served were draftees; only 4,000 volunteered. There was a black officer training camp at Des Moines with 1,250 students. The 92nd Division that served in France had black enlistees while initially 92 per cent of its officers were white, a ratio that fell to 58 per cent when the war ended.[128]

The Department of War sought a merit-based military. To ensure that each soldier received assignments and ranks that reflected his abilities, the Department of War assigned Dr Robert Yerkes, president of the American Psychological Association, to head a team of experts that devised the intelligence quotient (IQ) test. Around 1.5 million enlisted men and 33,000 officers took the tests.

3.4 Marine Personnel, 1914–1920[129]

Year	Total	Officers	Personnel
1914	10,386	336	10,050
1915	10,286	338	9,948
1916	10,601	348	10,253
1917	27,749	776	26,973
1918	52,819	1,503	51,316
1919	48,814	2,270	46,564
1920	17,165	1,104	16,061

The Western Front extended 475 miles from the North Sea through Belgium and France to the Swiss border. On each side, the belligerents constructed elaborate networks of trenches and bunkers divided by a 'no-man's land' of earth and rotting bodies churned by millions of artillery shells. The tactics consisted of 'creeping' artillery barrages that preceded mass attacks that the enemy usually decimated with machine guns, rifles and artillery. Each side proclaimed any capture of enemy ground a 'victory' even if it was measured in hundreds of yards that cost thousands or tens of thousands of lives to take. A British Army study found that artillery inflicted 58.51 per cent of casualties, machine gun and rifle fire 38.98 per cent, and bayonets less than 1 per cent.[130]

The Americans entered the war at an especially dismal time for Allied prospects. Starting on 5 May 1917, ever more of France's army went 'on strike', with eventually 68 of 112 divisions refusing to budge from their trenches to attack the enemy. The Germans prudently ceased fire on any front with striking French soldiers, to deprive them of any reason to fight. President Raymond Poincaire replaced Marshall Robert-George Nivelle with Marshall Henri Petain as the French army's commander. Petain was revered among soldiers and civilians alike for commanding the army that defended Verdun from German attacks that persisted from 21 February to 18 December 1916. Petain spent months visiting each division, listening to complaints, promising better pay, food and leave, and demoting inept officers, while having 23,385 mutineers tried and convicted, with 412 executed.[131]

***

Wilson insisted that America would fight in the war not as a formal 'ally' but as an 'associated power'. The United States would coordinate operations with the other Western Front belligerents: France, Britain and Belgium, but would exclusively command any American troops and ultimately decide where and how they would deploy and fight. The army to be established in France was called the American Expeditionary Force (AEF).

As for who would lead AEF, Major General John Pershing was the obvious choice.[132] On 2 May 1917, Army Chief of Staff General Hugh Scott informally passed him the word and summoned him to Washington. There, on 10 May 1917, first Scott and then Secretary of War Baker interviewed him. Two days later, Pershing received command of a division, the prelude to AEF command presented by President Wilson at the White House on 26 May 1917. Pershing's secret written orders were to head all American land forces in France and Britain that would cooperate with but stay autonomous from other Allied forces: 'the forces of the United States are a separate and distinct component of the combined forces, the identity of which must be preserved.'[133] Among Pershing's greatest challenges over the next eighteen months was resisting pressure from the British and French high commands to breakup America's swelling army and feed it to their hard-pressed fronts.

In his memoirs, Pershing marveled at his life:

> From the day of my entrance into West Point up to middle age I had hoped the time would come when I could return to civil life while still young enough to take up law or go into business. But successive assignments that offered chances for active field duty and adventure had held me in the army. Now there had come an opportunity for service to the country such as fallen to ... but few men ... Throughout my career I have never ceased to wonder whether, after all, we are not largely the creatures of fate.[134]

Pershing swiftly assembled a staff of 186 personnel, including 59 officers and 128 clerks, split among Personnel (G-1), Intelligence (G-2), Operations (G-3), Supply (G-4) and Training (G-5), the kernel for an army that eventually surpassed 2 million troops. Toward the top of his staff list was George S. Patton, who received promotion to captain on 15 May 1917 and the following day orders to join Pershing in Washington. Patton initially would command his headquarters troops and serve as an unofficial advisor and trouble-shooter. Around this time, Pershing and Nita agreed to marry as soon as the war was over.

During their time in France, Pershing and Patton repeatedly had to discourage schemes by Nita and Beatrice to join them as violations of military policy.

Pershing, Patton and the rest of the staff journeyed by train to New York on 27 May 1917, and the following day packed aboard a merchant ship that on 8 June 1917 docked in Liverpool, England where they boarded a train for London. Awaiting them was an official reception that included British Secretary of State for War Edward Stanley, 17th Earl of Derby; General John French, the home island commander; and American Ambassador Walter Page. The next day, King George V received Pershing at Buckingham Palace. On 13 June 1917, Pershing's headquarters transferred by train, boat and train to Paris. The following day Patton led a group to pay homage to Napoléon in his tomb at Les Invalides.

Pershing established his headquarters in a huge, beautiful mansion with a garden at 73 Rue Varennes. Patton found a three bedroom apartment at 40 Rue D'Artois three blocks off the Champs-Élysées and a block from the Grand Palais. In a typical day,

> I ride from eight to 9 [am]. I inspect barracks & kitchen from 9 to ten [am]. Attend to various jobs in my capacity as adjunct from 10 [am] to 12.30 [pm]. Eat lunch from 12.30 to 1.30 [pm]. Do a thousand things from 1.30 [pm] to seven. Drill the clearks from 7[.00] to 7.30 [pm]. Eat dinner from 7.45 to 8.30 [pm]. Read the 3 Musketeers from 8.30 to 10.30 [pm] and so to bed. I have a rubber bath [tub] and take a bath every morning.[135]

Building and sustaining an army that eventually reached 2 million men demanded a stunning array of related professions and industries. Patton informed his father-in-law that:

> We run railroads and build them. Build docks, charter ships, houses, hotels, factories. We buy coal, wood, movable houses. Horses. Automobiles. Aeroplanes. Clothes. Move troops. Make telegraph lines and almost every other sort of human occupation. We have a hell of a time finding office space for all other clearks and officers. Each day we think that the town will not hold another man then ten more come and we tuck them in.[136]

Patton adored and modeled himself on Pershing. He regretted that he 'was so occupied that I saw him only at meals and occasionally when I accompanied him on visits of inspection, such of that to the British front in July 1917.' Nonetheless, he thrilled that: 'Distance [from the

United States] makes Gen. Pershings job infinitely hard but he is doing it and there is no one else who could. He is a very great man and getting greater all the time.' After World War I, he paid this tribute to Pershing's greatest feat:

> It is to his iron resolution to form an American Army that we owe the great heritage of a victorious America, victorious in her own right and by her own means. But for him her man power would have been bled white to fill the depleted ranks of allied units, where their valor would have been unmarked and their achievements unheralded.[137]

In May 1943, while planning the Sicily invasion, he wrote to Pershing that:

> Whatever ability I have shown or shall show as a soldier is the result of a studious endeavor to copy the greatest American soldier, namely yourself. I consider it a priceless privilege to have served with you in Mexico and France.[138]

Yet Patton did gripe that Pershing

> works his staff too hard. Sunday is just like any other day and if this war is to last three years more as we think that will be more than men can stand. It is true the British staff works all day and every day but a Britisher never works very hard. He is less intense than we are so stands it better.[139]

In his rare time off, Patton enjoyed Parisian cafes, restaurants, theater and museums. He eagerly accepted an offer for an airplane flight from Colonel William 'Billy' Mitchell, who headed America's budding army air force. Elated, he wrote to Beatrice that: 'I had always thought it would frighten me but it did not. One feels perfectly safe and the machine seems steady as a church. The entire country spreads out like a map beneath.'[140]

Patton terribly missed Beatrice and tried to write her daily. To her, he could confess all the self-doubts, depressions, animosities and failures that he masked from his colleagues. The nearly incessant work far from a combat zone was flaying his always fragile confidence: 'Speaking of fate, I was very low in my mind yesterday. There seemed no future in my job and I was disgusted with the daily grind.'[141] Beatrice suffered the deaths of her father and mother while Patton was in France, and all he could do was send his deepest condolences and regrets.

He remained deeply in love with Beatrice and astounded that she returned his love despite all his faults. Those feelings inspired these lines of poetry:

> You never can tell about a woman …
> You are never certain that they love you
> You are often very certain that they don't
> For a man may argue still that he has the strongest will
> But a woman has the strongest won't.[142]

Patton's first important mission was organizing military police to keep order as ever more American units reached France. For that he consulted the British and French provost marshals; he set standards for acceptance and training for each division's 200 military police. He was disappointed by most American troops who appeared in rear echelon billets where they underwent more training: 'Men did not look smart, officers were lazy, troops lacked equipment and training, were listless.' Organizing, housing, training and equipping, and arming an army that would eventually number 2 million men was a Sisyphean torment to Patton and his colleagues: 'We are working long hours but apparently not doing much though of course we are but it is like a rat chewing an oak tree because there is so much to do.'[143]

Touring a stretch of frontline gave Patton a much needed grand view of his endeavors and left him exhilarated:

> I have just returned from a most interesting trip where I saw the working of over a million men from the inside. It is stupendous and fine. The more one sees of war the better it is. Of course there are a few deaths but all of us must pay 'the piper'.

He identified the ruthless key to minimizing American deaths and maximizing German deaths:

> A man has so many chances to shirking in a charge and only iron discipline will get them over the top. Lots of men are shot by their own officers in each attack. If they hang back a second they get it. No questions are asked.[144]

Patton would perform that grim murderous act in a future battle.

***

The French assigned the Americans three ports where ships disgorged troops, equipment and supplies, St Nazaire near the Loire river mouth, La Pallice near Rochefort, and Pauillac on the Gironde river where they were transferred to trains that carried them to the front. Admiral William Sims commanded the Atlantic fleet whose flotillas protected the convoys steaming back and forth across the ocean. Eventually the Atlantic fleet numbered 373 vessels, including 85 destroyers that with their speed and maneuverability were the most effective warships against submarines. Sims and British First Sea Lord John Jellicoe split the ocean into zones then deployed and coordinated their forces among them. Of the 2,079,880 American troops that crossed the Atlantic, American ships conveyed 952,581, British ships 1,006,987, British-leased Italian ships 68,246, and French, Italian, and other nationalities 52,066.[145]

The first significant contingent of American troops to reach France was the 15,000-man 1st Division that began disembarking at St Nazaire on 26 June 1917. Pershing had three 1st Division companies lead a parade on the Champs Elysee on 4 July 1917. Later that day, contrary to legend, it was not Pershing but his aide Colonel Charles Stanton who proclaimed before the general's tomb, 'Lafayette, we are here!'[146]

Pershing moved his headquarters to Chaumont, a small crossroads and cross-rails city in Lorraine, in September 1917. For officers, he established a General Staff College with a three-month curriculum of classes on all aspects of command, including administration, logistics, intelligence, strategy, tactics and leadership. After basic training, a battalion deployed at a quiet sector of the front to season and patrol for a few weeks.

Pershing's key notion of leadership and war was this: 'Military genius is really only the capacity to understand and apply simple principles founded on experience and sound reasoning.'[147] He was a cavalryman used to rapid movements that outflanked and routed or cutoff and destroyed the enemy. Trench warfare with its massed attacks and fruitless slaughter appalled him. He insisted that his troops be trained according to the 1911 and 1917 Field Regulations that emphasized movement and firepower against the enemy's weakest points. He emphasized to his officers and men that

> victory could not be won by the costly process of attrition, but it must be won by driving the enemy out into the open and engaging him in a war of movement. Instruction in this kind of warfare was based upon individual and group initiative, resourcefulness, and tactical judgment.[148]

In this Pershing and Patton were in perfect accord.

Soldiers mostly carried either the .30 caliber Springfield M-1903 rifle or American Model 1917 Enfield rifle, with total production surpassing 2.5 million. As for artillery, only 130 of 3,499 guns and 8,400 of 8,116,000 rounds were American made. Most common were the French 75-millimeter field and 155-millimeter heavy guns. The Americans relied on British factories for 1.5 million helmets.[149]

America's air force gradually expanded.[150] The army and navy had separate air wings with planes initially used for transporting light but important items and reconnaissance, but each soon developed combat squadrons. By the war's end, the Naval Air Service numbered 18,756 personnel including 1,656 pilots, and had flown 5,691 missions, attacking 43 enemy submarines. Pershing split the Air Service Section from the Signal Corps and made it the separate Army Air Service on 4 March 1918. During World War I, five men headed the Air Service, most famously Lieutenant William 'Billy' Mitchell from 30 June to 3 September 1917. Mitchell had extensive experience as a pilot with the Signal Corps' Air Service Section. Americans mostly flew French Nieuport 28s and Spad 13s. Most pilots and mechanics received training in Britain and some in France or Italy. Around ninety combat veterans transferred from the French army's Escadrille Lafayette for American pilots who volunteered before the United States joined the war.

Pershing wanted his troops' behavior to reflect their nation's ideals. To encourage that he issued this proclamation:

> For the first time in American history the American army finds itself in European territory. The good name of the United States and the maintenance of cordial relations require perfect deportment of each member of this command. It is of greatest importance that the soldiers of the American army shall at all times treat the people of France, especially the women, with the greatest courtesy and consideration.[151]

Yet Pershing was a pragmatist not an idealist. Crimes like robbery, rape and murder rose with the number of troops. He expanded the military police and justice system to arrest and try criminals and punish convicts; the system numbered 463 officers and 15,912 men by 1 November 1917.[152] A chronic problem he faced was casualties far from the frontline. Indeed, various diseases inflicted more losses than combat. Most rampant were venereal diseases that afflicted 259,612 soldiers or 5 per cent of the total and 27.7 per cent of 1,000 soldiers. To fight that Pershing had the army issue condoms and pamphlets with advice on how best to avoid it in France, while in the United States the Department of War worked with local officials to have prostitutes arrested and brothels shut down near bases.[153]

Colonel George Marshall was not initially on Pershing's staff. Pershing summoned him in July 1917, after observing his brilliance at organization and planning as 1st Division's chief of staff.[154] Patton and Marshall became friends during this time. Two decades later, as army chief of staff, Marshall would be critical in advancing Patton's career.

***

Within a month of reaching Paris, Patton had an encounter that would be crucial to his career although he dismissed it at the time:

> One hot July [1917] day I was drowsing … at GHQ … Suddenly my slumbers were disturbed by an orderly who told me to report to the Operations Officer … There a certain Major [Fox Conner] introduced me to a French officer and directed me to listen to his story and report my conclusions. This Frenchman was a Tank enthusiast who regaled me for several hours with his lurid tales of the value of his pet hobby as a certain means of winning the war. In the report I submitted … I said, couching the remarks in the euphemistic jargon appropriate to official correspondence, that the Frenchman was crazy and the Tank not worth a damn.[155]

Gradually, Patton warmed to the notion. In mid-September 1917, he wrote: 'There is a lot of talk about "Tanks" here now and I am interested as I can see no future in my present job.'[156] Then, on 3 October 1917, he learned that Pershing was considering him among others to establish and lead an American tank corps. He wrote to Pershing a request to select him, citing a long list of his qualifications:

> The duty of 'tanks' and more especially of 'light tanks' is analogous to the duty performed by cavalry in normal wars. I am a cavalryman … I believe that I have quick judgment and that I am willing to take chances. Also I have always believed in getting in close to the enemy and have taught this for two years at the Mounted Service School where I had success in arousing the aggressive spirit in the students. I believe I am the only American who has ever made an attack in a motor vehicle.[157]

Pershing became interested in tanks shortly after arriving in Paris, and established a committee headed by Colonel Leroy Eltinge to collect key information and draft a plan for an American Tank Corps.[158] In late

September 1917, Eltinge and his committee issued a report that called for a two division corps with one manning 375 to 600 heavy tanks and the other 1,200 to 1,400 light tanks. The heavy battalion would receive the British Mark 1, a 28-ton behemoth 32.6 foot long, 13.9 foot wide and 8.9 foot tall, with a 105 horsepower engine that drove up to 3.7 miles per hour with a 23-mile range, was armed with 2 Hotchkiss 6-pounder cannons and four .303 Vickers machine guns; and manned by a commander/ brakeman, driver, two gearsmen and four gunners.[159] The light battalion would receive the French Renault, with a 6.5 ton weight, 16 foot long, 5.9 foot wide, and 7 foot tall, with a 39 horsepower engine that drove up to 4.3 miles per hour with a 37 mile range, and was armed with a 37-millimeter cannon in a revolving turret, and two man crew, one driving and the other directing and firing the cannon. French Schneider tanks were twice as heavy as a Renault, 13.6 tons, 20.9 foot long, 6.9 foot wide and 7.7 foot tall, with a 60 horsepower engine that could propel it 5 miles per hour for 50 miles and were armed with a 75-millimeter cannon in the front and an 8-millimeter machine gun on each side. French tank battalions assigned to Pershing's First Army deployed Schneiders.[160]

The Tank Corps Heavy Division first organized at Camp Meade, Maryland, then transferred to Bovington Camp near Wareham, England where the British trained and equipped it. Only one Heavy Division fought in the war, 301st Battalion in the British sector during the battle of the Selle on 17 October 1918.

Pershing asked Patton to develop and lead the Tank Corps' Light Division at Bourg, France, on 9 November 1917. Patton eagerly accepted. The next day, Pershing's headquarters officially issued Patton that command with Lieutenant Elgin Braine his deputy. Bourg was 30 miles by rail south of Chaumont, Pershing's headquarters.

To command Tank Corps, Pershing tapped Brigadier General Samuel Rockenbach. That was a solid choice. Rockenbach was a VMI graduate, who served as a staff officer in the Spanish-American War, then headed a company against Filipino guerillas during the insurrection against American rule in the Philippine. He attended the War College in 1912 and served as quartermaster in the Mexico expedition. Pershing admired Rockenbach for his administrative skills and sanguine character.

At first Patton's decisive problem-solving and Rockenbach's gruff, skeptical characters clashed. For Patton, Rockenbach was

> the most contrary cuss I ever worked with. As soon as you suggest any thing he opposes but after about an hours argument comes round and proposes the same thing himself. So in the long run I get my way but

> at a great waste of breath. It is good discipline for me for I have to keep my temper.[161]

Eventually, they established a good working relationship in which the latter largely backed the former's ideas about training, organizing, and deploying the Tank Corps in combat, and tried to expedite all the recruits, equipment and supplies that Patton needed. Rockenbach was America's member of the Inter-Allied Tank Committee formed in April 1918, that met at Versailles the first day of each month to share information, allocate resources, recommend reforms, and coordinate operations.

Patton and Braine first developed an understanding of tanks by visiting the British and French tank schools, deployed regiments, repair shops and factories, taking copious notes of all relevant details and ideas, and learning how to drive and repair the tanks. Patton wrote to Beatrice that 'I am having an interesting and difficult time organizing them as everything is new and there is no precident to go on. I have to originate every thing [*sic*].'[162]

Patton began the two week training course at the French Tank School at Chamlieu in Compiegne Forest on 19 November 1917. He found that learning to drive a Renault tank was

> easy to do after an auto, and quite comfortable though you can see nothing at all ... They go about as fast as one can run and turn like lightening. It is funny to hit small trees and see them go down. They are noisy but easy riding.[163]

Amidst the course, British 3rd Army led by General Julian Byng launched an attack led by 378 Mark IV heavy tanks at a stretch of German trenches near Cambrai on 20 November 1917.[164] Although the army gained 4 miles, that cost them 179 tanks on the first day, 65 from enemy fire, 71 from mechanical breakdowns, and 43 for other reasons along with 75,000 casualties while inflicting 54,000 on the enemy. This was the first large-scale tank attack and Patton would later visit the corps to learn its lessons.

Patton sent Rockenbach a fifty-eight-page report titled *Light Tanks* on 1 December 1917. One section recommended improving the Renault with a bulkhead between the engine and cannon, an internal self-starter, a hand accelerator, leather helmets and a speaking tube for the crew, better tail and rear lights, a higher viewing slit for the driver, and easier ways to adjust the belt and grease the bearings; the French later adapted these innovations.

As for organization, Patton recommended that a platoon number five tanks with three men each, one tank with a 3-inch cannon, two with 6-pounder cannons, and two with machine guns. A company would number three platoons and a headquarters with

> two officers, a first sergeant, company clerk, ten drivers, twenty privates, mess sergeant, one mechanic, two motorcyclists, ten chauffeurs, and three cooks – a total of 2 officers and 51 men, with an additional tank equipped for signals, a tank for the company commander, eight tanks for support, training, and reserve, five trucks for ammunition, two trucks for gasoline and oil, one truck with a trailer for baggage, one kitchen truck with a trailer, one automobile, and two motorcycles. A company would thus have, all told, 5 officers and 96 men, 25 tanks and 12 vehicles. A battalion should have three companies, plus a battalion headquarters and a repair unit. Headquarters personnel would include a major in command, two lieutenants ... A battalion would then consist of ... 18 officers and 331 men, 77 tanks and 42 vehicles.[165]

Tactics involved massing tanks and troops for breakthroughs at vulnerable enemy positions. Tanks and troops would support each other as they advanced, with one or the other proceeding as appropriate to eliminate any threats from enemy machine guns, cannons, or riflemen. Tanks would mostly lead to flatten barbed wire entanglements and overrun trenches, while firing the cannon or machine gun at enemy troops. Patton identified six critical tank missions:

> 1. facilitate infantry advance by cutting wires ahead of the infantry;
> 2. prevent hostile infantry from manning the trench parapet when the preparatory barrage lifted;
> 3. prohibit machine guns and trench cannon from attacking the infantry;
> 4. help mop up, neutralizing strongpoints and blockhouses by masking them with fire and smoke bombs;
> 5. guard against counterattack by patrolling;
> 6. push on at own initiative beyond the final objective – but only after the infantry consolidated that position – in order to seek every opportunity for pursuit.[166]

As a cavalryman, he understood the key element of light tank warfare:

> Mobility is a most essential feature in all arms and is the chief place where the light tank has an advantage over the heavy. The latter must

> always be moved by rail while the light tanks can be moved by autotruck and by trailer ... To get the full value from light tanks they must have maximum mobility.[167]

Recruiters would find appropriate men 'among those who had mechanical experience, who had driven automobiles or motorcycles' along with 'blacksmiths, foundry hands, gasfitters, and plumbers.' The training course would last two months and involve all elements of warfare including driving, repairs and combat. First, two companies would be trained and they in turn would 'instruct two more companies, perhaps as many as four companies, and at the end of three [more] months, six companies or two battalions would be trained.'[168]

The day after submitting his report, Patton was traveling between Paris and Amiens when his automobile ran into a closed train crossing guard. He wrote to Beatrice that,

> I had my usual yearly accident and I carelessly put my head through the front window and cut an artery on my left temple and cut a hole at the point of the jaw on the right side about an inch long and deep.[169]

Once again, Patton cheated death and acquired his latest scars to prove it.

Patton welcomed the first two companies of his tank battalion at Bourg on 17 February 1918. The next day, he began vigorously training them to be tankers and better soldiers in a daily series of drills, classes, calisthenics, inspections, games, firing ranges, and pep talks. He wrote a pamphlet titled *Tank Drill and Training Manuel* in which he explained:

> Success in battle presupposes the destruction of the enemy. This is brought about by killing and wounding his men so as to reduce his strength and destroy his morale. The above happy results may only be looked for when the training has been intelligent and thorough, so that the men are educated in what to do and have the discipline to do it.[170]

Patton and Rockenbach spent much of March 1918 in Britain with a week at the tank training center at Wareham, gathering information and ideas. Later that month they returned to the continent for a week at France's tank training center at Martingy-les-Bains. Patton found the French

> certainly nice and do everything they can to help us. They are some soldiers too. Personally I like them better than the British possibly

> because they do not drink Tea. Which to my mind is a most hellish and wasteful practice ... I have hardly spoken a word of English for a week and am quite surprised at my fluency. I can now easily understand conversations between Two French who I happen to overhear. Which is a test of any language.[171]

Gradually, Patton's ranks caught up to his swelling duties. He was promoted to major on 26 January 1918, lieutenant colonel on 30 March 1918, and colonel on 17 October 1918. Rockenbach greatly appreciated Patton's leadership. In his April 1918 efficiency report, he lauded Patton for the 'splendid results obtained by this officer in the Tank School' that 'show him to be zealous and of good judgment and intelligence. His command is well disciplined and ever soldierly in appearance.' Overall, Patton was 'energetic, efficient, does much good work with little assistance. Qualified and especially fitted to command a tank brigade.'[172]

Patton steadily equipped his troops with everything they needed except, to his frustration, tanks. The Light Division was supposed to get most of its Renaults from French factories along with a portion from American factories. Patton sent Braine with blueprints to the United States to find a manufacturer and shipper. Braine dutifully accomplished that mission but production and transportation bottlenecks delayed the arrival of American-made Renaults until after the armistice. During World War I, American factories turned out only seventy-nine tanks of which fifteen reached France.[173]

Patton finally received his first ten tanks by train on 23 March 1918. He drove seven and a subordinate three of the tanks off the train. Swelling his elation was the French officer who delivered the tanks saying how impressed he was at the unloading that 'would take us 15 hours and we did it in just three.' Patton found the entire experience thrilling: 'It was a beautiful moonlight night and ideal for the purpose. When the procession of ten started across the fields I was delighted as I have been living on high hopes for four months.'[174]

Maintaining, repairing, and, above all, maneuvering tanks was now central to training. New companies of troops arrived to be quartered, equipped, and instructed. By 28 April 1918, he had enough companies to officially inaugurate 1st Light Tank Battalion. More batches of Renaults arrived. Patton longed to lead his battalion against the enemy, but his troops were not yet fully prepared for combat. Instead, he traveled to stretches of the front where French and British tank battalions operated.

Although the training camp was behind the lines dangers lurked. One day, Patton was observing soldiers fire a 37-millimeter gun when a

> defective round exploded in the muzzle, wounding two or three men. The next round exploded in the breach, blowing the head off the gunner. The men were reluctant to fire the next round, so it was incumbent on me ... to do so. I fired three rounds without incident. This restored the confidence of the men in the weapon. I must admit that I was never in my life been more reluctant to pull a trigger.[175]

***

The Western Allies suffered an enormous blow when a communist revolution led by Vladimir Lenin, overthrew Russia's government in early November 1917. The communists negotiated a cease-fire with Germany that began on 2 December 1917 and the Treaty of Brest-Litovsk on 3 March 1918. Under the treaty, Russia ceded its empire over Estonia, Latvia, Lithuania, Poland, Belorussia and Ukraine to Germany or Austria, and formally granted Finland independence; those lands included one third of the Russian Empire's population and half of its industry.

That freed the Germans and Austrians to transfer millions of their troops from the Eastern to their respective Western and Italian fronts. The hope in Berlin was that Germany's army could mass enough men for an offensive in early 1918 that smashed through the enemy lines before the American army's steady buildup reached a decisive level. By March 1918, General Erich Ludendorff, the German commander, had deployed 3,575,000 troops split among 192 divisions along the Western Front.

The Germans launched on 21 March 1918, the first of five short intensive offensives, with each punching through and capturing different stretches of the front but without a decisive breakthrough.[176] Each time the Allies managed to rush enough reserves to contain the Germans with the latest maze of trenches backed by massed artillery. The first offensive captured the most ground when it ended on 5 April 1918, followed by ones from 9 to 29 April, 27 May to 5 June, 9 to 13 June, and 15 to 17 July 1918. The Germans suffered 688,341 casualties while inflicting 865,374, including 433,000 on the French, 418,374 on the British, 7,000 on the Portuguese, and 5,000 on the Italians.

The Germans wielded new tactics to take all that ground and kill, wound, and capture a couple hundred thousand more soldiers than they lost. They abandoned the self-devastating mass human wave attacks preceded by mass artillery barrages. Each infantry company was split into fourteen-man Storm Trooper (*Sturmtruppen*) assault groups trained to infiltrate the enemy line and find positions to enfilade the defenders. Preceding attacks, artillery barrages were now shorter and more focused through three phases, first against the enemy's command and communication posts, then enemy artillery batteries, and finally weak parts of the enemy defenses. Those precise artillery and storm trooper attacks depended on intelligence gathered by airplanes and patrols then carefully analyzed and applied to battle plans by commanders at each appropriate level.

The Americans experienced their first large-scale fighting when the Germans attacked 26th Division in its sector around Seicheprey beginning 20 April 1918. The 1st Division launched the American army's first offensive when it attacked the Germans at Cantingy from 28 May 1918, captured the town and then repelled a series of counterattacks. The Americans suffered 1,603 casualties and inflicted slightly more, around 1,400 dead and wounded and 250 captured. The Americans fought their first prolonged campaign at Belleau Wood from 1 to 26 June 1918, when two army divisions and a marine brigade captured its objectives while suffering 9,777 casualties and inflicting around 10,000. Then, on 18 July 1918, during their attack near Château-Thierry, the Americans inflicted more than twice as many casualties as they suffered, 5,326 to 1,908.

The American Expeditionary Force numbered 1.3 million troops by August 1918. As the divisions arrived, Pershing assigned them to an expanding command structure. He established I Corps with its headquarters at Neufchâteau several miles behind the front on 15 January 1918 and designated First Army with three corps on 10 August 1918. Meanwhile, Patton's 1st Brigade of the Tank Corps steadily expanded and by early September 1918 included 326th and 327th battalions with 50 officers and 900 enlisted men and 174 Renaults split between them.

Pershing's worst frustration was dealing with Allied commanders and bureaucracy. France's red tape and bureaucrats dismayed him:

> After a few contacts with their system one marveled that the French had managed to get along so well in supplying their armies during three years of war. The French are very intelligent and have a highly organized government, but from the practical viewpoint they often become deeply

> involved in nonessential details and lose sight of the main objective. I have always likened the average French bureau official to a certain narrow type of quartermaster who … regarded all government property under his charge as his own, and when he finally issued it always made the recipient feel that he was being specially favored.[177]

French General Ferdinand Foch was the Supreme Allied commander who presided over the Supreme War Council of army commanders including Pershing. All along, Pershing sternly resisted pressure by the other generals to breakup his swelling army and transfer his divisions to their fronts crumbling under Germann assaults. During the 2 May 1918 meeting, Foch demanded that 'America give us 120,000 infantrymen and machine gunners in May [1918] – the same number in June [1918], with a supplement of 50,000 infantrymen and machine gunners.' Pershing replied with the greatest possible emphasis:

> Gentlemen, I have thought the program over very deliberately and will not be coerced … America declared war independently of the Allies and she must face it as soon as possible with a powerful army … the morale of our soldiers depends on their fighting under their own flag.[178]

First Army deployed 216,000 troops, 1,681 cannons, and 267 tanks in an arc around a sector called the St Mihiel salient that the Germans had occupied since September 1914 and fortified with extensive networks of trenches and forts. At the salient's west end south of Verdun, General Beaumont Buck's V Corps faced east, followed by French General Ernest Bondlat's Colonial Corps (48,000 troops, 1,329 cannons and 278 tanks) west and south of St Mihiel, then General Joseph Dickman's IV Corps and General Hunter Liggett's I Corps facing eastward. The Meuse river ran behind most of V Corps and the French Corps except for a German foothold west of the river at St Mihiel. The Moselle river split I Corps' western two thirds from its eastern one third. Brigadier General Billy Mitchell commanded 1,481 aircraft with American, French, British and Portuguese pilots to support the offensive with reconnaissance, bombing and strafing attacks on the enemy lines while fending off enemy fighters and bombers. The American contingent included twelve pursuit, twelve observation, and three bombing squadrons or about one third of the total.

Allied headquarters assigned Pershing's army the mission of eliminating that bulge.[179] For that, Pershing moved his headquarters from Chaumont to Neufchâteau to be closer to the front. Then, on the offensive's eve, Foch insisted that Pershing split his army and sent a corps west to aid a French offensive in the Aisne river valley. Once again Pershing resisted enormous pressure, finally winning with these words:

> Marshal Foch, you may insist all you please, but I decline absolutely to agree to your plan. While our army will fight wherever you may decide, it will not fight except as an independent American army.[180]

He then presented Foch a letter signed by President Wilson with those orders.

Pershing resumed planning the offensive with his staff. Headquarters initially assigned Patton's brigade to V Corps. Patton prepared for his offensive by reconnoitering the landscape between the lines where his battalion would attack:

> I was out on patrol in No man's land last week. It was most interesting and was not at all exciting. We went along with the 'Burglars Crawl' for about a mile and a half till we came to the Bosch wire. This we examined and the Bosch whistled at us and we whistled back and having seen what we wanted went home. No one shot at us but we saw some bosch walking along about 100 m. [meters away] Both sides were anxious not to disturb the others.[181]

Headquarters scrubbed that attack and shifted Patton's brigade to IV Corps headquartered at Toul. Initially, two tank brigades would support 42nd Division's assault, Patton's and the French IV Battalion of twenty-five Schneider medium tanks led by Major Charles Chanoine, then they were transferred to support 1st Division's 84th Brigade commanded by General Douglas MacArthur.

After reconnoitering that ground, Patton briefed his officers:

> From a tactical point of view the present operation is easy ... Remember that you are to make paths in the wire and put out machine gun nests for the infantry ... never get more than a hundred and fifty yards ahead of them and never let them get ahead of you ... No tank is to be surrendered or abandoned to the enemy. If you are left alone in the midst of the enemy keep shooting. If your gun is disabled use your pistols and squash the enemy with your tracks. If your motor is stalled and your gun broken still the infantry cannot hurt. You hang on, help will come ... As long as one tank is able to move it must go forward.[182]

The battle began before dawn on 12 September 1918 with a four-hour artillery barrage that fired 1.1 million shells on the German lines. After the barrage ended at dawn, Patton led his first tank assault. With an officer and three runners, he strode among his slowly advancing tanks, urging them onward and untangling any indecisions and hesitations along the way. On one stretch, two of the most acclaimed American commanders of World War II had an extraordinary encounter and displayed enormous courage to their troops:

> I walked right along the firing line of one brigade. They were all in shell holes except the general ... who was standing on a little hill. here I met Gen. [Douglas] MacArthur ... he was walking about too. I joined him and the creeping barrage came along toward us, but it was very thin and not dangerous. I think each one wanted to leave but each hated to say so, so we let it come over us. We stood and talked but neither was much interested in what the other said as we could not get our minds off the shells.[183]

World War II's history would have subsequently read quite differently had that day a stray shell obliterated Patton and MacArthur.

After the shelling ended, Patton 'asked him if I could attack the next town Pannes. He said sure so I started. All the tanks but one ran out of gas.' Patton climbed atop that tank with his officer and a runner and they rumbled slowly forward on the cratered road with infantry trailing far behind. His two men jumped off to chase a stray German who fled into a house, and there they found thirty other demoralized Germans who surrendered. Patton continued forward with the tank with the infantry following. Suddenly,

> I saw paint fly off the side of the tank and heard machine guns so I jumped off and got in a shell hole...The tank had not seen me get off and was going on. The infantry was about 200 m. back of me and did not advance ... I was on the point of getting scared as I was ... ahead of the infantry and all alone in the field. If I went back the infantry would think I was running and there was no reason for me to go ahead alone ... Finally I decided that I could get back obliquely. So I started ... As soon as the [machine guns] I would lay down and beat the bullets.[184]

Unscathed, Patton rejoined the hunkered down troops and ordered them to follow him forward, but they refused to budge. The tank he had ridden was still steadily advancing toward the enemy. He dashed forward several hundred yards, reached the tank, banged on the side, and ordered it to withdraw. As they reached the infantry four more tanks rumbled up and he led the five toward the enemy, this time followed by the infantry. They deployed around Pannes where, exhausted, they awaited reinforcements.

After catching his breath, Patton

> walked along the battle front to see how the left battalion had gotten on. It was a very long way and I had had no sleep for four nights and no food that day as I lost my sack chasing a boshe ... I found 25 tanks [that] ... had taken the town [Nonsard] and only lost 4 men & 2 officers but they were all out of gas. The major of the left battalion was crying because he had no more gas. He was very tired and had a bullet through his nose. I comforted him and ... started back seven miles to tell them to get more gas ... it had been raining two hours and the mud was bad ... I met an officer who was sight seeing and he gave me a lift. This was luckey [*sic*] as the car got caught in a jam and went slower than the men on foot and an air plane dropped a bomb on the road and killed two soldiers who had been walking just behind me ... I got a motor cycle and got the gas and reported to the Corps.[185]

Patton's first battle was an exhausting, perilous but ultimately exhilarating experience. He had

> proved to my own satisfaction that I have nerve. I was the only man on the front line except gen. MacArthur who never ducked a shell. I wanted to but it is foolish as it does no good. If they are going to hit you they will.

He lost relatively few men and machines for advancing around 7 miles and capturing the 'towns of Nonsard, Pannes, and Benny ahead of the infantry, and the town of Joinville unaided by any infantry.' In all,

> 5 men killed, 4 officers and 15 men wounded. Of them 2 were killed while inside tank, none was wounded there. Of the 174 tanks entering the battle, 3 were destroyed, 22 were ditched so badly that they were out of action all day, 14 had serious mechanical troubles.[186]

Patton's heroic leading of his men from the front enraged Rockenbach who blistered him for not directing the battle from the rear. Patton defended his behavior by arguing that only at the front could he clearly see what was going right and wrong, and what was needed and unneeded. Only by asserting his rank and leading charges could he get fearful, confused officers and soldiers alike to advance and attack under fire.

The Americans decisively won the battle of St Mihiel. First Army inflicted 22,550 casualties including 2,000 killed, 5,500 wounded and 13,250 prisoners, and captured 443 cannons and 752 machine guns while suffering around 7,000 casualties. Mitchell's air force flew 3,000 sorties, fired 30,000 rounds, shot down around 50 enemy planes and lost 40 pilots.

***

St Mihiel was the America army's warmup to the Meuse Argonne campaign that far surpassed it in its scale of troops, territory and time, and decisively ended the war.[187] First Army's three corps massed between the Aisne and Meuse rivers, and included 500,000 troops, 2,000 cannons, 900,000 tons of ammunition and 345 tanks. Three roads led from the rear to the front, and were jammed with men, machines and horse-drawn wagons.

The toughest fight would be I Corps' on the left north through the Argonne Forest and then north-east to the Meuse. On its right, V Corps had a much smaller forest, Bois de Cheppy, to battle through. III Corps had a salient across the Meuse at Verdun but yielded it to the attached French Corps. III Corps had more open ground to attack before crossing the Meuse around Dun. Patton's tank brigade would fight with I Corps' 28th and 35th divisions in the narrow Aire river valley, crowded by the Argonne Forest westward and Bois de Cheppy Forest eastward. When the offensive began, the brigade numbered 834 troops and 145 tanks. First Army's offensive was part of attacks by 160 divisions with 2.5 million Allied troops along much of the frontline with 60 divisions in reserve to exploit any breakthroughs.

***

Patton patrolled the no man's land he would fight through and found the terrain easier but the enemy far more numerous and the weather just as rainy:

> I fancy our next show will be less easy than the first that is if the bosch fight and I think they will. The ground however is better for us being less of a swamp than the St. Mihiel salient proved to be. Still as it has been raining all the time it may get muddie here too.[188]

Patton's *Memorandum on Plan for the Use of Tanks* for headquarters explained his intention to split his two battalions between the two infantry divisions. On each side he would mass his armor in depth on a 2-mile wide front accompanied by infantry to smash through the enemy line after which the tanks would split in two with the column nearest the river pushing ahead and the other column curling to block retreating enemy troops. The worst challenge was sustaining the offensive by conveying enough gas by truck to the advancing tanks. Engineers had to clear roads of obstructions and tire puncturing objects. The only insurmountable barrier was the river that kept tanks on either side from supporting those on the other if they bogged down.

Patton and his staff overcame rail and truck bottlenecks to bring all 345 tanks and 20,000 gasoline gallons to the front by 23 September 1918. Each tank began with a full load of gasoline plus two 2-liter cans attached to the back. Patton would again defy Rockenbach's orders and lead from the front, dashing with an officer and initially six runners from one stalled company to the next to rally the tankers and troops to overcome anything impeding them, including cowed or confused leaders.

The offensive began at dawn on 26 September 1918 with a massive artillery barrage as Patton's tanks and the infantry slowly advanced. Fog initially aided the attack, but German rifle, machine gun, and cannon fire steadily got deadlier as sunlight dispersed it. When a tank company got stuck crossing a wide trench and a couple of hundred or so infantry dispersed to hug any cover, Patton hurried over and ordered the men to shovel a portion of the trench so the tanks could cross as machine gun bullets whizzed past. Twice as bullets killed and wounded one after another among them, troops panicked and

> started to run but we hollered at them and called them all sorts of names so they staid [*sic*]. But they were scared … and acted badly, some put on gas masks, some covered their face with their hands but none did a damn thing to kill Bosch. There were no officers but me … I think I killed one man here. He would not work so I hit him in the head with a shovel. It was exciting for they shot at us all the time but I got mad and walked on the parapet. At last we got five tanks across and I started them forward and cursed and waved my stick and said go on. About 150 dough boys started but when we got to the crest of a hill the fire got fierce. We all lay down.[189]

Patton admitted that he

> felt a great desire to run. I was trembling with fear when suddenly I thought of my progenitors and seemed to see them in a cloud over the German lines looking at me. I became calm at once and saying aloud, 'It is time for another Patton to die', called for volunteers and went forward to what I honestly believed to be certain death. Six men went with me.[190]

Bullets killed four of the men when

> I felt a blow in the leg but at first I could walk so went about 40 ft when my leg gave way. My striker the only man left yelled, 'Oh god the colonels hit and there aint [*sic*] no one left.' He helped me to a shell hole and we lay down and the Bosch shot over the top.[191]

The bullet had sliced through Patton's hip and exited near his rectum. He lay there nearly an hour as shots sporadically buzzed overhead. Finally, medics reached him with a stretcher and carried him to a rear first aid station where later he was trucked to a distant hospital.

Rockenbach took over and directed a series of attacks with diminishing numbers of tanks over the next week. On 5 October 1918, with only 17 tanks and 81 men fit for duty, he called a halt. In all, of 757 enlisted men when the offensive began, 16 were killed and 118 were wounded; of 55 officers, three were killed and 18 were wounded, including Patton,[192]

Patton slowly recovered. He wrote to Beatrice that his 'wound is still full of bugs so they can't sew me up. It is most provoking.' He noted with mingled horror and pride that 'Six captains out of seven were hit the first three days and 30 Lieutenants out of 35 also got hit, we ended up after 14 days with 80 men and 6 officers out of 800.' Most vitally, the tank corps established its reputation for not giving ground. They only went forward. And they are the only troops in the attack of whom that can be said. With mingled relief and pride, he informed Beatrice that: 'You know I have always feared I was a coward at heart but I am beginning to doubt it.'[193] Pershing reassured Beatrice that her husband

> was exceptionally gallant and was leading a body of men to attack a machine gun nest when he was shot in the leg ... he has received all sorts of praise from those who know of the incident. You are to be congratulated and should be prouder of him than ever.[194]

***

The campaign ground on with steady American advances. Meanwhile, Pershing fought his latest battle with Foch over strategy, and this time lost. The Americans advanced faster than the French and were poised to capture Sedan on 10 November 1918, when Foch ordered Pershing to halt his army and let France's Fourth Army capture that city. For the

French, honor demanded that they retake Sedan where Germany had inflicted a crushing defeat on France during the Franco-Prussian War of 1870–1871.

Meuse-Argonne was America's deadliest and most prolonged battle in the nation's history. First Army suffered 26,277 American dead and 95,786 wounded, and 70,000 French casualties, while inflicting around 126,000 casualties, including 28,000 dead, 42,000 wounded and 55,000 prisoners, and captured 879 cannons. Despite First Army's losses, a steady stream of reinforcements doubled its size to 1,031,000 troops, including 135,000 French.

On 11 October 1918, Pershing split his men between the First Army and newly established Second Army commanded respectively by generals Hunter Liggett and Robert Bullard. That made him an army group commander with equal status to Henri Petain and Douglas Haig.

***

Germany's alliance, Western Front and government collapsed. Bulgaria signed an armistice on 29 September 1918, Turkey on 31 October 1918 and Austria-Hungary on 4 November 1918. Allied armies punched through the Western Front and advanced toward Germany. Worsening turmoil roiled Germany as a series of communist led mutinies erupted at naval bases in Kiel, Wilhelmshaven, Helgoland, Borkum and Cuxhaven from 29 October to 8 November 1918.

Kaiser Wilhelm II and Chancellor Max von Baden agreed to send Vice Chancellor Matthias Erzberger and a delegation to meet near Compiegne with the Allied delegation led by Marshall Foch. After the German delegates arrived on 8 November 1918, the Allies presented them an armistice document and gave them seventy-two hours to sign it. Meanwhile, a group of liberal and socialist leaders at Berlin declared Germany a republic on 9 November 1918. Kaiser Wilhelm II fled to exile in the Netherlands on 10 November 1918 and von Baden transferred the chancellorship to Friedrich Ebert, the Social Democratic Party leader. After learning of that revolutionary change of government, Erzberger signed the document.[195]

The 11 November 1918 armistice required Germany to evacuate France, Belgium, Luxembourg and the former French regions of Alsace and Lorraine that it had won after the Franco-Prussian War; withdraw all its troops 30 miles east of the Rhine river; let Allied troops occupy Germany west of the Rhine with bridgeheads at Cologne, Coblenz, Mainz and Strasbourg; hand over 5,000 locomotives, 150,000 railroad cars, 150 submarines, 5,000 cannons, 30,000 machine guns and 3,000 trench mortars; and sail its surface fleet to Scarpa Flow off northern Scotland where the Royal Navy would control it. The Allied naval blockade would continue until Berlin completely complied.

Pershing criticized the armistice for coming when the Allies were poised to crush the German army and invade Germany. Then the Allies could have forced the Germans to agree to unconditional surrender:

> Our success had been so striking since the beginning of the November 1st attack that I felt full advantage should have been taken of the possibility of destroying the armies on our front and seizing the region upon which Germans largely depended for her supply of iron and coal ... If unconditional surrender had been demanded, the Germans would, without doubt, have been compelled to yield, and their troops would have returned to Germany without arms, virtually as paroled prisoners of war. The surrender of the German armies would have been an advantage to the Allies in the enforcement of peace terms and would have been a greater deterrent against possible future German aggression.[196]

Although disappointed at the war's abrupt end, Pershing and his men could take enormous pride in what they had accomplished. America's Expeditionary Force eventually numbered 2,084,000 men in 49 divisions, with 1,390,000 men including 61,061 officers and 1,354,067 enlisted troops in 29 divisions split between 2 armies deployed on the front. Indeed, by November 1918, America's number of troops far surpassed France's 1,668,000 in number. The Tank Corps in France numbered 752 officers and 11,277 troops, and that in the United States numbered 484 officers and 7,700 split between Camp Polk, Louisiana and Camp Colt, Pennyslvania. The AEF officially fought for 150 days, and captured 63,000 enemy troops, 1,500 cannons, 10,000 machine guns and mortars, 485,00 square miles of territory, and deployed across 101 miles or a quarter of the frontline, and suffered 122,500 dead, including 48,909 from combat and the rest from disease and accidents, and 237,135 wounded. The army awarded 95 men with Medals of Honor and 6,154 men with Distinguished Service Crosses. Sergeant Alvin York committed the most renowned feat when he killed 25 Germans and captured 132 in one day. By the end of World War I, the American Air Service's 45 squadrons included 20 pursuit, 18 observation, and 7 bomber squadrons with 58,009 personnel. They shot down 755 enemy aircraft and 76 balloons while suffering 357 planes shot down along with 235 killed, 130 wounded, 145 captured and 654 who died from noncombat causes. Seventy-one pilots became aces by shooting down five or more planes, with Eddie Rickenbacker the highest with twenty-six kills.[197]

America's losses were horrific but much less compared to most other belligerents. America's dead were 0.4 per cent of the nation's population, 2.7 per cent of American troops and 1.2 per cent of all war dead. The highest death tolls for a nation were Serbia's 5.7 per cent, Turkey's 3.7 per cent, France's 3.4 per cent, Romania's 3.3 per cent, Scotland's 3.1 per cent, Germany's 3.0 per cent, Austro-Hungary's 1.9 per cent, Britain and Ireland's 1.6 per cent, Italy's 1.6 per cent, New Zealand's 1.5 per cent and Australia's 1.2 per cent. The worst total deaths included Germany's 2,037,000, Russia's 1,811,000, France's 1,398,000, Austro-Hungary's 1,100,000, Britain's 723,000, Italy's 578,000 and the British Empire's 198,000. In all, 9,450,000 soldiers and at least 6,000,000 civilians died during the war, more than 15,450,000 altogether,[198]

3.5 Total Combat Casualties of World War I[199]

Country	Killed	Prisoner	Wounded	Total
France	1,398,000	446,300	2,000,000	3,844,300
Belgium	38,000	10,203	44,686	92,889
Portugal	7,000	12,318	13,751	33,069
Italy	578,000	530,000	947,000	2,055,000
Britain	723,000	170,398	1,662,625	2,556,014
British Empire	198,000	21,263	427,587	646,850
Romania	250,000	80,000	120,000	450,000
Serbia	278,000	70,423	133,148	481,571
Greece	26,000	1,000	21,000	48,000
Russia	1,811,000	3,500,000	1,450,000	6,761,000
United States	114,000	4,480	205,690	324,170
Total Allies	5,421,000	4,846,376	7,025,487	17,292,863
Germany	2,037,000	617,922	4,207,487	6,861,950
Austro-Hungary	1,100,000	2,200,000	3,620,000	6,920,000
Bulgaria	88,000	10,623	152,390	251,013
Turkey	804,000	250,000	400,000	1,454,000
Total Central Powers	4,029,000	3,078,545	8,379,418	15,486,963
Grand Total	9,450,000	7,924,921	15,404,905	32,779,826

The number of men mobilized for the war was unprecedented. The Americans put 4.3 million in uniform or 4.3 per cent of the population and sent half overseas. Naturally the Europeans massed far more, France 7.9 million, Britain 8.4 million, Germany 13.2 million and Russia 18 million. In each European country the portion of manhood mobilized was several times larger than in the United States.

The Central Powers were far more financially adept at funding the war and killing the enemy than the Allies. The Allies and Central Powers respectively spent around $140 billion and $80 billion from 1914 to 1918. It cost the Central Powers just $11,344.77 to kill each enemy soldier, three times less than the Allies expenditure of $36,485,48. The Central Powers killed 35 per cent more troops than they suffered killed and captured as much as 38 per cent more than they lost as prisoners.[200]

***

Wilson devoted himself to making the war that just ended history's last war. On 8 January 1918, he had presented before Congress his fourteen point peace plan with eight that adjusted current boundaries to reduce ethnic animosities that provoked conflict while six were principles to guide international relations including freedom of the seas, self-determination for all peoples, open diplomacy, outlawing of imperial wars, and, most vital, an organization for all nations to peacefully resolve their differences.

3.6 Government War Budgets and National Debt[201]

Country	Budgets, 1914–1918 ($)	Debts, 1914–1919 ($)
United States	35,721,000,000	24,144,000,000
Germany	32,388,000,000	15,135,000,000
Britain	45,307,000,000	30,432,000,000
France	30,009,000,000	25,423,000,000
Russia	11,778,000,000	N/A
Italy	12,982,000,000	7,364,000,000

Wilson insisted on leading America's delegation that negotiated with the Allies a peace treaty to present Germany. On 15 December 1918, they reached Paris, greeted by exuberant crowds lining the streets. He later experienced the same mass jubilation when he visited London and Rome. That adoration exacerbated his already bloated ego and belief he was the world's secular savior. He spent nearly six months in Europe, mostly negotiating the treaty as a member of the Big Four along with prime ministers Georges Clemenceau of France, David Lloyd George of Britain and Vittorio Orlando of Italy. His colleagues sought to impose a harsh peace on Germany that extracted immense financial reparations and straitjacketed its military. Although Wilson favored a generous, forgiving peace, he grudgingly yielded to their demands for vengeance and spoils in return for the other three reluctantly accepting his idea for a League of Nations. Germany's reparation bill was eventually calculated at 132 billion gold Reichsmarks, and Allied troops would occupy its industrial Ruhr and Saar regions until it was paid, while its army was reduced to 100,000 troops and its air force and navy were abolished. After protesting those harsh terms, Germany's delegation signed the treaty at Versailles Palace on 28 June 1919, five years after the assassination that precipitated World War I.

Ironically, back in Washington, Wilson failed to convince more than two thirds of the Senate to ratify the Treaty of Versailles. Most opponents objected to the clauses that committed the United States to joining the League of Nations, fearing that membership would entangle America in unnecessary expenses, conflicts and wars. So, the League of Nations convened in 1920 without the world's greatest economic power that could have worked with the other great powers to keep the peace.

World War I shifted the global financial balance of power. When the war began in 1914, Americans owed foreign investors $3.7 billion more than they were owed. During World War I, most foreign investors sold off their assets in the United States, often at fire sale prices, while American financiers lent money mostly to the French and British governments. In 1919, America's net foreign investments were $11 billion. New York replaced London as the world's financial capital.

***

Meanwhile, Patton emerged from the hospital on 28 October 1918 and resumed command of his brigade. With the war ended, he and 2 million other American soldiers endured mostly tedium and homesickness as they awaited official word to return to the United States. Elgin Braine, Patton's deputy and now a major, took over the tank school at Bourg while Patton focused on administering his brigade and giving lectures on tank warfare to various military and journalist audiences.

Patton recommended three of his men for the Medal of Honor and sixteen for the Distinguished Service Cross. Rockenbach recommended that Patton receive a Distinguished Service Cross for extraordinary valor in combat. The citation that accompanied the award on 16 December 1918 declared that Patton

> displayed conspicuous courage, coolness, energy, and intelligence in directing his brigade … Later he rallied a force of disorganized infantry and led it forward behind tanks under heavy machine gun and artillery fire until he was wounded. Unable to advance further, he continued to direct the operations of his unit until all arrangements for turning over the command were completed.[202]

Patton certainly was pleased with getting the Distinguished Service Cross, but believed he merited the Medal of Honor 'which I missed getting this time on account of all the witnesses getting killed or being Bosch' but swore he would earn a Medal of Honor in the next war.[203]

Patton composed a list of nine 'Tactical Conclusions' for tanks with this key:

1. Infantry and tanks must work closely together with each benefiting from the other's strengths and overcoming its weaknesses;
2. Infantry without or with limited tank support should still advance;
3. Tanks were too valuable in fire power and too weak in mechanical power to be used for reconnaissance;
4. Officers must reconnoiter on foot the ground they will attack;
5. Enemy artillery most threatened tanks;
6. Tanks must attack mass in depth on narrow fronts at the enemy line's most vulnerable places. To reinforce infantry's crucial role, he later added the maxim, 'tanks can take nearly anything. They can hold absolutely nothing.'[204]

Patton applied to Pershing on 10 February 1919, for permission to return with his tank brigade to the United States rather than be transferred to Trier, Germany, as a provost marshal for the occupation. He cited being away from home for two and a half years during which his wife suffered the loss of her parents and was in poor health. Pershing granted him permission on 23 February 1919. Three days later, he departed on a train packed with 30 of his officers, 1,470 of his men, and their equipment in 36 cars bound for Marseilles. They embarked on a ship on 1 March 1919 and reached New York on 17 March 1919. Patton's family was among thousands waiting to greet the returning troops at dockside.[205] Patton's World War I experience was now literally behind him but echoed the rest of his life, informing, inspiring and haunting him.

Chapter 4

DOLDRUMS

'I am convinced that as good as Leavenworth is it is still only a means not an end ... I have worked all the problems of the two years since I graduated and shall continue to do so.

However I dont [*sic*] try for approved solutions anymore [*sic*] but rather to do what I will do in war.'

'It is much better to be a lone wolf than a coyote.'

George S. Patton

The army's rapid massive military buildup from 130,000 troops in April 1917 to 3.7 million troops in November 1918 was followed by just as rapid a demobilization. By June 1920, the army numbered just 200,000 troops. The 1920 National Defense Act authorized an army of 300,000 troops but the 1921 National Defense Act reduced the army to 12,000 officers and 125,000 troops. By 1922, America's army ranked in manpower number seventeenth in the world and there it stayed for eighteen years. During the interwar years, professional officers struggled to adjust to those cutbacks, reductions in rank and stymied chances for promotion and distinction.

After returning in February 1919, Colonel George S. Patton and his brigade were stationed at Camp Meade, Maryland. General Samuel Rockenbach returned to command the Tank Corps with an authorized strength of 154 officers and 2,508 men for 1919. Patton served on the Tank Corps Technical Board that investigated and reported ways to improve tank technology. They visited production and repair facilities, and talked to hundreds of veterans, managers and engineers. It was largely Patton's recommendations that filled the final report including improved or added

> periscopes, fan belts, a handrail for the engine compartment, a bracket wheel for the sun pinion, how to prevent a clutch from sticking, the radiator, exhaust manifold brake drum, speedometer cable ... munition storage system, the driver's location, the engine, the eye-slits, the foot accelerator, the round clearance of the axles, the movable roof, the pistol ports, the antiaircraft protection, the seat suspension, the small arms ammunition racks, and the placement of tools

along with 'the Browning tank machine gun be equipped with special ammunition designed to increase the tank's firepower.'[206]

The most important recommendation was for a new tank design called the Christie Gun Mount developed by Walter Christie of the Front Drive Motor Company in Hoboken, New Jersey. The tank included both interchangeable trends and thick tires that let it travel on earth and concrete. On 15 June 1920, the Ordnance Corps signed a contract with Christie to build a prototype.

The National Defense Act 1920 established the Air Service, Chemical Warfare Service and Department of Finance but abolished the Tank Corps and assigned the division to the infantry. That eliminated Patton's rank as colonel and he briefly reverted to captain on 30 June 1920, but the next day, 1 July 1920, was promoted to major. Rockenbach retained Patton and Lieutenant Colonel Henry Mitchell respectively to command the 304th and 305th Tank brigades.

***

During his latest stint at Fort Meade, Patton met and developed a deep friendship with the man who would be his commander throughout World War II.[207] Dwight D. Eisenhower was then a lieutenant colonel and second in command of the 305th Tank Brigade.[208] Eisenhower, nicknamed Ike, was easy to like. He was naturally amiable and enjoyed being with like-minded colleagues in common endeavors. He had a broad, infectious grin that put most others at ease. He had an all-American boy guilelessness that caused some to underestimate his intelligence, ambition and toughness. He never led men in combat yet through luck and multi-talents rose steadily through the ranks to become a five-star general and then president. He was born in Denison, Texas in October 1890, but grew up in Abilene, Kansas as the third of six rambunctious brothers. The Eisenhowers had a low income as the father was a mechanic in a creamery and the mother managed their small farm. Eisenhower was a roughneck boy and teenager, who loved baseball, football, hunting and fishing, and an occasion fistfight. He was very bright, very good at mathematics, and became adept at poker and bridge. He enjoyed reading, especially history and biographies of great men, although to relax he favored dime cowboy and detective novels. He was 5 feet and 11 inches tall, and 145 pounds when he graduated from high school. He became addicted to tobacco at a young age and during World War II daily chain-smoked four cigarette packs. Although he was handsome and athletic, he was shy around girls.

Unlike Patton, Eisenhower had not originally wanted to pursue a military career but sought a West Point or Annapolis appointment for a free university degree. He passed West Point's entrance exam and entered in 1911. He was not a natural soldier and racked up scores of demerits for breaking various rules. He was heartbroken when an injured knee forced him off the football team. He was just an above average student. Of 164 classmates in 1915, he graduated 61 in academics and 125 in discipline. Although Omar Bradley was among his classmates, they were just acquaintances.

To his chagrin, Second Lieutenant Eisenhower missed the Mexican expedition and World War I's frontlines in France. Nonetheless, by May 1917, his diligence at mostly staff and supply assignments along with being a winning football coach for post teams got him promoted to first lieutenant and then captain. When he was posted at Fort Sam Houston, he met at the Officer's Club and soon fell in love with Mamie Doud, a pretty flirtatious young woman from a wealthy merchant family in Denver that regularly vacationed in San Antonio. They married in November 1916.

He entered what was then called the Army Service School and later the Command and General Staff College at Fort Leavenworth, Kansas in December 1917. Before he could finish the course, he was abruptly transferred to the United States Tank Corps at Fort Meade, Maryland in February 1918. His job was to help train and equip the 301st Tank Battalion that eventually expanded into the 305th Heavy Tank Brigade. The brigade outgrew Camp Meade, already crowded with other regiments, and was transferred to Camp Colt, outside Gettysburg, Pennsylvania. His commander, Colonel Ira Welborn, was so impressed with Eisenhower's organizational and training skills for what became a 10,600 man brigade, that he got him swiftly promoted to major then lieutenant colonel. The brigade's worst deficiency was tanks. Factories were slow to turn out the British-designed Mark VIII Liberty tanks along with French designed Renaults for Patton's light brigade in France. The heavy brigade was moved to Fort Dix, New Jersey in December 1918, the month following the armistice. After that rapid buildup, Eisenhower's job now was to reduce the brigade to a skeleton and redeploy it back to Fort Meade in March 1919. For his efforts, Eisenhower received a Distinguished Service Medal in 1924.

Meanwhile, Eisenhower received his first independent command in 1919, the mission to organize and lead a motorized task force across the country. The expedition included 24 officers, 258 men and around 60 military vehicles including various trucks, automobiles and motorcycles, but no tanks. They departed Washington on 7 July 1919 and 3,251 miles later reached San Francisco on 1 September 1919. Eisenhower's successful leadership of that expedition earned him his first national headlines and Patton's interest in meeting him.

Eisenhower naturally looked up to Patton, who was five years older and a combat veteran of the Mexican expedition and World War I with a Distinguished Service Cross for extraordinary valor in battle. He described Patton as 'fundamentally so avid for recognition as a great military commander that he will ruthlessly suppress any habit of his that will tend to jeopardize it.'[209] That was true to a point. During and after World War II, Patton would cross the line several times that indeed jeopardized his career and each time Eisenhower, then his commander, had to penalize him. Patton's flamboyant personality and wealthy lifestyle of a Washington townhouse, servants, automobiles, polo, fox hunts and clubs was nearly as dazzling. Eisenhower recalled that:

'From the beginning he and I got along famously. Both of us were students of current military doctrine. Part of our passion was belief in tanks – a belief at the time derided by others.'[210] They debated tank designs and tactics. They dismantled a tank, examined each part, and thought of ways to improve its efficiency.

Sharing dangers and escaping death deepened their bond. Twice their experiments nearly killed them. One day an overheated machine gun began spewing bullets at them. Another day, they were nearly decapitated when a cable linked between two moving tanks snapped and the halves shot their way. Eisenhower recalled that:

> We were too startled at the moment to realize what had happened but then we looked at each other. I'm sure I was just as pale as George. That evening after dinner, he said, 'Ike, were you as scared as I was?' 'I was afraid to bring the subject up,' I said. We were certainly not more than five or six inches from certain death.

Patton predicted that international problems and injustices caused by

> the Treaty of Versailles had practically guaranteed the outbreak of another great war within something like a quarter century ... 'Ike,' he'd say, 'This [next] war may happen ... This is what we'll do. I'll be Jackson, you'll be Lee ... I don't want to do the heavy thinking; you do that and I'll get loose among our ... enemies.[211]

In this, Patton was astonishingly prescient.

Patton and Eisenhower advocated rapidly advancing massed tanks followed by infantry either to outflank or punch through key weak points of enemy lines then circling and cutting off the retreat. They wrote up their ideas in separate articles published by *Infantry Journal* in 1920, Patton's 'Tanks in Future Warfare' in May and Eisenhower's 'Infantry: Its Role, Capabilities, Limitations, and Relation to other Arms' in November 1919. Anticipating their future attendance, they worked together to solve problems from instruction manuals of Fort Leavenworth's Command and General Staff College. General Fox Conner, John Pershing's operations and plans chief in France, was a fellow innovator. A highlight during this time was Patton, Eisenhower and Fox inspecting the Tank Corps then dining together and exchanging ideas. Eisenhower later reflected that:

> These were the beginnings of a comprehensive doctrine that in Patton's case would make him a legend. Naturally, as enthusiasts, we tried to win converts. This wasn't easy but George and I had the enthusiasm of zealots.[212]

Those halcyon days of experimenting with tank doctrine and design were fleeting. The trouble was that their innovative solutions to strategic and tactical challenges violated the army's orthodox 'answers'. General Charles Farnsworth, the infantry commander, despised tanks. He summoned Patton and Eisenhower separately to castigate each of them for advocating what the army considered heresy. Eisenhower recalled him telling them that their ideas

> were not only wrong but dangerous and that henceforth I would keep them to myself. Particularly I was not to publish anything incompatible with solid infantry doctrine. If I did, I would be hauled before a court-martial ... George, I think, was given the same message. This was a blow. One effect was to bring George and me even closer.[213]

Atop that blow, they soon received different postings that. separated them for two decades.

The Tank Corps' elimination and Farnsworth's threats deeply depressed Patton and he requested a transfer back to the cavalry. On 4 September 1920, he was ordered to join 3rd Cavalry at Fort Myers near Washington. During this time, Pershing issued Patton the Distinguished Service Medal for the administrative brilliance he displayed organizing the Light Tank Brigade and the Silver Star for his heroism at the Rubio ranch shootout during the Mexico expedition. That briefly sparked his spirits.

Like countless combat veterans, Patton had trouble adjusting to a peacetime army and cramped home life with his wife and two young daughters. The girls viewed him as a mythic hero when he was away at war and a monster after he returned. He treated them like miniature soldiers rather than beloved companions and disciplined them severely when they disobeyed his commands. Second-born Ruth Ellen later insightfully recalled:

> I realize now that he was in considerable pain at the time; worried about his future in the tank corps of his creation; and having a hangover from the war, which is a very real thing. A man goes from the command of thousands of men where his judgment means victory or defeat, life or death, to the shrinking command of a handful of men, and the narrowing horizons of peacetime duty … and the tender trap of home and family and it is a letdown.[214]

Patton's home life became more stressful when his son, named George Smith Patton IV, was born on 24 December 1923. Patton was tough on his namesake and only son, but at times could be supportive. In 1939, while the son was at boarding school, he wrote to his father for advice about how to handle a bully who the other kids admired. Patton replied:

> Your frank and manly letter was very pleasing to me … It never pays to fight an underdog. You can fight for them but never against them. It is quite understandable that one should run around raising h-l, but it gets no where and betrays a lack of self-confidence. A man who is confident does not run around with a gang. It is much better to be a lone wolf than a coyote.[215]

After Beatrice, Patton's closest relationship was with his father who always gave him unconditional love and encouragement. He was crushed when his father died on 10 June 1927. Military duties prevented Patton from being present for his death or burial. He wrote movingly of his belated visit:

> The morning I arrived I wore my uniform and went alone to his grave … For an hour I stood there and the knowledge came to me that the grave no more held Pap than does one of his discarded suits hanging in a closet. Suddenly I seemed to see him in the road werring his checked overcoat and with his stick which he waved at me as he used to do when he was impatient and wanted to go somewhere … His soul was with me … Oh! darling Papa. I never called you that in life as both of us were too self-contained … I never did much for you and you did all for me.

In a long elegy extolling his father to his family and friends, Patton recalled that he

> always expressed to me his belief that the very fortunate career I had had in the army was Fate and that I was being especially prepared for some special work … When I used to bemoan the fact that wars were getting scarce and all the time I had spent getting ready would be wasted for lack of opportunity he used to reassure me with the greatest confidence that I would yet be in the biggest war in history.

His father's predictions were certainly prescient. Pershing wrote Patton a consoling letter:

> No one could meet your father without feeling his personality, and no one could know him … without recognizing his high character and great ability. I know the high esteem … you … held for him and … understand fully the reasons for your great admiration and affection.[216]

Four years later, as his mother's health deteriorated, he wrote her these moving and revealing words:

> Here with your things before me you are very near. I never showed you in life the love I really felt nor my admiration for your courage and sporting acceptance of illness and losses. Children are cruel things. Forgive me. I always prayed to show my love by doing something famous for you, to justify what you called me when I got back from France, 'Your hero son.'… Nothing you ever did for me was anything but loving. I have no other memories of you but love and devotion. It is so sad that we must grow old and separate … I loved and love you very much.
>
> Your devoted son
> G.S. Patton Jr[217]

Patton's duties were mostly dull routine broken by occasional ceremonies. He and 3rd Cavalry provided an escort for the car with presidents Warren Harding and Woodrow Wilson during the presidential inauguration parade for the former on 4 March 1921. They also escorted the coffin of the 'unknown soldier' from the Capitol to his tomb at Arlington Cemetery on 11 November 1921, three years after armistice. On most weekends, Patton played polo or steeplechased.

Patton kept penning verse in his spare time and eventually selected thirty poems for publication with this foreword:

> These rhymes were written over a period of years for his own amusement by a man who having seen something of war is more impressed with the manly virtues it engenders than with the necessary and much exaggerated horrors attendant upon it. They are offered to the public in the hope that they may counteract to a degree the melancholy viewpoint so freely expiated upon by most writers.[218]

Patton kept earning high overall marks in his efficiency reports from his superiors. For 1920, Colonel William Rivers rated Patton 'superior' in value to the army and in 'mental energy' but 'below average' in tact and overall an

> officer of more than usual power mental and physical. I estimate him to be of good habits – pleasing personality – has many attributes of a natural soldier and is much interested in his profession. Good type of officer to have in command.

Patton succeeded in raising his rating for 1921, receiving 'superior' overall, 'above average' in field duties, and 'average in tact'. Rivers lauded him as an

> officer of superior mental and physical qualities, a high class man devoted to his profession ... keen on military studies and keeps well abreast of the times by intelligent industry. Studious man fond of study and readings, yet Major Patton can take a horse, or a saber, or a rifle and equal or surpass any man ... in his squadron.

In 1922, an inspector generals' report commended Patton 'for the excellent condition of equipment, fine appearance of men and animals, and cleanliness and orderliness of Barracks and stables.'[219]

Patton completed the advanced cavalry course at Fort Riley in 1923 and the School of the Line, later renamed the Command and General

Staff School, at Fort Leavenworth in 1924. He graduated toward the top of both classes, most impressively at Fort Leavenworth where he was 25 of 248 students with an 88.948 grade average; Colonel Charles Bundel and General Harry Smith respectively deemed him 'a superior officer of marked ability' and 'one of the ablest and best officers of his grade in the service.'[220]

Patton's high score got him into the elite General Staff Corps and transfer to I Corps headquarters at Boston where he served as a G-1 or personnel officer. Colonel Charles Roberts rated him 'superior' and 'an experienced, well educated, accomplished officer. Excellently fitted for General Staff work or high command.'[221] After eight months he returned to his 3rd Cavalry troop at Fort Myer. He did not stay long.

Patton was transferred to the Hawaiian Division commanded by General William Smith at Fort Shafter in Honolulu in March 1925, and remained there until April 1928, During that time he served successively in the G-1 Staff, G-2 Intelligence, and G-3 Operations and Plans sections. Lieutenant Colonel John Murphy rated Patton 'superior' and explained that he

> served as my assistant during the Grand Joint Army and Navy Exercises April 1925. I had an excellent opportunity to observe the manner in which he performed his duties as a general staff officer. His tactical judgment is superior, he is well balanced, and he is a quick and enthusiastic worker. Major Patton is well educated along tactical lines and he would be a superior Chief of Staff, G-2 or G-3 of a Corps during combat

and 'an excellent commander of combat troops during war.'[222]

General Smith did transfer Patton from G-3 to G-2 after he wrote a scathing report when officers failed properly to implement instructions he issued them during a training exercise. At Fort Shafter, Patton first received training in army-navy amphibious operations, essential knowledge later during World War II for landings he planned and commanded in Morocco and Sicily.

While in Hawaii, Patton received the Treasury's silver Life Saving Medal of Honor 'in recognition of the gallant conduct displayed by you in bravely rescuing three boys from drowning in Salem Harbor, Massachusetts, August 21, 1923.'[223] Major General Edward Lewis, the Hawaiian Division's commander, awarded him the medal in a public ceremony. Patton had saved the boys from their sinking boat while he and Beatrice were sailing in the harbor.

When Patton learned that Eisenhower was attending Fort Leavenworth's Command and General Staff College, he sent him his extensive notes. Eisenhower put those notes to good use in helping him graduate first in his class and wrote to Patton with his deep appreciation for that. Patton replied:

> You are very kind to think that my notes helped you though I feel that you would have done as well without them. If a man thinks war long enough it is bound to affect him in a good way. I am convinced that as good as Leavenworth is it is still only a means not an end that we must keep on. I have worked all the problems of the two years since I graduated and shall continue to do so. However I dont [*sic*] try for approved solutions any more but rather to do what I will do in war.[224]

The Department of War transferred Patton to head the Plans and Training Division of the Office of the Chief of Cavalry in Washington in April 1928; he arrived on 7 May 1928. In a series of reports over the next few years, he advocated incorporating ever more trucks and armored cars into cavalry regiments to the point where they surpassed horsemen in personnel, cost and importance. In November 1928, he was detached to the Department of War's Mobilization Plan. He deepened relations with two colleagues that he first met in France during World War I; now Deputy Chief of Staff General Fox Conner, a renowned soldier's soldier and decorated World War I veteran, and General Adna Chaffee who commanded 1st Cavalry Division and advocated transforming it into an armored division; both generals highly esteemed Patton. Yet, in 1931, Chief of Staff Douglas MacArthur was forced to dissolve what was then called the Mechanized Force when Congress failed to fund it. During these years Patton renewed acquaintances with two men who would decisively affect his commands during World War II, Henry Stimson, then the secretary of state, and Dwight D. Eisenhower, reduced in rank to captain like virtually all post-World War I officers. He attended the Army War College in Washington from September 1931 to June 1932 and emerged a distinguished graduate. He became second in command of 3rd Cavalry Regiment at Fort Myers on 8 July 1932.

***

Patton may have chafed at the lack of a war to fight but at least he had a secure job, paycheck, housing and status for himself and his family.

America's economy imploded in October 1929 with the stock market's collapse that initiated a vicious cycle of ever more bankruptcies, layoffs, poverty, homelessness, malnutrition and despair. The mass greed of unbridled speculation mostly with borrowed money during the 1920s caused the stock market to skyrocket with the gap between a company's stock price and underlying genuine value steadily widening. That mass greed turned to mass panic as speculators frenzily tried to sell their stocks before the price plummeted, thus precipitating the collapse. President Herbert Hoover, inaugurated on 4 March 1929, responded to the Great Depression mostly with bromides that sooner or later the market would correct itself as entrepreneurs capitalized on chances to make money, and hired and paid workers. By 1932, the economy was half its size three years earlier and one of four workers was jobless.

Around 3 million men were World War I veterans. In 1924, the World War Adjusted Compensation Act issued veterans a certificate that they could redeem for money in 1945. Largely communists eventually mobilized 17,000 veterans and thousands of their family members to march on Washington and demand the immediate redemption of their certificates. They called themselves the Bonus Expeditionary Force (or BEF), a play on the American Expeditionary Force (or AEF) that John Pershing established in France. They camped in a 'Hooverville' at Anacostia Flats across the Potomac River. From there each day they marched across the bridge to protest before the White House and Capitol. On 15 June 1932, the House of Representatives voted 211 to 176 to redeem the certificates but the Senate voted 62 to 18 against that bill. Congress then adjourned. Although most marchers departed for their distant homes, the most radical and desperate remained to daily protest.

Violence erupted between protesters and police on 28 July 1932, with numerous injuries and a veteran killed by a policeman. Hoover told Secretary of War Patrick J. Hurley to expel the protestors from Washington back to their camp. Hurley had Army Chief of Staff General Douglas MacArthur implement that order. MacArthur personally led 12th Infantry and ordered Patton to join him with his 3rd Cavalry.

Patton had commanded the regiment just twenty days when he received that order. He dutifully obeyed. He and 231 of his mounted men proceeded the infantry toward the protesters and pushed them back. Some radicals threw stones and swung clubs while the cavalrymen slashed with their sabers. Finally, the protestors broke and streamed across the bridge.

MacArthur disobeyed his instructions and ordered the troops across the bridge to rout the marchers from their camp and then burn it. Patton vividly recalled that:

> When we crossed the bridge at the Navy Yard the infantry was in front and had to use grenades to force the spectator crowd out of the way. The cavalry formed at the north end of the camp with its right flank on the river, while the infantry moving south along the edge of the water turned by the left flank and started to clear the camp. At this moment we were ordered to halt as the Marchers said that if they were given an hour they would withdraw. During this hour many left but some set fire to their tents. When the time was up the infantry moved forward in a long line of skirmishers, using grenades from time to time … It speaks volumes for the high character of the men that not a shot was fired. In justice to the marchers it should be pointed out that had they really wanted to start something they had a great chance here but refrained.[225]

During the fighting, two protesters died and fifty-five were injured along with sixty-nine injured police and soldiers.

That action against the bonus marchers was the only peril Patton faced during the 1930s. Meanwhile, the Japanese, Italian, and German governments asserted a series of military aggressions that challenged the League of Nations. They shared versions of fascism, an ideology devised by Benito Mussolini that advocated an authoritarian, one-party state led by a charismatic dictator who promoted nationalism, subjected all individuals to the state, developed the economy with massive investments in infrastructure and industries, and a partnership between the public and private sectors, and conquered a territorial empire.[226] Although Mussolini called fascism a totalitarian ideology, that instead describes communism in which the Communist Party totally controls the people and economy after nationalizing all private property, eliminating markets and imposing five year economic plans. Fascist states upheld private property and markets with the power to nationalize them if necessary as in a war.

In the late nineteenth century, Italy, Germany and Japan had transformed from absolute into constitutional monarchies that guaranteed civil rights, elections and parliaments while maintaining royal families with limited powers. Despite those revolutionary liberal institutional and legal changes, the political cultures of those countries remained authoritarian. In each country, fascist movements exploited that flaw to take power in the 1920s and 1930s.

That transformation occurred first in Italy where Mussolini founded and led the Italian Fasces Combat (Fascist) Party. On 31 October 1922, King Victor Emmaneul III named Mussolini prime minister after he threatened to lead his Fascist Party to Rome and violently overthrow the government. In one of history's most cowardly capitulations, the king did so even though Italy's army numbered 500,000 troops and Mussolini's Fascist Party held only 2 of 535 Chamber of Deputy seats or 0.45 per cent of the total. In June 1923, Mussolini got the Chamber of Deputies to pass the Acerbo Law that granted him dictatorial powers with which he outlawed all political parties except the Fascist Party and rendered Parliament and a twenty-eight-member Fascist Grand Council mere rubberstamps for his decisions. Mussolini declared himself Italy's 'Duce' or all-powerful leader. He expanded Italy's military, and invested in Italy's railroad, electricity and manufacturing industries that stimulated the economy.

Japan's version of fascism differed from those of Italy and Germany which had charismatic dictators. Japanese worshipped their emperor as a demi-god but current Emperor Hirohito, like his predecessors, held only ceremonial and cultural power. Beginning in 1925, Japan's fascists manipulated or created a series of crises to suspend civil liberties and amass more power in an Imperial War Council of three civilian and three military leaders presided over by the emperor. The council reached decisions by consensus that the government and military dutifully fulfilled without question or hesitation. Of the three, only Japan's fascism was emotionally totalitarian with its power to inspire not just its soldiers, sailors and airmen but even civilians to fight to the death rather than surrender. German and Italian soldiers did give up after being surrounded and depleting their supplies.

Adolf Hitler admired and emulated Mussolini in how he established and led the National Socialist Workers' Party (Nazi Party) to power. The Great Depression discredited the Weimar Republic that replaced the constitutional monarchy as World War I ended. Hitler's Nazi Party won ever more seats in Germany's Parliament or Reichstag, from just 2.62 per cent of the total in May 1928 to 18.25 per cent in September 1930, 37.27 per cent in July 1932 and 33.69 per cent in November 1932. Although only one in three Germans voted for the Nazi Party, it was the largest in the Reichstag. Hitler demanded that President Paul Hindenburg appoint him chancellor, and he complied on 30 January 1933. Hitler allied the Nazis with the National People's Party to hold most Reichstag seats with which they passed the Enabling Act on 23 March 1933, that granted him dictatorial powers. Hitler abolished the other parties. When Hindenburg died on 2 August 1934, Hitler abolished that office and declared himself Germany's 'Führer' or all-powerful leader.

Tokyo was the first of the three to violate the international laws against imperialistic or aggressive war established by the 1919 League of Nations Covenant and reinforced by the 1927 Kellogg-Briand Pact. Japan had acquired a small empire in north-east Asia after winning short wars against China from 1894 to 1895, and took the island of Formosa (Taiwan); against Russia from 1904 to 1905, and took Korea, Sakhalin Island's southern half, and control over the Manchurian railroad in north-east China including the right to defend it with an army; and against Germany from 1914 to 1918, and took its Shantung Peninsula sphere of influence in China and the western Pacific island groups of the Marshalls, Marianas and Carolines.

Militants in Japan's army deployed along Manchuria's railroad provoked a crisis that Tokyo wielded as an excuse to conquer all of north-east China. On 18 September 1931, the Japanese murdered some Chinese near the railroad, set off a small bomb on the track, and claimed they had killed saboteurs. With that the army overran Manchuria.

China's government was then at Nanjing and led by Generalissimo Chiang Kai-shek, who headed the National (Kuomintang, KMT) Party. He could merely protest Japan's conquest of Manchuria and appeal to the League of Nations to force Tokyo to withdraw. China had been convulsed by civil war since 1911 when revolutionaries inspired by Sun Yat-sen overthrew the Chiang Dynasty but failed to establish a unified government. Instead, warlords took over regions. Sun had established the Nationalist Party and eventually embraced Chiang, a general, as his right-hand man. The Nationalists initially allied with the Chinese Communist Party when it was founded in 1922. Chiang became the KMT's head when Sun died in 1925, and in 1927, he directed the Nationalist army to attack the Communists. The Nationalists routed the Communists who withdrew to Yanan in northern central China near Mongolia. Chiang's army was too overextended and weak to fight the Japanese in Manchuria.

The League of Nations dispatched a five-man commission led by Victor Bulwer-Lytton to investigate Japan's takeover of Manchuria. The Lytton Commission's report, issued on 2 October 1932, condemned Japan's imperialism in Manchuria. Tokyo denounced the report and demanded that the League of Nations repudiate it. When they upheld the Lytton Report, Japan withdrew from the League of Nations on 24 February 1933.

France and Britain were the League of Nation's two most powerful countries but their governments and peoples had no interest in rallying the other members to impose economic sanctions against Tokyo let alone threaten military action. American Secretary of State Henry Stimson reacted to Japan's conquest on 7 January 1932, by protesting and declaring the United States would not recognize it. The failure of the League of Nations and the United States to work together to back their principles with economic and military sanctions encouraged Japan, Italy and Germany to commit a series of increasingly aggressive acts that culminated with World War II.

Italy went to war against Ethiopia in October 1934 and completed its conquest by 19 February 1937; the League of Nations temporarily imposed limited economic sanctions then lifted them after six months. On 7 March 1936, Hitler ordered his army to march into Germany's Ruhr industrial region in violation of the Treaty of Versailles; the League of Nations did nothing. In July 1937, Tokyo used the excuse of a shootout between Japanese and Chinese forces near the Marco Polo Bridge outside Beijing for an all-out invasion that conquered much of eastern China; the League of Nations did nothing. On 12 March 1938, Hitler engineered Germany's annexation of Austria in violation of the Treaty of Versailles; the League of Nations did nothing. In summer 1938, Hitler threatened war against Czechoslovakia if it did not cede its western Sudetenland region where most people spoke German. British Prime Minister Neville Chamberlain got French Premier Edouard Daladier and Italian Duce Mussolini to accept Hitler's demand and force Czechoslovakia to transfer Sudetenland to Germany in September 1938. After returning to London, Chamberlain declared, 'We have peace our time!' Hitler's army took over the rest of Czechoslovakia from 14 to 23 March 1939. Hitler and Mussolini formed a 'Pact of Steel' military alliance on 22 May 1939. Germany, Italy and Japan formed the 'Tripartite Pact' military alliance on 27 September 1940.

President Franklin Roosevelt viewed each of these aggressions with increasing alarm but could do little. Most Americans and members of Congress wanted the government to appease rather than confront foreign imperialism. They believed that an 'America first' or 'isolationist' policy would protect the nation from foreign aggression. Congress reinforced that attitude with laws in 1935, 1936, 1937 and 1939 that increasingly restricted the president's power to extend economic or military aid to aggression victims.[227]

***

During these years, Patton paid little attention to the worsening aggression and tighter alliance among fascist Japan, Germany and Italy. He was mostly concerned with his professional duties and personal interests. To his delight, he was promoted to lieutenant colonel on 1 March 1934. He received orders to return to Fort Shafter in Hawaii and serve as a G-2 intelligence officer in May 1935. Despite the idyllic setting, this period was his emotional nadir for a natural warrior in a barebones peacetime army. He started drinking heavily with effects compounded by his previous concussions. His daughter Ruth Ellen wrote that:

> Whatever had happened to his head, it cut down on his capacity to carry alcohol and whereas he had never shown his liquor in his whole life, just a couple of drinks would make him quite tight. This upset Ma no end … and she told him so. Ma had never criticized Georgie in his life and that upset him and he got very disagreeable … Sometimes he would take an extra drink while she was looking at him; just to 'show her'.[228]

Then 50 years old, he had a brief affair with 21-year-old Jean Gordon, a pretty, vivacious friend of his daughter and Beatrice's half-sister. Gordon had stopped to visit during a voyage from the United States to Japan. The affair ended when she reembarked. Beatrice found out about the affair and seriously considered leaving him but chose to stay. She explained why to Ruth Ellen:

> Your father needs me. He doesn't know it right now, but … he needs me more than I need him … I want you to remember this: that even the best and truest of men can be be-dazzled and make fools of themselves … I stuck with him because … I love him and he loves me.[229]

The Pattons stayed at Fort Shafter until June 1937, when he transferred to the Cavalry Board at Fort Riley, Kansas. On 28 July 1937, a horse kicked and broke Patton's leg then as he recovered in the hospital he contracted phlebitis and a pulmonary embolus that kept him mostly bedridden for dreary month after month. He was finally well enough to return to service on 2 February 1938. That year he served as the Cavalry School's Executive Officer from 8 February, was promoted to colonel on 1 July 1938, commanded 5th Cavalry at Fort Clark, Texas on 24 July, and returned to Fort Myers, Washington, to resume command of 3rd Cavalry on 10 December 1938. During these years, his daughters married army officers, Beatrice to Lieutenant John Waters in 1934 and Ruth Ellen to Lieutenant James Totten in July 1940.

***

During his latest sojourn in Washington, Patton and Army Chief of Staff George Marshall developed a relationship of mutual respect. Of America's World War II military leaders, Marshall likely contributed the most to victory for his brilliance at organization and grand strategy.[230] He was a 1901 Virginia Military Institute graduate and captain of the corps; first in his class at Fort Leavenworth's School of the Line in 1907; the chief operations and plans officer first for 1st Division then for General John Pershing during World War I; and Pershing's aide from 1919 to 1924. While he was assistant commandant of Fort Bennings' Infantry School from 1927 to 1932, he revamped the training course to emphasis fire and movement strategy and tactics. But he also understood that strategy and tactics were only as good as the supplies that sustained him; he was a genius at finding and sending supplies. Biographer Ed Cray explained that: 'Logistics governed Marshall's War Department. They determined global strategies. They set timetables for campaigns in the field. The clamor for supplies never ceased.'[231] President Roosevelt appointed Marshall the army chief of staff on 1 September 1939, the same day that war erupted in Europe when Hitler ordered Germany's army to invade Poland.

At rare times, Patton could be as brilliant at social strategy as he was at military strategy. He seized a chance to ingratiate himself with Marshall. Learning that the chief of staff's home at Fort Myer was being renovated, he wrote to Marshall that:

> it occurs to me that you will have no place to stay. All my family are away, but my house is open and running, and I am there. I can give you a room and bath and meals, and should truly be delighted to do so.

Marshall was happy to accept his offer. Patton excitedly wrote Beatrice that:

> I have just consummated a pretty snappy move. Gen. George Marshall is going to live at our house!!! He and I are batching it. I think that once I get my natural charm working I won't need any letters [of recommendation from General Pershing or other high ranking officers to boost his career].[232]

Patton accomplished that mission. During those days, Patton and Marshall found common views on an array of military issues, especially the army's vital need to develop armored warfare. They shared many meals together and Patton took him out on his sailboat on the Potomac. He wrote to Beatrice that Marshall 'does not seem to have many friends.' When Marshall received promotion to lieutenant general, Patton sent him eight silver stars. Marshall thanked him for his 'thoughtfulness and generous gesture.' After Marshal and his wife Katharine were established in their own home, Patton and Beatrice invited them to parties and accompanied them to social events.[233]

***

The foreign ministers of two tyrannies, Hitler's Nazi Germany and Joseph Stalin's Communist Soviet Union, signed two treaties on 23 August 1939. The public treaty was a non-aggression pact. In the secret treaty, they conspired to conquer and split Poland between them. The German army invaded western Poland on 1 September 1939. Prime Minister Chamberlain finally abandoned appeasement and asked Parliament to declare war against Germany on 3 September 1939. France's government declared war against Germany that same day. On 17 September 1939, the Soviet Red Army invaded eastern Poland. With its army decimated and nation overrun, Poland's government surrendered on 5 October 1939. The Germans and Soviets respectively occupied and exploited the western two thirds and eastern one third of Poland. By mutual agreement, the Soviets also conquered Estonia, Latvia and Lithuania, and warred against Finland.

Although France had a 1-million-man army with much of its deployed in the Maginot Line of fortresses along the border with Germany, Paris did not order an attack even though most of Germany's army was fighting in Poland. Instead, for half a year a 'phoney war' prevailed in which neither side attacked the other. Nor did Paris or London declare war against Moscow even through Soviet imperialism was just as blatant, destructive, and actually conquered more countries than Germany's. The British deployed an army in northern France that eventually numbered 390,000 troops.

The 'phoney war' ended in April 1940, when Berlin and London asserted the same strategic idea. Germany's industry depended on iron ore from mines in northern Sweden that was transported by rail to the ice-free port of Narvik, Norway, then shipped to German ports. The two leaders dispatched task forces to seize Narvik. The Germans arrived first and repelled the British while other German forces captured Bergen, Stavanger and Trondheim, and later Oslo. The Germans also occupied Denmark whose government surrendered to avoid the devastation of an inevitable defeat.

Meanwhile, five Panzer armies in two groups massed east of the Ardennes forest in eastern Belgium. The blitzkrieg came on 10 May 1940, when those armies punched through the Belgium army and raced west while paratroopers landed on several fortresses ahead. Other German armies along the French border launched limited attacks to pin down and divert attention from that breakthrough. The Panzer armies cut through northern France to reach the English Channel at Abbeville, thus splitting the British Army and a French army northward and most French forces south-east.

Chamberlain resigned as prime minster and Winston Churchill took his place on 10 May 1940. Churchill's decisive leadership could not change the Battle for France. The Germans drove back the British and French to a pocket around Dunkirk. Churchill ordered its evacuation and by 4 June 1940, ships bore 338,226 troops, two thirds British, to Britain. France's government fled Paris for Bordeaux. The Germans cut off and devastated the French armies in eastern and central France, pursued the remnants south, and captured Paris on 10 June 1940. Mussolini declared war against France on 11 June 1940 and sent Italy's army into southeastern France. France's government surrendered on 25 June 1940.

Hitler split France between northern and western zones that German troops would occupy, a southeastern Italian zone, and a rump, puppet French state in the center and south with its capital at Vichy and General Philippe Petain its president. Hitler then sought to conquer Britain in two stages. The first aimed to control the seas around and the sky above Britain. 'Wolfpacks' of submarines sank scores of supply ships sailing to or from Britain as bombers attacked British airfields and cities while Messerschmidt 109 and Fulkwulf 190 fighter planes swirled in dogfights with British Spitfires and Hurricanes. The British eventually won the air battle by shooting down nearly twice as many enemy planes as they lost – 1,733 to 915, but the Battle of the Atlantic persisted until the war's end.

Unable to vanquish Britain, Hitler turned against the Soviet Union. He massed 3.8 million troops and 3,795 tanks on the border defended by 2.9 million Soviet troops and 11,000 tanks, with millions more Soviet troops deployed elsewhere. He launched the blitzkrieg on 22 June 1941. German Panzer armies circled and destroyed Soviet armies and drove eastward. Over six months, they killed or captured more than 4.5 million Soviet troops while suffering 1 million casualties. Yet, despite those stunning victories, by December 1940, the German onslaught bogged down in deep snow and freezes just a dozen miles from Leningrad and a score of miles from Moscow.

***

When war erupted in Europe in September 1939, America's military was just 1 per cent of the economy while the regular American army numbered 189,838 personnel in 9 divisions with varying degrees of organization and 2 cavalry divisions but no armored division. Tank units had only 1,500 personnel. The army air force had 1,750 mostly obsolete planes. Roosevelt worked closely with Congressional leaders to expand the army to 269,023 personnel for 1940.

The German blitzkrieg that conquered France and besieged Britain in summer 1940 transformed American public opinion. Isolationism had prevailed since World War I's end and deepened during the Great Depression even as fascist Japan, Italy and Germany become more belligerent and imperialistic. Now most Americans and members of Congress realized that the nation had to prepare for a worsening world war that seemed ever more likely to engulf the United States.

Roosevelt called on Congress to draft and pass the Selective Service and Training Act. The Senate voted for a version by 58 to 31 on 28 August 1940, the House 283 to 149 for a different version on 7 September 1940 and both approved a reconciled version that Roosevelt signed into law on 14 September 1940. The law required all men between ages 21 and 35 to register, and if drafted serve one year in the regular army and ten years in reserve. On 20 December 1940, Congress approved an amendment that expanded those required to register from age 18 to 64, and those picked from 20 to 44. The initial law would expire after a year. When the Service Extension Act appeared on the floor on 12 August 1941, the House voted in favor by just 1 vote, 203 to 202, a sign of lingering popular isolationism. The Senate approved by acclamation. Roosevelt signed it into law on 18 August 1941.

Roosevelt was able to get Congress to repeal the 'neutrality laws' of 1935, 1936, 1937 and 1939 that prevented the president from sending economic and military aid to countries that were attacked by aggressors. The Lend-Lease Act passed the House of Representatives by 260 to 135 on 8 February 1941, the Senate by 60 to 31 on 8 March 1941, and Roosevelt signed it into law on 11 March 1941. Under lend-lease, the United States eventually distributed $51.1 billion in military and economic aid to its allies, including $31.9 billion to Britain, $11.3 billion to the Soviet Union, $3.2 billion to France, $1.6 billion to China, and $2.6 billion to an array of minor countries. That aid was decisive in preventing the Germans from defeating the Soviet Union then transferring all their military on that Eastern Front to the Western Front. It was also crucial in relieving severe shortages of food and fuel in Britain and equipping British armies, navies and air forces.[234]

Roosevelt sought to bolster public support for helping Britain, China, the Soviet Union and other victims of fascist aggression by articulating a set of principles for international relations worth fighting for. In doing so, he emulated his predecessor Woodrow Wilson whose Fourteen Points justified America's participation in World War I. For that, he met with Churchill at Argentia, Newfoundland from 9 to 12 August 1941, during which they embraced a set of liberal international principles diametrically opposed to authoritarian fascism and totalitarian communism. What they called the Atlantic Charter included self-determination for all peoples, freedom of the seas, disarmament of aggressors, no territorial gains through imperialism, global economic cooperation and territorial adjustments only with the consent of people living there. Roosevelt and Churchill established both a partnership and friendship that overcame all the challenges confronting the alliance over the next three years.[235]

Meanwhile the draft enabled the army's ranks to expand to 1,462,315 troops in 1941 and eventually 8,267,958 troops in 1945. The average soldier was 26 years old, 5 foot and 8 inches tall, and 150 pounds. As for education, one in three completed sixth grade, one in four high school, and one in ten attended college for at least a semester. Monthly pay ranged from $50 for privates to $96 for master sergeants. Medal of Honor winners earned a monthly $2 bonus.

4.1 Army Personnel, 1939–1947[236]

Year	Total	Officers	Enlisted
1939	189,839	14,489	175,353
1940	269,023	18,236	250,697
1941	1,462,315	99,536	1,362,779
1942	3,075,608	206,422	2,869,186
1943	6,994,472	579,576	6,414,896
1944	7,994,750	776,980	7,212,770
1945	8,267,958	891,663	7,376295
1946	1,891,011	267,144	1,623,867
1947	991,285	132,504	858,781

4.2 Navy Personnel, 1939–1947[237]

Year	Total	Officers	Enlisted
1939	125,202	12,023	113,179
1940	160,997	13,604	147,393
1941	284,427	29,092	225,335
1942	640,570	69,564	571,006
1943	1,741,750	179,676	1,562,074
1944	2,981,365	276,153	2,705,212
1945	3,380,817	331,379	3,049,438
1946	983,398	141,161	842,237
1947	498,661	52,434	446,227

4.3 Marine Personnel, 1939–1947[238]

Year	Total	Officers	Enlisted
1939	19,432	1,380	18,052
1940	28,345	1,800	26,545
1941	54,359	3,339	51,020
1942	142,613	7,138	135,475
1943	308,523	21,384	287,139
1944	475,604	32,788	442,816
1945	474,680	37,067	437,613
1946	155,679	14,208	141,471
1947	93,658	7,506	85,547

Transforming those men into soldiers, equipping them with uniforms, weapons, and supplies, and training officers to command them was a daunting challenge. During World War II, Army Ground Forces Command alone gave basic training to 2,700,000 troops and specialized training to 108,000 officers and 229,000 enlisted men.[239]

Training troops was as much about psychological as physical conditioning, of learning to obey instantly without question, of understanding and mastering one's fears, of killing and maiming others to reduce the odds of oneself or one's comrades being killed or maimed. The motivation to fight was for one's buddies and self-esteem first and one's nation and ideals second.

Training officers is far more complex and time consuming than training the soldiers they will command. Lower ranking officers must not only be as physically tough and skilled at combat as their men, but must also excel as leaders, tacticians and administrators. One key lesson was that soldiers tend to mirror the outlooks and behaviors of their noncommissioned and commissioned officers. At all times, officers should be confident, calm, firm and precise in their orders and appearance, and should avoid being either overly friendly and cheerful or harsh, vulgar, and angry. In combat, officers should usually stay behind the frontlines to direct operations and only rarely lead attacks.

***

Supplying troops all they needed was a constant headache. Each soldier in the field consumed 66.8 pounds of supplies daily, including 33 pounds of oil, gasoline, and grease, 8 pounds of ammunition, 7.3 pounds of construction materials, 7.2 pounds of rations, and the rest medical, signal and other things. Each month in Europe the army had to replace an average 36,000 small arms, 2,400 vehicles, 700 mortars and 500 tanks.[240]

A military is only as powerful as the economy that supplies it. That in turn depends on the national government mobilizing and paying for all those vital supplies. For that, Roosevelt established an array of federal institutions. He had already established the seven-member National Defense Advisory Committee chaired by General Motors president William Knudsen in May 1940, and transformed it into the Office of Production Management with the power to coordinate and allocate production among industries and corporations. He established the Office of Scientific Research and Development chaired by brilliant MIT professor Vannevar Bush. That organization's most vital program was the top secret Manhattan Project that developed the atomic bombs. America did not have a national intelligence agency, only intelligence divisions in the state, war and navy departments that failed to work together. Roosevelt rectified that by tapping William Donovan, a Medal of Honor World War I veteran, Wall Street lawyer, and international businessman to head an organization first called the Coordinator of Information then Office of Strategic Services (OSS) that would conduct covert operations overseas including espionage, sabotage and guerrilla operations with local resistance groups. Other prominent organizations were the offices of Price Administration, Economic Stabilization, and Production Management, the War Production Board, National War Labor Board, War Shipping Administration, War Manpower Commission and Defense Plant Corporation. Presumably, these bureaucracies resolved more problems than were caused by the inevitable overlap, red tape and inertia.

To pay for fighting a global war, Roosevelt wielded the same combination that Woodrow Wilson had for World War I, Congressional laws that raised taxes, Treasury department sales of war bonds, and the Federal Reserve's expansion of the money supply. World War II cost America $288 billion at the time but with interest payments on loans and veterans benefits including health care and education the eventual price was $664 billion. The federal budget skyrocketed more than ten times until $8,841,224,000 in 1940 to $98,302,937,000 in 1945, and the national debt nearly four times from $40,439,532,000 to $258,682,187,000. But the economy also more than doubled from $99,700,000,000 to $211,900,000,000 and the jobless rate plummeted from 14.6 per cent to 1.9 per cent as all that government spending finally ended the Great Depression with full employment and regular paychecks. Government spending was around 20 per cent of the economy in 1940 and 52 per cent in 1945. As such, virtually every working American helped vanquish the fascist powers during World War II.

As a result, American industrial production kept up with the incessant and voracious military demand in Europe, the Pacific and other fronts. Indeed, America's economy surpassed all others in mass production, finance, innovation and invention, and nearly doubled in size during World War II while the enemy economies steadily diminished. One huge advantage was that the enemy never inflicted any significant bombing damage on the United States aside from Pearl Harbor. Even more vital was America's cultural superiority in entrepreneurship, pragmatism, experimentation, applied science, and problem-solving.

4.4 Federal Government, War and Navy Budgets, and National Debt, 1939–1947[241]

Year	Federal Budgets ($)	War Department ($)	Navy Department ($)	National Debt ($)
1939	8,841,224,000	695,256,000	672,722,000	40,439,532,000
1940	9,055,269,000	907,160,000	891,485,000	42,967,531,000
1941	13,254,948,000	3,938,943,000	2,313,058,000	48,961,444,000
1942	34,036,861,000	14,325,508,000	8,579,589,000	72,442,445,000
1943	79,367,714,000	42,525,563,000	20,888,349,000	136,696,090,000
1944	94,986,002,000	49,438,330,000	28,537,634,000	201,003,387,000
1945	98,302,937,000	50,490,102,000	30,047,152,000	258,682,187,000
1946	60,326,042,000	27,986,769,000	15,164,412,000	269,422,099,000
1947	38,923,379,000	9,172,139,000	5,597,203,000	258,286,383,000

An array of dual use new or more sophisticated previous technologies drastically shaped World War II, including live-saving medicines like quinine, plasma, sulfur drugs and penicillin; detection devices like radar and sonars; air power enhancements like self-sealing tanks, belly tanks and chaff; propellants like rockets and jet engines; metals like reinforced aluminum and stainless steel; and explosives like nuclear energy.

Cryptography was a crucial Allied advantage. American and British cryptographers were able respectively to crack Japanese and German diplomatic and military codes, and so gain critical information about the enemy's power and plans. The codenames for those operations were Ultra and Enigma for the German and Purple and Magic for the Japanese codes. The most decisive use of that intelligence was the Battle of Midway from 4 to 7 June 1942, when the American navy sank four Japanese aircraft carriers while losing one, and so turned the Pacific war's tide for the Allies.

4.5 National and Personal Income in United States Dollars and Jobless Rates, 1929 and 1932–1945[242]

Year	Gross National Income ($)	Per Capita Income ($)	Jobless Rate (%)
1929	103,100,000,000	847	3.2
1932	58,000,000,000	465	23.6
1933	55,600,000,000	442	24.9
1934	65,100,000,000	514	21.7
1935	72,200,000,000	567	20.1
1936	82,500,000,000	643	16.9
1937	90,400,000,000	701	14.3
1938	84,700,000,000	651	19.0
1939	90,500,000,000	691	17.2
1940	99,700,000,000	754	14.6
1941	124,500,000,000	934	9.9
1942	157,900,000,000	1,171	4.7
1943	191,600,000,000	1,401	1.9
1944	210,100,000,000	1,518	1.2
1945	211,900,000,000	1,515	1.9

Yet another challenge was organizing armies with vast number of troops.[243] That required generals to expand their minds from the peacetime emphasis on regiments to the wartime emphasis on divisions as the most important building block unit in the military hierarchy. An American infantry division numbered 22,000 troops split among four regiments and two brigades until June 1941, when it was reduced to 15,514 personnel in three regiments with no brigade. From July 1943, an infantry division numbered 14,253 personnel in 3 regiments, with 5,221 men split among 27 rifle companies of 6 officers and 187 enlisted men. A rifle company had three rifle platoons of three twelve-man rifle squads each with ten men carrying Garand .30 caliber M1 semi-automatic rifles with an eight bullet clip, one with an M1918 30.05 Browing Automatic Rifle (BAR), and one with a M1903 bolt action sniper rifle, and a thirty-six man heavy weapons platoon with two .30 caliber and one .50 caliber machine guns, three 60-millimeter mortars and three bazookas. America's Garand M1 is generally acclaimed as the best World War II rifle for its accuracy, reliability and rate of fire. Each division had an artillery regiment with two battalions armed with twelve 105-millimeter howitzers and one battalion with twelve 155-millimeter howitzers. With its larger calibers, American artillery was more cumbersome to transport than German artillery but, with its 'Time on Target' tactic of massed, concentrated fire against enemy infantry more deadly and accounted for more than half of all casualties ground forces inflicted during World War II. Every American infantry division was completely mechanized with halftracks and trucks that carried all personnel, weapons, munitions, equipment and other supplies. That made American armies the war's most mobile, an advantage Patton exploited more than any other general.

From 1939 to 1943, a German infantry division numbered 17,200 personnel split among 3 regiments each with 3 battalions. Heavy losses and dwindling manpower reserves forced Berlin to reduce a division's strength to 12,769 personnel, around 1,500 fewer than an American division. German infantry divisions suffered an even worse disadvantage versus American divisions. Most German divisions had limited motorized support and had to rely on horse-drawn wagons, and only a few were fully mechanized. In June 1943, Berlin bestowed the name Panzergrenadier on its mechanized infantry divisions and tried to equip more of them.

German divisions did have two advantages. One was a more efficient ratio of officers to other personnel, with only 2.68 per cent to America's 7 per cent portion. Of course, that could become a handicap if too many were killed or wounded and replaced by neophytes.

Another was withdrawing devastated divisions from the front to the rear where recruits were integrated into the ranks. The Americans kept their divisions at the front longer and fed them recruits who were killed or wounded at high rates from their lack of experience and protective comrades; veterans tended to shun rather nurture the replacements for their lost friends.

American armored divisions in March 1942 included 14,620 officers and men, 252 medium tanks, and 158 light tanks. The tanks and 4,848 officers and men were split between 2 regiments, each with 2 medium and 1 light tank battalions, while 2,389 personnel formed a 3-battalion armored-infantry regiment and 2,127 personnel manned a 3-battalion armor-artillery regiment. The remaining troops were headquarters staff, engineers or supply. The armored infantry rode in M-3 half-tracks and the armored artillery crews manned fifty-four self-propelled 105-millimeter cannons. From September 1943, armored divisions numbered more personnel – 10,937, and fewer tanks 263, including 186 mediums and 77 lights. To allow more tactical flexibility, each armored battalion now had two medium and one light tank companies. A company had seventeen tanks, five each in three platoons and two tanks for headquarters.

American army commanders often attached a tank battalion to each infantry division to bolster its tactical flexibility and firepower, and sometimes an infantry battalion to an armored division to bolster the power to take and hold positions. General Lesley McNair explained those different approaches to coordinating tanks and infantry:

> The big question in my mind is the relative merit of tank battalions attached to infantry divisions vs. infantry battalions attached to armored divisions. I lean toward employing armored divisions for exploitation and tank battalions attached to infantry divisions for … infighting.[244]

Worsening production and manpower shortages forced German armored divisions to diminish in personnel and tanks as their American counterparts expanded. In 1944, a full-strength German armored division numbered around 190 tanks split among two Mark IV and one Mark V or Mark VI battalions; companies were supposed to have twenty-two tanks but those dwindled as production and manpower fell further behind combat losses.

Military technologies and weapons determine tactics.[245] Not just German Mark VI 'Tiger' tanks with their 88-millimeter cannons but also German Mark IV and Mark V Panther tanks with their long 75-millimeter cannons outgunned American 'light' M-3 Grants with their 37-millimeter cannons and 'medium' M-4 Shermans initially with their short-barreled 75-millimeter cannon and from 1944 a long 76-millimeter cannon. A Panther had thicker front armor, 120 to 76 millimeters, and a larger although much less durable engine than a Sherman, that gave it a slight edge in top speed, 27 to 25 miles per hour; however, a Sherman's engine lasted five times longer than a Panther's before it needed an overhaul. Tigers had even larger engines and thicker armor but broke down even sooner than Panthers. That prompted Patton's judgment that probably dismayed his tankers and food soldiers that had to fight them: 'Their famous Tiger [tank] is ... a poor piece of artillery and a bad tank.'[246]

As for anti-tank guns, although America's 105-millimeter cannon was more powerful than Germany's 88-millimeter field cannon, it was less effective. For hand-carried anti-tank weapons, German Panzerfausts were twice as powerful as American bazookas. Indeed, Americans enjoyed turning captured Panzerfausts against their original owners.

American M-26 Tank Destroyers had long 75-millimeter cannons but thin armor and an open turret that made them easily destroyed not just by enemy tanks and cannons, but by troops with Panzerfausts and even grenades tossed inside. They were best deployed in camouflaged positions overlooking open space where German tanks might attack. They also were good for firing at buildings or pillboxes before troops attacked them. For Patton, tank destroyer flaws and limitations rendered them more a burden than asset. To a visiting army inspection team led by General Brehon Somervell, he argued:

> I definitely recommended the cessation of the construction of tank destroyers and the replacing of the tank destroyer battalion in an infantry division by a tank battalion. I also reiterated my request for two co-axial machine guns in each tank.[247]

No one influenced the development of American tank warfare doctrine more than Patton. Essentially, he adapted cavalry tactics and strategy to tanks. Given the crucially different capabilities in movement, armor and firepower of American and German tanks, Patton instructed his tankers to avoid fighting German tanks head to head, a duel they would likely lose. Instead, America's tankers should fire phosphorus shells to mask themselves as they raced off in wide enveloping movements to fire shots aimed low at the Panzer tracks. After disabling the Panzers, the Americans should speed ahead after radioing air or artillery attacks on the stranded enemy.

Naval power would be critical in both the European and Pacific theaters with arrays of warships including aircraft carriers, battleships, cruisers, destroyers and submarines protecting vast convoys of troops and supply ships that landed armies on distant shores. Patton led amphibious invasions of Morocco and Sicily. In the Pacific, the Americans began the war behind the Japanese in the number and quality of their aircraft carriers but swiftly surpassed them culminating with the seventeen *Essex* class super-carriers with a 20,000 mile cruising range, 33 knot top speed, and up to 100 aircraft aboard. Landing troops on enemy shores required a variety of vessels. LSTs (Landing Ship, Tank) were the largest at 328 feet and could carry 2,000 ton, including 50 tanks and 500 troops. LCIs (Landing Craft, Infantry) were 158 feet long and could carry 18 tanks or 200 troops. LCVP (Landing Craft, Vehicle or Personnel) were 35 feet long and could carry two tanks or twenty-five men. DUKWs were 2.5 ton six-wheeled amphibious armored trucks that could carry 5,000 pounds of cargo or twenty-five troops.

The battle for naval supremacy in the Atlantic lasted from the European war's start in September 1939 and ended only with Germany's defeat in May 1945. The battle's essence pitted German submarines against Allied anti-submarine ships and planes. Germany's objective was to destroy enough enemy war and merchant ships that Britain, starved of protection and supplies, was forced to surrender. During those years, German submarines sank 175 allied warships and 2,825 merchant ships while Allied planes and ships sank 781 of 1,131 submarines, killing around 33,000 of 40,000 crew. Altogether the submarines destroyed 14,500,000 tons of Allied merchant shipping or 18,565 tons for each lost submarine. Yet, the Allies managed to produce more ships and sent more troops and supplies across the Atlantic than they lost, thus ultimately winning that battle albeit at a tremendous cost in lost ships, sailors and supplies.[248] The ability of American shipyards to build standard designed Liberty and larger and better designed Victory cargo ships was essential to winning the war. The production became increasingly efficient with a Liberty ship's construction time plunging from 230 days to 24 days. Eighteen shipyards built 2,710 Liberty ships from 1941 to 1945, and 531 Victory ships from 1943 to 1946.[249]

New technologies applied to war can drastically change outcomes for those who first master them, and thus spur all belligerents to join and win that race. Shortly after the Wright brothers invented the airplane in 1903, farsighted military leaders in America and Europe sought to develop it to enhance communication, transportation, reconnaissance and firepower. General John Pershing acquired eight planes for his Punitive Expedition into Mexico, but mechanical and supply problems grounded them. During World War I, the belligerents swiftly built up air forces with arrays of increasingly powerful planes that fought each other or bombed enemy positions. After World War II, Italian General Gulio Douhet and American General Billy Mitchell were leading advocates for developing and making central to warfare fleets of massive bombers that destroyed cities, troops, and ships.

Aviation experienced exponential growth during the interwar era. America's army and navy steadily deployed ever more powerful warplanes, and that development accelerated during World War II. By 1943, American ground and carrier based fighters and bombers surpassed those of the Axis powers. In Europe, land-based P-51 Mustangs replaced obsolete P-40s to devastate German Messerschmitt-109s and Focke Wulf-190s in dogfights; the Americans shot down three German planes for every one lost among themselves. P-38 Lightning and P-47 Thunderbolt fight-bombers ravaged enemy troops, tanks, trucks and trains. B-17 and B-24 strategic bombers destroyed European cities. In the Pacific, F6F Hellcats replaced mediocre F4FWildcats to fly from airfields and carriers to outfight Japanese Zeros while B-29s with 3,500-mile ranges and 20,000-pound bomb loads destroyed Japanese cities. The C-47 was World War II's best cargo and paratrooper plane. The navy upgraded some warplanes that began the war inferior to their Japanese equivalents to surpass them in quality like second generation Dauntless and Helldiver dive bombers and Avenger torpedo bombers. American pilots received three times more training before being committed to combat than enemy pilots.[250]

The Combined Chiefs of Staff ensured that each army fighting in Europe was partnered with a Tactical Air Force. For instance, Patton's Third Army and General Otto Weyland's XIX Tactical Air Command worked closely together. America's fighter-bombers accounted for more than half of all destroyed German tanks. From 6 June 1944 to 8 May 1945, American fighter-bombers and fighters flew 212,731 sorties and fired 24 million rounds of .50 caliber bullets against German targets.[251]

At times, Patton and other ground commanders sought heavy bombers to join fight-bombers in destroying the enemy forces before them. For instance, around 12 per cent of Eighth Air Force's sorties were tactical support. Strategic and fighter-bombers avoided attacking targets within 1,000 and 300 respective yards of friendly troops. The danger of using strategic bombers for tactical strikes was that American B-17s and B-24s and British Lancasters that unleashed their 'dumb bombs' from 12,000 feet against relatively small targets below almost invariably missed and often killed civilians and at times Allied troops. For instance, during D-Day strategic bombers dumped 2,944 tons of bombs from several hundred yards to several miles behind the German positions on the coast.[252]

Bombing enemy cities into rubble was euphemistically called 'strategic bombing'. In Europe, American General Carl Spaatz and British General Arthur Tedder insisted that round-the-clock bombing by America's Eighth Air Force at day and Britain's Bomber Command at night could defeat Hitler's regime. In the Pacific, General Curtis LeMay asserted that strategic bombing could defeat Japan. Those advocates were wrong. Hitler's regime endured 131 cities and towns destroyed along with 400,000 lives and 7,000,000 people rendered homeless, only finally to collapse after nearly 5 million American, British, Soviet and other Allied troops overran the country and its allies and conquests. Japan's regime was preparing its soldiers and civilians to fight to the death against an American invasion after enduring 64 cities and 400,000 lives destroyed, and millions of people homeless by conventional bombs, and only surrendered after atomic bombs destroyed Hiroshima and Nagasaki.

Allied strategic bombing inflicted vast incalculable economic damage to the Third Reich and forced Berlin to divert 1.2 million Germans into anti-aircraft units and 1.8 million workers to repairing bomb damage, especially to the transportation and oil industries. Yet American and British airmen suffered 160,000 dead, wounded and captured. The 6-month casualty rate for 1,000 airmen was a horrendous 89 per cent with 712 killed or missing and 175 wounded. In 1944 alone, German flak gunners shot down 6,400 Allied planes and damaged 27,000. The British Lancaster bomber was especially vulnerable with 3,349 of 7,374 shot down or wrecked. With just one emergency exist, they were death traps for crew with four of five dying after their plane was hit and began to plummet to earth; B-17s had four exits that let three of five jump free with a parachute.[253]

Patton delighted in the fighter bombers that blasted the enemy as his troops advanced or defended, but the destruction of Europe's beautiful cities by carpet bombing disgusted and saddened him. He argued that

> indiscriminate bombing has no military value and is cruel and wasteful, and that all such efforts should always be on purely military targets and on selected commodities which are scarce. In the case of Germany, it would be on oil.[254]

Among the ironies of carpet bombing was that the rubble it left behind was easily defended by the Germans against advancing Allied troops.

***

The ultimate question for commanders is how best to war against the enemy.[255] For that, the American Army Field Manual's 1939 edition presented this core maxim:

> The ultimate objective of all military operations is the destruction of the enemy's armed forces in battle. Decisive defeat breaks the enemy's will to war and forces him to sue for peace which is the national aim.

The Manual did note that: 'An objective may sometimes be gained through maneuver alone; ordinarily it must be gained through battle.'[256]

The model American generals for George S. Patton, Dwight D. Eisenhower and Omar Bradley were respectively John Pershing, Ulysses S. Grant, and William Sherman who emphasized the destruction of enemy forces by whatever appropriate means, although virtually continuous movement and fire against the enemy's most vulnerable strategic and tactical positions was essential. The character of Pershing, Grant and Sherman also provided a vital model. Each was a cool professional, at once ruthless and compassionate. Grant famously demanded 'unconditional surrender' from the enemy generals whose armies he had defeated and surrounded.

War games that pitted armies against each other across regions of the United States were the best way to give all soldiers from the lowest private to the highest general vital training in large-scale operations. Patton was tapped to serve as an umpire at Fort Benning's war games from 12 to 25 April 1940, then at Fort Beauregard's from 5 to 25 May 1940. In each game, tank units outmaneuvered and beat infantry units. As umpire Patton learned many lessons for handling both tanks and troops, especially for coordinating their movements and attacks.

Amid the games, Marshall established a separate armored corps within the army in May and named General Adna Chaffee the commander on 10 July 1940. Chaffee's 1st Armored Corps included the 1st Division at Fort Knox, Kentucky and 2nd Division at Fort Benning, commanded respectively by generals John Magruder and Charles Scott. When cancer forced Chaffee to resign, Marshall replaced him with General Jacob 'Jake' Devers.

A critical turning point in Patton's career came on 29 July 1940, when he received command of 2nd Armored Division's 2nd Armored Brigade that included 2 light tank regiments, 1 medium tank regiment, 1 field artillery regiment, 1 engineer battalion, 350 officers, 5,500 troops, 383 tanks, 202 armored cars and 24 105-millimeter cannons.[257] He wrote Marshall a thank you letter and received this reply:

> I am glad the arrangement is pleasing to you, for I thought it would be just the sort of thing that you would most like to do at the moment. Also, I felt that no one could do that particular job better. I am looking forward to seeing you and having a talk with you before you leave for the South.[258]

Patton proudly wrote to his old commander John Pershing that: 'This command is a very fine one and I am most fortunate to have landed it.'[259] He was promoted to brigadier general on 2 October 1940.

Patton invited his old friend Dwight D. Eisenhower, now a lieutenant colonel, to join his staff. Eisenhower replied that 'it would be great to be in the tanks again and even better to be associated with you again.' But Eisenhower wanted to be a combat commander not a staff officer, which had straightjacketed his career until then: 'I suppose it's too much to hope that I could have a regiment in your division, because I'm still almost three years away from colonelcy … I think I could do a damn good job of commanding a regiment.' Patton promised to welcome him either as a staff officer or regimental commander, but added: 'If you get a better offer in the meantime, take it as I can't be sure, but I hope we can get together.'[260] Neither post opened and Eisenhower took another position.

Meanwhile, Patton began training his brigade by instructing the officers in tank warfare strategy and tactics through long maneuvers in the surrounding countryside. He received two extraordinary messages on 4 April 1941, promotion to major general and command of 2nd Armored Division. Patton expanded his division to number 776 officers and 10,121 men by March 1941.[261]

During 2nd Armor's buildup, Patton received a visit from Secretary of War Henry Stimson; the two had enjoyed morning horse rides and talks during Stimson's time as Secretary of State from 1929 to 1933. Patton arranged a series of combined tank, infantry, artillery and dive bomber maneuvers for Stimson to observe, and the secretary of war found 'the synchronization astonishing.'[262] Like Marshall, Stimson would back Patton with commands and promotions despite the controversies he provoked during World War II.

Patton split his division in columns on parallel roads from Fort Benning 170 miles to Panama City, Florida and then back by different routes in mid-December 1941. The division then numbered 392 officers, 6,079 troops and 231 tanks. Part of his training program emphasized maintenance and he was delighted that only one tank broke down along the way. The return included a simulated attack on Fort Benning.[263]

Patton was eager to pit 2nd Armored against 'enemy' forces in three war games that Marshall organized for 1941.[264]

The first was between the two Second Army Corps at Camp Forrest, Tennessee in June 1941. In the first round, Patton's division got poor marks when he failed to coordinate his maneuvers with the infantry division and lost 135 vehicles that umpires ruled the defenders had destroyed. That criticism spurred him to extraordinary plans and efforts for the next round. For that, Patton swung 2nd Armored Division in a wide flanking movement that captured General Cortland Parker at his 5th Infantry Division command post. That ended the round after nine hours rather than the scheduled two full days. Patton proudly wrote Stimson that despite the long march of up to 110 miles 'every fighting vehicle in the division, except two tanks and a scout car, got to the place it was supposed to be in time to deliver the attack.'[265] In his efficiency report, General Charles Scott, who now commanded 1st Armored Corps, rated Patton 'superior', number five of sixty generals that he had evaluated, and a 'most energetic and capable commander who is quick in his decisions and vigorous in their execution.'[266]

The second game pitted 'Blue' Third Army with 240,000 troops led by General Walter Krueger against 'Red' Second Army with 160,000 troops led by General Ben Lear in September 1941 and unfolded over northern Louisiana and eastern Texas. Patton's 2nd Armored Division was with the 'Red' army the first round and the 'Blue' army the second round. To his officers, Patton explained that he expected them and their troops to make 'mistakes down in Louisiana, not over in Europe, and if it doesn't work, find out we need to make it work.'[267] Each time, Patton launched 2nd Armored Division in wide flanking maneuvers that captured most of his objectives but with heavy losses. In the second round, 2nd Armor Division advanced over 400 miles to 'capture' Shreveport within four days, forcing the umpires to cancel the scheduled week-long game the following day. Among the observers was Omar Bradley:

> Patton broke all the old-fashioned rules, smashing his mechanized forces ever onward with dazzling speed and surprise. He was criticized by the umpire-general for his unorthodoxy, for leaving his command post and prowling the 'front lines,' for running his divisions 'roughshod' over the enemy. But it was clear to anyone in the U.S. Army with eyes to see that we had on our hands one of the most extraordinary fighting generals the Army had ever produced.[268]

Elated, Krueger wrote to Patton that: 'I was constantly impressed by the high morale, technical proficiency, and devotion to duty of the personnel of 2nd Armored Division ... Your leadership has produced a fighting organization.' Patton mingled praise and criticism to his officers, pointing out 'certain tactical errors of which we were guilty' but wanted to 'congratulate all of you ... and it is my fond belief that we will get better and better.'[269]

The third war game took place between General Hugh Drum's 'Blue' First Army and General Oscar Griswald's 'Red' provisional army in South Carolina and North Carolina in November 1941. The 1st Armored Corps led by General Scott, including Patton's 2nd Armored Division and Bruce Magruder's 1st Armored Division fought for the Red Army in the first round and the Blue Army in the second. In the first round with the Red Army, Patton's 2nd Armored captured Columbia, South Carolina on the third day. Patton's 2nd Armored suffered losses and he had to withdraw during the second round as anti-tank guns devastated his tanks. Magruder did worse; his division not only suffered heavy losses but he was captured. Scott wrote Patton that:

> I desire to commend you, the officers and all enlisted men ... for the esprit de corps, the energy, the endurance, the initiative, and the fighting spirit evidence throughout this most strenuous and exacting work ... [I]n the most difficult situations, when the enemy was pressing from all sides, when our own and the enemy's tactical dispositions were obscure, and when exacting and intricate night maneuvers were ordered, I could always count on you ... being in the right place at the right time to meet any hostile opposition.[270]

Marshall carefully studied each of the three war games with Patton foremost in mind. He concluded that:

> Patton is by far the best tank man in the army. I knew this from the First World War. I watched him closely when he commanded the first tanks we ever had. I realize he is a difficult man but I know how to handle him.[271]

***

While Hitler's Third Reich appeared to be the worst threat facing the United States, Japan would actually launch the first attack, and it was devastating. The Japanese had conquered Manchuria from September

1931 and warred against China with the goal of conquering it from July 1937. Roosevelt had managed to circumvent the Neutrality Laws and authorize $100 million in military aid for China in 1938; he also authorized Colonel Claire Chennault to form a voluntary air force of Americans to fight with the Chinese against the Japanese; finally, he called on American businesses voluntarily to stop selling war goods to Japan. In June 1940, Tokyo took advantage of France's defeat to pressure the Vichy regime into basing military forces in northern Vietnam in June 1940. Roosevelt responded with an executive order that forbad American businesses from selling scrap metals, aviation fuel, and machines tools to Japan.

Roosevelt authorized Secretary of State Cordell Hull to begin negotiations with Ambassador Kisaburo Nomura in January 1941. The two talked past each other for the next ten months until 26 November. Hull insisted that the Japanese withdraw from all their conquests since 1931, while Nomura demanded that the United States recognize those conquests.

Tokyo pressured Vichy to let it deploy military forces at bases and ports in southern Vietnam in July 1941. Roosevelt responded on 24 July 1941, by having Treasury Secretary Henry Morgenthau freeze Japan's financial assets in the United States. That freeze prevented Tokyo from buying American products, most vitally petroleum that supplied 80 per cent of Japan's consumption. At the time, Japan had eighteen months' worth of oil in storage tanks but once that was exhausted Japan's military and economy would grind to a halt.

Japan's Imperial War Council authorized Admiral Isoruku Yamamoto to plan a massive offensive across the Pacific with the initial attack to destroy America's fleet at Pearl Harbor, on Oahu Island of the Hawaiian Islands. The fleet against Pearl Harbor included six aircraft carriers with 414 warplanes, 2 battleships, 2 heavy cruisers, 1 light cruiser, 8 oil tankers, 23 submarines, and 5 mini submarines commanded by Admiral Chuichi Nagumo. At Pearl Harbor were 8 battleships, 8 cruiser, 300 destroyers, 4 submarines, and 73 auxiliary naval vessels, along with 380 warplanes at nearby Henderson air field.

Nagumo's fleet departed Etorofu Island in the Kurile Islands north of Japan on 26 November 1941 and steamed in radio silence until early morning on 7 December, when it halted 250 miles north of Pearl Harbor. Nagumo ordered two waves of attacks that sank four battleships, damaged four battleships and three cruisers, destroyed 188 warplanes and damaged 159 others, killed 2,403 military personnel and wounded 1,178 people, while losing only 29 planes. Had Nagumo ordered a third wave that destroyed the oil storage tanks, he would have crippled Oahu as an American military base and forced the withdrawal of most navy and army forces to San Diego, California, 2,621 miles north-east. Nagumo was disappointed that America's two aircraft carriers in the Pacific were not at Pearl Harbor and feared that they lurked nearby and would attack his fleet. So, he departed. That Japanese victory would have been decisive had the fleet conveyed an army powerful to invade and conquer Honolulu.

Pearl Harbor was the opening attack of a brilliant series of Japanese offensives. On 8 December1941, a Japanese air attack destroyed much of the American air and naval forces defending the Philippines; although eight hours earlier, the commander, General Douglas MacArthur, had learned of the Pearl Harbor attack, he did nothing to prepare for an attack on his own forces. From then through to May 1942, the Japanese conquered America's Philippines, Britain's Malaya, Singapore and Burma, and the Netherlands' and Indonesia.

Meanwhile, Roosevelt asked Congress for a war declaration against Japan on 8 December 1941, which the Senate approved by 83 to 0 and the House by 388 to 1. Hitler and Mussolini declared war against the United States on 11 December 1941. Congress reciprocated that same day. With the United States now a belligerent, the war had truly become global.[272] Patton finally got the war he had both predicted and desired.

Chapter 5

NORTH AFRICA

'Use steamroller strategy, that is make up your mind on a course and direction of attack and stick to it. But in tactics do not steamroller. Attack weakness. Hold them by the nose and kick them in the arse.'

'The eyes of the world are watching us; the heart of America beats for us; God is with us. On our victory depends the freedom or slavery of the human race. We shall surely win.'

'After having spent thousands of casaulties making a breakthrough, we were not allowed to exploit it.'

'Sir, all I want to tell you is this – I will leave the goddamned beaches either a conqueror or a corpse.'

George S. Patton

Pearl Harbor at once appalled and exhilarated British Prime Minister Winston Churchill. He commiserated with the Americans for their horrendous loss of lives and warships, yet he was exultant that with the United States now an ally: 'We had won the war [World War II] … How long the war would last or in what fashion it would end no man could tell.'[273] After giving his condolences to President Franklin D. Roosevelt, he suggested that they and their Joint Chiefs of Staff meet as soon as possible to begin planning how to crush the Axis power. Roosevelt readily agreed.

Churchill and his Joint Chiefs of Staff journeyed to Washington for intensive discussions and key decisions from 22 December 1941 to 14 January 1942. The first was to establish in Washington the Combined Chiefs of Staff from each nation's Joint Chiefs of Staff. The American chiefs included George Marshall for army, Ernest King for navy,

Henry 'Hap' Arnold for air, and Roosevelt's military advisor Admiral William Leahy, and for the British John Dill for army, Dudley Pound for navy and Charles Portal for air.

Roosevelt and Churchill agreed that their two nations should lead a democratic crusade of as many other countries as possible against the fascist powers. To that end, they gathered envoys of twenty-six countries at the White House on 1 January 1942, and they signed the Declaration of the United Nations that espoused the Atlantic Charter's liberal ideals.

That done, the Americans and British reached a swift consensus on one key strategic question and stalemated on another. The Allies would first defeat Germany and Italy, which posed the worst immediate threat, then go after Japan. The trouble was for defeating Germany and Italy, the Americans and British had diametrically opposed strategic outlooks. The Americans dismissed Italy as a secondary enemy and sought the fastest way to defeat Germany which they insisted involved landing overwhelming forces in northern France and fighting straight to Berlin. The British wanted an indirect approach via the Mediterranean Sea and southern Europe that first knocked Italy out of the war and defeated German forces along the way. Eventually, the Allies would head north toward Germany, possibly via north-east Italy and the Ljubljana Gap across the Alps.

Among Churchill's paradoxes was how such a brilliant man could be so deluded at grand strategy. He continuously advocated his 'soft European underbelly' approach for Allied offensives and rejected the northern France strategy that he insisted would be a blood-soaked debacle. That was bizarre enough given that mountainous Italy, which the Allies invaded in September 1943, and the mountainous Balkans, which Churchill wanted to invade, were 'soft' for defenders not attackers, while most of northern France was relatively flat and so ideal for rapid tank-led advances. The only 'soft' Axis place for invaders on the Mediterranean Sea was southern France. Yet Churchill adamantly opposed landing there, asserting that would be just as disastrous as one in Normandy. Fortunately, he was as wrong about both northern and southern France as he was tragically wrong about Italy. And Churchill was not alone in his strategic delusions. Chief of Staff Alan Brooke and most of Britain's high command vigorously backed him.

Americans and Britons also had different approaches to planning. American commanders tend to give subordinates general instructions for ends, means, and whens to allow them the flexibility to adapt creatively to subsequent shifting opportunities and threats. British commanders tend to minutely plan operations that subordinates implement. In that, generals George S. Patton and Bernard Montgomery epitomized their respective national differences.

British prejudices were another strain on the alliance. Although Churchill was overjoyed at being and working with the Americans on a global crusade, most of his high command did not share his enthusiasm. They barely concealed their contempt for their American counterparts who they dismissed as rank amateurs. Chief of Staff Alan Brooke was especially critical, although he confided his most scornful remarks to his diary.

***

Meanwhile, Patton was determined to prepare his men's minds, bodies and skills for combat. He assembled 2nd Armored on 20 December 1941 to review their three war games and prepare them for future combat:

> Tactically I made mistakes, both in training and in operations, which I am now correcting through further education of myself and the officers of this division ... Put your heart and soul into being expert killers with your weapons. The only good enemy is a dead enemy ... Battle is not a terrifying ordeal to be endured. It is a magnificent experience wherein all the elements that have made man superior to the beasts are present: courage, self-sacrifice, loyalty, help to others, devotion to duty ... Remember that these enemies, whom we shall have the honor to destroy, are good soldiers and stark fighters. To beat such men, you must not despise their ability, but you must be confident in your own superiority.[274]

Patton received command of 1st Armored Corps on 15 January 1942. Anticipating that his first combat was likely in North Africa, Patton requested desert in which to train his men. In April 1942, he received orders to transfer his corps from Fort Benning to what became the Desert Training Center and later Camp Pendleton, California, a vast expanse of the Mohave Desert. His headquarters and the barracks were near Indio. He acclimated and toughened his men by requiring them to run a mile within ten minutes while carrying a rifle and full backpack. In the first twenty days, he conducted 'thirteen major tactical exercises, including with two nights in the desert.'[275] Meanwhile, one of his closest friends was promoted to a key position at Army Chief of Staff George Marshall's headquarters.

Dwight D. Eisenhower had developed into an outstanding army administrator in the two decades since he and Patton had enthusiastically tried to develop tank design and doctrine. Among Eisenhower's highlights were graduating first in his class from Fort Leavenworth's Command and General Staff College in 1926 and the War College in Washington in 1928, then serving as the chief aide for General Douglas MacArthur when he was army chief of staff in Washington from 1933 to 1935, and Philippine President Manuel Quezon's military advisor in Manila from 1935 to 1939. Eisenhower hated serving MacArthur, a flamboyant narcissist who took credit for anything that went well and blamed others for any mistakes. Yet, to handle such an egotistical and erratic commander, Eisenhower bolstered his natural diplomatic skills, skills that would be crucial for him as the commander of allied armies whose governments often had divergent interests and whose generals often had towering egos. Among those skills was knowing when to be conciliatory and compromising, and when to be tough and stand one's ground. After returning to the United States in December 1939, now Lieutenant Colonel Eisenhower commanded 15th Regiment's 1st Battalion at Fort Lewis, Washington from May 1939 to March 1941. He was promoted to colonel and became a staff officer for Geneal Walter Krueger, Third Army's commander at Fort Sam Houston; he became a brigadier general in October 1941. After Japan's attack on Pearl Harbor and America's war declaration, Army Chief of Staff George Marshall summoned Eisenhower to Washington to be chief of operations and planning.

Patton and Eisenhower resumed their friendship, for now expressed through letters. In May 1942, Patton penned Eisenhower these poignant and prescient lines:

> Sometimes I think that your life and mine are under the protection of some supreme being or fate, after many years of parallel thought, we find ourselves in the situations we now occupy. But remember that my fate largely depends on you, because in this distant locality, one can very easily be forgotten ... I stick my neck out, but I trust to your great powers of discernment and persuasion to see that no one drops an ax on my neck.[276]

Eisenhower would indeed save Patton's career from his own follies over the next three and a half years.

***

A devastating defeat eventually enabled the British to win their tug-of-war with the Americans over grand strategy. German General Erin Rommel launched his Afrika Korps in an offensive that routed

General Neil Ritchie's British Eight Army in Libya, captured Tobruk with 35,000 prisoners on 11 June 1941, and advanced as far east as El Alamein, Egypt, just 90 miles from Alexandria; overall Rommel's blitzkrieg inflicted 75,000 casaulties and 600 lost tanks on Eighth Army.

Churchill was with Roosevelt at the White House on 21 June 1941, when Marshall appeared with news of the Tobruk disaster. Roosevelt somberly asked Churchill, 'What can we do to help?' They discussed various options and settled on one. An American armored division would reinforce Eighth Army in Egypt.

Marshall and his staff debated who should lead that division. Eisenhower recalled that

> my mind immediately turned to one of my oldest friends, Major General George S. Patton, Jr. who was not only a tank expert but an outstanding leader of troops. I was astonished to find my choice flatly opposed by a considerable portion of the staff, but I was convinced that this was due entirely to Patton's rather bizarre mannerisms and his sometimes unpredictable actions. He conformed to no pattern – a circumstance that made many fearful of his ability to fit into a team. Such doubt had no influence with me because of my confidence in his fighting heart and he would provide effective leadership for combat troops.[277]

Marshall enthusiastically approved Eisenhower's choice and had Patton summoned to Washington on 21 June 1941.

Patton accepted the offer and Marshall sent him to the War College to plan the operation. Soon Patton reported that dispatching two divisions would be more appropriate. Marshall ordered him to return to 1st Armored Corps. Patton feared that he had offended Marshall. Actually, Roosevelt, Churchill and the Combined Chiefs of Staff decided to send Eighth Army 300 Sherman tanks rather than an armored division.

Marshall dispatched Eisenhower to London on 24 June 1941, to head America's swelling military forces in Britain and convince Churchill and his military advisors to adapt a northern France invasion strategy then codenamed Roundup. Eisenhower established his headquarters for what was called the European Theater of Operations (ETOUSA) at 20 Grosvenor Square in London's ritzy Mayfair neighborhood. The Allied Force Headquarters (AFHQ) with American and British officers was at Norfolk House at 31 St James Street, Westminster.

Meanwhile, Roosevelt accepted Churchill's arguments to postpone an invasion of France and instead land an American army in French Northwest Africa then drive east and crush Rommel's Afrika Korps against Britain's Eighth Army. American officers and men were green, and better ripened against second rate French and colonial troops in North Africa than against veteran German troops in France.

Roosevelt, Churchill and the Combined Chiefs of Staff formally authorized that campaign, codenamed Torch, on 24 July 1941.[278] Chief of Staff Ernest King and Army Chief of Staff Marshall flew to London to begin planning Torch and appoint a commander. On 26 July 1941, Marshall informed Eisenhower that he would command that army. Eisenhower named General Mark Clark his deputy. Marshall and King then returned to Washington.

Planning for Torch unrolled in both Washington and London. The first key question was where to invade. Landings in Tunisia that captured the ports of Tunis and Bizerte would deprive the Germans and Italians of their supply ports and trap Afrika Korps at the end of its 1,000-mile long tether. Eisenhower explained the most important reason why the planners rejected that proposal:

> A successful direct landing in the Bizerte-Tunis area would have yielded great results, but that locality was far outside the range of fighter support, and British experiences in running convoys to Malta had been only little short of disastrous, this particular project was quickly given up as beyond the bounds of justifiable risk.[279]

Another fear was that Spain's fascist Generalissimo Franciso Franco might join the Axis, capture Gibraltar, and cut off the expedition. They agreed that the expedition should seize Morocco on the Atlantic Ocean and Algeria on the Mediterranean Sea to intimidate Spain.

Marshall and Eisenhower agreed that Patton should command the Moroccan invasion. Marshall summoned Patton to Washington for a briefing on 30 July 1941, then flew him to London to join Eisenhower and the planning team at Norfolk House on 6 August 1941. Over two weeks, as Patton attended sessions, he grew more disillusioned with Eisenhower for delaying tough decisions, and when he did decide, favoring British over American commanders to lead the most vital operations. He worried that 'Ike is not as rugged mentally as I thought; he vacillates and is not a realist.'[280]

The planners devised a daring and complex massive invasion by 3 task forces totaling 117,000 troops, with 3 of 4 soldiers American. General Charles Ryder commanded Eastern Task Force with 23,000 British and 10,000 American troops against Algiers; General Lloyd Fredendall Central Task Force with 39,000 American troops against

Oran; and Patton Western Task Force with 33,000 American troops against Casablanca, Mehida and Safi.

Patton flew back to Washington on 21 August 1941. Over several days, he had prolonged talks with Secretary of War Stimson, Army Chief of Staff Marshall, and other key military leaders. He also had a last poignant meeting with General Pershing at Walter Reed Hospital. As they reminisced over their campaigns in Mexico and France, Pershing told him:

> I can always pick a fighting man and God knows there are few of them. I am happy they are sending you to the front at once. I like generals so bold that they are dangerous. I hope they give you a free hand...When I left I kissed his hand and asked for his blessing. He squeezed my hand and said, 'Goodbye George, God bless, and keep you and give you victory.'[281]

That was their last time together, although Pershing would outlive Patton.

Patton assembled a headquarters staff whose key personnel included General Geoffrey Keyes as deputy, Colonel Hobart Gay as chief of staff, Colonel Paul Harkins as assistant chief of staff, Colonel Percy Black as intelligence (G-2) chief, Colonel Kent Lambert as operations (G-3) chief, Colonel Walter Muller as logistics (G-4), Captain Dick Jenner and Lieutenant Alexander Stiller as aides, Sergeant George Meeks as orderly, and Sergeant John Mims as driver. Most of those men stayed with Patton as he commanded II Corps, then Seventh Army and finally Third Army. The key newcomer was Oscar Koch, a brilliant intelligence analyst who soon replaced Black as G-2 chief.[282]

Meanwhile, another British military disaster reinforced the arguments for Torch.[283] On 19 August 1941, the British launched a raid by 6,058 troops of Canada's 2nd Division along with 100 commandos and 50 American rangers conveyed or supported by 252 warships, and 74 air squadrons to seize Dieppe, a French fishing port on the English Channel. The 1,500 German defenders and the Luftwaffe decimated the attackers, killing 907, wounding 2,460, and capturing 1,946, knocking out 18 tanks, sinking a destroyer and 33 landing craft with 550 killed sailors and shooting down 106 planes while suffering 311 killed, 280 wounded and 48 downed planes. That failure bolstered the British military's belief that the Germans would destroy any cross-channel invasion and thus the Allies should confine their operations to the Mediterranean basin.

Patton spent most of his time in Washington trying to plan the operation with Admiral Kent Hewitt whose fleet would convey his corps to Morocco and sustain it there. At first Patton disliked Hewitt who differed with him over how to assemble and organize supplies and when landing conditions were unacceptable. After Patton erupted in fury against him and his staff, Hewitt complained to Chief of Naval Operations Admiral King. King urged Army Chief of Staff Marshall either to subdue or replace Patton. When Marshall asked for his advice on what to do, Eisenhower defended his friend, dismissing the complaints as 'nothing more than George's flair for the dramatic' and

> suggesting that if his personality was causing any difficulty in conferences the issue could be met by sending him out with his troops and allowing his staff members to represent him in the completion of planning details.[284]

Marshall promised King he would talk with Patton. When Marshall summoned Patton at 8.00 am on 21 October 1941, he was 'friendly and helpful' and 'told me to influence Hewitt but not to scare him.'[285] Patton felt that 'Marshall lacks imagination but has an unusual mind.' Patton met Hewitt later that morning to make amends and forge a good working relationship. President Roosevelt greeted Patton and Hewitt at the White House that afternoon. Patton recalled that Roosevelt 'greeted us with "Come in, Skipper and Old Cavalryman, and give me the good news."' The three discussed various problems but Patton's key point was, 'The Admiral and I feel we must get ashore regardless of cost, as the fate of the war hinges on our success.' To that Roosevelt replied, 'Certainly you must.'[286] As Patton left, he tried to reassure Roosevelt by melodramatically promising, 'Sir, all I want to tell you is this – I will leave the goddamned beaches either a conqueror or a corpse.'[287]

Of the three task forces, Patton's faced the worst challenges. One was hitting beaches on the open, tempestuous Atlantic Ocean rather than the relatively calm Mediterranean Sea for the other task forces. Another was having to split his command among three dispersed landings while the other task forces massed their respective forces at Oran and Algiers. Eisenhower recognized those challenges. He wrote Marshall that 'If Patton faces any real resistance, he is going to have a tough time of it because landing problems alone are enough to occupy his full attention.'[288]

Patton seesawed emotionally between elation and worry over his mission and his ability to accomplish it. For his 22 October 1941 diary entry, he wrote: 'When I think of the greatness of my job and realize that I am what I am, I am amazed, but on reflection, who is as good as I am. I know no one.' Five days later, he wrote:

> Every once in a while the tremendous responsibility of this job hits me like a ton of bricks, but mostly I [am] not in the least worried. I can't decide logically if I am a man of destiny or a lucky fool, but I think I am destined.[289]

***

Word of two British Eighth Army victories, one limited, the other crushing at El Alamein on Egypt's north-west coast dispelled some of the concerns permeating Torch's planners.[290] After taking command of Eighth Army on 10 August 1941, General Bernard Montgomery had his troops construct elaborate defenses of mine fields, barbed wire, pillboxes and trenches. Eighth Army repelled an attack by Rommel's Afrika Korps on 31 August 1941. Montgomery then built up Eighth Army for a massive attack that he launched on 23 October 1941 that pitted his 195,000 troops, 1,029 tanks, 435 armored cars, 908 cannons and 1,451 anti-tank guns against Afrika Korps' 116,000 troops, 547 tanks, 192 armored cars, 552 cannons and 1,062 anti-tank guns. Rommel was on leave in Germany when Eighth Army's onslaught began and hurried back to retake command of Afrika Korps from his deputy, General Georg Stumme. Rommel's military genius could not prevail against such overwhelming odds. By 11 November 1941, Eighth Army had crushed Afrika Korps, inflicting as many as 9,000 dead and 15,000 wounded, capturing 49,000, and knocking out 500 tanks while suffering 13,500 casualties and 332 destroyed tanks. Rommel escaped with just 36 tanks and 80,000 troops.

Yet Montgomery failed vigorously to pursue and destroy Afrika Korps remnants. Had he done so, he would have spared half a year and 100,000 Allied casualties that it took to complete North Africa's capture by May 1943. Nonetheless, Britons celebrated Montgomery as a hero for his victory.

Montgomery would become Eisenhower's most troublesome subcommander and Patton's greatest rival.[291] He would provoke controversy for other delayed limited victories at Caen, Falaise, and crossing the Rhine and outright defeats at Arnhem. Montgomery was a plodder who only attacked after prolonged massive buildups with overwhelming strength against the enemy.

Eisenhower wrote to Marshall this acute assessment that Montgomery

> is unquestionably able, but very conceited ... [H]e is so proud of his successes to date that he will never willingly make a single move until he is absolutely certain of success – in other words, until he has concentrated enough resources so that anybody could practically guarantee success.[292]

Yet during World War II, Eisenhower would repeatedly cave into Montgomery's demands for massive supplies and reinforcements for his proposed campaigns at the expense of Patton, a far superior general who would have scored decisive victories that eventually captured Berlin and defeated Germany had he wielded those same massive resources for his own ambitious strategies. Eisenhower's tendency to side with Montgomery and other British leaders enraged most American generals who griped that 'Ike is the best general the British have.'[293]

Bernard Montgomery was the fourth of eight children of a father who eventually became an Anglican bishop and a bullying, unaffectionate mother who frequently canned him.[294] He attended Sandhurst Royal Military College and after graduating in September 1908, was assigned to the Royal Warwickshire Regiment posted in India until 1913, when it returned to England. He was a first lieutenant when his regiment was sent with the British Expeditionary Army to France in August 1914 after World War I erupted. In October 1914, during the Battle of Ypres, he was shot in the lung and knee, and later evacuated to Britain where he received the Distinguished Service Order for valor and was promoted to captain. After recovering, he worked as a staff officer in London and was promoted to major. In 1916, he returned to the front where he served as 47th Division's chief of staff until the war ended. From 1919, he worked his way up as a staff officer at the battalion, regiment and division level in Britain, Egypt and India, and in rank to brigadier general, then in 1938, he was promoted to major general and given command of 8th Division in Palestine. He was transferred to command 3rd Division in Britain in 1939.

Montgomery was very bright but not as much as he believed himself to be. He was cocky, boastful, arrogant, condescending and pontificating. Most of his colleagues thought him insufferable but his troops adored him for attending their needs and insisting on high standards for physical fitness and technical and tactical skills while ignoring strict rules of dress. He was indifferent to women all his life until he was 38 when he married a widow with two small boys and had a son with her; an illness killed his wife in 1937 and he had relatives raise his sons.

Montgomery's division was in the II Corps commanded by General Alan Brooke and part of the nine division British Expeditionary Force that deployed in northern France in May 1940. The German blitzkrieg shattered the British, French, Belgium and Dutch armies. When Brooke was recalled to London, he tapped Montgomery to lead II Corps. Montgomery received accolades for his skilled handling of first the division then corps in staving off German attacks. Montgomery and his corps' remnants were among the 350,000 British and French troops evacuated from Dunkirk in June 1940.

During World War II, Montgomery had one key military backer, General Alan Brooke who first commanded him when heading II Corps in France and then as imperial chief of staff. Like Montgomery, Brooke was condescending, especially to Americans, but was as introverted as Montgomery was extroverted. General Frederick de Guingand was Montgomery's chief of staff. He was kind but his boss was abrasive.

Bernard Montgomery was Britain's version of General George McClellan who bedeviled President Lincoln and the Union cause during the Civil War with his narcissism, delays, demands, slow buildup for set-piece battles with overwhelming forces, and failure to ruthlessly follow up any victories. Montgomery could have destroyed Rommel's Afrika Korps by an unrelenting swift pursuit after El Alamein just as McClellan could have inflicted the same on Lee and his rebel army after Antietam.

Biographer Nigel Hamilton noted Montgomery's paradox:

> The very virtues which gave his leadership its inspiring quality – absolute conviction, insistence on proper planning, ruthless professionalism – made him an infuriatingly opinionated and stubborn ally.[295]

***

Torch's critical question was whether the 120,000 French troops deployed in France's North African colonies would resist or embrace the invaders. Elaborate and daring espionage and counterespionage preceded and accompanied Torch. The key American player was Robert Murphy, the roving ambassador to French North Africa. Murphy talked General Charles Mast, who commanded 16,000 troops defending Algiers, into secretly organizing as many French officers as possible to support the allied invasion. Mast explained that General Henri Giraud, then hiding in Vichy France, was the best choice to head the French army. Giraud fought heroically in both world wars; he had recently escaped from a German prisoner of war camp. Murphy journeyed to London with his intelligence reports on French North Africa. British Secret Service agents extracted Giraud from France.

Eisenhower dispatched his deputy General Mark Clark on a perilous mission in late October 1942. Clark flew to Gibraltar then boarded a British submarine that took him to the coast near Algiers. There he and six commandos paddled a rubber raft ashore to a villa where Murphy and Mast waited. Clark assured Mast that the Americans were coming and would support him, Giraud, and others who abandoned the Vichy regime to join the allies. During the meeting, the police appeared to search the house but did not find the conspirators who hid in the cellar. Clark and the commandos paddled back to the submarine which conveyed them to Gibraltar.

Eisenhower transferred his headquarters to Gibraltar on 5 November 1942. He faced a crisis when Giraud appeared before him and demanded command of Allied forces in French North Africa. Eisenhower asserted all his vast diplomatic skills into trying to convince Giraud to accept a key but subordinate rank in the Allied command.

Although Mast had secretly promised to surrender, he faced three potentially overwhelming obstacles to doing so. His immediate superior was General Louis Koeltz who commanded the region and above him was General Alphonse Juin who commanded all French troops in North Africa. Then, just days before the invasion, Admiral Jean-Francois Darlan, Vichy's military commander and Petain's designated successor, paid an unexpected visit to visit his son stricken with polio.

Murphy did what he could to ensure the French embraced rather than resisted the invasion. A few hours before H-Hour, he made this pitch to Juin:

> I am happy to say that I have been instructed by my government to inform you that the American and British armies of liberation are about to land ... Our talks over the years have convinced me that you desire above all else to see the liberation of France, which can come about only through cooperation with the United States.

Juin grudgingly agreed with Murphy but explained that he was under Darlan's command. Murphy then met with Darlan and made the same argument. Darlan angrily warned Murphy that his troops would resist the invaders.

Beginning at midnight on 7 November 1942, the BBC broadcasted every half hour to Vichy France and north-west Africa a recorded speech by Roosevelt and then French translation that proclaimed: 'We come among you solely to destroy your enemies and not to harm you. Do not obstruct, I beg of you, this great purpose. *Vive la France, eternelle.*'[296]

***

The Eastern and Central Task forces had massed in the Firth of Clyde in northern Scotland. They departed on 22 October 1942 and approached their respective landing sites after midnight on 8 November 1942. Each would capture its port after overcoming limited resistance.

Eastern Task Force was mostly British although commanded by American General Charles 'Doc' Ryder. Before dawn, two British destroyers packed with 662 American rangers and 74 British marines steamed into Algiers' harbor. Searchlights illuminated them for French gunners to target. One destroyer withdrew but the other docked and rangers secured the position. Meanwhile, regiments of America's 9th and 34th Infantry and Britain's 78th Infantry divisions landed unopposed at beaches a few miles east and west of Algiers and converged on the city. Juin surrendered at 6.00 pm that day.

General Lloyd Fredendall commanded the task force that targeted Oran. Fredendall split General Terry Allen's 1st 'Big Red One' Division and General Orlando Ward's 1st Armored Division into brigades that landed at undefended beaches either east or west of Oran with 200,000 inhabitants and General Robert Boisseau's French 10,000 defenders. Colonel William Darby's 1st Ranger Battalion captured the artillery battery at Arzew 25 miles east. A battalion of 509th Paratrooper Regiment landed on Oran's airport. Two British destroyers packed with a battalion of American troops churned into Oran's harbor. French gunners sank both of them, killing 189 Americans and wounding 157 along with 113 Royal Navy dead and 86 wounded. The east and west brigades converged on Oran. Boisseau surrendered on 10 November 1942.[297]

***

Western Task Force departed Norfolk on 24 October 1942 for a fourteen-day zigzag journey across the Atlantic Ocean. The fleet included the aircraft carrier *Ranger* and an escort carrier with 108 planes between them, 1 battleship, 3 heavy cruisers, 14 destroyers, and 36 transport ships packed with 33,834 troops and supplies. Patton and his staff joined Hewitt aboard his flagship, the heavy cruiser *Augusta*. En route, Patton, Hewitt and their staff worked out lingering campaign details. Patton reported to Marshall that

> relations between the Army and Navy in this convoy could not possibly be more satisfactory. Admiral Hewitt and his chief of staff, Admiral Hall, have shown the utmost cooperation and the finest spirit. I desire to bring this to your attention because prior to leaving I had some doubts. These doubts have been removed.[298]

He was enraged to see that the mass printed proclamation in French that explained that the Americans came as friends to liberate the population failed to include accents and ordered his intelligence section to redo it correctly. During his down time, Patton read history, did calisthenics, and ran 480 steps in place.

Napoléon's proclamations to his troops before and after campaigns and battles greatly inspired Patton. Using similar rhetoric, he issued this to his men:

> Soldiers: We are to be congratulated because we have been chosen as the units of the United States Army best trained to take part in this great American effort ... It is regrettable to contemplate the necessity of fighting the gallant French who are at heart sympathetic toward us, but all resistance offered must be destroyed. However, when any of the French soldiers seek to surrender, you will accept it and treat them ... respect ... When the great day of battle comes, remember your training, and ... above all that speed and vigor of attack are the sure roads to success, and you must succeed – for to retreat is as cowardly as it is fatal ... Americans do not surrender. During the first few days and nights after you get ashore you must work unceasingly ... A pint of sweat will save a gallon of blood. The eyes of the world are watching us; the heart of America beats for us; God is with us. On our victory depends the freedom or slavery of the human race. We shall surely win.[299]

Of Patton's three landings, the key was General Jonathan Anderson's 19,000 troops of 3rd Infantry Division and a 2nd Armored battalion to come ashore at Fedala, 15 miles north-east of Casablanca, and then barrel down the coast to capture that city. General Lucian Truscott with 9,000 troops including a 9th Infantry Division regiment and a 2nd Armored Division battalion would land near Mehdia to capture nearby Port Lyautey and its airfield 90 miles north-east of Casablanca.

General Ernest Harmon with 6,500 troops of a 9th Division regiment would take Safi, 141 miles south-west of Casablanca to block any French forces coming from Marrakesh 96 miles inland. As for strategy and tactics, Patton told his officers:

> Use steamroller strategy, that is make up your mind on a course and direction of attack and stick to it. But in tactics do not steamroller. Attack weakness. Hold them by the nose and kick them in the arse.[300]

Western Task Force split into three flotillas to land troops at their widely separated sites. Harmon's swiftly secured Safi against light and brief resistance with few casualties. Patton lauded Harmon's decisive, courageous leadership that won a series of victories over several days:

> The landing at Safi ... went as planned ... Harmon, showing tremendous drive and initiative, captured the harbor...He immediately landed a light armored battalion and moved it out on the Marrakech road where enemy forces of about 40 trucks and a number of armored cars were advancing. Our navy and bombers engaged this force, and it lasted long enough to allow the light armored battalion to build up sufficient strength to check the French advance ... On the 10th ... he attacked Marrakech column and destroyed a large number of trucks and armored cars ... [then] started to march on Casablanca ... completing a night march of 90 miles without lights and arriving at dawn ... The bridge across the river ... was defended. Harmon was just deploying to attack when he received my message that the French had ceased firing ... With great personal courage he went forward with one scout car, waving a dirty white towel, and informed the French officers on the far side that the war was over.[301]

As such, Harmon displayed all the Pattonesque initiative, creativity, and bravery that Patton continually sought to inspire in his officers.

Truscott's troops needed three days to secure Mehdia and Port Lyautey. Heavy waves limited how many of the 9,000 troops and 881 vehicles could get ashore. Although outgunned, the French fought tenaciously and only surrendered on 10 November 1942 after expending most of their ammunition and suffering over 400 dead, while inflicting 79 killed and 250 wounded on the Americans. Truscott admitted that the landings and firefights rattled the inexperienced troops and sailors, and had they faced more and better trained and armed enemy troops the battle might have been 'a disaster'.[302]

At Casablanca, around 10,000 French troops were garrisoned in and around the city while the French fleet anchored in the harbor included the battleship *Jean Bart*, a light cruiser, seven destroyers and eight submarines. Admiral Francois Michelier and General Emile Bethouart respectively headed those naval and army forces. Murphy and Mast had secretly recruited Bethouart to collaborate with the Allies. When Bethouart got word of the pending landing, he urged Michelier to order the navy to stand down and sent several trusted officers to try to convince Morocco's resident general, General Auguste Nogues, who resided at Rabat to join the Allies. Michelier had Bethouart arrested, while Nogues angrily rejected those entreaties.

General Jonathan Anderson's 3rd Division landed along 4 miles of beach centered at Fedala 15 miles north-east of Casablanca. Just 8,000 troops got ashore the first day through heavy waves and fire from shore batteries with 46 cannons and protected by 2,500 troops. Meanwhile, the battleship *Massachusetts*, *Augusta* and two other cruisers, and half of the destroyers deployed within range of Casablanca harbor and opened fire at the French warships. A dogfight between Wildcats launched from the two carriers and French fighter planes resulted in respective losses of five and seven warplanes. The American fleet sank one light cruiser, four destroyers and seven submarines, and silenced *Jean Bart* with its 16 inch guns.

With exhilaration and frustration, Patton described the fight for Casablanca harbor and his first attempt to join his men ashore:

> We have had a great day so far and have been in a naval battle since eight. At 7.15, six enemy destroyers came out of Casablanca; two were on fire. All ships in range opened on them and they went back. The [battleship] Massachusetts had been shelling the [battleship] Jean Bart for about thirty minutes. I was going ashore at eight and my boat was on the davits with all our things, including my white [ivory-handled] pistols. I sent an orderly to get them, and at that moment a light cruiser and two big destroyers came out of Casablanca, tearing up the coast close to shore to try to get near our transports. The *Augusta* speeded up to twenty knots and opened fire. The first blast from the turret blew our landing boat to hell, and we lost everything except my pistols. Then we went back into the fight with the French ships, and fired hard for about three hours. I was on the main deck when a shell hit so close that it splashed water all over me, and later, on the bridge, one hit even closer.[303]

Patton and three aides crammed into a boat at 12.42 pm and jumped onto the beach at 1.20 pm.

The following day, Patton recorded a typical war day of near constant movement, problem-solving, death-dodging, and leading by example:

> I got out of the Hotel before dawn ... The beach was a mess and the officers were doing nothing. We tried since the previous day to have the lighters use the beach, but Emmitt never told them. As a result they were beached half the time ... I cursed and at last got a launch off to catch the boats and show them into the harbor ... Just as I got the launch out a boat turned over and downed 16 men ... The French bombed the beach and later strafed it. One soldier who was pushing a boat got scared and ran onto the beach...I kicked him in the arse with all my might and he jumped up and went to wor. Some way to boost morale. As a whole the men were poor, the officers worse. It is very sad.[304]

At Fedala, naval guns and fighter bombers knocked out most shore batteries while troops captured most of the French positions on 9 November 1942; by the evening 20,000 troops but only 5 tanks had reached shore as 6 foot waves slowed and imperiled landing. On 10 November 1942, most of the Americans moved south to overrun the two airfields and engulf Casablanca from its land sides, although one French battery still sporadically shelled troops and supplies on the beach. Patton sent Colonel William Wilber with a white flag into Casablanca to urge Michelier and Bethouart to surrender or else suffer a devastating bombardment and attack. Michelier had had Bethouart arrested for treason the first day and now refused to see Wilbur, who returned to the beach. There Wilber asserted command of four tanks and an infantry company that captured that last enemy battery; Wilber later received a Medal of Honor for his heroism.

Piling on Patton's challenges was Eisenhower's 10 November cable that read:

> Dear Georgie –
>
> Algiers has been ours for two days, Oran's defenses crumbling rapidly ... The only tough nut left is in your hands. Crack it open quickly and ask for what you want.[305]

He also complained that Patton was not feeding him regular reports on his operations. To that Patton replied, 'I regret you are mad with me over my failure to communicate, however, I cannot control interstellar space and our radio simply would not work.'[306]

The previous day, Clark and Giraud flew to Algiers to negotiate with Darlan for a ceasefire. On 10 November 1942, they struck a deal whereby Darlan would govern French North Africa as a neutral region. Darlan sent an order to all French forces in North Africa to cease fire and cooperate with Allied forces. Not all officers initially received or obeyed that order, although most did. Learning that Petain's regime had repudiated his order, Darlan demanded that he be allowed to revoke it. Clark essentially put him under arrest to prevent him from canceling the ceasefire.

That word reached the Vichy officers at Casablanca just in time. Patton ordered 3rd Division and a 2nd Armored battalion to prepare to attack Casablanca following a naval and air bombardment at 7.30 am on the morning of 11 November 1942. At 4.30 a French officer appeared at Patton's headquarters with the message that Rabat had surrendered and Casablanca was likely to do so soon. Patton sent him into Casablanca to inform Admiral Michelier that he would launch a massive air, naval, and ground attack against Casablanca if he did not immediately surrender. Patton received Michelier's word that he would surrender at 6.40 am and called off the pending attack.

Patton and his staff went ashore to Casablanca's Hotel Miramar where they met Michelier and Nogues at 2.00 pm. At times Patton was as exemplary a diplomat as he was a commander. Torch planning required task force commanders to impose on the French commanders Treaty C that required them to disarm their troops and let American forces occupy the colonies. Michelier and Nogues argued that only the French army could subdue the 11 million Moroccan Arabs who otherwise would likely revolt against the Americans, thus preventing them from fighting Axis forces far eastward. In a dramatic gesture, Patton ripped the treaty in half and asked them to give their word as officers and gentlemen that they would maintain the ceasefire. They agreed. In a letter to Secretary of War Stimson, Patton explained his diplomacy's how and why:

> We had a fairly hard fight and lost some good men, but we inflicted very severe casualties on our late enemies … When the French came in to make terms, my sporting sense of not wishing to triumph over a gallant enemy induced me to have a guard of honor to receive the French officers. This made a very happy impression upon them and was, I believe, a precursor of the excellent entente which has existed ever since … I decided the best way to avoid an Arab uprising was to allow the French to retain their arms and man all their works … the French agreed to what I asked them … I said, 'Gentlemen, we have now settled everything, but there is one disagreeable formality which we should go through.' They all looked very worried. I then produced some champagne and suggested a toast.[307]

Eisenhower flew to Algiers on 13 November 1942, and met with the four key French commanders, Darlan, Nogues, Giraud and Juin at the St George Hotel. He got them to agree that Darlan would head the provisional government, Giraud would command the military, and Nogues would remain Morocco's resident general. The ceasefire would continue indefinitely with no formal surrender. Most French commanders haughtily rejected Giraud's attempts to assert command over them. Then, on 24 December 1942, Fernand Bonnier de la Chapelle, a French resistance fighter, shot to death Darlan. Eisenhower made Giraud the provisional leader.

***

The Allies conquered Morocco and Algeria with relatively light losses of 526 Americans and 574 British troops killed, an escort carrier, 4 destroyers, 2 sloops, 6 troopships, and a minesweeper sunk, while the French suffered 1,346 dead, 1,997 wounded, 1 light cruiser, 5 destroyers, and 6 submarines sunk while the Germans and Italians respectively lost 8 and 2 submarines. Western Task Force suffered the heaviest losses with 337 killed, 637 wounded, 122 missing, and 71 captured along with 5 transport ships although none held troops; shells and waves wrecked or beached around 150 of 378 landing craft. They inflicted on the French 462 dead and 200 wounded, sank 1 light cruiser, 7 destroyers and 7 submarines, and silenced battleship *Jean Bart*'s 16-inch guns.[308]

Historian Rick Atkinson offered this assessment of Torch and American military and diplomatic power:

> The truth was that a callow, clumsy army had arrived in North Africa with little notion of how to act as a world power. The balance of the campaign – indeed the balance of the war – would require learning not only how to fight but how to rule ... As for combat, Torch revealed profound shortcomings in leadership, tactics, equipment, martial elan, and common sense. Certain features of the invasion, such as amphibious assaults and attacks on an enemy's flanks would be polished by harsh experience and provide a template for Allied offensives throughout the war. But the U.S. army was simply inept at combined arms – the essence of modern warfare, which requires skillful choreography of infantry, armor, artillery, airpower and other combat forces.[309]

Hitler reacted decisively to Torch. He ordered ten German and six Italian divisions to overrun Vichy to ensure Marshal Philippe Petain's puppet regime remained loyal. Admiral Jean Laborde, who commanded the French fleet at Toulon, had rejected Darlan's command to steam his ships to French North African and join the Allies. After the German and

Italian divisions began their invasion, Laborde ordered his captains to scuttle their ships that included three battleships, seven cruisers, thirty-two destroyers, ten submarines and nineteen other vessels. Hitler established the Fifth Panzer Army initially led by General Walther Nehring in Tunisia, and sent a steady stream of troops, tanks and supplies. In November 1942 alone, 176 tanks, 131 cannons, 1,152 vehicles and 13,000 tons of supplies unloaded in Tunisia. Fifth Panzer Army soon fielded 150,000 troops.[310]

Torch was at once a brilliant success and a bungled chance for a decisive, quick, far less costly victory. The original plan might have triumphed earlier had America's best general, Patton, headed II Corps that took Algiers then advanced to Tunisia while lackluster, timid Fredendall lead the Morocco invasion. Even better, had Patton's task force landed at Bizerte rather than Morocco, it would have captured lightly held Tunisia, prevented 100,000 German reinforcements from landing there, and severed Afrika Korps' routed remnants from its supply source thus forcing its surrender or evacuation from Tripoli. Mark Clark, then Eisenhower's deputy, much later confessed that:

> We had been unquestionably timid (although far less than Washington) in the scope of our original invasion of Africa. Had we struck out boldly and landed forces far to the east, even in Tunisia ... we would have almost certainly been successful.[311]

***

Despite all of Torch's shortcoming, Churchill expressed its strategic value with these typically eloquent words: 'Now this is not the end. It is not even the beginning of the end. But it is, perhaps, the end of the beginning.'[312]

Securing Morocco and Algeria was the invasion's first stage. Eisenhower issued orders for the second phase on 13 November 1942. General Kenneth Anderson was to combine the Eastern and Central Task forces with a French corps into the British First Army, and lead it east, with British V Corps, from 5 December 1942 commanded by General Charles Allfrey, following the 560-mile coastal road from Algiers to Tunis, while General Alphonse Juin's French XIX Corps and General Fredendall's American II Corps advanced on parallel roads far inland. Ideally, First Army would join forces in Tunisia with General Bernard Montgomery's Eighth Army driving west.

For two weeks, those Allied forces made steady progress until they literally ran into a wall of mountains defended by Fifth Panzer Army. The Dorsal Mountains run north-south through central northern Tunisia. That was where the Allies advance bogged down, with V Corps in the north; XIX Corps in the center; and II Corps in the south. Nehring launched a series of attacks on the Allies from 25 to 30 November 1942 that blunted their advance.

Axis troops would fend off and launch spoiling attacks along the front for the next six months. Three advantages empowered them to hold out that long superior generalship, troop fighting prowess, and shorter supply lines from ports. The Axis armies received a steady stream of reinforcements and supplies from Tunis and Bizerte that were at most 100 miles from the furthest position while the Allied supply line stretched from the allied front 500 miles west to Algiers on three routes, one coastal along the potholed mostly dirt road and rickety one track railroad, and two interior roads just as wretched. Winter rains washed out stretches of the three roads and the railroad. Reinforcements and supplies trickled to the front. Bad weather also limited Allied air support for troops on the front.

***

With mingled frustration and relief, Patton could only read reports about that distant fighting. He wrote to Beatrice that

> I get fed up sitting here and seeing the war is lost but it may all work out for the best as some goats will have to be found soon and they are all ranked higher than me ... Well, any how I am having a lot of fun and am still young enough to learn.[313]

Diplomacy occupied much of Patton's time during the next four months. He met numerous times with Nogues, Michelier, and other French military and civilian leaders and paid respectful visits to the sultan and leading Moroccan political and religious leaders. He sought to develop friendly, trustful relations with all the leaders. To that end, he joined them for meals at their palaces and hunts for boars and other wild beasts in the countryside.

Patton recognized the perilous situation the Allies faced in French North Africa. The 21 million mostly Muslim Arabs resented this latest invasion atop prolonged French colonial rule. What kept them from revolting depended much more on soft psychological than hard physical power:

> As I see it, the French position in Morocco rests almost entirely on the mythical supremacy of France, which at the present time is represented to the Arab mind by Darlan ... Anything which is said in the United States to destroy this mythical French authority could have and probably will have a very adverse effect on the Arab. I am convinced that the Sultan ... is wholly for us, but he is not the authority or means of controlling the Arab tribes whereas ... French prestige, nebulous as it may seem ... can and will maintain order.[314]

Patton was wrong about Darlan; the Arabs had no loyalty to him and did not revolt when he was assassinated. Yet the rest of Patton's assessment was correct.

After two months of observing and interacting with Arabs, Patton wondered if

> arrested development does not apply to man. Certainly, between 600 and 800, the Arab race developed remarkable ability as conquerors, as scholars, and as lovers – or were they great only in comparison with the unutterable stupidity of the Dark Ages? It were folly to pursue this line of thought, else we would inevitably shatter an idol by concluding that at Tours, Charles Martel saved Europe by beating second-rate opponents ... The fatalism attributable to Koranic Law may well be the basis for Mohammedan decadence. If man is unsuccessful, he does not bestir himself. It is the Will of Allah.[315]

Patton tried to ensure that his troops remained sharp in behavior and appearance. He issued these instructions on 15 November 1942:

> I fully appreciate the danger and hardships you have been through ... [E]ach of you, is a representative of a great and victorious army. To be respected ... you must inspire respect. Stand up, keep your clothes buttoned, and your chin straps fastened. Salute your officers and the French officers, now our allies. Keep your weapons clean and with you. Your deeds have proven that you are fine soldiers. Look the part.[316]

Patton's orders bore results. General Jacob Devers was a West Point classmate and friend of Patton. After leading an inspection tour the North African fronts, Devers wrote Beatrice that, 'George's troops were by far the best looking group of soldiers that I saw in all my travel.' He did worry that Patton 'seemed a little depressed' at not being allowed to fight Rommel but was 'demonstrating at all times that he was a soldier's solder.' In his final report, he lauded Patton for establishing 'excellent relations with the French and the natives' and 'of all commands visited, General Patton's was the finest.'[317]

Patton was indeed depressed for being forced to play proconsul in Morocco with his war talents squandered far from the frontline in Tunisia. With bitter humor he wrote to a friend that:

> I think sometimes that I am a cross between a one-time soldier, a pseudo-statesman, a jack-legged politician and a crooked diplomat. I walk a soapy tightrope in a rainstorm with a blasting furnace on one side and a pack of ravenous tigers on the other.[318]

Patton flew to Gibraltar in mid-November to meet Eisenhower at this headquarters and discuss an array of strategic and political issues. Throughout the war, Patton griped about Eisenhower's leadership, especially his lack of decisiveness, rare visits to his commanders and the front, and tendency to favor British over American commanders. This 17 November diary was typical: 'Ike lives in a cave in the middle of the rock – in great danger. His chief of staff, G-2, and G-4 are British, and so are many of his words. I was disappointed in him. He talked of trivial things.' In a letter to Beatrice, he quipped, 'I truly fear that London has conquered Abilene.'[319] His view of Eisenhower improved after a conference three months: 'Ike certainly makes a fine impression when he talks. I was proud of him. I think I could do better in the same job, but I seem to lack something which makes the politicians trust Ike.'[320] What Patton lacked, of course, was the tact, patience, and humility that Eisenhower naturally exuded. That was why Patton and Eisenhower were such different generals, respectively America's best combat and political leaders of World War II.

***

The conference between President Roosevelt, Prime Minister Churchill, and the Combined Chiefs of Staff at Casablanca from 14 to 24 January 1943 was among the war's most consequential. Roosevelt and Churchill resolved a major diplomatic problem and made two key decisions.

The diplomatic problem was that generals Charles de Gaulle and Henri Giraud each insisted that he was the Free French Force's commander and detested the other. Roosevelt and Churchill found both French men arrogant and demanding. For now, they deferred choosing between them. Roosevelt did get them to be photographed by reporters shaking hands as a sign of Allied unity.

Roosevelt and Churchill agreed to a policy of unconditional surrender for all three Axis powers – Germany, Japan and Italy.

Churchill preferred to keep that policy secret for fear that it would encourage their leaders literally to fight to the death. So, he was surprised but backed Roosevelt when he announced the policy at a press conference. As will be seen, that declared policy would be catastrophic for Italy's fate.

The other key decision was what to do after the Allies completed their conquest of North Africa. America's military leaders favored holding North Africa while massing allied forces in Britain for an invasion of northern France in May 1944. Britain's leaders adamantly insisted on a series of offensives throughout the Mediterranean basin starting with Sicily that Churchill called Europe's 'soft underbelly'.

Speaking for the Americans, Eisenhower gave a brief off the cuff pitch that impressed no one, whether they favored or opposed it. British Chief of Staff Alan Brooke silently and contemptuously dismissed Eisenhower's 'ridiculous plan'. Ashamed of his poor presentation, Eisenhower hastily existed, claiming he had vital duties to fulfill elsewhere. Brooke then delivered an articulate, detailed argument for the Mediterranean strategy. When Army Chief of Staff Marshall asked how that would defeat Germany, Brooke replied:

> The Germans have forty-four division in France. That is sufficient strength to overwhelm us on the ground and perhaps hem us in ... Since we cannot go into the Continent in force until Germany weakens, we should try to make the Germans disperse their forces as much as possible.[321]

Roosevelt and Churchill devised a compromise whereby the Allies invaded Sicily in July 1943 and France in May 1944. Army Chief of Staff George Marshall complained bitterly that strategically 'the Mediterranean was a blind ally to which American forces had only been committed because of the President's insistence that they should fight the Germans somewhere.'[322] Eisenhower later wrote that 'General Marshall and I shared the belief that everything done in the Mediterranean should continue to be subsidiary to and in support of the main purpose of attacking across the Channel in early 1944.'[323]

What the Americans did not then anticipate was that after Sicily's conquest Churchill and his commanders would argue the next logical strategic step was invading the Italian peninsula across the Messina Straits. The Americans viewed the Italian peninsula as a strategic deadend and could not understand the British determination to fight there. But eventually they knuckled under to that strategy.

Although during the conference Patton was present for many official and social events he felt sidelined: 'I wish someone would listen to me. I have something which makes people reluctant to question me, perhaps I always have an answer based on truth and not bootlick.'[324] Patton's self-assessment was correct. Eisenhower sent him a letter 'in which he advises me to be more circumspect and less flip in my conversation in military matters.' In a reply that he never sent, Patton explained that:

> For years, I have been accused of indulging in snap judgments. And Honestly, this is not the case because … I am a profound military student and the thoughts I express, perhaps too flippantly, are the result of years and study … I have been fortunate in long and intimate associations with many eminent men … I am not sufficiently over-awed in the presence of high personages and therefore speak too freely, whereas others less used to associating with the great may speak with more reticence and in consequence give the presence of considered thought, whereas their hesitation is really due to embarrassment.[325]

For Patton, the conference's highlight happened when he accompanied Eisenhower to the airport on 16 January 1943. As Eisenhower was about to board his plane, he pinned a Distinguished Service Medal on Patton and mentioned he was considering making him his deputy.

Famous people do not always live up to their reputations when observed first hand. For instance, Patton was unimpressed with Churchill, who, although they 'got on well', struck him as 'cunning rather than brilliant, but with great tenacity… He is easily flattered.'[326] Nor did Patton impress everyone who met him. British Chief of Staff Alan Brooke expressed the view among many of his colleagues that:

> I did not form any high opinion of him … A dashing, courageous, wild, and unbalanced leader, good for operations requiring thrust and push but at a loss in any operation requiring skills and judgment.[327]

Patton attended a lecture series by Montgomery on lessons from his campaign during a conference at Tripoli in mid-February 1943. In his first encounter with Montgomery, Patton described him as 'small, alert, wonderfully conceited, and the best soldier – or so it seems – I have met in this war.'[328] That generous appraisal by one flamboyant general of another was fleeting. Patton increasingly scorned Montgomery as he competed with him to reveal to the world who was the superior general first in Sicily then across France and into Germany.

***

The Tunisian front remained stalemated. Kesselring replaced Nehring with General Hans-Jurgen von Arnim, a more aggressive and experienced tank commander, as Fifth Panzer Army's commander on 20 February 1943. The 120,000 Axis troops deployed from the sea south along the Dorsal Mountain range to the desert, blocked Anderson's 120,000-man British First Army, with Allfrey's 120,000-man V Corps north, Juin's 50,000-man XIX Corps central, and Fredendall's 90,000-man II Corps southward.

Eisenhower did not directly command Allied forces in Tunisia. The Combined Chiefs of Staff created an intermediary command, the Eighteenth Army Group of the First and Eighth armies led by General Harold Alexander on 20 January 1943. Montgomery's Eighth Army did not reach Tunisia until three months after First Army's arrival.

Ater his El Alamein victory, Montgomery spent nearly two months building up Eighth Army before his next advance. Vastly outgunned, Rommel withdrew Afrika Korps before Montgomery's slow advance, fighting occasional delaying battles. Eighth Army marched into Tripoli, Libya, Afrika Korps' chief supply port, on 23 January 1943. Rommel withdrew Afrika Korps to southeastern Tunisia where he established the 30-mile Mareth Line below Gabes between the sea and rugged Matmata Mountains on 15 February 1943. With reinforcements, Afrika Korps numbered 50,000 German and 35,000 Italian troops. Eighth Army would not approach the Mareth Line in strength until 6 March 1943. That gave Rommel and Arnim plenty of time to combine forces for a devastating attack on the Americans.

The American army's worst deficiency was leadership. Most officers from second lieutenants to generals lacked leadership skills. Worst of all was II Corps' commander, Lloyd Fredendall, who proved to be not just inept but cowardly. While his troops literally starved for supplies at the front, he deployed an engineer battalion to build a complex bomb-proof tunnel complex for his headquarters at Tebessa, 65 miles from the front. He scattered his three divisions' brigades and regiments at various passes and valleys along a 40-mile front that they did not fortify.

Fredendall's II Corps was nicely placed to punch east toward the sea at Gabes and Sfax to cut off and bag Afrika Korps, but Fredendall thought not of an active defense let alone a decisive offense. Instead, he dithered inside his bunker. Yet, even had he suggested it, Alexander, backed by Eisenhower, would have rejected it. Eisenhower had accepted having American troops play a supporting role to the British who would inflict the decisive blows against the enemy.

Arnim and Rommel devised a plan to crush II Corps between them in two phases.[329] On 14 February 1943, Armin's 10th Panzer Division dashed through Faid Pass to rout its defenders, then, the next day, Rommel's 21st Panzer Division punched through Gafsa; the Germans inflicted 2,546 casualties, and knocked out or captured 103 tanks, 280 vehicles and 18 cannons while suffering a few hundred casualties. Rommel took command of both the 10th and 21st Panzer divisions to pursue II Corps to Kasserine Pass where in a series of attacks from 19 to 22 February 1943, the Germans degraded and finally routed the Americans, killing 3,300, capturing 3,000, knocking out or capturing 183 tanks, 616 vehicles and 208 cannons while suffering 989 killed or wounded and 608 captured and just 20 lost tanks, 67 vehicles and 14 cannons. In the first large-scale battle between them, the Germans inflicted a humiliating and costly defeat on the Americans, driving them 85 miles back from Faid Pass to Thala. Among the American losses was Patton's son-in-law, Lieutenant Colonel John Waters who was captured.

The British seized on the devastating defeat at Kasserine Pass to 'prove' their prejudice that Americans were poor soldiers, leaders, tacticians and strategists, and thus must be relegated to secondary roles as British forces plotted and spearheaded campaigns. Alexander informed Britain's Joint Chiefs of Staff that:

> My main anxiety is the poor fighting ability of the Americans. They simply do not know their job as soldiers and this is the case from the highest to the lowest … Perhaps the weakest link…is the junior officer, who does not lead, with the result that their men don't really fight.[330]

In contrast to British condescension, Rommel offered this realistic assessment:

> Although it was true the American troops could not yet be compared to the veteran troops of the Eighth Army, yet they made up for their lack of experience by more flexible command … The tactical conduct of the enemy's defense had been first class. They had recovered quickly after the first shock and had soon succeeded in damming up our advance by grouping their reserves to defend the passes and other suitable points.[331]

Although appalled by Fredendall's defeat, Eisenhower was loath to replace him amidst a campaign. Instead, he, accompanied by his aide Harry Butcher and General Ernest Harmon, visited Fredendall at his bunker. There he could not overlook Fredendall's cowardice and ineptness. Eisenhower relieved him to return to the United States to train troops, then asked Harmon to replace him. When Harmon refused, Eisenhower offered the command to his deputy Mark Clark who also refused. Only then did Eisenhower turn to Patton.

Patton eagerly accepted and arrived at Fredendall's headquarters to replace him on 6 March 1943.[332] There Omar Bradley awaited him, assigned by Eisenhower to be his 'eyes and ears' for his volatile friend. Having a headquarters spy in his camp angered Patton, but he sought to coopt Bradley by getting Eisenhower officially to make him II Corps' deputy commander. This was the beginning of a dynamic and at times strained relationship among the three that militarily was largely a success in North Africa, Sicily, and across northern France to Germany's heart.[333]

Omar Bradley was a West Point classmate of Eisenhower and thereafter like him missed serving on World War I's frontline and instead for the next quarter of a century worked a series of staff and training assignments at higher ranks, increasingly in Washington.[334] Although he only graduated 44 of 164 among his classmates, he was very bright. He was especially adept at mathematics with which he boosted his income by playing poker and the stock market.

Bradley was Patton's foil in personality and strategy. Bradley was self-effacing and straight-laced, and favored methodical infantry-led rather than free-wheeling tank-led campaigns. His favorite past general was William Tecumseh Sherman whose victories depended on outmaneuvering enemy armies and inflicting far more casualties than he suffered. As for his contemporaries, he extolled George Marshall above all: 'No man had a greater influence on me personally or professionally. No man served his country more nobly or perfectly, or sought so little credit.'[335]

Patton and Bradley first got to know each other during nearly a year at Fort Benning from 1940 into 1941 when they were respectively training tankers and infantry. Patton liked Bradley and considered him a friend. Later, after Bradley replaced him as Seventh Army's commander, Patton expressed his deep gratitude to him for serving as his deputy, writing that 'I never enjoyed service with anyone as much as with you and trust that some day we can complete our warlike operations.'[336] The word 'warlike' may have been a Freudian slip. With his tightly controlled emotions, Bradley provided emotional ballast for Patton's volatility. Yet Bradley secretly loathed Patton and revealed that only in two autobiographies published after Patton's death.[337] Jealousy explains most of Bradley's feelings. Patton was brilliant, photogenic and rich, while Bradley was merely a competent general who lived modestly on his paycheck and had a hangdog face. Yet Patton's profanity and boasts genuinely offended Bradley who masked his disgust. Throughout the war, Patton apparently was oblivious to Bradley's animosity toward him, and was delighted when Eisenhower approved his request to make Bradley Seventh Army's deputy commander. He viewed Bradley as 'a very sound and extremely loyal soldier.'[338]

***

Over several days, Patton visited each II Corps division to inspect the troops and speak with officers, trying to infuse them with fighting spirit. In a proclamation, he explained:

> Our duty … is plain. We must utterly defeat the enemy. Fortunately for our fame as soldiers, our enemy is worthy of us … The justice of our cause … makes us confident … The reputation of our army, the future of our race, your own glory, rest in your hands. I know you will be worthy.[339]

Among Patton's firm beliefs was that looking like a soldier was crucial to being a soldier. He issued orders that the men express pride in themselves as American fighting men by dressing and saluting properly. Henceforth every soldier had to wear the regulation uniform including leggings, a necktie and a helmet on duty, and enlisted men and officers would be respectively fined $25 and $50 for any violations. Although that provoked grumbling in the ranks, Bradley approved the psychology:

> Each time a soldier knotted his necktie, threaded his leggings, and buckled on his heavy steel helmet, he was forcibly reminded that Patton had come to command the II Corps, that the pre-Kasserine days had ended, and that a tough new era had begun … these Patton reforms promptly stamped his personality upon the corps. And while they did little to increase his popularity, they left no doubt in anyone's mind that Patton was to be the boss.[340]

Bradley recounted an odious act that Patton committed against a subordinate officer, in this case General Terry Allen, 1st Division's commander. When he inspected Allen's headquarters, he was angered to see slit trenches beside the tents. He believed that slit trenches revealed cowardice rather than prudence in sparing unnecessary lives and limbs from enemy bombs or shells. To make that point,

> he said, 'Terry, which one is yours?' When Allen pointed out his slit trench, Patton strode over, unzipped his fly and urinated into the trench. Imperiously rezipping his fly, Patton sneered at Terry: 'Now try to use it.' With this earthy GI gesture, Patton had virtually labeled Allen a coward in front of his own men. I was no less shocked than Terry, and I had to wonder if this was indeed good leadership.[341]

Nonetheless, Bradley mostly lauded Patton to their boss. Eisenhower praised Patton for his 'buoyant leadership and strict insistence upon discipline' that

> rapidly rejuvenated the II Corps and brought it up to fighting pitch. Moreover, the troops were now fortified by battle experience and had a much higher appreciation of the value of training, discipline, and speed in action. Our losses in tanks, personnel, and equipment were rapidly made good.[342]

Patton's longstanding dream was to outgeneral and rout Rommel. Before Montgomery's victory at El Alamein, he wrote: 'I should like particularly to be in a position to beat Marshall Rommel because, since no one has licked him yet, I will get more credit when I do, and I feel perfectly confident that I will.'[343] Two realities rendered that an impossible dream. The most vital was that illness forced Rommel secretly to return to Germany for hospitalization on 9 March 1943. General Giovanni Messe replaced him as commander with Afrika Korps, renamed the First Italian Army. Messe was a competent, experienced general, having commanded an Italian army on the Russian front. Hitler promoted Arnhem to command both Fifth Panzer and First Italian armies.

Yet even had Rommel remained, generals Alexander and Montgomery were determined to confine American commanders and their troops to supporting roles while the British led all campaign planning and implementation. With reinforcements, II Corps now numbered 88,473 troops split among four divisions, and they were now ready and eager to avenge Kasserine Pass. Instead, Alexander gave Patton the limited strategic mission of making diversionary attacks on the Germans before them while Montgomery's Eighth Army launched a massive assault on the Mareth Line on 16 and 17 March 1943. Patton bitterly observed that Alexander's strategic

> instructions definitely prohibit an American advance to the sea. In other words, we continue to threaten the enemy's right flank, but we do not participate in cutting him off. In brief, this is to pinch us out so as to insure a British triumph ... The more I think about the plan of pinching us out the madder I get.[344]

For that Patton ultimately blamed Eisenhower:

> God damn all British and all so-called Americans who have their legs pulled by them ... Ike is more British than the British and is putty in their hands. Oh God, for John J. Pershing.[345]

This campaign was the first in which Patton and Montgomery commanded different fronts initially with opposite results. Italian First Army blunted Eighth Army's attacks over two days, and Montgomery withdrew his troops to regroup. Meanwhile, Patton unleashed a two-pronged offensive on 17 March 1943, with Allen's 1st Division, spearheaded by Colonel William Darby's ranger regiment and backed by Manton Eddy's 9th Infantry Division, punching from Gafsa 75 miles through El Guettar to Sened Pass on the road to Gabes, while Ward's 1st Armored Division backed by the 34th Infantry Division captured Faid Pass and fought toward Sfax.[346] Alexander's orders prevented II Corps from fighting to the sea and cutting off First Italian.

After First Italian Army drove back Eighth Army, Arnim launched 10th Panzer Division against Allen's 1st Division at El Guettar on 23 March 1943. The Americans repelled the attack and Patton ordered a series of counterattacks on both the Gabes and Sfax routes over the next two weeks. The fiercest and most prolonged fighting was on the El Guettar front, where the 1st and 9 Division slugged it out with the 10th and 21st Panzer and Italian Centauro divisions. During that time, Patton's troops inflicted as much damage as they suffered, around 6,000 killed, wounded, and captured Germans and Italians along with 37 knocked out or captured tanks to 5,893 American casualties and 22 tanks.[347] With one exception, his division commanders took a series of enemy positions when and where Patton ordered, with the how up to them.

Patton fumed at Ward's cautious advance toward lightly defended Maknassy Pass. By the time his troops reached the foot, reinforcements swelled the defenders. Ward ordered one attack after another, but the enemy repelled each. Enraged, Patton 'called Ward on the phone and told him to personally lead the attack on the hills and take them.' After he calmed down, he got second thoughts:

> Now my conscience hurts me for fear that I have ordered him to his death, but I feel that it was my duty. Vigorous leadership would have taken the hill the day before yesterday … As a result of the above orders, the 1st Armored attacked led by Ward, and gained a temporary foothold on top of the ridge but were unable to maintain it, due to the fact that they had wasted so much time that the position was too thoroughly organized to be held with the troops available. I therefore ordered 1st Armored to quit attacking and consolidate.[348]

Patton hurried to Ward's command post and subjected him to his typical good cop / bad cop mix of critiques, exhortations, and instructions.

> [I] told him that he lacked drive and trusted his staff too much in that he presumed orders were carried out and did not take the trouble to find out that they were. He admitted this. I also told him that if he failed I would relieve him. He took it very well. I decorated him with the Silver Star for his action in leading the attack. I believe his action would have merited the DSC except for the fact that it was necessary for me to order him to do it.

Patton remained worried about Ward and 1st armored: 'Ward lacks force. His division has lost its nerve and is jumpy. I fear that all our troops want to fight without getting killed.'[349] Of course, Patton's latter point is actually how wars are won but what he meant was his men's reluctance to take extraordinary risks to destroy the enemy. Patton relieved Ward on 4 April 1943 and replaced him with Ernest Hamon.

Complicating Patton's command and stoking his ire was Alexander's visit to his front on 29 March 1943. After he listened to Patton's summary of the situation and glanced at operational maps, Alexander ordered him to change a planned 1st Armored attack. Patton contained his rage and followed orders as Alexander returned to his headquarters. The attack failed. Incensed, Patton fired off a letter to the army group commander:

> I feel that I must respectively call General Alexander's attention to the fact that in the United States Army we tell officers what to do, not how to do it, that to do otherwise suggests lack of confidence in the officer … I feel that for the honor and prestige of the U.S. Army I must protest.[350]

As Patton visited various divisions, he narrowly escaped enemy shellings and strafings. For instance, one day 'I went to the front and sat on forward face of a hill … Shortly after I left the place where I had been sitting was struck by a salvo of 150 [shells].' Another day 'I had to get out twice and run for cover when the air strafed me.'[351] He suffered a terrible loss when his aide Captain Richard Jenson was killed during a German bombing raid on 1 April 1943.

Patton vented his rage and sorrow against Air Marshall Arthur Coningham by accusing him of failing to protect his troops from enemy bombing and strafing attacks. He did not cite Jenson's death but instead a German assault by 161 warplanes in 51 sorties that killed 15 and wounded 55 men. Coningham angrily retorted that the real problem was that Patton was a fool and American troops were not battleworthy. Patton angrily complained to Eisenhower who had air chiefs British General Arthur Tedder and American General Carl Spaatz visit Patton at this headquarters to assess the situation. Amid their talk, '4 German planes flew right down the street not 50 feet from the window, firing machine guns and dropping small bombs. No one was hurt.' When Tedder asked him how he arranged that demonstration, Patton replied, 'I'll be damned if I know, but if I could find the sonsabitches who flew those planes, I'd mail … them a medal.'[352]

Patton demanded that Coningham apologize to him and his troops. Eisenhower had Coningham visit Patton at his headquarters. Patton regarded Coningham with contempt and refused to shake hands with him. Coningham said, 'I want to apologize and do what I can to make amends.' Patton replied that, 'I am willing to accept your apology and forgive you for indicating that I was a fool … but I cannot accept an oral apology for calling 60,000 American soldiers unbattleworthy and failing in their duty.' Each angrily defended himself until Patton pointed out that had he said what Coningham had, 'I would now be a colonel and on my way home.' That sobered Coningham, who apologized and asked what he could do. Patton insisted on a written apology to his men. When Coningham agreed, Patton shook his hand and said, 'It is always easy to be generous to a gentleman who admits his mistakes.' In his diary, Patton wrote that: 'We parted friends and I think we will now get better air support than ever before. I was rather proud of myself, as I was firm, but moderate.'[353]

***

Meanwhile, Montgomery finally broke the Mareth Line from 20 to 28 March 1943, with a divisionary attack on the front while two corps filed 100 miles west through the desert beyond the mountains to smash into the enemy rear. Italian First Army withdrew to the Wadi Akarit Line 30 miles north of Gades.

With II Corps prepared to drive to the sea, Alexander ordered Patton to stand down. That infuriated Patton who later condemned what he saw as high command's strategic and moral double standard:[354] While leading from the front on the Gabes road, Patton himself met a British patrol on 7 April 1943, when he had expected to direct an attack against Germans. Alliance diplomacy had missed an extraordinary chance to cut off most of Messe's army by forcing Patton to support rather than lead the offensive. He complained that,

> After having spent thousands of casaulties making a breakthrough, we were not allowed to exploit it. The excuse is that we might interfere with the Eighth Army ... when the Eighth Army is in trouble, we are to expend our lives gladly; but when the Eighth is going well, we are to halt so as not to take any glory ... and Ike falls for it. Oh! For a Pershing.[355]

Eisenhower, meanwhile, was dazzled by Patton's performance, writing his diary that: 'Among the American commanders, Patton I think comes close to meeting every requirement made on a commander.'[356]

***

All along, Patton kept dodging death:

> My car got hit while I was in it. A 155 shell hit the spot I had been sitting in two minutes after I left it, and another salvo threw mud over me. An Arab just missed me – unfortunately I missed him ... Enemy planes pursued me down the road, which is a form of sport I am not interested in. Also I was in the first vehicle going through a mine field. I got through all right, but the next vehicle blew up.[357]

To his regret, Patton was taken away from the campaign before the Allies destroyed the Axis armies. On 15 April 1943, Eisenhower informed him that he would command one of the two invading armies, first called the Western Task Force that on D-day would become Seventh Army, with Montgomery's Eighth Army the Eastern Task Force. Patton was to turn over II Corps to Bradley and proceed to Rabat where he and his staff would plan Seventh Army's landing.

Patton's campaign was a limited victory. His advanced troops remained far from the ultimate goals of the costal ports of Sfax and

Gabes that would have blocked the Axis army retreat from the Mareth Line. He summed up his Tunisian campaign:

> I have been gone 43 days, fought several successful battles, commanded 95,800 men, lost about ten pounds, gained a third star and a hell of a lot of poise and confidence, and am otherwise the same.[358]

He could claim that his campaign was victorious since it took and held ground, and diverted enemy forces from the major attack by Eighth Army. However, the strategic results were meager. His greater success was transforming II Corps' morale and combat prowess from dismal to functional, and that was a stunning achievement in just a few weeks.

Bradley offered this assessment:

> Patton's forty-two day tour in Tunisia had gained him much notoriety, contributing to his growing legend, but it had not been his finest hour. It was no fault of his own. He had been thrust into Fredendall's job with no warning and had to make do with Fredendall's staff and a deputy corps commander [Bradley] also new to the scene. He had restored discipline to the corps and to a large extent its self-confidence. But Patton, severely tethered because of Alexander's lack of faith in our soldiers, had little opportunity to show its battlefield prowess. II Corps had not done particularly well even in its limited role.[359]

He summarized the campaign's strategic worth and limits:

> Our II Corps materially assisted Monty's breakthrough by initially drawing off the 10th Panzer Division, some Italian troops and considerable Axis air. But our follow up operations were unimpressive. Allen's Big Red One, having checked the 10 Panzer attack, ran out of steam and dug in, fending off savage but minor assaults. Ward's 1st Armored Division remained bogged down near Maknassy, unable to complete its mission of taking the heights near the town – a failure that so infuriated Patton that he ordered Ward personally to lead the attack. Ward did so and was slightly wounded by a ricocheting rock, but he failed to take the hills ... Farther north, Doc Ryder's 34th Division, ordered to 'make noise' toward Fondouck but not to run grave risks, encountered unexpectantly heavy resistance, broke off the attack, and withdrew without having accomplished anything of consequence.[360]

Army Chief of Staff Marshall alleviated some of Patton's disappointment at not being allowed to finish the campaign as II Corps' commander with these words:

> You did a masterful job in reorganizing the II Corps and joining with the Eighth Army to drive the Germans out of southern Tunisia ... You set a stiff pace for Bradley, but he seems to be following through in excellent style. I realize that the planning you are now occupied with is a poor substitute for active combat, but it is of the utmost importance, and as you know, you turn will come again soon.[361]

Bradley took over II Corps on 16 April 1943. Pressure by Patton and Bradley finally got Eisenhower to give II Corps a significant role in the final offensive by shifting it to the coast to capture Bizerte. After a prolonged siege by II Corps, General Fritz Krause surrendered Bizerte on 9 May 1943. Meanwhile, Anderson's First and Montgomery's Eight Armies battled their way toward Tunis, capturing it on 7 May 1943. Arnim had retreated to the Bon Peninsula where he surrendered on 13 May 1943. Although there was never an exact count, the Axis lost around 250,000 troops, including 100,000 Germans, in Tunisia. From Torch's landings on 8 November 1942 to the surrender on 13 May 1943, the Americans suffered 18,221 casualties, including 2,715 dead, 8,978 wounded and 6,528 missing, the British 35,940 casualties and the French 16,180, for 70,341 altogether.[362]

The Allies had won a decisive victory. As vital, American troops, officers and generals alike had become hardened and skilled veterans, at least those that survived physically and emotionally. Patton learned vital lessons from his Torch landings and II Corps campaign that he would assert in a series of dazzling offensives in Sicily, northern France, and Germany. But at crucial times ahead, orders to halt and supply shortages stunted his victories and advances, while several times, his own erratic behavior nearly got him cashiered and sent home in disgrace.

Chapter 6

ACROSS SICILY

'To conquer, we must destroy our enemies. We must not only die gallantly, we must kill devastatingly. The faster and more effectively we kill, the longer you will live to enjoy the priceless fame of conquerors.'

'We can go twice as fast as the British and hit harder …

Our method of attacking all the time is better than the British system of stop, build up, and start.'

'This is a horse race in which the prestige of the U.S. Army is at stake. We must take Messina before the British.'

'Soldiers of the Seventh Army, born at sea, baptized in blood, and crowned in victory, in the course of 38 days of incessant battle and unceasing labor, you have added a glorious chapter to the history of war.'

George S. Patton

Generals Dwight D. Eisenhower and Harold Alexander, the respective theater and 15th Army Group commanders for Sicily's invasion, originally envisioned landings at opposite ends of the island, with Eighth Army at Syracuse and Seventh Army at Palermo, eventually to converge at Messina.[363] That strategy changed radically during a planning conference at Hotel St Georges in Algiers on 29 April 1943 attended by British generals Alexander and Oliver Leese, admirals Andrew Cunningham and Bertram Ramsey, air marshals Arthur Tedder, Arthur Coningham and Philip Wigglesworth, and four other high ranking officers with Patton and staff officer General Arthur Nevins the sole Americans.[364] Montgomery was not present, likely to avoid confrontation with Patton, but over the previous weeks he had

George Patton, his mother Ruth Wilson Patton, and his sister Anne "Nita". He had an idyllic boyhood on a ranch a dozen miles east of Los Angelas. He learned to shoot, ride, and hunt before he could read and write because dyslexia delayed his development.

George Patton's father and namesake. Patton adored his father who was a successful businessman, lawyer, and district attorney.

George Patton as a United States Military Academy cadet (1904-09) at West Point, New York. He entered after a year's preparation at the Virginia Military Institute (VMI), then flunked math his first year and had to repeat that year but eventually graduated a respectable 46 of 103 classmates.

Lieutenant George Patton steeple chasing. He won fifth place in the 1912 Olympics' Pentathlon that included shooting, riding, fencing, swimming, and running contests.

Lieutenant George Patton during the Punitive Expedition during which he first made the headlines with a shootout at a ranch where he killed General Julio Cardenas and possibly one or two others of three Villistas slain.

General John Pershing, the model soldier and commander for Patton when he served under him during the Punitive Expedition and World War I campaigns.

General John Pershing inspects Captain George Patton's troops, Chaumont, France, 1917.

Major George Patton as commander of what will be the Tank Light Division.

George Patton with First Light Tank Division.

The Patton family in Washington, D.C. in 1929. Clockwise from left: Beatrice, George, daughters Beatrice and Ruth Ellen, and son George IV.

President Franklin Roosevelt, Prime Minister Winston Churchill, and the Combined American and British Chiefs of Staff. Roosevelt and Churchill developed a deep friendship as well as partnership leading the western alliance during World War II. However, they and their respective joint chiefs of staff differed sharply over grand strategy, with the Americans favoring landings in northern and southern France that linked for a drive east into Germany that captured Berlin while the British promoted an indirect approach through what they insisted was "Europe's soft underbelly" in the Mediterranean that first knocked Italy out of the war.

George Patton and Dwight Eisenhower. They had been friends since 1920 and after becoming Patton's commander, Eisenhower repeatedly saved his career when Patton endangered it through controversial behavior and remarks.

George Patton with Admiral Kent Hewitt aboard the heavy cruiser *Augusta*. They collaborated planning during the Morocco and Sicily landings. Patton complained of Hewitt's excessive caution. Hewitt complained of Patton's quick temper and profanity.

George Patton and Bernard Montgomery greeting each other with Omar Bradley observing. Beneath the conviviality was a fierce rivalry.

George Patton with his "War Face."

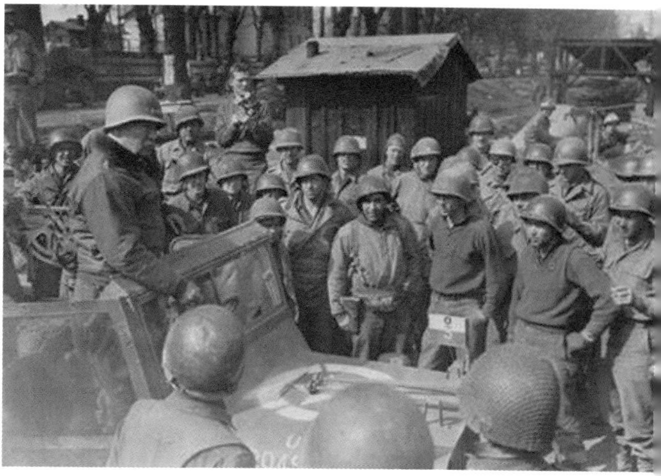

George Patton addressing his Third Army troops.

Patton during one of his regular visits to wounded soldiers. In Sicily, he slapped, cursed, and ejected two soldiers suffering from combat fatigue at two separate hospitals. He accused them of malingering but committed a court martial offense in striking them off a battlefield. The incidents caused Eisenhower to promote Bradley over Patton.

During the battle of the Bulge, Patton with General Anthony McAuliffe, who commanded besieged Bastogne, after 4th Armored fought its way into the town.

George Patton, Omar Bradley, and Dwight Eisenhower, the respective Third Army, Twelfth Army Group, and Supreme European commanders in Bastogne. During the battle of the Bulge, Eisenhower gave Montgomery command of Bradley's Twelfth Army Group First and Ninthe Armies north of the Bulge while confining Bradley to command south of the Bulge. Bradley and Patton deeply resented that choice and much more later Montgomery's claim that he won the battle of the Bulge.

Patton contemplating the Rhine River that his troops had recently crossed, beating Montgomery by a day.

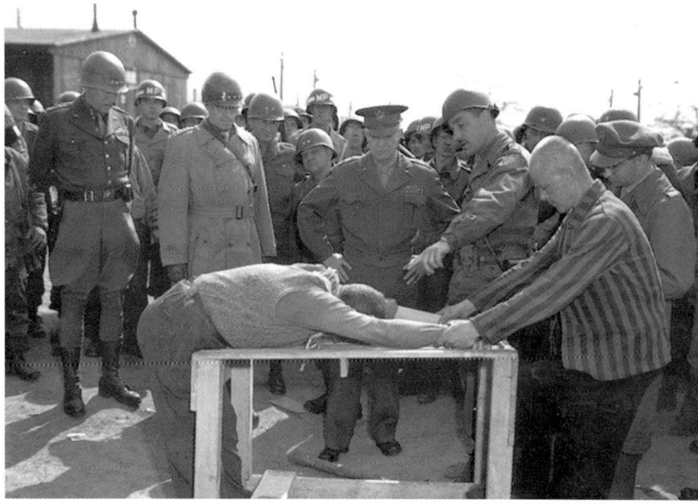

Patton, Bradley, and Eisenhower at the Ohrdruf concentration where some inmates demonstrate Nazi torture techniques.

Patton at a victory parade in Boston after the war in Europe ended.

George Patton's grave at the head of 5,070 fellow fallen American soldiers, Hamm Military Cemetery, Luxembourg.

convinced Alexander and most of the others to relegate Seventh Army to guarding Eighth Army's left flank as it won the glory of driving north along the coast to Messina, and cutting off and capturing the enemy army. As Montgomery's spokesman, Leese delivered an in-depth report that explained and justified the strategy.

The British split over the proposal. Admiral Cuningham worried that,

> From the naval point of view, the massing of so many ships in the Siracusa area is to invite disaster, and besides, the chief merit of amphibious attack is to do so on a broad front and disperse enemy effort. I am definitely opposed to the plan.

Alexander replied, 'But from our viewpoint, that is, the army, it is necessary, we must do it.' Of course, the army that Alexander spoke for was the British Eighth. At one point, Cunningham suggested, 'Why not ask Eisenhower? After all, he is commander in chief.' No one seconded that idea.[365]

All along, Patton seethed but suppressed his temper. When Alexander asked him what he thought of the plan, he bit his tongue and tersely fibbed: 'General, I don't plan – I only obey orders.'[366] The conference ended in stalemate. Over the next couple of days, Alexander and Montgomery talked Eisenhower into the revised plan.[367]

General Bedell Smith, Eisenhower's chief of staff, called Patton with the bad news on 2 May 1943. Patton vainly protested. Smith later admitted that

> the reason everyone yields to Monty is because Monty is the national hero and writes direct to the Prime Minister; and if Ike crossed him, Ike might get canned. Also that ... Alex is afraid of him.[368]

Patton griped to his staff that: 'This is what you get when your Commander-in-Chief ceases to be an American and becomes an ally.'[369] Throughout World War II, Patton bitterly confided complaints that the British were trying to hog the glory to his diary with entries like this: 'So far, this war is being fought for the benefit of the British Empire and for post-war considerations.'[370]

The plan deprived Seventh Army of a major port from which to unload supplies and reinforcements. Instead, Seventh Army would land along a 70-mile front with three minor fishing ports, Scoglitti east, Gela central and Licata west. There were three small airfields with Comiso and Biscari near Scoglitti, and Ponte Olivo near Gela. Admiral Kent Hewitt would command the fleet conveying Seventh Army to the beaches and provide firepower as he had during the Morocco landings. Unfortunately, despite their previous experience working together, they did not get along much better this time. Patton complained that Hewitt 'as usual cannot decide anything and is full of querulous reasons for failure.' At one point Hewitt so exasperated Patton that he privately denounced him as 'a perfect fool.'[371]

Patton's Seventh Army eventually included two corps, initially Omar Bradley's II Corps with Terry Allen's 1st Division and Troy Middleton's 45th Division, and from 15 July 1943, General Geoffrey Keyes's Provisional Corps with Hugh Gaffey's 2nd Armored Division, Lucian Truscott's 3rd Division and Manton Eddy's 9th Division. Patton shifted two units between the corps as needed, William Darby's Ranger brigade and Matthew Ridgway's 82nd Airborne Division.

Patton had ensured that Bradley commanded II Corps. That elated Bradley, who recalled:

> I was pleased to be working again in harness with Patton. By now we understood one another perfectly and professionally we worked in complete harmony ... Patton, as always, was impatient with planning. His mind was fixed on attack and not the logistics, and he was content to leave the details to his deputy army commander, General Keyes, and the rest of us.[372]

Patton shifted his Seventh Army headquarters from Rabat, Morocco to Mostaganem, Algeria on 26 April 1943. At Mostaganem, he mixed planning with rehearsals like landings and maneuvers by his units, inspections, and exhortations to inspire his troops. He took pride that:

> The training we do over here is very much more realistic than any thing I have ever seen. We actually fire ball cartridges over each other's heads, actually blow up wire, and actually do lots of other things along the same lines.

He admitted to Chief of Staff General George Marshall that: 'When I went through it personally, it frightened me to death.'[373]

As always, Patton tried psychologically to prepare his men for combat. As the invasion neared, he issued this proclamation:

> We must remember that victories are not gained solely by selfless devotion. To conquer, we must destroy our enemies. We must not only die gallantly, we must kill devastatingly. The faster and more effectively we kill, the longer you will live to enjoy the priceless fame of conquerors.

Before the 45th Division, he exclaimed:

> Battle is the most magnificent competition in which a human being can indulge, It brings out all that is best; it removes all that is base. All men are afraid in battle. The coward is the one who lets his fear overcome his sense of duty. Remember that the enemy is just as frightened as you are ... The attacker wins ... Pride is the greatest thing a man can have ... We Americans are a competitive race...We love to win. In this next fight, you are entering the greatest sporting competition of all times ... for the greatest prize of all – victory.[374]

Patton, Montgomery and their staff met at Algiers to coordinate their plans on 7 May 1943. Although disappointed for his army's secondary role, Patton was genial and cooperative. He even expressed a grudging respect for the general who politically outmaneuvered him: 'Monty is a forceful, selfish man, but still is a man. I think he is a far better leader than Alexander and that he will do just what he pleases, as Alex is afraid of him.'[375]

Patton's staff was just as letdown as he was but he 'straightened them out by the simple method of showing a confidence which I don't feel, although I am pretty confident. I believe it my fate, and to fulfill it, this show must be a success.'[376]

Patton was just as generous toward Eisenhower, despite regretting his surrender to Montgomery on strategy for Sicily. He confided to his diary that in a letter to Marshall about Eisenhower:

> I largely overstated his merits, but I feel I owe him a lot and must stay with him. I lied to a good cause. As a matter of fact, I know no one except myself who could do any better than Ike, and God knows I don't want his job.[377]

Strangely, Eisenhower did not reciprocate the good will and support. During a meeting between them a few days before the invasion, he castigated Patton for a litany of faults but at 'no time did Ike wish us luck and say he was back of us.' He dismissed Patton as 'a great leader but a poor planner.' To that, Patton replied, 'except for Torch, which I had planned and which was a success, I had never been given a chance to plan.' Eisenhower threatened to replace Patton with Bradley if the invasion 'turned into a slugging match.' Patton protested that 'I would like to finish one show.' He could not 'make out whether he thinks Bradley is a better close fighter than I am or whether he wants to keep in with General Marshall, who likes Bradley.' Atop those attacks and threats, 'Ike has never asked me to a meal since I have been here.' Nonetheless, Patton's gratitude for commanding Seventh Army let him swallow Eisenhower's aggression and ill manners: 'I would not change places with anyone. I know am leading 90,000 men in a desperate attack and eventually it will be over 250,000 [men]. If I win, I can't be stopped. If I lose, I shall be dead.'[378]

***

General Albert Kesselring commanded Axis forces in Italy. On the peninsula, General Heinrich von Vietinghoff headed the German 10th Army deployed mostly in the south. In Sicily, Italian General Alfredo Guzzoni led the Axis forces that initially included Italy's 200,000-man Sixth Army with four regular Italian divisions and five Sicilian coastal divisions, along with two German divisions, the Hermann Göring Division and 15th Panzergrenadier Division commanded respectively by generals Paul Conrath and Eberhard Rodt, each with about 15,000 troops. After the invasion, Kesselring dispatched 29th Panzergrenadier Division and 1st Airborne Division to Sicily. German troops committed to defending Sicily peaked at around 62,000.[379]

Preceding the Sicily invasion were several operations designed to deceive, discourage and diminish the enemy. British intelligence took a homeless Englishman who died, dressed him in a naval uniform, gave him a fictitious name, handcuffed a briefcase filled with false secret documents to his wrist and dumped him off the Spanish coast. The hope was that Spanish officials would recover his body, read the documents that referred to a pending Allied invasion in the eastern Mediterranean, and share that 'intelligence' with Berlin. Astonishingly, that actually happened although it did not divert German reinforcements from Sicily. Meanwhile, Air Chief Tedder directed a bombing campaign against thirty enemy air, infantry and supply bases on Sicily and southern Italy, with American daylight and British nighttime missions. Some squadrons dropped millions of leaflets calling on people to overthrow the Mussolini regime and fight the Germans who 'will fight to the last Italians.' After a massive bombardment, a task force captured Pantelleria Island with its airfield and 11,000 Italian troops around midway between Tunisia and Sicily on 11 June 1943. Fighter planes based at Pantelleria's airfield escorted bombers against enemy positions. The Allies wrested air superiority from the Axis by 1 July 1943.

To convey, protect, and supply Seventh and Eighth armies, the American and British navies respectively committed 845 and 1,614 vessels, with 31 from other Allies.[380] Eighth and Seventh armies embarked at their respective ports beginning on 6 July 1943 and by early 10 July appeared off their landing sites. No naval artillery barrage preceded the landings because there were no significant fortifications ashore. Instead, 1,500 British 1st Airborne Division paratroops and glider troops and 3,400 American 82nd Airborne Division paratroopers descended in the dark around midnight on 9 July 1943. High winds with gusts up to 35 miles per hour and pilot errors led to the wide dispersal and heavy losses among them.

Montgomery's two corps came ashore along a thirty mile stretch of south-east Sicily. Miles Dempsey's XIII landed around Avola south of Syracuse then advanced north to capture that vital port, while Oliver Leese's XXX landed around Pacino at Sicily's south-east tip then advanced westward to link with Seventh Army.

Seventh Army embarked in Malta on 6 July 1943; Patton was with Hewitt aboard his flagship, the heavy cruiser *Monrovia*. Just before dawn on 10 July 1943, 45th Division landed at Scoglitti, Darby's 3rd Ranger Battalion at Gela and 1st Division along the beach stretching 3 miles eastward, and 3rd Division at Licata; a 2nd Armored battalion landed at each beach.

Lucian Truscott's 3rd Division at Licata and Troy Middleton's 45th Division at Scoglitti faced little resistance and swiftly routed the enemy to secure beachheads a couple of miles deep. The Hermann Göring Division and Livorno Division counterattacked Darby's rangers in Gela and Terry Allen's 1st Division on the nearby beach. The armada's cannons combined with the infantry's small arms eventually drove off the attackers with heavy losses.

The fighting at Gela was so confused and the beach so chaotic the first day that Patton stayed aboard the *Monrovia*. That chaos persisted the second day as scattered units of American troops fought off, flushed out or advanced against German and Italian troops. Patton, his chief of staff General Hobart Gay, aide Major Alexander Stiller, and two guards packed into an amphibious scout car and churned toward shore. As they landed two shells exploded in the water around 30 yards behind them. Patton recalled that

> I intended to go to the headquarters of the 1st Division, about three miles to the southeast along the coast road. As we got into Gela, we noticed a flag on the left and decided to call on Colonel W.O. Darby, commanding the Rangers. This was very fortunate because, had we proceeded down the road, we should have run into seven German tanks, which at that moment were advancing toward the town. As we arrived … Darby and … Gela were being attacked.[381]

Guzzoni hurled the Hermann Göring Division and the Italian Livorno division against Gela. American anti-tank gunners ashore and naval guns knocked out sixteen German tanks rumbling toward the beach and the rest hastily retreated out of range. Patton sent word to Allen

> to close the gap between Gela and 1st Division and to send a company of tanks to help Darby. This was done. Darby counterattacked at once to his left and took five hundred prisoners. We also destroyed the seven tanks east of Gela.[382]

Patton was in the thick of the fighting.

> [He] personally helped lay some 4.2s [mortar rounds] at a range of about 900 yards on enemy infantry. The white phosphorus was remarkable in its effect and seemed to make them quite crazy as they rushed out of the ravine, shrilling like dervishes with their hands over their heads [in surrender]. On that same day we used it at about 3000 yards against tanks with some effect.

Patton then drove along the beach to 1st Division where he met General Theodore Roosevelt, the deputy commander, and 'talked to him about his failure ... to carry its objective last night. The chief reason ... is that the division attacked without antitank guns and without moving their artillery up.' Then Allen joined them and as they discussed the situation fourteen German planes passed over head dropping bombs as antiaircraft guns ashore and on ship opened fire. Fragments hit within a dozen feet of the generals and 'we saw two bombers and one other plane shot down.' After agreeing on an attack plan for the next day, Patton returned to Gela

> without incident except I think it is quite unusual for an Army Commander and his Chief of Staff to travel some six miles on a road parallel to the front of two armies and about equally distant from the two. It was quite a lonesome feeling, but not very dangerous. It is good for self-esteem.[383]

A potential catastrophe lay on Gela's beach where Patton witnessed

> the most stupid thing I saw soldiers doing. There were about 300 500-pound bombs and seven tons of 20-mm high explosive shells piled on the sand, and these soldiers dug themselves foxholes in between the bombs and boxes of ammunition. I told them that if they wanted to save the Graves Registration burials, that was a fine thing to do, but

> otherwise they better dig a foxhole somewhere else. About that time ... two bombers came over and strafed the beach and all the soldiers jumped right back in the same holes they dug. I continued walking up and down and soon shamed them into getting up.[384]

Patton

> got back to the *Monrovia* at 7.00 o'clock, completely wet. This is the first day in this campaign that I think I earned my pay. I was well satisfied with my command today. God certainly watched over me today.[385]

He later received the Oak Leaf Cluster to his Distinguished Service Cross for his ceaseless and decisive action that day.

Patton ordered Mathew Ridgway to fly the rest of his 82nd Airborne Division from its base in Tunisia and parachute inland. He sent word to his army and the navy commanders to hold their fire when 82nd Airborne Division passed over for their drop during the night of 11 July 1943: 'Flights will pass between 2230 and 2400 hours approximately. Length of flight approximately forty minutes. Flights will drop parachutists or release gliders.'

There were 198 Italian and 283 German warplane strafing or bombing attacks against the troops or ships on 11 July 1943, mostly against the American armada that sank the destroyer USS *Maddox*, two LSTs and a supply ship. The latest wave of attacks came at 9.50 pm that evening. Gunners at sea and ashore were hair-triggered for other enemy attacks despite being informed of the 82nd Airborne Flight's flight. Tragically, they opened fire and shot down 23 of 144 planes, killed 81 and wounded 118 paratroopers with 68 missing and presumed dead.[386]

The fighting was nearly as fierce on 12 July 1943. The 15th Panzergrenadier Division attacked 3rd Division as most of the Hermann Göring Division withdrew to regroup and resupply. The 3rd Division staved off a series of attacks then counterattacked, driving back 15th Panzergrenadier Division. After a firefight, 45th Division captured Biscari airfield from a Hermann Göring Division regiment. Seventh Army rounded up 4,400 prisoners by that day's end.

That same day, Eisenhower joined Patton on the *Monrovia,* not to praise Seventh Army's progress but to blister him for not sending him up to date campaign reports, going ashore the previous day to command tactical firefights rather than stay at his headquarters to direct his army's broad strategy, and being 'too prompt in my replies, and should hesitate more, the way he does.' Patton defended himself against the charges.[387] The next day, Patton received a 'wire from Ike, cussing me out' for the airborne tragedy and demanding 'an investigation and ... punishments for those guilty of firing on them.' The harsh criticism hurt Patton's feelings and shook his confidence. That night he wrote in his diary that

> every possible precaution was taken by this headquarters to obviate firing on our own airborne troops ... As far as I can see, if anyone is blamable, it must be myself, but personally I feel immune to censure.

He worried that 'Ike is looking for an excuse to relieve me.'[388]

***

As in Tunisia, Hitler reinforced rather than withdrew from an imperiled front. He had Kesselring shift 1st Airborne Division and 29th Panzergrenadier Division from the mainland to Sicily with General Hans Hube to command all German forces. Hube and Guzzoni coordinated their operations in a fighting withdrawal of the four German and four Italian divisions north-east to a hedgehog defense and eventual evacuation to the mainland.

While Seventh Army advanced inland and captured its objectives, Montgomery's Eighth Army stalled before Catania and the slopes of nearby Mount Etna. That gave Seventh Army the opportunity to push north-east on Highway 124 around Mount Etna to the sea and cut off the enemy. The American 45th and British 51st divisions were both battling toward Caltagirone and Vizzini on that road. Montgomery sought victory for Eighth Army and insisted that Alexander and Eisenhower agree to shift the boundary westward so that route now lay in Eighth Army's zone.

Patton was furious when he learned that Eisenhower and Alexander had approved Montgomery's demand:

> Alexander ... directs that the Seventh Army protect the rear of the Eighth Army, thus putting the Americans in a secondary role, which is a continuation of such roles for the whole campaign and may find the war with us being overlooked.[389]

Bradley was even more enraged when he learned of the switch. He condemned Montgomery's demand and Alexander's acquiesce as 'the most arrogant, selfish, and dangerous move in the whole of combined operations in World War II.'[390] He explained that:

> Seventh Army was poised to break out. We had secured our beachhead, firmed up our front and got our armor and artillery ashore. Our supply lines was running smoothly over the beach, and the enemy air attacks had subsided ...We had reached the main road north faster than the British. The enemy front before us was soft from his withdrawal ... We were in ideal position for a fast run to the north coast.[391]

Bradley blamed Patton for not protesting Alexander's order, attributing his reticence to his ignorance of

> British Army protocol – that by tradition, an 'order' from a superior was open to challenge, a basis for discussion. He had been trained to obey explicitly an 'order' from a superior... 'My God,' I said to Patton, 'you can't allow him to do that!' Patton replied with curious lameness that it was too late to change the orders.[392]

Part of Patton's timidity was the fear that Eisenhower would fire him if he protested.

Eighth Army's takeover of the route forced Bradley to withdraw 45th Division to Gela, then head north. Patton's Seventh Army would merely guard Eighth Army's now much further western flank. Montgomery ordered General Leese's XXX Corps to fight its way along that route but the Germans and Italians soon blunted that advance. To his credit, Leese later admitted that

> it was an unfortunate decision not to hand over it to the Americans ... they were making much quicker progress than ourselves ... We were still inclined to remember how slow the American progress was in the early stages of Tunisia, and I for one certainly did not realize the immense development in experience and technique which they had made in the last weeks of the North African campaign. I have a feeling now that if they could have driven straight up the road, we might have had a chance to end this frustrating campaign sooner.[393]

Patton flew to Tunis to meet Alexander on 17 July 1943 and explained 'that it would be inexpedient politically for Seventh Army not to have equal glory in the final stage of the campaign' and presented 'a map showing our proposed operation.'[394] Fortunately, General Albert Wedemeyer, one of Chief of Staff Marshall's closest advisors, happened to be visiting Alexander's headquarters and backed Patton. Alexander reluctantly approved Patton's plan.

Patton ordered Bradley's II Corps' divisions to capture Termini Increase on the coast and the key crossroad city of Enna then head east toward Messina while Keyes's Provisional Corps' division overran western Sicily and captured Palermo before turning east to reinforce II Corps. The number of Italian prisoners swelled so rapidly that Bradley paroled 33,000 Sicilian conscripts to go home after pledging to fight no more. That clever act inspired countless more Italians to surrender hoping for the same treatment.

Seventh Army's rapid advance and rout of enemy forces elated Patton. He attributed that success to his determination that from

> the initial successful assault on the beaches ... we have continued to push along several days ahead of our assumed schedule. This has been due to the fact that having once got the enemy started, we have not let him stop, but have ... kept on his heels. It is also due to the fact that the Italians and Germans spent tremendous effort in time, labor, and money building defensive positions

that his advanced troops bypassed and cutoff, then rear echelon troops forced the defenders to surrender.[395]

Yet Patton still steamed when he pondered the additional allied death and destruction caused by the transfer of that key route from Seventh Army to Eighth Army:

> I think the British have the bear by the tail in the Messina peninsula and we may have to go in and help. Had they let us ... take Caltragirone and Etna ourselves, instead of waiting for them, we would have saved two days and been on the north coast now. Alex[ander] has no idea of either the speed or power of Americans armies. We can go twice as fast as the British and hit harder, but to save British prestige, the XXX Corps had to take the envelopment, and now I think they are stuck ... Our method of attacking all the time is better than the British system of stop, build up, and start.[396]

Each day Patton drove from one corps, division and regiment to the next, inspecting and exhorting, dodging various dangers and marveling at historic sites along the way. He related a typical day in a letter to Beatrice:

> we ... are attacking right now... and having quite a war. We have captured more thousands of prisoners ... and destroyed a lot of tanks. The enemy has been booby trapping his dead, which has made our men very mad, with the result that there are more enemy dead than usual ... I drove over one of our battlefields and smelled dead men for some ten miles It is a very strong disgusting odor. Our losses have been relatively

> small, but we have lost some good men. The town I am in is probably known to you as the Germans have broadcasted that they recaptured it. They damned near [*sic*] did, but we beat hell out of them. I was right in the middle of it and had a swell time. Some came pretty close but I earned my pay and probably saved the situation. Monty is trying to steal the show and with the assistance of Devine Destiny [Eisenhower] may do so but to date we have captured three times as many men as our cousins ... My CP [command post] is on the site of a pagan temple ... No one here knows any thing [*sic*] about it except Pliny wrote about it.[397]

Keyes informed Patton that his troops would capture Palermo on 21 July 1943 and asked him to join him for a victory parade into the city. Patton replied, 'You took it. You enter and I will enter it after you.' He lauded Keyes for moving his corps 'faster against heavier resistance and over worse roads than did the Germans during their famous blitz.' He generously attributed Keyes with 'most of the credit' for the successful offensive and 'handed it out to him via the press.' Keyes's triumphant entrance into Palermo was his life's proudest moment.[398] Seventh Army's Palermo campaign cost merely 272 American casualties, including 57 killed, 170 wounded and 45 missing while killing 2,900 and capturing 53,000 enemy troops.[399]

Triumphantly, Patton reached Palermo on 22 July 1943, joined Keyes and Gaffney to congratulate and toast them with a flask, then made the Royal Palace his headquarters. It was not quite fit for a conquering general but would amply due:

> I am in the King's room and there are ... seven anterooms between my room and the State dining room. My bed has three mattresses on it but it is uncomfortable, and there is a bathroom with warm water, also electric lights. Many fine oil paintings on the walls and much gold furniture, mirrors ... There is a grand staircase – very dirty. All sorts of retainers live in holes about the place and all give the Fascist salute. [Major Alexander] Stiller has no flair for history and said he was sure he could find a nicer place in some good boarding house. I prefer the historical lift of sleeping in a royal bed and cleaning my teeth in glass etched with the Arms of Savoy.[400]

Patton directed Bradley and Keyes to fight eastward on two parallel roads, Route 113 along the coast and Route 120, 15 miles or so inland, with Messina the objective. Both routes were narrow, winding, mostly mountainous roads. Middleton's 45th and Truscott's 3rd divisions fought along the coast road while Allen's 1st and Eddy's 9th divisions advanced along the interior road. On both routes, combat engineers performed marvels rebuilding demolished bridges, and clearing rubble from destroyed village streets and obstructions from roads.

***

Alexander ordered Patton and Montgomery to join him at Syracuse airport on 25 July 1943, to sort out their respective zones and coordinate their offensive. When Alexander was delayed, Patton and Montgomery amiably forged an understanding on those issues. That was actually the first and last time during the pre-campaign planning and actual campaign in Sicily that Alexander had made such an effort, and after he arrived he was peeved that they resolved those questions without him. Patton described him as

> a little mad, and, for him, a little brusque. He told Monty to explain his plan. Monty said he and I had already decided what we were going to do, so Alex got madder and ... said there were supply difficulties.

Later Alexander assured Patton that '15th Army Group is completely Allied in mind and favors neither army. I know this was a lie, but said I felt that he was right – God pardon me.' After agreeing on an array of other issues 'the meeting broke up. No one was offered any lunch and I thought Monty was ill bred both to Alexander and me. Monty gave me a 5 cent lighter. Some one must have sent him a box of them.'[401]

Patton invited Montgomery to join him at his Royal Place headquarters on 28 July 1943, ostensibly for a second round of strategizing but mostly to show off what a superior general and host he was. He had a military escort with sirens blaring convey Montgomery from the airport to the palace, where they met in the king's council room followed by an elaborate lunch in the royal dining room. With Eighth Army still bogged down before Catania and Mount Etna, Montgomery recognized that he would lose the race to Messina so he conceded what he could not win. Indeed, only Seventh Army driving into the Axis rear could liberate Eighth Army from its stalemate. Patton knew Montgomery was trying to lull him into complacency. He wrote to Middleton that, 'This is a horse race in which the prestige of the U.S. Army is at stake. We must take Messina before the British. Please use your best efforts to facilitate the success of our race.'[402]

***

Allen's 1st Division captured the fortress town of Enna from 15th Panzergrenadier Division on 26 July 1943, then pushed to take Nicosia two days later. The campaign's most prolonged battle was for Troina that raged from 31 July to 6 August 1943, when the Americans finally expelled the Germans. Triona's capture forced Hube to withdraw his army into a tighter position north of Mount Etna. Eighth Army troops marched into an abandoned Catania on 5 August 1943.

Despite 1st Division's victories, Bradley felt that Allen and his deputy, General Theodore Roosevelt lacked 'the inner toughness to impose the discipline or training or the willingness to take orders from and play on the same team with higher command.' He received Patton's permission to replace Allen with General Clarence Huebner on 7 August 1943. Bradley described that act as 'one of my most unpleasant duties of the war.'[403]

When German troops rebuffed attacks by Truscott's 3rd Division on the coast, Patton had battalions packed in transports and landed toward the enemy rear at Sant'Agata on 8 August 1943, Brolo on 11 August, and at Falcone east of Cape Milazzo on 15 August. The results were mixed. None of the landings had enough troops or were far enough in the German rear to be decisive. Indeed, the last one landed alongside in the rear of Truscott's advanced guard. Patton complained that:

> We are having a good deal of trouble in getting the Navy to go in for amphibious operations ... They appear to have no idea of the value of time or the need for improvisation. If they can't get everything they want, they say they can't move. I think this is the result of many years during which all officers who lost a ship were tried [by court martial]. It is true that they have had two destroyers smashed by bombs ... but we have had many thousands of men hit.[404]

Truscott's 3rd Division fought its way into Messina and secured the city during the evening of 16 August 1943. Learning of the capture, Patton hurried to get there the next morning. He almost did not make it:

> On the way, the enemy shelled the road from the Italian side [of the straits]. One of these shells hit the second car behind me, wounding all the occupants ... The next car behind that ... had all four tires blown off without injuring ... anyone in it. In the town of Messina we met three British tanks and a few men who had arrived at 10:00 o'clock under the command of a general. It is very evident that Montgomery sent these men for the purpose of stealing the show ... I think the general was quite sore that we had got there first, but ... the race was

> clearly to us ... We then went to the town hall and saw the Mayor, the Chief of Police, etc. I had Truscott to do the honors as he had captured Messina.[405]

The Germans withdrew most of their troops before the jaws of the Seventh and Eighth armies snapped shut on them. Hube organized a brilliant withdrawal over a week from 9 to 16 August 1943 that steadily thinned and contracted the front to five rearward lines and eventually ferried across the Messina Straits 39,851 German troops, 14,772 wounded, 9,789 vehicles, 51 tanks, 163 cannons, 1,874 tons of fuel and ammunition and 16,791 tons of equipment. Separately, Guzzoni managed to evacuate 62,000 Italian troops, 3,000 sailors, 227 vehicles and 41 cannons.[406]

Nonetheless, Seventh Army captured 122,204 soldiers – although nearly all, 118,700, were Italians, along with 3,504 Germans. Overall, the Germans only suffered around 29,000 casualties including 4,325 killed, 17,944 wounded and 6,663 captured, along with 78 lost tanks and armored cars, 287 cannons, and 3,500 vehicles. The Italians lost around 2,000 dead, 5,000 wounded and 137,000 captured.[407]

Allied losses were far less. The American army suffered 8,781 casualties, including 2,237 dead, 5,946 wounded and 598 captured, and the navy 1,030 with 546 killed and 484 wounded. The British Army suffered worse casualties, 11,843, with 2,082 killed, 7,137 wounded and 2,644 captured, and the navy 729, with 314 killed, 411 wounded and 1 missing. The worst Axis losses were aircraft with some 600 German and 140 Italian airplanes shot down or destroyed on the ground to 375 lost Allied airplanes.[408]

The Allied victory in Sicily was limited rather than decisive because most Axis soldiers escaped. General Harold Alexander, 15th Army Group commander, ultimately was responsible for that failure. The core problem was forcing Seventh Army to be Eighth Army's western shield rather than an independent spear. Initially Patton and Eisenhower envisioned Seventh Army landing near Palermo and fighting east along the north coast road while Eighth Army landed near Syracuse and fought up the eastern coast road. Had that happened, the two armies would have cut off and captured far more German and Italian troops. Instead, Alexander succumbed to Montgomery's pressure to relegate Seventh Army to landing on the south coast bereft of a major port to guard Eighth Army's left flank as it headed toward Messina. Typically, Patton's generalship swiftly overcame those disadvantages and within days was poised to punch around Mount Etna, seize Messina, and bag the Axis army. Eager to grab that glory for himself, Montgomery convinced Alexander to transfer that key route from Seventh to Eighth Army but failed decisively to exploit it. The Germans contained Eighth Army for another three weeks. Meanwhile, Patton, unable to fight north-east, talked a reluctant Alexander into letting him overrun the island's thinly held western half then drive eastward toward Messina. Patton beat Montgomery into Messina, but by then nearly all the German and many Italian troops escaped across the straits to Italy's mainland.

Montgomery's flaws as a general and strengths as a politician were also vital reasons for the limited victory. What he failed to win on the battlefield he won in backstage intrigues with Alexander backed by Eisenhower to make Seventh Army Eighth Army's lackey. Bradley offered this assessment:

> Monty, typically, had been too slow, too methodical in his post-landing tactics. He had given the enemy too much time to reinforce his line and get entrenched. In short, Monty's revised plan for the invasion of Sicily, forced on the Allies in early May – a plan that only Monty really liked – has failed abysmally.[409]

The Allied high command failed to consider an alternative strategy that would have reaped an even greater victory. The German and Italian generals were stunned and relieved that the Allies never landed near Reggio in Calabria at the Italian peninsula's toe to block any Axis withdrawal across the Mesina Straits. Kesselring observed that a 'secondary attack on Calabria would have enabled the Sicily landing to be developed into a devastating victory.' General Vietinghoff further explained:

> From the German standpoint it is incomprehensible that the Allies did not seize the Straits of Messina, either at the same time as the [invasion] landing or in the course of initial action … On both sides of the Straits… this would have been possible without any special difficulty.[410]

Typically, only Patton saw that critical strategy. On 12 August 1943, he proposed dropping the 82nd Airborne Division in Barcelona to cut off the retreat of the 15th and 29th Panzergrenadier divisions. Army Group Commander Alexander approved the plan but Air Chief Arthur Tedder rejected it.[411]

***

After pressuring the Americans into backing a Sicily campaign, Churchill and his commanders immediately advocated invading the Italian peninsula. Churchill opened his campaign during a conference of Mediterranean commanders in Malta in May 1943, Eisenhower recalled that:

> Churchill was at his eloquent best in painting a rosy picture of the opportunities that he foresaw opening up to us with the capture of Sicily. He insisted, in the conference discussions, that he had no intention of interfering with preparations for the cross-Channel attack in 1944, but he was concerned that I understand the desire of the two governments that the Allied forces should quickly exploit any opportunities arising out of the fall of Sicily ... However, he did not propose in my hearing any campaign on a major scale, with the Balkans or even northern Italy, as a minimum objective.[412]

Eisenhower finally succumbed on 17 July 1943, and had his staff send the Combined Chiefs of Staff a recommendation that the Allies invade Italy after completing Sicily's conquest. The American chiefs reluctantly and the British chiefs enthusiastically approved.

That decision was among the war's worst blunders.[413] In doing so, they committed enormous resources of men, weapons, equipment, and, especially, limited numbers of landing craft, on a campaign that would prove to be literally and figuratively a dead end for the Allied cause. Had the Allied instead asserted that vast military power in either southern or northern France, they could have defeated Germany before 1944 ended.

The Sicilian campaign's greatest result was political not military. The British argued for invading Sicily then Italy as a one-two punch to knock Benito Mussolini' regime out of the war. That strategy worked, although the Allies bungled Italy's transformation from enemy to ally. Mussolini's series of costly and usually disastrous wars against Ethiopia, Albania, Greece, and Britain and France alienated not just most Italians but eventually most of his fellow Fascist Party colleagues. In February 1943, Mussolini fired his cabinet ministers as scapegoats, including Galeazzo Ciano his foreign minister and son-in-law. Ciano began conspiring with a group of other Fascist leaders to overthrow Mussolini, mostly vitally General Pietro Badoglio and Dino Grandi.

Mussolini's dictatorship was far from totalitarian. Unlike in Germany where Hitler had the military swear personal allegiance to him, Italy's military pledged loyalty to the king, not il Duce. Mussolini had abolished all political parties except the Fascists and transformed Parliament into a ceremonial institution by stripping the appointed Senate's powers and turning the popularly elected Chamber of Deputies into the appointed Chamber of Fasces and Corporations. The Grand Council was the twenty-eight-member Fascist institution that previously rubberstamped Mussolini's appointments and decrees.

The invasion of Sicily on 11 July 1943 and bombing of Rome on 19 July, emboldened the conspirators to act. On 24 July, Dino Grandi proposed before the Grand Council a vote of no-confidence on Mussolini. The Grand Council debated the resolution into the night. Grandi's condemnation of Mussolini was the most searing:

> You believe you have the devotion of the people. You lost it the day you tied Italy to Germany. You believed yourself a soldier – let me tell you, Italy was lost the very day you put the gold braid of a marshall on your cap ... In this war we have already a hundred thousand mothers who cry: 'Mussolini assassinated my son.'

The Grand Council voted for no confidence, 19 to 8, with one abstention early on 25 July. Later that morning, with Badoglio beside him, Victor Emmaneul summoned Mussolini to tell him that the general would replace him quietly endured il Duce's tirade, then replied: 'The game is over, Mussolini ... You have to go. There's no other course open to me.' Mussolini declared, 'Sire, this is the end of Fascism', then strode out. Police arrested Mussolini as he departed.[414]

Had the king and general then declared that Italy would withdraw from the war into neutrality and gave Hitler thirty days to withdraw German troops, they would have spared their nation mass death and destruction. Instead, for two weeks they dithered. They did not immediately secretly try to negotiate peace with the Allies, partly stymied by the unconditional surrender policy that Roosevelt and Churchill had announced at the Casablanca Conference in January 1943. Meanwhile, fearing that Italy would flip sides, Hitler diverted reserve German divisions into the peninsula.

It was not until mid-August that Badoglio sent General Giuseppe Castellano secretly to the American ambassy in Lisbon, with the message that Italy would like to negotiate a peace treaty with the Allies. Upon learning of that initiative, Eisenhower sent General Walter Bedell Smith his chief of staff and Brigadier General Kenneth Strong to negotiate with him. Castellano flew back to Rome with the Allied terms. On 30 August 1943, Victor Emmaneul and Badoglio agreed to an armistice only if an Allied army landed in Italy to fight the Germans.

They sent Castellano to Sicily where negotiations resumed at Cassibile near Syracuse. Smith and Castellano signed the Armistice of Cassibile on 3 September 1943.

Although Victor Emmanuel ratified the treaty, he and Badoglio hesitated openly to declare their decision and order the Italian army to resist the Germans. Upon learning of the armistice, Hitler ordered the German army to disarm the Italian army. Most Italian commanders acquiesced. Badoglio reassured Hitler that Italy remained loyal.

Word that the king and prime minister were waffling enraged Eisenhower, He sent Badoglio a warning that if he did not comply with the treaty, he would publish all their secret negotiations and terms, thus exposing them to Hitler's wrath. Eisenhower broadcasted on 9 September 1943 the message that: 'The Italian government has surrendered its armed forces. All Italians who now act to help eject the German aggressors from Italian soil will have the assistance and support of the United Nations.' He later explained that 'I announced the surrender at six thirty that evening and Badoglio, in fear and trembling, finally decided an hour and a half later that he had to follow suit.'[415] The king, prime minster, their families and an entourage fled from Rome and eventually reached safety behind Allied lines to be the latest government in exile.

***

For the Italian campaign, General Alexander commanded two armies, Mark Clark's American Fifth and Bernard Montgomery's British Eighth Army. Montgomery began the invasion by sending XIII Corps across the Messina Straits to occupy undefended Reggio on 3 September 1943. General Heinrich von Vietinghoff, the German Tenth Army's commander in southern Italy, had withdrawn his forces north in anticipation of Allied landings there. As XIII Corps advanced against sporadic and limited resistance up the coast, Eighth Army task forces occupied the key ports of Taranto on 9 September 1943, and Brindisi and Bari on 11 September.

Air power determined Fifth Army's landing zone. Army Chief of Staff Marshall wanted a landing in Naples bay while Clark advocated a site near Gaeta 50 miles north of Naples. Air Marshall Tedder opposed either target because they were beyond range of fighter planes that would escort bombers. The Combined Chiefs of Staff settled in Salerno 50 miles south of Naples. Clark and his staff began planning that operation, codenamed 'Avalanche'.

When asked to study and comment on the plan, Patton foresaw that it courted disaster.

> I was very tactful, but could not help calling his attention to the fact that the plan uses the Sele River as a boundary between the British X Corps and the U.S. VI Corps, with no one actually on or near the river. I told him that just as sure as 'God' lives, the Germans will attack down that river.[416]

As usual, Patton was prescient about what the enemy would do and why he would do it. And as usual, those he warned treated him like Casandra.

Salerno bay has a crescent of nice beaches with the city central but backed by steep mountains from which the Sele river flows down into the sea. Fifth Army landed on 9 September 1943. The Germans swiftly took the high ground, hemmed in the Allied troops, and attacked down the Sele valley to nearly destroy Fifth Army. With massive bombing and reinforcements, Fifth Army finally drove back the Germans and linked with Eighth Army. The Allied armies in Italy scored two victories on 1 October 1943, when Eighth Army and Fifth Army respectively took Foggia and Naples.

After that the Italian campaign became a blood-soaked stalemate with minor Allied advances after vast expenditures of lives and munitions. When the war ended twenty-one months later, the Allied armies were no further than the Po river valley's southside. Over 608 days of fighting, the Allies suffered 312,000 casualties or 40 per cent of their total for Europe, with 23,501 dead among 120,00 American casualties. They inflicted 435,000 German casualties, with 48,000 killed, and most of the rest captured, and most of them in the war's last chaotic weeks. Fifth Army alone captured 212,000 prisoners. Along the way, the fighting devastated countless Italian cities and towns, killed around 150,000 civilians, and wounded hundreds of thousands more physically and psychologically.[417] Military historian Basil Liddel Hart spoke for most in the profession when he condemned the Italian campaign as 'tactically the most absurd and strategically the most senseless campaign of the whole war.'[418]

As for his Sicilian campaign, Patton issued on 22 August 1943, this proclamation to his troops:

> Soldiers of the Seventh Army, born at sea, baptized in blood, and crowned in victory, in the course of 38 days of incessant battle and unceasing labor, you have added a glorious chapter to the history of war ... As a result of

> this combined effort, you have killed or captured 113,350 enemy troops. You have destroyed 265 of his tanks, 2,324 vehicles, and 1,162 large guns, and in addition have collected a mass of military booty running into hundreds of tons. But your victory has a significance above and beyond its physical aspect – you have destroyed the prestige of the enemy.[419]

For himself, Patton identified this essential lesson:

> It is desirable ... to have different personalities for corps commanders. Keyes is very dashing. Bradley and Middleton are more methodical. All three are infinitely loyal and of superior effectiveness.[420]

As usual after a victorious campaign, Patton felt mingled elation and melancholy, pride and humility. He worried that: 'As I fought a perfect campaign and a second DSC, I may have fulfilled my destiny, but hope not. Some one must win this war and also the peace.'[421]

Chapter 7

DOG HOUSE

'[T]here was only one good German and that was a dead one.'

'[H]e was a horrid, bloody mess and was not good to look at, or I might develop personal feelings about sending men to battle.'

'[S]ince it is the evident destiny of British and Americans, and, of course, the Russians, to rule the world, the better we know each other, the better job we will do.'

George S. Patton

Patton did not long savor his brilliant Sicily campaign. Before and during the campaign he committed his career's most controversial acts that caught up to him.

The worst came from pep talks he gave before the invasion when he called on the troops 'to kill the enemy wherever we found them' because 'the more we killed then the less we'd have to kill later' and 'that there was only one good German and that was a dead one.'[422] That speech appalled Colonel Homer Jones, Seventh Army's judge advocate. He urged Seventh Army's Chief of Staff General Hobart Gay to get Patton to explain that his order was metaphorical not literal or else 'we might have remarks misinterpreted and have violations of international law.'[423] If Patton heard that advice from Gay, he did not follow it. General Albert Wedemeyer recorded more nuanced remarks by Patton before 45th Division on 29 June 1943:

> He admonished them to be very careful when the Germans or Italians raised their arms as if they wanted to surrender ... The enemy soldiers had on several occasions shot our unsuspecting men or thrown grenades at them. Patton warned ... watch out for this treachery and 'kill the S.O.B.s' unless they were certain of their real intention to surrender.[424]

Sure enough, Patton's words provoked at least two known massacres. Captain John Compton ordered a firing squad to execute thirty-six captured snipers. Sergeant Horace West sub-machine gunned thirty-four Italian and two German soldiers who had surrendered. Military courts tried both men. Compton received an acquittal after citing Patton's order for his defense. West received life in prison for his mass murder but served only a year and was released with the rank of private. Three other massacres did not result in prosecutions, including a busload of German prisoners, sixty Italian prisoners and several Sicilian looters in a factory.[425]

Patton learned of Compton's massacre shortly after it happened when Bradley, deeply upset, informed him. His reaction was to dismiss and cover it up.

> [He] told Bradley that it was probably an exaggeration, but in any case to tell the officer to certify that the dead men were snipers or had attempted to escape or something, as it would make a stink in the press and also would make the civilians mad. Anyhow, they are dead, so nothing can be done about it.[426]

Learning of that and other massacres, three reporters demanded an explanation from Patton. He asked them to keep it secret and promised quietly to issue an order forbidding such killings. The Inspector General Division investigated the massacres and Patton's role in them and concluded that he was not culpable and criticized the defense lawyers of 'quite unethical methods' for trying to blame him.[427]

Patton's other controversial behavior pales beside inciting mass murders. His most upsetting duty was visiting hospitals and trying to exude confidence and gratitude with often gruesomely maimed men. Those visits always deeply affected him with mingled sorrow and inspiration, guilt and pride. He struggled to control those tortured feelings: 'I saw one poor devil missing a leg. I asked him how he felt and he said fine, since you came to see me. I suppose I do some good but it always makes me choke up.' Another time, he: 'Stopped at an evacuation hospital and talked to 350 newly wounded. One poor fellow who had lost his leg cried; another had lost his leg. All were brave and cheerful.' Among his most horrific encounters was a soldier with 'the top of his head blown off and they were just waiting for him to die. He was a horrid, bloody mess and was not good to look at, or I might develop personal feelings about sending men to battle.'[428] During two visits in Sicily, he slapped and cursed soldiers that he believed were malingering.

The first happened on 2 August 1943, after Private Charles Kuhn appeared at the hospital to complain of exhaustion. A medical exam found him suffering a 'psycho-neurosis anxiety state' and a doctor treated him with sodium mytal. This was the third time during the Sicilian campaign that he entered a hospital to receive that diagnosis and treatment. At that point Patton

> came into the tent with the commanding officer and other medical officers ... The General spoke to the various patients in the receiving tent and especially commended the wounded men. Then he came to Pvt. Kuhn and asked him what was the [*sic*] matter. The private replied, 'I guess I can't take it.' The General immediately flared up, cursed the soldier, called him all types of a coward, then slapped him across the face with his gloves and finally grabbed the soldier by the scruff of his neck and kicked him from the tent. The soldier was immediately picked up by corpsmen and taken to a ward tent. There he was found to have a temperature of 102.2 degrees and he gave a history of chronic diarrhea.[429]

Patton was so outraged by what he believed was Kuhn's cowardice that he issued this memo on 5 August 1943:

> It has come to my attention that a very small number of soldiers are going to the hospital on the pretext that they are nervously incapable of combat. Such men are cowards and bring discredit on the army and disgrace to their comrades, whom they heartlessly leave to endure the dangers of battle while they ... use the hospital as a means of escape. You will take measures too see that such cases are not sent to the hospital but are dealt with in their units. Those who are not willing to fight will be tried by Court-Martial for cowardice in the face of the enemy.[430]

The second incident involved Private Paul Bennett who had endured combat until 6 August 1943, when his friend was killed in action. Thereafter he could not sleep and was nervous. Although he wanted to remain with his unit, his officer sent him to the hospital on 10 August 1943. Once again, Patton arrived and spoke with each wounded man, expressing gratitude for his courage and hope he would soon recover. When he came to Bennett who was sitting on a bed, he demanded to know why he was there.

> [Bennett] replied, 'It's my nerves,' and started to sob. The General then screamed at him, 'What did you say?' Bennett said he couldn't take the shelling any more and kept sobbing. Patton cursed and slapped him

> twice, demanded that doctors, 'Don't admit this yellow bastard: there's nothing the matter with him. I won't have the hospitals cluttered up with these sons of bitches who haven't got the guts to fight.' He then yelled at the private: 'You're going back to the front lines and you may get shot and killed, but you're going to fight. If you don't, I'll stand you up against a wall and have a firing squad kill you on purpose. In fact,' he said, reaching for his pistol, 'I ought to shoot you myself, you Goddamned whimpering coward.'

Patton strode from the tent demanding that the doctor send the private back to the front.[431]

Four reporters informed European Theater Commander Dwight D. Eisenhower of the incidents. He urged them not to reveal the story and promised to open an investigation and privately punish Patton if it was true. On 17 August 1943, Eisenhower had Dr Frederick Blesse, a brigadier general and chief surgeon, deliver to Patton the investigation report with his cover letter describing it as

> shocking in its allegations against your personal conduct. I hope you can assure me that none of them is [*sic*] true; but the detailed circumstances communicated to me lead to the belief that some ground for the charges must exist. I am well aware of the necessity for hardness and toughness on the battlefield. I clearly understand that firm and drastic measures are at times necessary in order to secure the desired objectives. But this does not excuse brutality of the sick, nor exhibition of uncontrollable temper in front of subordinates.

He noted that 'I am extremely proud ... that the personal services you have rendered the United States and the Allied cause during the past weeks are of incalculable value.' Then came the threat that produced gut-wrenching dread in Patton: 'I must so seriously question your good judgement and your self discipline as to raise serious doubts in my mind as to your future usefulness.' Finally, he assured Patton that at 'Allied headquarters there is no record of the attached report or of my letter to you, except in my own secret files.'[432] To his aide Harry Butcher, Eisenhower explained his mixed feelings for the incidents:

> in any army one-third of the soldiers are natural fighters and brave. Two-thirds inherently are cowards and skulkers. By making the two-thirds fear possible public upbraiding such as Patton gave ... the skulkers are forced to fight.

Thus, Patton's method 'was deplorable but the result was excellent.' He told Blesse that: 'Patton is indispensable to the war effort. One of the guarantors of victory.'[433]

Eisenhower handled the slapping incidents with political and psychological finesse:

> I determined to keep Patton. I first wrote him a sharp letter of reprimand in which I informed him that repetition of such an offense would be cause for his instant relief ... [and] that ... his retention as a commander in my theater would be contingent upon his offering an apology to the two men whom he had insulted. I demanded that he also apologize to all the personnel of the hospital present at the time of the incident. Finally, I required that he appear before the officer and representative groups of enlisted men of each of the divisions to assure them that he had given way to impulse and respected their positions as fighting soldiers of a democratic nation.

To his relief, 'Patton instantly complied, and I kept in touch with results again through a series of observers and inspectors.'[434]

Patton truly believed that his behavior was correct and the best method to fight what he called malingering. He explained that to General John Lucas on 20 August 1943, who Eisenhower sent to convey his off-the-record order to apologize to the two privates he slapped, everyone who witnessed the incidents, and to the troops of each Seventh Army division. Patton dutifully called in the privates separately to explain why he behaved as he did then apologized and shook hands with them; made similar remarks before the doctors and nurses in each hospital; and finally before troops of each division he gave a speech that vaguely referred to the incidents but mostly lauded their accomplishments.

Patton saved his most profuse apology for Eisenhower: 'I want to commence by thanking you for the additional illustration of your fairness and generous consideration in making your communication' about the complaints

> personal. I am at a loss to find words with which to express my chagrin and grief at having given you, a man to whom I owe everything and for whom I would lay down my life, cause for displeasure with me. I assure you that I had no intention of being either harsh or cruel in my treatment of the two soldiers ... My sole purpose was to try and restore in them a just appreciation of their obligation as men and soldiers.[435]

Eisenhower later made this key distinction:

> Soldiers will not follow any battle leader with confidence unless they know he will require full performance of duty from every member of the team. When bullets are flying and every man's safety and welfare depend upon every other man in the team doing his job, men will not accept a weakling as their leader. Patton's offense, had it been committed on the actual front, within an assaulting platoon, would not have been an offense. It would merely have been an incident of battle … But because of the time and place of his action, Patton's offense was … serious … more so because of his rank and standing. Thus to assault and abuse an enlisted man in a hospital was nothing less than brutal.[436]

Eisenhower wrote General Marshall, the chief of staff, on 24 August, that stressed: 'Patton … has conducted a campaign where the brilliant successes scored must be attributed directly to his energy, determination, and unflagging aggressiveness.' He then explained that Patton continued to 'exhibit some of those unfortunate personal traits of which you and I have always known. His habit of impulsive bawling out of subordinates, extending even of personal abuse of individuals.' He alluded to the two slapping incidents, but insisted that after sternly talking to him,

> I believe that he is cured – not only because of his great personal loyalty to you and to me but because fundamentally he is so avid for recognition as a great military commander that he will ruthlessly suppress any habit of his own that will tend to jeopardize it.[437]

Marshall put Patton on a list of officers who would permanently receive their current promotions. Patton became a full-fledged major general on 4 October 1943 along with these kind words from Eisenhower:

> I am delighted … You have lived up to every one of the expectations I have held for your during the past 25 years, and I know that every government job the government may give you during this war will be performed with the same dash, energy, and determination that have characterized all your actions during the past 10 months.[438]

Patton visited Eisenhower at his headquarters in Algiers on 16 October 1943. Eisenhower used the occasion to offer an assessment of Patton shared by many familiar with psychology and him. That night Patton recorded in his diary that during dinner, Eisenhower

> said I was always acting a part, that it was probably due to my having an inferiority complex. This amused me a lot but I agreed. The truth is that I have too little of such a complex – in fact I look down my nose at the world and too often let them know it.[439]

In contrast to Eisenhower, Bradley's feelings toward Patton became unequivocal. During several months working together, he increasingly despised Patton for his bravado and profanity. Patton's attempt to whitewash the Compton massacre and his slappings of the soldiers provoked Bradley to loath him. Yet Bradley professionally masked his true feelings then and over the next two and a half years until Patton's death.

***

Meanwhile, a series of summits and other diplomatic conferences unfolded that shaped both the military campaigns that would eventually defeat the Axis powers and determined the world's postwar fate.[440]

Churchill held out for his Mediterranean 'soft underbelly' strategy until his summit with Roosevelt in Washington from 12 to 25 May 1943. There he reluctantly accepted Operation Overlord to invade northern France on 1 May 1944. During the summit in Quebec from 17 to 24 August 1943, he agreed that Overlord should have priority over all other campaigns for troops, landing craft, munitions, and all other resources. Then Churchill got cold feet and during the Cairo Conference from 22 to 26 November 1943, he tried to weasel out of Overlord and resumed his specious arguments for a Mediterranean basin strategy, including the capture of Rhodes. That enraged America's Joint Chiefs of Staff. Marshall spoke for them when he asserted, 'Not one American is going to die on that goddamned beach.'[441] Faced with united opposition from the president and his Joint Chiefs of Staff, Churchill bitterly accepted Overlord, That done, Roosevelt and Churchill sought an agreement on other key strategic and political issues before their pending summit with Stalin at Tehran. They also discussed strategy and military aid with Chiang Kai-shek, China's generalissimo who joined them for the summit.

Roosevelt, Churchill, and Stalin met at Tehran, Iran from 28 November 1943 to 1 December 1943. For Stalin, the most vital issues were Overlord and Anvil, the simultaneous invasions of northern and southern France. Roosevelt enthusiastically and Churchill grudgingly promised an invasion on 1 May 1944. Stalin then asked who would command Overlord. Roosevelt and Churchill sheepishly admitted that they had not yet decided but that the president and prime minister would respectively pick the supreme command and his deputy. They then discussed and cut deals on other key questions. Stalin tentatively agreed that the Soviet Union would go to war against Japan three months after Germany's defeat. Roosevelt and Churchill reluctantly accepted the Soviet takeover of Estonia, Latvia and Lithuania, which had broken free from the Russian empire to become independent countries after World War I; their condition was that a plebiscite in each country would determine whether a majority wanted to remain independent or return to Russian rule.

Roosevelt had to choose a Supreme Commander for Overlord, and that posed a dilemma. The two top choices were Army Chief of Staff George Marshall and European Theater Commander Dwight D. Eisenhower. Both wanted the job but neither lobbied for it. Marshall was brilliant at advising, planning, organizing and implementing, and had impeccable character. Although he had never directly experienced combat, he knew war first hand as chief of operations for 1st Division then for General Pershing during World War I. His personality was aloof and he played no favorites and tolerated no fools. He repeatedly stood up to Prime Minister Winston Churchill and General Bernard Montgomery when their demands were strategically unsound or politically unpalatable. Yet Roosevelt worried that toughness might strain relations between American and British leaders. Eisenhower was a first-rate administrator and his genial personality put others, even the worst prima donnas or aristocratic snobs at ease. Roosevelt was aware that many if not most British leaders thought him a second-rate general.

Roosevelt made his choice on his way back from the Tehran conference. When Eisenhower met him at the Tunis airport on 6 December 1943, Roosevelt cheerfully exclaimed, 'Well, Ike, you are going to command Overlord.' He later explained to Marshall that: 'Well, I didn't feel I could sleep at ease if you were out of Washington.'[442] Eisenhower was overjoyed at the news, then chagrined to learn who Churchill chose as Overlord's planner and ground commander. After mulling generals Harold Alexander and Louis Mountbatten, Churchill tapped Bernard Montgomery on 24 December 1943.

***

Unfortunately, Patton's two slapping incidents were not quietly forgotten. Instead, in mid-November 1943 Drew Pearson broke the slapping story in this 'Washington Merry-Go-Round' column for the *Christian Science Monitor*. That provoked a political storm as mostly anxious parents, especially mothers, worried for their sons, demanded that the president and their senators and representatives investigate and punish Patton. On 24 November 1943, Secretary of War Henry Stimson asked Eisenhower to provide him all official reports on the incidents. Patton wrote Stimson a letter that at once justified and apologized for his behavior. By mid-December, the White House alone had received around 1,500 letters mostly demanding justice but some justifying Patton's acts. Patton was crushed when he learned that General John Pershing, his mentor, had denounced the slappings. However, a Gallup Poll revealed that four of five Americans wanted Patton kept in army command.[443]

Gradually, Patton's latest controversy subsided. In his December 1943 efficiency report, Eisenhower rated Patton 'superior' and five of twenty-four lieutenant generals, 'outstanding as a leader of an assault force. Impulsive and almost flamboyant in manner. Should always serve under a strong but understanding commander.'[444]

Yet, Patton's two slapping incidents cost him command of America's First Army that would invade Normandy alongside Britain's Second Army, and later command of the Twelfth Army Group of First and Third Army. Eisenhower informed Marshall that he had chosen Omar Bradley, Patton's subordinate, for those subsequent commands but would let Patton command Third Army that would begin fighting in France two months after the invasion. He explained that

> Bradley … is … the best rounded combat leader I have yet met in our service. While he possibly lacks some of the extraordinary and ruthless driving power that Patton can exert at critical moments … he is among our best.[445]

Eisenhower faced a dilemma in juggling commands between Bradley and Patton:

> I foresaw some possibility of friction advancing Bradley to the highest American ground command in Overlord because I was also planning to use Patton in that operation, provided he concurred in the new arrangement, which would involve a reversal of the relative positions the two men had held in the successful Sicilian campaign. Both were my intimate friends of many years' standing and I knew that either would

> accept any assigned duty. I was hopeful…that Patton, who for certain types of action was the outstanding soldier our country had produced, would wholeheartedly support the plan I had in mind. I had a frank talk with him and was gratified to find he thoroughly agreed that the role for which he personally was ideally suited for was that of an army commander.[446]

Bradley was bitter to learn of Patton's assignment:

> Our roles in North Africa and Sicily were now reversed; I was his boss. Had it been left up to me, I would not have included Patton in Overlord. I did not look forward to having him in my command. He had shown in Sicily that he did not know how to run an army; his legendary reputation (now badly tarnished) was the product of an uncritical media buildup. But Ike insisted on Patton for his undeniable drive.[447]

Patton would not receive official word that he would command Third Army until late January 1944. Meanwhile, he spent the intervening months in limbo mostly at Seventh Army's headquarters at Palermo's royal palace; he was bored, anxious for his future, and reading lots of history, especially on the Punic Wars, between routine staff meetings and inspections. On Torch's anniversary, he noted sadly to Beatrice that: 'We have been at it just a year to day and in all that time I have only been in battle 72 days out of 365.'[448] He took a series of essentially site-seeing trips by hopping flights to Egypt, Palestine, Corsica, Italy, Malta and other Allied possessions in the Mediterranean, hobnobbing with local commanders and reveling in the ancient history. On 1 January 1944, he was officially relieved of Seventh Army's command. That compounded his fears that his career was effectively dead.

Eisenhower summoned Patton to London for a meeting on 26 January 1944. In his diary, Patton wrote that he:

> Called on Ike at office and found I am to command Third Army … in support of Bradley's First Army – not such a good job, but better than nothing … Well, I have an army and it is up to me. As far as I can remember this is my twenty-seventh start from zero since entering U.S. Army. Each time I have made a success of it, and this one must be the biggest.[449]

Eisenhower had his driver, Kay Summersby, give him a tour of London. Summersby was smitten with Patton, calling him the 'most glamorous, dramatic general I ever met … a man's man and yet he unfailingly treated women with an eighteenth century flourish.' He rode beside her in the front seat where 'his ramrod back never once unbent, never touched the seat' and muttered 'those sonsofbitches' as he witnessed the devastation caused by German bombers, but each time apologized to her for his language. His only flaw was 'the world's most unfortunate voice, a high-pitched womanish squeak.'[450]

Patton's duties were secretly to organize and train Third Army while publicly pretending to command a fictitious First Army Group that would invade the Pas-de-Calais region of France with the shortest distance across the English Channel. To promote that deception, engineers constructed fake bases with inflatable tanks and trucks in south-east England. Patton established his headquarters at Peover Hall near Knutsford, England 20 miles south-west of Manchester. Third Army already existed in the United States and General Walter Krueger commanded it before Eisenhower transferred it to Patton.

Third Army received orders to transfer to England on 1 January 1944. Over the next half year, convoys of transports crossed the Atlantic and deposited men, weapons, and supplies at Liverpool, Bristol, and smaller west England ports. Patton welcomed the first contingent, a headquarters staff of thirteen officers and twenty-six soldiers on 29 January 1944. As the components arrived, Patton deployed them in camps spreading across the surrounding countryside. His corps commanders eventually included generals Troy Middleton for VIII, Gilbert Cook for XII, Wade Haislip for XV and Walton Walker for XX. His staff included General Hugh Gaffey as chief, General Hobart Gay as deputy chief, Colonel Paul Harkins as the deputy's deputy, and colonels Frederick Matthews for Personnel (G-1), Oscar Koch for intelligence (G-2), Halley Maddox for operations (G-3), Walter Muller for logistics (G-4) and Nicolas Companole for civil affairs (G-5).

As always, Patton tried to prepare his troops emotionally as well as technically and physically for combat. He spoke before each new unit that arrived, explaining what war was like and how to fight to win. In a typical speech, he asserted these key points to boost their patriotism, pride, and devotion to their common cause:

> All real Americans love the sting and clash of battle. America loves a winner. America will not tolerate a loser. Americans despise a coward. Americans play to win. That is why America has never lost and will never lose a war ... Death must not be feared. Death in time comes to all of us. And every man is scared in his first action ... The real hero is the man who fights even though he is scared ... An army is a team, lives, sleeps, fights, and eats as a team ... Every single man in the Army plays a vital role ... We want to get this thing over ... The shortest road home is through Berlin and Tokyo.[451]

The XIX Tactical Air Command, led by General Otto Weyland was attached to Third Army. Weyland flew Patton in various warplanes and explained their strengths, weaknesses, and how best to wield them tactically with ground forces. That began an outstanding partnership between the generals and their commands. XIX Tactical Air Command would excel at three missions, bombing enemy troops and depots far ahead of Third Army's advancing troops and tanks, bombing enemy troops immediately before Third Army attacks, and covering Third Army's open flanks as it raced across the countryside.

Dwight D. Eisenhower headed both the Supreme Headquarters Allied Expeditionary Force (SHAEF) for operations across France into Germany, and the European Theater of Operations (ETO). The former was initially headquartered at Norfolk House in St James Square while the later was at Grosvenor House in Grosvenor Square.

Overlord was the codename for the Normandy invasion. Eisenhower was Overlord's supreme commander in title and its figurehead in practice. Churchill and his high command insisted that his inner command circle were British including General Arthur Tedder as deputy chief, Admiral Bertram Ramsay as naval chief, General Trafford Leigh-Mallory as air chief, and General Bernard Montgomery as Overlord's ground commander who would plan and implement the campaign. Typically, Eisenhower did not resent but warmly embraced all of them except Montgomery, who remained condescending toward him. Indeed, his other British chiefs genuinely liked Eisenhower not just as a person but increasingly appreciated his managerial leadership style. They scorned Montgomery not just for his arrogance but later as the campaign in France unfolded, for the timid generalship behind his bluster. In his diary, Tedder wrote that 'the problem is Monty who can be neither removed nor moved to action.'[452]

Montgomery and his staff minutely planned Overlord at London's St Paul's School, from which he had graduated. To his credit, he did make two changes from the original plan, expanding the number of first-wave divisions from three to six, and the expanse of beachheads from 25 to 50 miles. The Germans undoubtedly would have swiftly contained and destroyed the earlier limited invasion much as they nearly did at Anzio in Italy. Now each division would spearhead a corps.

Meanwhile, Churchill continued trying to undercut Overland with schemes for invasions elsewhere in the Mediterranean like Yugoslavia and Rhodes. Yet he rejected the planned invasion of southern France's Rivera, codenamed first Anvil then Dragoon. That such a brilliant statesman and student of military history would be so deluded in his grand strategy was among Churchill's most perplexing paradoxes. Fortunately, rational American strategic thinking persisted and eventually prevailed. The original plan was for Overland and Anvil to occur simultaneously to tie down German troops on both fronts, then punch through enemy lines and join forces in eastern France. The swift capture of a large port on each front was deemed critical to victory, Cherbourg in Normandy and Marseilles in the Riviera. The diversion of landing craft to the Anzio landing 30 miles south-west of Rome on 22 January 1944, forced Eisenhower to postpone the Riviera invasion nearly two and a half months to mid-August 1944.

Eisenhower and the Overlord planners had to contend with an array of other strategic and political challenges far beyond Normandy's beaches. There was the Pacific war where American naval, ground and air forces demanded enormous amounts of personnel, supplies, weapons, ships and landing craft.

Montgomery assembled the key commanders including Eisenhower, Bradley, and Patton at St Paul's on 7 April 1944, and over two hours presented his plan while pointing at a large relief map of Normandy. Patton was pleased that:

> During Montgomery's lecture, it was interesting to note that I was the only Army commander of the four Army commanders involved to be mentioned by name. The other three he mentioned by number [of the army].[453]

A few days later, he wrote to Beatrice that:

> I have a feeling, probably unfounded, that neither Monty nor Bradley are too anxious for me to have a command. If they knew what little respect I had for the fighting ability of either of them, they would be even less anxious for me to show up.[454]

Patton's feeling was indeed solidly founded. Bradley did not want Patton in his command and Montgomery did not want Patton as a rival general for victories, glory and popular acclaim.

***

During the hectic, stressful months before D-Day, Patton and Eisenhower shared some scarce leisure time together. Eisenhower recalled that Patton

> would spend the evening with me at my quarters and though this usually involved the certainty of sitting up till the wee hours of the morning, conversation with him was always so stimulating that it was difficult to remember that the work day began before dawn.[455]

Then Patton stirred his latest controversy, this one a tempest in a teapot, while speaking off the record at the Welcome Club for American Soldiers run by local ladies in Knutsford. Geoffrey Mould of the Ministry of Information had invited him to attend the club's opening. He thought he was just there to preside until the chair asked him to say a few words. He explained that he was there secretly and neither his photo nor remarks should be recorded, then said:

> Until today, my only experience in welcoming has been to welcome Germans and Italians to the 'Infernal Regions'. In this I have been quite successful. I feel that such clubs as this one are a very real value because I believe … that … since it is the evident destiny of British and Americans, and, of course, the Russians, to rule the world, the better we know each other, the better job we will do.[456]

The idea that the Americans, British and Russians would rule the post-war world conflicted with President Roosevelt's vision of a United Nations of all countries dedicated to collective security, peace and prosperity led but not dominated by the Four Policemen that included China along with the other three. The British Press Association reported Patton's remarks and soon they appeared in American newspapers. Isolationist-leaning senators and representatives criticized Patton and called for a congressional committee to debate America's postwar role.

Eisenhower and Marshall exchanged their latest letters on Patton, with both concluding that his military brilliance was more vital than his controversial remarks. Marshall again let Eisenhower deal with Patton as he thought best while emphasizing that 'Patton is the only available Army Commander for his present assignment who has had actual experience fighting Rommel and in extensive landing operations followed by a rapid campaign of exploitation.'[457] In other words, Patton was indispensable to victory in northwestern Europe.

Eisenhower again let Patton off with a reprimand rather than dismissal. In his diary, Patton wrote that Eisenhower had his chief of staff Bedell Smith call to 'give me a verbal order from Ike that I am never to talk in public without first submitting what I am going to say to Ike and himself for censorship.' Patton complained that 'I have caught nothing but hell for nearly a year now. All I want to do is win this war and everyone seems to think that all I want is notoriety which I despise.'[458]

Patton met Eisenhower at his headquarters on 1 May, abjectly apologized for his latest indiscretion, and offered to resign. To Patton's immense relief, Eisenhower replied that: 'Since the War Department has placed the decision of relieving you on me, I have decided to keep you ... Go ahead and train your army.' He added that he did so

> solely because of my faith in you as an able battle leader ... I expect you to ... exercise extreme care to see that while you are developing the morale and fighting spirit, you will not be guilty of any further embarrassment to your superiors or yourself.[459]

Eisenhower recalled that Patton

> was stirred to the point of tears. At such moments General Patton revealed a side of his makeup that was difficult for anyone except his intimate friends to understand. His remorse was very great, not only for the trouble he had caused me but ... for the fact that he had vehemently criticized me to his associates when he thought I might relieve him. His emotional range was very great and he lived at either one end or the other. I laughingly told him, 'You owe some victories, pay off and the world will deem me a wise man.'[460]

Despite Patton's latest indiscretion, Eisenhower still highly esteemed him. In his latest efficiency report, he rated Patton 'superior' and number two as an army commander and number eight overall, 'a brilliant fighting leader' but 'impulsive and quick tempered, likely to speak in public in an ill-considered fashion.'[461]

On the train back to Manchester and then a car to his headquarters, Patton calmed himself by reciting poetry to himself then concluding: 'I am destined to achieve some great thing – what, I don't know, but this last incident was so trivial in its nature, but so terrible in its effect, that it is not the result of an accident but the work of God.'[462]

Chapter 8

ACROSS FRANCE

> 'Of course, Monty does not want me in as he fears I will steal the show, which I will.'
>
> 'Some goddam fool once said that flanks have got to be secure. Since then sonsofbitches all over the globe have been guarding their flanks. I don't agree with that. My flanks are something for the enemy to worry about, not me. Before he finds out where my flanks are, I'll be cutting the bastard's throat.'
>
> George S. Patton

Patton was among the audience of army commanders and chiefs of staffs along with King George V and Prime Minister Winston Churchill when General Bernard Montgomery presented Overlord's latest version at St Paul's school on 15 May 1944. Afterward, although Churchill still feared the worst, he finally expressed guarded confidence in the invasion:

> Gentlemen, I am hardening to this enterprise. I repeat, I am hardening to this enterprise. Let us not expect all to go according to plan. Flexibility of mind will be one of the decisive factors. We must not have another Anzio. Risks must be taken.[463]

Ideally, Overlord was the opening campaign of a series that eventually overran Germany and destroyed Hitler's Third Reich.[464]

Although Germany's army remained formidable, it was spread thin from the Atlantic to the Russian steppes and from the Mediterranean to Scandinavia. In May 1944, 193 German divisions fought in the Soviet Union, 28 in Italy, 26 in the Balkans, 18 in Norway and Denmark, 8 in Finland, and 59 in France, Belgium and the Netherlands.[465] Two

German army groups commanded by Gerd von Rundstedt defended northern France. General Erwin Rommel's Group B included General Friedrich Dollman's 7th Army in Normandy and Britanny and General Hans von Salmuth's 15th Army in Pas-de-Calais from the Seine river to Belgian border. General Johannes von Blaskowitz's Group G included 1st Army and 19th Army that respectively defended the Bay of Biscay and southern France.

Rundstedt and Rommel disagreed over how best to defend northern France. Rundstedt favored keeping armored divisions inland to race to any invaded beach. Rommel favored deploying them with infantry divisions along shore to destroy any invaders at the water's edge. Rommel argued that Allied air superiority would devastate any rearward armored divisions as they drove to the coast. Rundstedt countered that air and naval power would likely decimate any tanks dispersed on shore.

Both Rommel and Rundstedt along with Hitler believed that the Allied invasion would more likely attack Pas-de-Calais than Normandy so 15th Army numbered more troops and tanks than 7th Army. After assuming command of Group B, Rommel ordered his troops to build an elaborate defense complex along the coast that included 20,000 concrete bunkers and pillboxes, 500,000 sea and land obstacles and 6,500,000 mines on beaches and atop posts planted in the water to blow up landing craft. Behind the lines fortified supply depots were packed with provisions and munitions. Rommel's Army Group B numbered around 500,000 troops and 1,608 tanks, including 674 Mark IVs and 514 Mark V Panthers.[466]

For Overlord, the Allies had shipped across the Atlantic or produced in Britain an extraordinary array and amount of vital transport and supplies including

> 301,000 vehicles, 1,800 locomotives, 20,000 rail cars, 2.6 million small arms, 2,700 artillery pieces, 300,000 telephone poles, and 7 million tons of gasoline, oil, and lubricant SHAEF had calculated daily combat consumption, from fuel to bullets to chewing gum, at 41.298 pounds per soldier. Sixty million K-rations, enough to feed the invaders for a month, were packed in 500-ton bales.[467]

Engineers constructed two massive artificial harbors to be towed across the English Channel and anchored offshore, codenamed Mulberry A for First Army and Mulberry B for Second Army.

Meanwhile, British intelligence conducted several parallel operations to deceive Berlin. They had captured every German spy that parachuted into Britain and forced them to transmit false information back to their headquarters. As Overlord loomed, the disinformation included Patton heading First Army Group to land at Pas-de-Calais and seventy-nine divisions rather than the actual fifty-two divisions in Britain. Meanwhile, the Ultra program that cracked and read Germany's secret military code fed intelligence to Allied headquarters.

The Normandy landing, 'D-Day', was scheduled for 5 June 1944. Any landing could not take place any time. Just a few days each month the tide was low enough on Normandy's beaches to let landing craft avoid the thousands of mines atop posts just below water at full tide. Engineers would follow the first wave of infantry to clear paths through those forests of mines for the next assault as the tide rose.

From 1 April 1944, a bombing campaign aimed to destroy coastline defenses and rear echelon bridges, railroads, and supply depots. The Ninth Air Force included the IX Bomber Command and the IX and XIX Tactical Commands. The two tactical commands had 36,000 airmen and 1,500 aircraft split among five wings each with eighteen fight-bomber squadrons. The IX and XIX Tactical Commands, led respectively by generals Elwood Quesada and Otto Weyland, were respectively attached to the First and Third armies. That campaign cost the allies over 2,000 airplanes and 28,000 airmen.

Eisenhower faced a critical decision when a gale surged into the region on 4 June 1944 and persisted into 5 June. Eisenhower tentatively delayed the landing until 6 June then tensely waited for that day's meteorologist report. When the meteorologists concluded that the gale would finally abate the night before, Eisenhower tersely queried his key generals over what to do. Each guardedly wanted to invade. Eisenhower gave the go-ahead.

The invasion force included 174,320 troops, 20,108 tanks and other vehicles, 4,226 landing craft, 6,939 vessels and 11,000 aircraft. The ships were split into five task forces for five beaches along a 50-mile stretch of Normandy's coast. Minesweepers spearheaded each task force to clear paths through the mine forests. Before and after the airborne drops, the air force flew 14,674 bombing, strafing, reconnaissance, parachute drops and glider lifts just on 5 and 6 June 1944. Most bombs exploded beyond the coastal defenses, either harmlessly on fields and woods or destructively on homes and villages. The warships fired 140,000 shells before and during the landings, although, like the bombs, few scored direct hits.

Nighttime airborne landings behind enemy lines proceeded the seaborne landings to secure them against enemy counterattacks. The 82nd and 101st American Airborne divisions dropped west and south of Utah Beach, while the British 6th Airborne Division dropped south and east of Sword Beach. Meanwhile, the American and British task forces stopped 11 and 7 miles from shore. LSTs disgorged LCTs that churned along troop ships. Troops gingerly climbed down rope webs into the LCTs that, when filled, headed toward shore.

Omar Bradley's First Army landed at the two western beaches, with 4th Infantry Division of Lawton 'Lightening Joe' Collins's VII Corps at Utah Beach and 1st and 29th divisions of Leonard Gerow's V Corps at Omaha Beach. Miles Demsey's Second Army landed at the three eastern beaches, with 50th British Division and 3rd Canadian Division of Gerald Bucknall's XXX Corps respectively at Gold and Juno beaches, and 3rd British Division of John Crocker's I Corps at Sword Beach.

Allied troops pushed inland for several miles at each beach except Omaha, where the Americans crept forward only several hundred to a thousand yards inland against intensive German fire. During D-Day, the Americans suffered 6,577 casualties, including 1,465 dead, 3,184 wounded and 1,928 missing, and the British about 3,300 casualties. The 82nd and 101st Airborne divisions suffered the worst losses for American divisions with 2,499 casualties between them. The Allies inflicted around 10,000 German casualties. Naval losses were light; enemy mines sank a destroyer, a patrol boat, three LCTs and two LCIs. Allied warplanes shot down thirty-one enemy planes and lost seventy-one.[468]

With the beaches secure, the navy performed wonders. By 15 June 1944, the Americans disembarked 314,504 troops and 41,000 vehicles, and the British 314,547 troops and 54,000 vehicles. Yet, supply fell behind military demand and that crimped operations. The Allies landed 116,065 tons or 72.8 per cent of 159,350 tons planned. Shortages worsened after a gale devastated Normandy from 19 to 21 June 1944, sank or beached nearly 800 vessels, and most critically sank America's artificial harbor and damaged Britain's.[469]

Over the next six weeks, First and Second armies slowly fought inland as ever more divisions reinforced them. The greatest Allied victory was VII Corps' capture of Cherbourg with 39,042 prisoners on 29 June 1944, although it would take a month for engineers to clear the harbor of thousands of mines and 100 scuttled vessels so that supply ships could dock there.[470] The worst disappointment was Montgomery's failure to realize his boast that his men would capture Caen, 12 miles from the beach, by nightfall on D-Day; the German defenders repelled British attacks for the next two months.

Progress was glacial because much of Normandy's landscape is ideal for defenders. 'Bocage' are earth walls topped by thick hedges that surround farms. Germans crouching behind the earth walls and firing rifles and machines guns through the hedges could devastate attackers while enjoying nearly bullet-proof cover. First Army eventually developed tactics that let troops systematically capture one hedgerowed farm after another, although the pace was tedious. Engineers welded serrated steel 'teeth' to the front of Sherman tanks so they could slice through the hedgerows after mortar fire hit enemy troops within the hedgerows. White phosphorus shells were especially effective at burning out defenders. Infantry followed the tanks to toss grenades over and fire through the hedge at the enemy as they fled to a rear hedgerow, where the tactic was repeated. By mid-July 1944, First Army deployed over 500 modified Shermans dubbed 'rhinoceroses'.[471]

Each side committed more forces to the campaign. From 6 June to 23 July 1944, the Germans deployed 410,000 troops to Normandy and suffered 116,863 casualties. Meanwhile, by 29 July 1944, the Americans had deployed 903,061 troops, 176,620 vehicles and 858,436 tons of supplies, and the British 663,295 troops, 156,025 vehicles and 74,540 tons of supplies.[472]

***

Meanwhile, Patton impatiently readied Third Army for deployment. Eisenhower visited him and chatted with some of his troops on 26 June 1944. Patton confided to his diary these insightful impressions of Eisenhower's folksy leadership style:

> Ike made an inspection by walking through the ranks and talking briefly to numerous men. He tries to find points of common interest with them and is clever at it. Then he gets the loud speaker and tells the soldiers to fall out and gather around. He talks very familiarly to them, but uses I, mine, and me too much, usually exhorting them to fight well, 'So that we can end this war and I can go home and go fishing.' … The men seem to like it and usually clap and cheer a little. It is the style of an office seeker rather than that of a soldier…His theory is that by this method one gets on a level with the men. A commander cannot command and be on the same level … I try to arouse fighting emotions – he tries [for] votes – for what?[473]

They met again on 5 July 1944, with Eisenhower

> just back from the France and seemed cheerful, but a little fed up with Monty's lack of drive. He is swinging over … to take personal command of the fighting, but is still temporalizing. He cannot bring himself to take

> the plunge. His current plan is ... for four American Armies, with one small American army for Montgomery ... Why an American Army has to go with Montgomery, I do not see, except to save the face of the little monkey.[474]

Patton kept secretly fuming at Eisenhower's indecisive leadership:

'Ike is bound hand and foot by the British and does not know it. Poor fool. We actually have no Supreme Commander – no one can take hold and say that his shall be done and that shall not be done.' He was just as unsparing of Bradley and Hodges:

> I could break through ... in three days if I commanded. They try to push all along the front and have no power anywhere. All that is necessary now is to take chances by leading with armored divisions and covering their advance with air bursts. Such an attack would have to be made on a narrow sector.

Secretary of War Henry Stimson paid a visit to the front. At Cherbourg, Patton met with Stimson, an old friend and mentor, and shared his frustrations. Stimson gave him the sound advice 'not to criticize anyone, but let my actions speak for me.'[475]

Within a month, Patton would brilliantly implement his Normandy breakout strategy. He and his staff flew to Normandy on 6 July and set up headquarters at Nehou, within General Troy Middleton's VIII Corps district. After Third Army became operational, VIII Corps would transfer to it from First Army. Meanwhile, one by one the divisions of Third Army's other corps journeyed from England to designated grounds in Normandy where they continued to organize and train.[476]

Within days, Patton learned of two dramatic events that deprived him of his most esteemed rival enemy general and nearly the war against Germany itself. A strafing attack wounded Rommel on 17 July 1944 and forced him into a German hospital. Hitler replaced Rommel with General Gunther von Kluge. Once again, Rommel disappeared from his command just as Patton was about to square off with him. Then on 20 July 1944, a group of German officers tried to assassinate Hitler and take power in a coup, followed by surrendering the Allies.[477] During a conference of Hitler and his staff at his Wolf's Lair headquarters in East Prussia, Colonel Claus von Stauffenberg placed a time bomb in a briefcase under the table and excused himself. His driver took him to a nearby airfield where he boarded a plane for Berlin to join the other coup leaders and take over the government. The bomb exploded but a heavy table leg spared Hitler while killing four and wounding twenty others in the room. Hitler ordered the Gestapo to arrest Stauffenberg and the other conspirators, then summarily try and execute them. Eventually the Gestapo arrested over 7,000 suspects and shot 4,980 of them. Hitler had Rommel, who knew of but did not join the plot, commit suicide.

Hitler's near assassination bolstered Patton's fear that the war would end without him playing a decisive role. All he could do was supervise the transfer of Third Army's divisions to camps behind First Army's lines in Normandy. With that done, the Twelfth Army Group would form led by Bradley with Patton's Third Army along with First Army, now led by General Courtney Hodges, while Montgomery commanded the Twenty-First Army Group with General Henry Crerar's Canadian First Army and General Miles Dempsey's British Second Army.

Courtney Hodges was Patton's opposite as a commander, a low key plodder and lackluster leader.[478] His courage was unquestionable. He flunked out of West Point his freshman year, joined the army as a private, and displayed such leadership skills that he earned a second lieutenant's commission in 1909. He served with Pershing's Punitive Expedition in Mexico and America's Expedition Force in France. From there he methodically worked his way up the ranks by being a team player.

In a diary entry, Patton revealed some of the subtleties behind his leadership style's scowling face. He did not hesitate to threaten to fire deficient leaders but his bark was worse than his bite. He thought that Bradley and Collins

> are too prone to cut off heads. This will make division commanders lose their confidence. A man should not be damned for an initial failure with a new division. Had I done this with Eddy of the 9th Division in Africa, the army would have lost a potential corps commander … I shall be more conservative in the removal of officers and have told the corps commanders so orally.[479]

Patton and Bradley met Montgomery at his headquarters on 7 July 1944. Patton wrote that after lunch,

> Montgomery went to great length explaining why the British had done nothing. Caen was their D-Day objective, and they have not yet taken it. He tried to get Bradley to state that the Third Army would not become operational until the VIII Corps had taken Avranches. Bradley refused to bite because he is using me as a means of getting out from under the 21st Army Group.[480]

Eisenhower authorized Bradley on 14 July 1944, to activate Third Army and take command of Twenty-First Army Group whenever he believed the time was right. Patton was naturally eager to lead Third Army on campaign as soon as possible. As always, personal interests mingled with strategic interests in shaping relations among the commanders. Patton wrote in his diary that:

> Brad says he will put me in as soon as he can. He could do it now with much benefit to himself, if he had any backbone. Of course, Monty does not want me as he fears I will steal the show, which I will.[481]

Montgomery launched his latest offensive, this one codenamed Goodwood, on 18 July 1944. Like his others, his massive air and artillery bombardment followed by a massive ground attack soon sputtered to a halt. Montgomery called off his offensive on 25 July 1944, after his armies suffered 6,000 casualties and 400 destroyed tanks of 1,370 deployed for just a 6-mile advance into Caen's ruins north of the Orne river with Caen on the south bank still in German hands.

Meanwhile, Bradley's Normandy breakout, codenamed Cobra, unfolded in two phases culminating with First Army punching a hole that Third Army dashed through.[482] The first phase began on 3 July 1944 and ended on 14 July when Bradley called a halt after First Army captured the strategic crossroads town of St Lo, after suffering 40,000 casualties and advancing only 7 miles.

Patton fumed at the other army commanders and their stalled Normandy campaign: In mid-July 1944, he wrote:

> Sometimes I get desperate over the future. Bradley and Hodges are such nothings. Their one virtue is that they get along by doing nothing. I could break through [the enemy defenses] in three days if I commanded. They try to push all along the front and have no power anywhere. All that is necessary now is to take chances by leading with armored divisions and covering their advance with air bursts. Such an attack would have to be made on a narrow front.[483]

Bradley and Hodges embraced Patton's strategy for the second phase that began on 25 July 1944. A massive bombing and artillery bombardment of German defenses around St Lo preceded Collins's VII Corps attacking with his four divisions in a narrow front. Bradley had asked the air force to bomb along the German line. Bomber command rejected that for exposing their warplanes to continuous flack fire, and instead instructed Bradley to withdrew First Army 3,000 yards to avoid getting hit by bombs falling short during a standard fly over. Bradley withdrew First Army's most exposed divisions to 1,500 yards. On the night of 25 July 1944, 1,500 heavy bombers dropped 3,300 tons of bombs of which most hit Germans or uninhabited countryside. Tragically, erratic bombing inflicted 156 casualties including 30 dead on First Army on 25 July, and 111 dead and 490 wounded the next day; Lieutenant General Lesley McNair was among those killed.[484]

Bradley had scheduled Third Army's debut for 1 August 1944, but with First Army's breakthrough, he greenlighted Patton and shifted VIII Corps to his command on 27 July 1944. Patton was elated:

> [He] Felt much happier about the war [World War II]. He immediately visited the VIII Corps ... to arrange to takeover the corps, but conducted everything very casually so as not to get people excited at the change.[485]

The presence of Patton and his Third Army in Normandy was still top secret to keep the fiction that he commanded Fifteenth Army Group that would invade Pas-de-Calais.

Patton's first key goal was Avranches, a town near the coast hinging Normandy and Brittany. If Third Army smashed through at Avranches its divisions could fan out to encircle and destroy enemy forces in Britanny and Normandy. His initial strategy was that

> two armored divisions, preceded by a heavy artillery concentration using air bursts, and followed by two infantry divisions, could ... cut straight down the west coast to Avranches without the necessity of waiting for an air blitz.[486]

He modified that by broadening the attack to include Troy Middleton's VIII Corps on the coast road and Wade Haslip's XV Corps on a parallel inland road punching south. Middleton's VIII had the 4th and 6th Armored divisions along with two infantry divisions while Wade Haslip's XV Corps had three infantry divisions. Behind them in reserve was XII Corps initially commanded by Gilbert Cook until 19 August 1944, when Manton Eddy replaced him, and Walton Walker's XX Corps.

Patton recalled that the passage of

> Third Army through the corridor at Avranches was an impossible operation. Two roads entered Avranches; only one left it over the bridge. We passed through this corridor two infantry and two armored divisions in less than twenty-four hours. There was no plan because it

> was impossible to make a plan. I simply put the Corps and Division commanders at critical points and sent units through as they arrived. It was a hazardous operation, because the troops were jammed head to tail for miles, but there was no other way of attaining the necessary speed.

The critical element was the 'extremely effective use of veteran staff officers and by the active part taken by corps and division commanders who, on occasion, personally directed traffic.'[487] At times, Patton himself got out of his jeep it unsnarl traffic jams.

VIII Corps bagged over 8,300 prisoners while suffering 833 casualties during the three days it took to capture and secure Avranches.[488] As such VIII Corps set the Third Army standard ratio for enemy to friendly casualties that the other corps competed to emulate and surpass. After VIII Corps' breakthrough, Patton

> told Middleton to head for Brest and Rennes, with the 6th Armored Division and the 79th Infantry Division on Brest, and the 8th Infantry Division and 4th Armored Division on Rennes, and also to create a task force ... to go along the north coast of the Peninsula.[489]

Patton talked Bradley into letting VIII Corps overrun Brittany while he raced his three other corps eastward to rout and mop up scattered German forces before they could coalesce into a powerful defensive line. As VIII's divisions fanned out west and south-west from Avranches, Patton pointed XX Corps south toward the Loire then east to clear its north side while XV Corps, with XII Corps following, angled south-east then east toward Le Mans, the German Seventh Army headquarters.

During these hectic days, Patton was in near constant motion, unsnarling traffic jams and shaming hesitant officers to keep moving. On one prowl, he appeared before General Robert Grow and his 4th Armored Division staff as they paused with their lead tanks before a small river with a destroyed bridge that they feared was too deep to cross. Patton asserted leadership:

> Grow was not showing any life so I built a fire under him ... I asked him whether he had been down to the river, and he said, 'No'. So I told him that unless he did something, he would be out of a job. I then went down and looked at the river and was not fired at, although you could see a few Germans on a hill ... So I directed the division to advance and cross the river. The fact that the bridge was out didn't matter as the river was not over a foot deep.

Patton's example inspired Grow and thereafter his 'division was one of the boldest in Third Army, but since this was its initiation to battle, it needed just that sort of kick to get it started.'[490] Grow made up for lost time and, worse, Patton's wrath. On 1 August 1944, he raced 4th Armored Division 40 miles to encircle Rennes, the strategic crossroads of eastern Brittany. The 79th Division took the city on 4 August, Grow's 4th Armored Division would become Patton's most effective tank division.[491]

Patton triumphantly noted that by the eighth day of Third Army's offensive,

> the 83rd Division of VIII Corps was in the outskirts of St. Malo. The 6th Armored Division was close to but not in Brest. Dinan had been captured by an infantry combat team of the 8th Division, which then moved on up the Peninsula west of St. Malo to attack Dinard. The 4th Armored Division was in Vanne and was approaching Lorient. The 79th Division was across the river at Laval and the 90th across the river at Mayenne, while the 5th Armored was near Chateau Gontier and reconnaissance elements of another part of the 8th Division were in Chateaubriand.[492]

Patton's corps rapidly captured nearly all their objectives. Middleton's VIII Corps took Vanne on 5 August 1944, St Malo on 17 August, Granville on 2 September and Brest on 19 September. After overrunning Nantes and Angers on 12 August, Walker's XX Corps barreled up the Loire river valley's north side on parallel roads. Haslip's XV's Corps captured Mayenne on 4 August and the strategic crossroads city of Le Mans on 8 August. A key to Third Army's rapid advances was Patton's close coordination with General Otto Weyland's XIX Tactical Air Command whose P-47 Thunderbolts preceded road columns to bomb and strafe any enemy positions. For instance, just on 8 August, XIX Tactical flew 717 sorties and destroyed 29 locomotives, 137 train cars, 205 vehicles and 17 tanks, while gathering vital intelligence of enemy positions and strengths. A report issued on 16 August estimated that XII, XV and XX Corps faced 125,000 troops and 300 tanks while XIII Corps faced 38,330 German troops in Brittany.[493]

Hitler sought to stop Patton by cutting Third Army's supply line. He ordered Kluge to attack Mortain with five Panzer and one Panzergrenadier divisions and punch through to capture Avranches near the coast.[494] From 7 to 13 August 1944, the 30th Infantry Division valiantly staved off that onslaught. Hitler's angrily replaced Kluge with General Walter Model.

Patton anticipated that offensive. On 7 August 1944, his headquarters

> got a rumor last night from a secret source that several panzer divisions will attack west from … Mortain … on Avranches. Personally, I think it is a German bluff to cover a withdrawal, but I stopped the 80th, French 2nd Armored, and 35th in the vicinity of St. Hilaire just in case something might happen.[495]

That pause for three of his divisions is a fine example of Patton's prudence and flexibility that nearly always accompanied his hard driving advances. The key to generalship was reacting decisively to changing circumstances amid the fog of war. He always sought not just to grab any new opportunities but thwart any threats. And thwarting a threat usually led to new opportunities.

Bradley and Patton saw a golden opportunity in all those German troops and tanks attacking Mortain.[496] They worked out a plan with Montgomery for Patton to pivot Haslip's XV Corps north to Argentan where General Henry Crerar's First Canadian Army would join him to cut off the German army's retreat. Later at a press conference, Patton graciously conceded that the strategy did not originate with him, citing: 'Improvisation by General Bradley. I thought we were going east and he told me to go north.'[497]

Secretary of War Stimson was among those dazzled by Third Army's rapid advance west south, east and now north. Anticipating the capture of an entire German army, he wrote to Beatrice a glowing tribute of her husband:

> The attack in which he has been the commander of the leading forces bids fair to result in one of the most decisive victories that the American army has ever achieved, and the daring and energy by which his work has been characterized are so dramatic that they will never be forgotten.[498]

Tragically, that victory was limited rather than decisive. Haislip's XV Corps captured Argentan on 12 August 1944 but Crerar's two armored divisions and two infantry divisions stalled before Falaise 19 miles north. Patton sought Bradley's approval to punch forward to Falaise and sear shut the pocket. Bradley, backed by Eisenhower, refused, fearing that the retreating Germans would overwhelm rather than surrender to those blocking troops. Bradley explained that 'I much preferred a solid shoulder at Argentan to the possibility of a broken neck at Falaise. Patton recalled Haislip's patrols to the boundary and his men began to dig in on the shoulder.'[499]

Patton called General Leven Allen, Bradley's chief of staff, on 13 August 1944, and begged him to get Bradley to let Haslip shut the gap.

Later that day, Bradley did telephone General Frances de Guingand, Montgomery's chief of staff, for permission to redraw the lines so Patton could advance to Falaise. Montgomery refused to cede to Patton a victory that he was incapable of winning himself.[500] Patton later wrote that the halt order

> emanated from 21st Army Group and was either due to [British] jealousy of the Americans or to utter ignorance of the situation or to a combination of the two. It is very regrettable that the XV Corps was ordered to halt, because it could have gone to Falaise and made contact with the Canadians northwest of that point and definitely...closed the escape gap through which the Germans on August 13 were starting to with[draw].[501]

Each of Patton's points was correct.

At Bradley's Twenty-First Army Group headquarters, Major Chester Hansen confided to his diary the politics resolving around Montgomery that tragically shaped Allied strategy at Falaise and numerous other campaigns and battles:

> Montgomery has subscribed to the vice of extreme over-caution and has made the error of many commanders in denying sound tactics for the prestige value of the objective ... However, it would be folly to criticize Montgomery due to his great prestige position among the British and he occupies an almost professional immunity in his position. All of us are anxious that the SHAEF Operational Hqs come in soon and take command of the situation.[502]

As Supreme Commander, Eisenhower could have shifted the army group line to give Falaise to Twenty-First Group but wanted to avoid antagonizing Montgomery who sported two hats as ground commander and Twelfth Army Group commander. Eisenhower delayed establishing his headquarters in France and taking over ground command from Montgomery until 1 September 1944. Until then, Montgomery shamelessly wielded his ground commander authority to defend and enhance his Twenty-First Army Group authority. What Eisenhower did do was finally lift the shroud from Third Army so that Americans and other Allied populations could marvel that Patton rather than Hodges was behind the extraordinary advances over the previous weeks.

Hitler relented to Kluge's pleading and authorized him to withdraw forces from the Falaise gap starting on 14 August 1944. At least 40,000

Germans and perhaps as many as 100,000 streamed eastward from that partly sprung trap; among those who escaped were four of five corps and twelve of fifteen division commanders. Although the Germans left most of their heavy equipment and supplies behind, they would soon be refitted to kill and maim Allied troops on other fronts. First Canadian troops did not link with Third Army troops until 19 August 1944. The victory did result in 10,000 dead Germans, 50,000 captured, and 220 destroyed or captured tanks, 160 armored assault guns, 700 towed cannons, 130 antiaircraft guns and 5,000 motor vehicles, but could have crippled Germany's western front had it bagged those other 40,000 to 100,000 troops.[503]

Patton turned Third Army east and raced it forward. He saw another chance to cut off large numbers of Germans by rapidly advancing XII Corps to Chartres and XX Corps to Dreux, and then curling them north against the German rear. To do so, he needed Bradley's permission, which he got on 14 August 1944. To his diary, he wrote: 'It is really a great plan, wholly my own, and I made Bradley think he thought of it.' Patton immediately ordered his corps commanders to race forward. Then the next day, Bradley

> came down to see me suffering from nerves. There is a rumor, which I doubt, that there are five panzer divisions at Argentan, so Bradley wants me to halt my move … His motto seems to be, 'In case of doubt, halt.' I am complying with the order, and by tomorrow I can probably persuade him to let me advance … I wish I were Supreme Commander.[504]

Although bitter at the latest squandered strategic opportunity, Patton understood the political expedience of crediting Bradley for Third Army's dazzling advances. He generously attributed the 'operations which the Third Army have been fortunate enough to conduct in a successful manner' as

> largely the result of the efforts of General Bradley's Army prior to my arrival on the scene. I was simply fortunate in being able to exploit the successes he had initiated … Our chief success was due to the fact that we cut the armored divisions loose and did not tie them to the infantry. However, we always kept one combat team of infantry motorized so that in the event of a serious situation, they would be available in a few hours to the armored divisions.[505]

Bradley increasingly feared German troops south of the Loire river attacking Third Army's rear echelons north of that river and cutting off the advanced divisions. Patton reassured Bradley that XIX Tactical Air Command was patrolling that flank and the only enemy troops they found and attacked were fleeing eastward to escape being cut off by Third Army. To his staff, Patton insisted that:

> Some goddam fool once said that flanks have got to be secure. Since then sonsofbitches all over the globe have been guarding their flanks. I don't agree with that. My flanks are something for the enemy to worry about, not me. Before he finds out where my flanks are, I'll be cutting the bastard's throat.[506]

Bradley approved Third Army's advance but confined to its designated lane and forbidden to cut north before the Allied armies no matter how many Germans it might bag. Haislip's XV Corps reached Dreux on 17 August 1944, Walker's XX Corps Chartres on 18 August, and Cook's XII Corps Mantes on 19 August. Patton was generally satisfied with all his corps commanders except Cook who was slow and timid; with the excuse of Cook's ill health, Patton replaced him with General Manton Eddy on 19 August.

Bradley diminished the potential power of Third Army's advance for two weeks by refusing Patton's request to transfer 4th Armored Division from VIII Corps to join the eastward surge, worried that remaining pockets of Germans in St Nazaire and L'Orient somehow could attack VIII Corps' infantry divisions. Patton replied that infantry alone could besiege and eventually take those cities; tanks were useless in sieges but priceless in rapid advances.[507] Bradley relented in mid-August and released 4th Armored Division.

Eisenhower deprived Third Army of the chance to liberate Paris. The Parisian underground revolted against German occupation troops led by General Dietrich von Choltitz on 19 August 1944. Originally, Eisenhower wanted to bypass Paris because supplying its 2 million or so inhabitants with food, fuel, and other necessities would drain the Allied advance. But President Roosevelt and Prime Minister Churchill ceded to General Charles de Gaulle's demands that General Philippe LeClerc de Hautclocque's 2nd French Armored Division join forces with the resistance and free Paris. On 23 August 1944, Eisenhower transferred Leclerc's 2nd Armored Division from the Third Army to the First Army since Paris was in the latter's zone. Leclerc's 2nd Armored Division followed by 4th Infantry Division rumbled into Paris on 25 August 1944.

As Patton pushed his corps beyond the Seine, he made his latest brilliant proposal to Eisenhower and Bradley. Third Army should pivot north to cut off German forces defending the Seine river's east bank with

> the XX Corps from Melun and Montereau, the XII from Sens. This could be done faster than anything else. We would initially head toward Beauvais, and could have picked up the 4th Infantry Division, First Army, which was closing on Paris, the 79th Division, also First Army, from Mantes, and possibly the 5th Armored Division. After reaching Beauvais, we could have paralleled the Seine River and opened it to the British and Canadians, and thereafter taken our supplies across at Mantes, saving at least 50 percent of the haul necessary to take them via Montereau.

Patton called this 'the best strategical idea I ever had.'[508]

As they had for Falaise, Eisenhower and Bradley rejected that strategy with the same specious argument that it would trespass into Montgomery's Twenty-First Army Group's zone. To no avail, Patton argued that the point of war is to win as swiftly and cheaply as possible which his plan might do, not sooth the pride of any nation or narcissist.

***

Meanwhile, vital reinforcements joined the Allies on the Western Front. The stalemated, blood-soaked Italian campaign should have convinced Prime Minister Winston Churchill, his Chief of Staff Alan Brooke, and other ranking British commanders that their 'soft underbelly of Europe' strategy was utterly deluded. Instead, Churchill doubled down by pressuring Roosevelt and the American Joint Chiefs of Staff to invade the mountainous Balkans and even the island of Rhodes far in the eastern Mediterranean. If southern Europe occupied by Axis troops had a soft underbelly, it was southern France with mostly relatively flat or undulating ground far beyond the beaches and up much of the Rhone valley. Yet Churchill adamantly opposed Operation Anvil proposed by America's Joint Chiefs of Staff that would land an army on the French Rivera to capture the ports of Toulon and Marseilles, then surge up the Rhone valley into Burgundy to join Allied armies in northern France, ideally cutting off huge numbers of Germans still occupying south-west and central France.

Roosevelt and his chiefs rejected Churchill's proposals as literal and figurative deadends, and instead insisted that Anvil must go forward.[509] Anvil was originally conceived to land the same day as Overlord, but the Anzio landings south-west of Rome on 22 January 1944 consumed so many landing ships and craft that it was postponed. On 14 July 1944, the Combined Chiefs of Staff authorized Anvil, renamed Dragoon, to land on 15 August 1944. Even then Churchill protested and demanded that Anvil instead land in Brittany of all places! Fortunately, Roosevelt, backed by his Joint Chiefs of Staff and most British Joint Chiefs of Staff prevailed.

General Johannes Blaskowitz commanded Army Group G that included the First Army in south-west France and Nineteenth Army in south-east France. After the Normandy landing on 6 June 1944, Hitler had Blaskowitz withdraw ever more divisions to embattled German armies in northern France.

General Jacob Devers Sixth Army Group included General Alexander Patch's Seventh Army and General Jean-Marie de Lattre de Tassigny's First French Army. On 15 August 1944, troops from those two armies packed into 1,370 landing craft and surged ashore at four beaches along a 30 mile stretch of the Riveria with St Tropez central. They faced little resistance and swiftly captured their objectives along with 2,300 Germans while suffering 95 killed and 385 wounded. Within 24 hours, around 60,000 troops and 6,500 vehicles came ashore.

From the beachheads, two giant pinchers emerged. One headed west to capture Toulon on 26 August 1944 and Marseilles on 28 August, then headed up the Rhone valley to take Lyon on 3 September 1944. Meanwhile, the other pushed through the mountains to capture Grenoble on 22 August. The pincers joined to surge north into Burgundy and take Autun on 9 September, Dijon on 10 September and Langres on 13 September. Troops from Patton's Third Army and Lattre de Tassigny's First French Army met near Dijon in Burgundy on 12 September. Allied armies now stretched from the English Channel to Switzerland, a 500-mile front. But the Germans blunted any significant Allied advances on that front for the next five months.

Overlord and Anvil were stunningly successful campaigns. From D-Day to mid-September 1944, 2,168,307 troops and 460,745 vehicles disembarked in Normandy, and 380,000 troops and 69,312 vehicles in the Riveria. The Twenty-First and Twelfth Army groups suffered 224,569 casualties, including 39,961 killed, 164,400 wounded, and 20,124 missing, or around 1 of 10 men, while they inflicted over 300,000 casualties on the Germans and besieged another 200,000 in coastal fortresses. Of Allied losses, 30 per cent were killed, captured, or missing and 70 per cent wounded. Among the wounded, 45 per cent recovered and returned to their units and 11 per cent received light duties within 120 days, while 44 per cent were disabled. The Allies outnumbered the Germans by two and a half to one in cannons and twenty to one in tanks. As for air power, there were 5,059 American bombers, 3,728 fighters and 5,104 British warplanes compared to the Germans with 573 warplanes on the Western Front of 4,507 overall.[510]

Third Army's dash from the Falaise Gap to eastern France devastated and routed German forces in its way. From 28 July to 21 August 1944, Third Army inflicted 108,000 casualties and destroyed or captured 543 tanks and 680 cannons while suffering 15,629 casualties and 227 destroyed tanks and 64 cannons.

8.1 Comparison of Third Army Casualties Suffered and Inflicted, 28 July 1944 – 21 August 1944[511]

	Third Army	German Army
Killed	1,713	11,000
Wounded	7,928	49,000
Missing/Captured	1,702	48,000
Non-Battle	4,286	
Total	15,629	108,000

8.2 Comparison of Third Army and German Force Armor and Artillery Loses, 28 July 1944 – 21 August 1944[512]

Third Army		German Army	
Light Tanks	70	Medium Tanks	269
Medium Tanks	157	Panther or Tiger	174
Artillery	64	Artillery	680

During summer 1944, the Germans unleashed two new revolutionary weapons that forced the allies to shift their war plans.[513] German scientists and engineers pioneered long-range ballistic missiles tipped with explosives. The 27-foot tall V-1 rocket flew 400 miles per hour in a slight arc for 160 miles. The 42-foot tall V-2 rocket shot nearly straight up 2,200 miles per hour 60 miles then plummeted to earth so fast that it exceeded sound until it exploded on the ground.

The Germans launched two V-1s on 13 June 1944, with London the target, and eventually 9,619 others until Allied troops captured the last site within range on 29 March 1945. Of V-1s fired, 2,419 hit the city to kill 6,184 people and wound 17,981. Antwerp was the target for 4,248 V-1s. Anti-aircraft guns or fighter airplanes shot down around 2,200 V-1s. The Germans launched the first V-2 on 7 September 1944, with

Paris the target. Eventually, they fired 1,664 V-2s at Belgium, mostly Antwerp and Liege; 1,402 at Britain, mostly London; 76 at France, mostly Paris; 19 at the Netherlands and 11 at the Ludendorff Bridge spanning the Rhine at Remagen, Germany, after America's First Army captured it. There was no defense against V-2s because of their supersonic speed. The V-1 and V-2 bombardment campaign forced nearly 1.5 million people to evacuate London. They killed 2,754 people and wounded 6,523 in London, and killed 1,736 people and wounded around 4,500 in Antwerp and Liege.

Churchill and Britain's high command naturally wanted a campaign to overrun the V-1 and V-2 launch sites in northern France, and western Belgium and the Netherlands. Capture of that region was already designated for Twenty-First Army Group but overrunning V-1 and V-2 launch made that mission urgent. Montgomery added that to his arguments that Twenty-First Army Group receive priority for increasingly scarce supplies to while the Twelfth and Sixth Army groups stood down.

***

Allied armies in northern France faced a worsening crisis that ironically resulted from their rapid advance and buildup. By 1 September 1944, there were 2,189,307 Allied troops and 460,745 vehicles in 49 divisions and 6 armies in France. During combat a division consumed around 700 tons of supplies daily. Supplies came by ships from ports in Britain or America and were disgorged at Cherbourg and the Normandy beaches where 6,000 trucks called the Red Ball Express carried them to increasingly distant depots eastward. Of course, the Red Ball Express consumed gasoline to deliver gasoline, daily some 300,000 gallons. Around seventy trucks daily wrecked or broke down, and a lack of repair shops along the way caused thousands to be abandoned, with their usable parts and the supplies they carried looted. Around 1,400 3-ton British trucks had flawed pistons that required engine overhauls.[514]

Although a freight train could carry as much as 400 trucks worth of supplies, the Allied bombing campaign had destroyed hundreds of miles of track, hundreds of bridges, stations, and repair facilities, hundreds of locomotives and thousands of cars. Allied command deployed 18,000 workers, including 4,000 prisoners, to rebuild the rail system. By New Years Eve 1944, that effort had reconstructed 11,000 miles of track and 241 bridges.[515]

The most critical shortage was gasoline. The amount brought to France and distributed among the armies fell ever shorter of demand as the front advanced further east and the number of troops and vehicles expanded. The four northern allied armies needed 1.5 million daily gallons and increasingly got dwindling fractions of that. For instance, Third Army consumed from 350,000 to 400,000 gallons daily from 16 August to 2 September 1944, but only received an average 202,382 daily gallons, and only 25,390 gallons that last day.[516] The Pipeline Underwater Transport of Oil (PLUTO) network would eventually include twenty-one pipelines beneath the English Channel linking British and French or Belgian terminals, but the first link was not completed until mid-August.

Corruption compounded the shortages. Criminal groups within the military or civilian contractors stole supplies and sold them on the black market. For instance, around half of the 22 million gasoline cans landed in France were looted from D-Day to mid-September.[517] General John Lee commanded the Allied Services of Supply division, with 8,000 officers and 21,000 enlisted men, renamed the Communication Zone on 7 June 1944. Although Lee claimed to crack down on those thefts, he contributed to the supply drain by maintaining a huge headquarters staff eventually housed at the Hotel Majestic in Paris.

Complicating the supply crisis, another American army squeezed into the line on 5 September 1944, General William Simpson's Ninth Army between General Miles Demsey's Second Army and General Courtney Hodges's First Army. Inexplicably, Eisenhower and the Combined Chiefs of Staff approved creation of that new army with a huge bureaucracy rather than splitting its corps among existing American armies to aggrandize them.

Meanwhile, engineers swiftly cleared mines and sunken ships from Marseilles and Toulon, and supply ships began unloading there on 15 and 20 September 1944, respectively. That enabled General Jacob Devers's Sixth Army Group to enjoy a steady flow via truck convoys and the railroad north from Marseilles and Toulon while Montgomery's Twenty-First and Bradley's Twelfth Army groups competed for a diminishing flow.

Eisenhower moved his headquarters from London to Granville in Normandy on 1 September 1944. There Patton met Eisenhower, Bradley and Hodges on 2 September, and begged the Supreme Commander for enough gas to dash forward and punch through the Siegfried Line before the Germans fully manned it: 'Give me 400,000 gallons of gasoline and I'll put you in Germany in two days.'[518] Eisenhower rejected Patton's plea for Third Army to spearhead the advance. He insisted that his broad front strategy was the best way to victory and 'kept talking about the future great battle of Germany.' Patton tried to 'assure him that the Germans will have nothing left to fight with in Germany if we push now. If we wait there will be a great battle of Germany.'[519] Patton, of course, was prescient.

Time was of the essence. Ahead all along Germany's frontier was the West or Siegfried Line, a dense complex of mine fields, dragoon's teeth, rolls of barbed wire, and pillboxes that engineers had methodically constructed over years.[520] Pillboxes were up to 30 feet wide, 50 feet below ground, 30 feet above ground with exposed sides and roofs eight feet thick, several firing slits for cannons, machine guns and rifles, and usually defended by fifteen soldiers. Patton was determined that Third Army would reach and breach the Siegfried Line before the Germans fully manned it.

Eisenhower did let Patton secure crossings over the Meuse river and advance toward the Siegfried Line. To that end, he allocated Third Army 1,396,710 gallons from 3 to 6 September 1944.[521] Patton ordered XII Corps and XX Corps to race to the Meuse river then the Moselle. XX Corps captured Verdun on the Meuse on 1 September 1944 then pushed on toward Metz on the Moselle. Captured gasoline depots helped fuel Patton's offensive, with the largest 100,000 gallons by XX Corps on 3 September. Then, on 6 September, Eisenhower abruptly shut the gasoline tap. He did so after embracing a bold plan for a single army thrust from usually cautious Montgomery.

Patton later condemned Eisenhower's decision to halt Third Army and funnel nearly all available gas to Montgomery as 'the momentous error of the war.'[522] He lamented that high command had

> lost a victory before winter through their inability to keep us supplied with gasoline ... Ike is all for caution since he has never been to the front and has no feel of actual fighting ... Ike did not thank or congratulate any of us for what we have done.[523]

***

Montgomery's plan, codenamed Market Garden, was for three airborne divisions to land each at a key city with bridges over rivers, General James Gavin's 82nd Airborne Division at Eindhoven at the confluence of the Dommel and Gender rivers, General Mathew Ridgway's 101st Airborne Division at Nijmegen on the Waal and Grave on the Maas, and General Lewis Brereton's British 1st Airborne Division at Arnhem on the Rhine.[524] Meanwhile, General Brian Horrock's XXX Corps of General Miles Demsey's British Second Army would smash through the German lines and thrust up the road linking those cities. Within a week, Montgomery's troops would be across the Rhine river and German forces in his sector split asunder and forced to retreat.

Market Garden could advance Twenty-First Army Group to positions from which other offensives could overrun V-2 sites. Bradley explained the role of V-2s in Eisenhower's decision to approve Market Garden:

> I feel sure that Ike was reluctant to disapprove a plan that might stop the rain of these terror weapons on London. Moreover, at any time these weapons could be directed against our vulnerable supply bases. Finally, there was the human factor. The force of Monty's personality seemed to mesmerize Ike and befuddle his thinking. I think in this instance Ike in part to stroke his ego and keep peace in the family.[525]

Patton and Bradley scorned Montgomery as incapable of realizing his scheme and condemned it as a devious way to divert Twelfth Army Group's scarce gasoline and other supplies to his Twenty-First Army Group. Bradley pointed to

> any number of weaknesses in the plan. The principle was that Monty would be in complete charge. We would be putting all our money on a horse that looked good in the paddock but had a tough time getting out of the starting gate and had never shown well on a fast track. We had well noticed Monty's ponderous build-ups and long delays before mounting an attack, his apparent reluctance to take risks and pursue and exploit (at El Alamein, the Mareth Line, Chott Line, Sicily, Italy, Caen on D-Day, and Falaise Gap). Now he was asking us to believe that he could lead us straight through to Berlin in a single quick dash that would be one of the riskiest maneuvers in the history of warfare.[526]

The strategic priority should have been reopening Antwerp, Europe's largest port. Antwerp was 60 miles from the North Sea, connected by the Scheldt river estuary. The Germans had filled the Scheldt with mines and sunken ships, occupying the islands of Walcheren and South Beveland on the north shore. Antwerp could not reopen until engineers removed the Scheldt's obstructions, and that laborious, dangerous, time-consuming effort could not begin until troops captured Walcheren and South Beveland islands.

Although General Henry Crerar's First Canadian Army captured Antwerp on 4 September 1944, Montgomery failed to order a campaign to capture the Scheldt estuary's northern islands. Indeed, he failed to block Germany's Fifteenth Army from withdrawing 86,000 troops, 600 cannons and 6,000 vehicles from Walcheren and South Beveland Islands by 22 September.[527] Had Montgomery focused on trapping those troops along with 20,000 defenders left behind, he would have scored as decisive a victory as Market Garden became a costly diversion. On the islands, the Germans fended off attacks until the last pocket surrendered on 8 November 1944. The effort to clear the Scheldt estuary was not completed until 28 November, when the first supply ships docked at Antwerp.

Montgomery and his commanders nearly pulled off his plan. The operation unfolded from 17 to 25 September, with 82nd and 101st Airborne divisions capturing their cities and bridges while Horrock's corps fought its way through to them. However, the Germans counterattacked and decimated the 1st British Airborne Division and its remnants eventually withdrew to Horrock's advancing corps. Montgomery's troops punched a bulge in the enemy lines at the cost of 12,000 airborne and 1,500 ground force casualties, 261 aircraft and 658 crewmen shot down and 70 tanks destroyed while inflicting around 6,000 casualties.[528] Atop that, contrary to Montgomery's pledge that Market Garden would lead Twenty-First Army Group toward Berlin, the slender 60 mile salient actually pointed north toward the Netherlands.

For Bradley, the result was a strategic disaster:

> The ultimate cost of Market Garden cannot be measured in casualties alone. It diverted the force, thought, and planning required to open Antwerp at a time when the Scheldt could have been cleared with relative ease. It was a massive assault *in the wrong direction* at what was probably the most crucial moment on the German front, Had all the thought and effort it drained away from our eastern thrust been placed behind Hodges and Patton during the period September 10 to September 20, I am certain that both American armies could have maintained momentum and reached the Rhine River. Had this goal been achieved, we would have been in a far superior position to mount our final offensives on the heartland of Germany and would have been spared the tens of thousands of casualties we suffered to achieve that position.

Ultimately, Bradley blamed Eisenhower for losing that opportunity to shorten the war and Allied losses: 'In permitting Monty to launch Market-Garden, Ike committed his gravest tactical error of the war.'[529]

***

Meanwhile, Patton pushed his commanders to advance as far as they could then defend what they took with everything they had. When Bradley tried to halt him, Patton insisted:

> Don't stop us now, Brad. I'll make a deal with you. If I don't secure a couple of good bridgeheads east of the Moselle by the night of September 14, I'll shut up and assume the mournful role of defender.[530]

Patton was good to his word. Third Army did cross the Moselle river at several points, most vitally in a double envelopment of Nancy that XII Corps captured after a ten-day battle. That was the only significant victory for two months. After dashing 400 miles in August, Third Army battered forward just 25 miles from September through mid-December 1944. Meanwhile, Eisenhower weakened Third Army by transferring VIII Corps to First Army on 3 September, and XV Corps to Seventh Army on 29 September, then tried partly to compensate for those severe losses by assigning Third Army III Corps commanded by General John Milliken on 10 October 1944.

Bradley could have done more to aid Patton's advance but actually undermined it. He divvied Twenty-First Group's gasoline ration to favor plodding Hodge's First Army with 50.1 per cent or half, while sending 27.1 per cent to Patton's Third Army and 22.8 per cent to newcomer Ninth Army led by William Simpson.[531] He approved Hodges's plan to attack Germans defending the Hurtgen Forest, a strategically worthless region but seemingly threatening to nearby Aachen, that First Army had besieged and did not take until 21 October. The battle for the Hurtgen Forest bogged down First Army from 19 September to 16 December 1944, cost 33,000 casualties while inflicting 28,000, and failed to completely drive out the enemy. Bradley called off the campaign when the Germans launched their own offensive that would be called the battle of the Bulge.[532]

Had Bradley instead allocated Third Army half of Twenty-First Group's gasoline rations, Patton's corps would likely have breached the Siegfried Line before it was fully manned. Atop that Bradley acquiesced in Eisenhower's decision to transfer two corps from Third Army. That became the excuse to divert even less gasoline to Third Army thus sapping its power to eliminate nearby enemy positions let alone take strategic ones beyond the horizon.

Nonetheless, Bradley and Patton never worked better together than as the respective commanders of Twelfth Army Group and Third Army. Bradley had opposed Eisenhower's choice for Patton to head Third Army. He detested Patton for all the excesses and follies he committed in Sicily and feared enduring more in northern Europe. To his relief, the punishments that Eisenhower inflicted on Patton for his offenses finally reformed him. Bradley later wrote that

> George soon caused me to repent these uncharitable reservations, for he not only bore me no ill will but he trooped for 12th Army Group with unbounded loyalty and eagerness...we formed as amiable and contented a team as existed in the senior command. No longer the cocky martinet who had strutted around Sicily, George had now become a judicious, reasonable, and likeable commander.[533]

Of course, their common rival Montgomery also bolstered their bond.

Despite its abrupt slowdown, Third Army continued to inflict many times more damage to the enemy than it sustained. From 22 August to 24 September 1944, Patton's troops killed, wounded or captured 106,800 Germans while suffering 29,501 casualties, and destroying or capturing 680 tanks and 1,038 while losing 255 tanks and 39 cannons. Then from 25 September to 21 December 1944, Third Army inflicted 169,000 casualties, including 33,000 killed, 91,000 wounded, and 95,000 captured while suffering 73,830 casualties, including 5,723 dead, 26,985 wounded, 4,601 captured or missing and 36,521 non-combat losses from illness or injury, with trench foot most common.

As if supply shortages were not onerous enough, the weather was atrocious. Rain plagued offensive operations throughout autumn 1944 then turned to snow in the winter. Rivers ran so high, broad and fast that engineers could not bridge them with pontoons. Noncombat losses soared past combat losses. Although various illnesses and increasingly frostbite forced many soldiers temporarily into hospitals, trench-foot from soaked feet inflicted worse losses. On 21 November 1944, Patton issued this memorandum:

> The most serious menace confronting us today is not the German Army, which we have practically destroyed, but the weather which, if we do not exert ourselves, may destroy us through the incidence of trench foot ... To win the war we must conquer trench foot.[534]

He ordered his troops to dry and massage their feet and put on fresh socks as often as possible; they should wash dirty socks in their helmets. That order gave Third Army the lowest trench-foot rate per soldier of the Allied armies. As for total noncombat casualties from 1 September to 16 December 1944, Third Army's 42,088 compared to First Army's 50,867 and Ninth Army's 20,787.[535]

8.3 Comparison of Third Army Casualties Suffered and Inflicted, 22 August 1944 – 24 September 1944[536]

	Third Army	German Army
Killed	2,828	19,800
Wounded	14,790	40,000
Missing/Captured	2,846	47,000
Non-Battle	9,037	
Total	29,501	106,800

8.4 Comparison of Third Army and German Force Armor and Artillery Loses, 22 August 1944 – 24 September 1944[537]

Third Army		German Army	
Light Tanks	70	Medium Tanks	439
Medium Tanks	185	Panther or Tiger	241
Artillery	39	Artillery	1,038

8.5 Comparison of Third Army Casualties Suffered and Inflicted, 25 September 1944 – 21 December 1944[538]

	Third Army	German Army
Killed	5,723	33,000
Wounded	26,985	91,000
Missing/Captured	4,601	95,000
Non-Battle	36,521	
Total	73,830	169,000

8.6 Comparison of Third Army and German Force Armor and Artillery Loses, 25 September 1944 – 21 December 1944[539]

Third Army		German Army	
Light Tanks	58	Medium Tanks	426
Medium Tanks	165	Panther or Tiger	70
Artillery	13	Artillery	498

For Patton, autumn 1944 was the most tedious, frustrating time of the war. Most of Third Army's efforts during that time focused on capturing one place. Metz was Europe's most fortified city with an inner ring of fifteen fortresses and outer ring of twenty-six fortresses, each an elaborate three story concrete complex with one story above ground of interconnected bunkers festooned with revolving turrets slitted for cannons, machine guns and rifles, and two story underground warrens of rooms for supplies, barracks, bathrooms, water reservoirs, hospitals, electricity generators and command posts. Exposed outer walls and ceilings were 3 meters thick. Underground telephone lines connected the fortresses, letting commanders coordinate operations. Patton assigned Walker's XX Corps the mission of capturing Metz.[540] The siege lasted from 27 September to 22 November 1944 when the city's defenders surrendered, although several outlying forts held out until the last gave up on 13 December 1944.

With Metz secure, Patton launched Third Army toward the Sarre river. By 5 December 1944, his troops had captured four beachheads across the Sarre. Beyond was the Palatinate region with the Saar industrial complex, second to the Ruhr in importance for Germany's economy. Patton planned an offensive into the Palatinate region to begin on 18 December 1944. Then an event that Patton had sensed forced him to drastically change his plans.[541]

Chapter 9

ARDENNES

'As usual on the verge of action, everyone felt full of doubt except myself. It has always been my unfortunate role to be the ray of sunshine and the backslapper before action, both for those under me and also for those over me I can say with perfect candor that, at that time, I had no doubt as to the success of the operation.'

'Had the V and VIII Corps of the First Army been more aggressive, the Germans could not have prepared this attack; one must never sit still.'

'War requires the taking of risks and he won't take them ... If I could get more divisions I could win this war now.'

'The Kraut's stuck his head in a meatgrinder. And this time I've got the handle.'

George S. Patton

Patton's mind was as intuitive as it was rational. At times, he sensed things were going to happen before he had any hard evidence that they would. More often than not his gut instincts were prescient. Now he worried when he looked north at the Ardennes Forest, where First Army's VIII Corps of First Army with 68,822 troops in four divisions was spread thin along an 80-mile front. The commander, General Troy Middleton, had ordered his soldiers to dig in, stay warm and rest, assuming that the enemy troops manning the Siegfried Line opposite them were doing the same. Patton had a hunch that the Germans were planning a massive offensive through the Ardennes. On 25 November 1944, he confided to his diary that: 'First Army is making a terrible mistake in leaving VIII

Corps static, as it is highly probable that the Germans are building up east of them.'[542] Patton asked Colonel Oscar Koch, his intelligence chief (G-2), to investigate. Koch and his team compiled two reports that confirmed a German buildup and predicted an attack through the Ardennes. They forwarded the first report to Eisenhower's headquarters on 9 December 1944 and a more extensive report on 13 December, but they were ignored. Patton ordered G-3 Operations Chief Colonel Halley Maddox to prepare two contingency plans for Third Army to pivot north and punch the flank of a German offensive.[543]

The Cassandras were right. Adolf Hitler had mobilized, reinforced and massed before VIII Corps, Sepp Dietrich's Sixth Panzer Army and Hasso von Manteuffel's Fifth Panzer Army that together had 7 armored and 13 infantry divisions with 406,342 troops, 557 tanks, 667 self-propelled guns, 1,261 armored personnel carriers and 4,224 artillery pieces. Among them were Colonel Otto Skorzeny's 2,000-man mechanized regiment for long distance raids; around 150 of his men were fluent in American English, dressed in American uniforms, and given the mission to infiltrate far behind enemy lines to give conflicting orders, conduct sabotage, and assassinate high-ranking commanders including Eisenhower.

The massive assault came early on 16 December 1944 on five east-west roads and swiftly punched through and devastated the four American divisions.[544] The German offensive was no blitzkrieg or lightning war. Icy roads kept tanks and trucks from moving more than 10 miles per hour or else they would slide into off the road or into each other. Nonetheless, the German columns steamrolled slowly forward. At its height, the German bulge was 40 miles wide and 60 miles deep into the Allied line.

***

By chance, Bradley was conferring with Eisenhower at his headquarters at Versailles on 16 December 1944 when they learned of the attack. Bradley assumed it was a limited spoiling attack, but Eisenhower feared it was an all-out offensive. Eisenhower approved Bradley's request to rush the only reserve divisions, both airborne, the 82nd and 101st, by trucks to the front.

Patton's reaction when he learned of the attack was: 'Had the V and VIII Corps of the First Army been more aggressive, the Germans could not have prepared this attack; one must never sit still.'[545] Bradley summoned Patton and his key staff officers to Twelfth Army Group headquarters at Luxembourg on 18 December 1944 and asked him how he could help. Patton promised to dispatch two divisions north the following day and a third division the day after that. After getting of the phone with Bradley, Patton worked with his staff to issue orders implementing that strategy to his three corps commanders, Walton Walker of XX, Manton Eddy of XII and John Milliken of III.

Patton then relocated Third Army's headquarters to Luxembourg to coordinate operations with Bradley's headquarters. Bradley recalled that 'we worked in closest contact and saw each other daily, either at his headquarters or mine. We dined together and planned together. We had never been closer or worked in greater harmony.'[546]

Bradley, Patton, and their respective key advisors met with Eisenhower and his staff at Verdun on 19 December 1944. Eisenhower recalled:

> As the conference started, with everyone around a long table, I remarked: 'The present situation is to be regarded as one of opportunity for us and not of disaster. There is to be only cheerful faces at this conference table.' True to his impulsive nature, General Patton broke out with, 'Hell, let's have the guts to let the — – — go all the way to Paris. Then we'll really cut 'em off and chew 'em up.' Everyone, including Patton, smiled at this one, but I replied that the enemy would never be allowed to cross the Meuse.[547]

Eisenhower told Patton, 'George, I want you to command this move – under Brad's supervision of course – making a strong counterattack with at least six divisions. When can you attack?' Patton promptly replied, 'The morning of December 21, with three divisions.' That stunned Eisenhower who told Patton,

> Don't be fatuous George. If you try to go that early you won't have three divisions ready and you'll go piecemeal. You will start on the twenty-second, and I want your initial blow to be a strong one! I'll even settle for the twenty-third if it takes that long to get three full divisions.

Patton assured Eisenhower that he had already ordered his staff to prepare to pivot Third Army north and attack the German flank. He then explained on a wall map of the region his strategy to shift and initially attack with the 4th Armored, 36th and 80th divisions.[548] Done, he joyfully quipped: 'The Kraut's stuck his head in a meatgrinder. And this time I've got the handle.'[549]

The following day, Patton was with Bradley when he received a call from Eisenhower that infuriated them both:

> He told Bradley that he was putting Monty in operational control of the First and Nineth Armies, due to the fact that telephonic connections between Bradley and those two armies was difficult. As a matter of fact, telephonic communications were all right, and it is either a case of having lost confidence in Bradley or having been forced to put Montgomery in through the machinations of the Prime Minister [Churchill] with the hope that if he gives Monty operational control, he will get some of the British divisions in [the fight]. Eisenhower is unwilling or unable to command Montgomery.[550]

Bradley recalled that:

> This was the darkest of times for me. Giving Monty operational control of my First and Ninth armies was the worst possible mistake Ike could have made. Owing to Monty's caution and conservatism, it practically assured that we would fail to cut off the German salient with a bold thrust from the north. The enemy would escape in force as it had escaped from the Falaise Gap. I prayed for the souls of the dead American GI's, whose stubborn courage had already doomed the German offensive.[551]

Once again, Patton and Montgomery were directly competing to reveal who was the superior general, and once again Patton's brilliance would eclipse Montgomery's dithering. As he had in Sicily and at the Falaise Gap, Montgomery never toed the race line and instead tried to convince Patton to drop out. After talking with him on the phone, Patton told Bradley that

> Monty says that the First Army cannot attack for three months and the only attack that can be made is by me, but I am too weak; hence we should fall back to the Saar-Vosges line or even to the Moselle.[552]

Patton confided his frustrations to his diary:

> If Ike will put Bradley back in command of the First and Nineth Armies, we can bag the whole German army. I wish Ike were more of a gambler, but he is certainly a lion compared to Montgomery, and Bradley is better than Ike as far as nerve is concerned ... Monty is a tired little fart. War requires the taking of risks and he won't take them ... If I could get more divisions I could win this war now.[553]

Patton convened the commanders and staff of his III, XII and XX Corps at Luxembourg on 21 December 1944; although Eisenhower had transferred VIII Corps from First Army to Third Army on 19 December, its staff was too distant to attend. Patton adjusted plans, answered questions, resolved problems, and boosted morale before the attack:

> As usual on the verge of action, everyone felt full of doubt except myself. It has always been my unfortunate role to be the ray of sunshine and the backslapper before action, both for those under me and also for those over me. I can say with perfect candor that, at that time, I had no doubt as to the success of the operation.[554]

Patton's leadership during the battle of the Bulge dazzled Bradley:

> True to his boast at Verdun, Patton, having turned his Third Army ninety degrees, attacked on 22 December. His generalship during this difficult maneuver was magnificent, one of the most brilliant performances by any commander on either side in World War II.[555]

Witnessing how Patton's staff operated changed Bradley's mind:

> Until the Battle of the Bulge I did not share George's enthusiasm for his Third Army staff which, unlike those of both the First and Ninth Armies, lacked outstanding individual performers. Indeed, I had once agreed with the observation of another senior commander who said, 'Patton can get more good work out of a mediocre bunch of staff officers than anyone I ever saw.'[556]

Now Bradley was pleasantly surprised at the speed and efficiency that he observed.

Bastogne was the campaign's key strategic point, located in the Bulge's middle 25 miles west of the Seigfried Line and the hub for seven roads.[557] General Anthony McAuliffe's 101st Airborne Division reached Bastogne the evening of 19 December; his paratroopers and remnants of VIII Corps units numbered around 22,000 troops. General Heinrich von Luttwitz's XLVII Panzer Corps attacked the next day and soon encircled Bastogne. When Luttwitz sent McAuliffe a surrender demand, he famously replied with one word, 'Nuts!' The defenders blunted a series of attacks over several days.

Fourth Armor's advanced units fought their way through the German lines and into Bastogne's defense on 26 December. To Beatrice, Patton boasted that: 'The relief of Bastogne is the most brilliant operation we have thus far performed and is in my opinion the outstanding achievement of this war.'[558] Although that was debatable, Bastogne's relief did shift the battle's momentum. Thereafter the Americans mostly attacked and the Germans mostly defended.

Air power played a crucial role in winning the Battle of the Bulge. The Ninth Air Force took advantage of mostly clear skies from 23 to 31 December 1944, to fly 10,305 sorties and drop 6,969 tons of bombs that destroyed 207 armored vehicles, 2,323 trucks, 173 artillery positions, 620 railroad cars, 45 locomotives, 333 buildings and 7 bridges while losing 158 warplanes.[559] Clear skies also let the air force parachute critically needed supplies into Bastogne, thus enabling McAuliffe's troops to hold out until Patton's rescue.

XIX Tactical Air Force attached to Third Army flew vital reconnaissance, bombing, dogfight and supply missions every good flying day. For instance, on the day 4th Armored Division fought its way into Bastogne, XIX conducted:

> 558 sorties in 59 missions. They dropped 157 tons of bombs, and escorted medium and heavy bombers. They destroyed or damaged 312 motor vehicles, 34 armored vehicles and tanks, 26 gun positions, 61 buildings, 2 bridges, 2 supply dumps, and 83 stacks of ammunition. They also hit three marshalling yards and 14 rail lines. While XIX Tac lost 15 planes, they killed 22 German planes with 1 probable and 11 damaged.[560]

Meanwhile, the Germans pivoted ever more divisions against Third Army, which initially fought three but by 3 January 1945, battled twelve with 93,000 troops and 290 tanks and assault guns.[561] Patton recorded a gamble he made against the advice of his officers that resulted in a victorious battle on 30 December:

> Yesterday my luck held in a big way. I was launching two new divisions, but they were late getting to the assembly area, and every one [*sic*] urged that the attack be suspended. I insisted that they attack if it was only with their advanced guards. They did attack and ran right into the flank of a German attack. Had this not happened, things could have been critical. As it was we stopped the attack in its tracks.

He then honestly and modestly added: 'Historians will claim that such perfect timing was a stroke of jenius. It was just mulishness on my part. I had no idea the Germans were attacking.'[562] That day, he drove to Bastogne to pin the Distinguished Service Cross on General McAuliffe.

Patton issued this congratulatory New Year's proclamation to his troops:

> From the bloody corridor of Avranches, to Brest, thence across France to the Saar, over the Saar into Germany, and now on to Bastogne, your record has been one of continuous victory. Not only have you invariably defeated a cunning and ruthless enemy, but you have also overcome by your indomitable fortitude every aspect of terrain and weather ... The speed and brilliancy of your achievements is unsurpassed in military history.[563]

Later that day in a press conference at Luxembourg, he outlined his operations to the reporters then explained that

> sounds like what a great man George Patton is, but I did not have anything to do with it. I told [Chief of Staff] Gay and the staff, and they got the orders out. The people who actually did it were the younger officers and soldiers. When we think of those men marching all night in the cold, over roads they had never seen, and nobody getting lost and everybody getting to the place in time, it is a very marvelous feat. I know of no equal in military history...I take off my hat to them.[564]

As usual, Patton overcame numerous command problems in daily visits to stretches of the front. One day,

> I noticed another instance of the complete incapacity of inexperienced officers. Several ordnance trailers, each loaded with between 40 and 50 replacements ... were stuck on a slippery hill and not moving. There were a number of officers present, but none of them had enough sense to make the men dismount and push the vehicles until [Major Alexander] Stiller and I did so. Then the trucks got moving again.[565]

Yet, while Third Army's relentless attacks punched back the Germans the campaign was far from over. Bradley and Montgomery agreed for Third and First armies to join forces at Houffalize, the bulge's midsection. Patton disagreed with that plan, arguing instead that the two American armies should cut off the Germans at the Bulge's base. Eisenhower backed Montgomery and Bradley in rejecting that proposal. Patton confided to his diary that

> I want to attack to the north from Dietrich but Bradley is all of putting new divisions in the Bastogne fight. In my opinion, this is throwing good money after bad. In this weather, on the defensive, the Germans can hold us well enough so that we can never trap them there, whereas if we attack close to the base [of the Bulge], they will have to pull out and we will regain ground and probably catch ... many Germans.[566]

As with Messina and Falaise, Patton fulfilled his mission while Montgomery's turtle-like advance let most Germans escape. The two armies did not sear shut the bulge at Houffalize until 16 January 1945, one month after the Germans launched their offensive.

***

The Battle of the Bulge was not just the war's bloodiest for Americans, it inflicted one of ten casualties that the United States suffered during the entire war. The Americans endured 80,987 casualties, including 4,138 dead, 20,231 wounded and 16,946 missing from 16 December 1944 to 2 January 1945, and 39,672 casualties, including 6,138 dead, 27,262 wounded and 6,272 missing from 3 to 28 January 1945. Third Army suffered 50,630 casualties including 4,447 dead, 20,185 wounded, 3,228 missing and 22,770 noncombat casualties from 22 December 1944 to 29 January 1945. Estimates of German losses ranged from 81,834 to 103,900, with the Germans and Allies respectively citing those figures. At the very least, the Germans lost 12,642 dead, 38,600 wounded and 30,582 missing. Patton's Third Army recorded the higher figure of 103,990 including 24,200 killed, 63,200 wounded and 16,400 prisoners.[567]

9.1 Comparison of Third Army Casualties Suffered and Inflicted, 23 December 1944 – 29 January 1945[568]

	Third Army	German Army
Killed	4,447	29,700
Wounded	20,185	82,800
Missing/Captured	3,226	23,000
Non-battle	22,770	N/A
Total	50,626	135,500

9.2 Comparison of Third Army and German Force Armor and Artillery Loses, 23 December 1944 – 29 January 1945[569]

Third Army		German Army	
Light Tanks	72	Medium Tanks	322
Medium Tanks	264	Panther or Tiger	226
Artillery	28	Artillery	310

Strategically, the Bulge was a disaster for Germany both for the remaining war months and postwar decades. By massing and hurling all those troops and tanks against the western front, Hitler's weakened his Eastern Front. Had Hitler instead launched those two Panzer armies against the Red Army, he might have delayed the Soviet advance for months. That would have empowered the western Allies to drive east to liberate most of Germany, Austria and Czechoslovakia. At the Yalta summit in February 1945, that would have strengthened the diplomatic hands of Roosevelt and Churchill to insist on post-war occupation zones much further east, perhaps with just a token Soviet presence in Berlin and eastern Germany. That in turn would have given Western Civilization a vast strategic and political edge over the Soviet Union during the subsequent Cold War.

Although Allied victory in the Bulge was inevitable, how, when, and at what cost had many variants. For instance, the Germans missed capturing 2.5 million gasoline gallons at a depot outside of Stavelot on 17 December 1944. Had they seized that fuel the battle probably would have lasted longer with worse casaulties. The furthest German advance was 2nd Panzer Division to Celles 60 miles from the Siegfried Line starting point when they literally ran out of gas. First Army's 2nd Armored Division attacked and devastated 2nd Panzer Division on 25 December 1944. That battle might have gone the other way or lasted longer if German amor and truck gas tanks were full rather than empty. Then again, when Eisenhower learned of that loss he undoubtedly would have ordered bombers to destroy it on the first good flying day, which was 23 December 1944. That in turn would have slowed the advance of American forces that otherwise would have used that gasoline.

The Bulge's most haunting what if was Eisenhower embracing rather than rejecting Patton's plan to attack the German offensive's starting point rather than midsection and tip. That would have bagged more Germans sooner with fewer American casualties than what happened. A related question was Eisenhower letting Bradley alone direct the battle rather than split Twelfth Army Group between him and Montgomery south and north of the Bulge. Bradley would likely have accepted Patton's pleas and launched First Army a week earlier at the German starting line rather than midsection.

For the Bulge, Eisenhower sacrificed 'command unity' on the altar of 'allied unity', and in doing so inflicted on American forces countless unnecessary lost lives, opportunities, and time. As usual, he knuckled under to the demands of Montgomery, a plodding general but skilled, charismatic political fighter rather than the pleas of Patton, the war's most brilliant Allied general.

Typically, all along Montgomery shamelessly hogged credit for any advances and victories even though his timidity and tardiness when directing America's First Army delayed and diminished them. During a 7 January 1945 news conference, he paraded these blatant falsehoods:

> General Eisenhower put me in charge of the whole Northern front. I employed the whole available power of the British Group of Armies ... and today British divisions are fighting hard on the right flank of First U.S. Army. You thus have the picture of British troops fighting on both sides of American forces who have suffered a hard blow ... The battle has been most interesting; I think one of the most interesting and tricky battles I have ever handled, with great issues at stake.[570]

Atop that, Montgomery persisted in badgering Eisenhower to make him the western front's ground commander.

Those words enraged Patton and Bradley along with virtually anyone else who knew the true story. As Twelfth Army Group commander, Bradley conveyed to Eisenhower the collective disgust of his officers and enlisted men for Montgomery's lies and insults to America's soldiers. He warned: 'I cannot serve under Montgomery. If he is to be put in command of all ground forces, you must send me home.' He added that Patton would also resign if forced to serve under Montgomery.[571]

Eisenhower later wrote, 'This incident caused me more distress and worry than did any similar one of the war.' He assuaged some of the rancor by not naming Montgomery ground commander and by returning First Army to Bradley's Twelfth Army Group on 17 January 1945, although he did let Twenty-First Army Group keep Simpson's Ninth Army. He had a long talk with Churchill who agreed that Montgomery's remarks were unjust and must be corrected. In the House of Commons on 9 January 1945, Churchill declared:

> I have seen it suggested that the terrible battle which has been proceeding ... on the American front is an Anglo-American battle. In fact ... United States troops have done almost all the fighting ... Care must be taken in telling our proud tale not to claim for the British Army an undue share of what is undoubtedly the greatest American battle of the war.[572]

Montgomery's latest grandstanding and deceptions were just one reason the victory was bittersweet for Patton. He privately griped that 'Courtney Hodges and Omar Bradley got a DSM for their unsuccessful defense of the Bulge and I did not get one for successfully defending it.'[573] But Patton swiftly put that hurt behind him. Third and First Armies had eliminated the German bulge between them. Now they had to turn back eastward and somehow smash through the Siegfried Line.

Chapter 10

ACROSS GERMANY

'Have taken Trier with two divisions.

What do you want me to do, give it back?'

'Brad, for God's sake tell the world we're across ... I want the world to know that Third Army made it before Monty.'

'I think history will answer that for you.'

George S. Patton

As 1945 opened, Allied forces on the Western Front numbered seventy-three divisions including forty-nine American, twelve British, eight French, three Canadian, one Polish and forty-nine infantry, twenty armored and four airborne, with around 2 million troops overall. Two months later reinforcements swelled Allied forces to ninety-one divisions including twenty-five armored divisions and 2.5 million troops. The Germans numbered about 1 million troops.[574]

The question for Allied commanders, of course, was what to do with all their military might against the Third Reich. To determine that 'broad front' and 'narrow front' strategy devotees fought their latest tug-of-war. General Dwight D. Eisenhower, backed by President Franklin D. Roosevelt and the American Joint Chiefs of Staff, wanted each Allied army to keep attacking enemy forces before it to stretch the Germans to the snapping point and rapidly exploit any breakthroughs. The broad front strategy was largely risk free as long as each army received the reinforcements and supplies it needed. General Bernard Montgomery, backed by Prime Minister Winston Churchill, Chief of Staff Alan Brooke, General Harold Alexander and most British Joint Chiefs of Staff advocated a narrow front strategy that let Montgomery's

Twenty-First Army Group receive overwhelming land and air power to cross the Rhine river and drive toward Berlin while the American armies played merely supporting roles. Patton also favored a narrow front strategy, but with Third Army dashing toward Berlin. Either narrow front strategy risked being hemmed in and contained by converging German forces, as happened to Montgomery during his Market Garden campaign from 17 to 25 September 1944.

Atop the narrow front strategy, the British insisted that Montgomery take over from Eisenhower the role of 'ground commander' to direct all three army groups. As ground commander, Montgomery would shamelessly divert the lion's share of resources to his own Twenty-First Army Group while sidelining Twelfth and Sixth Army groups.

The latest battle over these conflicting strategies and commands came during a summit between Roosevelt and Churchill along with the Combined Chiefs of Staff in Malta from 30 January to 2 February 1945. Eisenhower did not attend because he was too busy fulfilling duties at his headquarters, recently moved to Rheims, France. But Secretary of War Henry Stimson was there alongside Army Chief of Staff George Marshall. The meeting was supposed to forge a consensus before the pending summit among Roosevelt, Churchill and Joseph Stalin with their respective chiefs of staff at Yalta, but the strategy and command disputes consumed the most time. Stimson and Marshall were concerned that Eisenhower had recently waffled on his broad front strategy by allocating disproportionate resources to Montgomery's Twenty-first Army Group. After a long talk with Marshall, Stimson wrote that:

> I myself have been worried lest he [Eisenhower] lose sight of the necessity of supporting sufficiently our national goals view where they were at variance with the British. That was the reason why I favored the appointment of Marshall for this European command ... but with Marshall's vigorous interposition at this conference he seems to have readjusted the balance and give [Eisenhower] a healthy boost.[575]

After Eisenhower sent word that he again upheld in principle the broad front strategy, Roosevelt promptly approved followed reluctantly by Churchill. The Americans also adamantly rejected the British proposal to replace Eisenhower with Montgomery as ground commander. To pressure Roosevelt to hold firm, Marshall actually threatened to resign if the president ceded that authority.

After their Malta summit, Roosevelt and Churchill flew with their respective entourages in separate planes to Yalta while support teams arrived by ship. America's delegation numbered 330, including 14 generals. During the conference from 4 to 11 February 1945, the Big Three made crucial decisions for ending the war and determining the post-war international order.

Naturally the Soviets had a vital interest in spreading their communist empire as far westward as possible, while the Americans and British had an even more vital interest in containing that inevitable advance as far east as possible. Boots on the ground were crucial in determining just where the frontiers would be formally drawn once the shooting stopped. And for that, the Soviet currently had an enormous advantage.

Stalin's hard power overshadowed the summit. When 1945 dawned, the Red Army's 2 million troops were mostly along a north-south line through central Poland on the Vistula river and through eastern Hungary, Romania and Bulgaria. On 17 January 1945, the Red Army began an offensive that devastated German forces before them, captured Warsaw, and crossed the Vistula at many places. When the Yalta conference began, the Red Army had advanced 100 miles to the Oder river just 40 miles east of Berlin.

Meanwhile, the Western Front remained west of the Rhine river with a couple of hundred miles separating the nearest Allied troops from Berlin. The Red Army's overrun of eastern and central Germany, including Berlin along with Austria, Czechoslovakia and Hungary appeared just a matter of weeks. The Soviet's 180 divisions vastly outnumbered the German's 80 divisions and enjoyed overwhelming advantages of 7 to 1 in tanks, 11 to 1 in infantry, and 20 to 1 in artillery.[576]

Stalin made a series of 'concessions' that either advanced Soviet interests or he had no intention of fulfilling. He promised 'free elections' for all the eastern European countries that the Red Army had 'liberated'. Actually, one by one, the communists imposed dictatorships in each of those countries. Roosevelt sought Stalin's firm promise to join the war against Japan three months after Germany's defeat. Although Stalin played hard to get, he was actually eager for the Red Army to expand the Soviet empire and sphere of influence in north-east Asia. He agreed to war against Japan in return for Japan's Kurile Islands and Sakhalin Island's southern half. He cynically recognized Chiang Kai-shek's Nationalist regime in Chungking rather than Mao Zedong's communist regime in Yanan as China's legitimate government, while he would give captured Japanese war supplies to the communists warring against the nationalists for power. Stalin agreed that France could have an occupation zone in Germany and Berlin as long as it came from the American and British zones. Stalin wanted United Nations memberships for all fifteen Soviet 'republics', which were actually satellites of Stalin's communist tyranny. Roosevelt and Churchill agreed to three seats for Russia, Ukraine and Belorussia. Stalin demanded $1 billion in annual reparations from Germany. Roosevelt and Churchill reluctantly agreed to $2 billion in total reparations while declining taking any for their own countries. The Big Three signed the 'Declaration on Liberated Europe' that promised 'a world order under law' and 'the right of all peoples to choose the form government under which they will live.'

As for Germany's occupation zones, the European Advisory Commission of American, British and Soviet envoys had split the county and Berlin into three with Berlin located in the Soviet zone. The understanding was that the Western and Eastern Allied armies would advance at different speeds to eventually destroy the Third Reich between them. With victory, the armies would advance or withdraw as necessary into their respective zones.

The summit ended with Stalin exultant at all his gains while Roosevelt and Churchill were fatalistic that they had taken and given what was necessary. They sharply differed over whether they believed Stalin would fulfill his promises, with Roosevelt optimistic and Churchill pessimistic. Churchill's gloomy forecast was prescient.

***

Meanwhile, the race among the Allied army commanders to get to and over the Rhine river shifted.[577] Eisenhower finally succumbed on 10 February 1945 to Montgomery's incessant demands that his Twenty-first Army Group be given all needed land and air power for a massive offensive that crossed the Rhine river and drove toward Berlin, while the American armies stood still. Montgomery would spend the next five weeks planning and massing forces and supplies for his operation, codenamed Operation Plunder.

Patton was determined that Montgomery, backed by Eisenhower, was not going to straitjacket the Americans to a supporting role in crossing the Rhine and overrunning Germany. He confided to his diary that:

> It is essential to get the First and Third Armies so deeply involved in their present plans that they cannot be moved north to play second fiddle to the British instilled idea of attacking with 60 divisions on the Ruhr plain.[578]

Fortunately, Bradley fully backed Patton on this.

Patton devised a two phase strategy to advance to the Rhine river. The first phase involved overrunning the Eifel region, starting by capturing the key crossroads towns of Prum and Bitburg on the Siegfried Line, then surging into the Moselle Valley from Trier to Koblenz at the confluence with the Rhine river. In the second phase, Third Army would cross the Moselle behind the Siegfried Line, overrun the Palatinate region, and capture Mannheim and Worms on the Rhine river.

Patton was not just adept at exploiting enemy mistakes, weaknesses and setbacks. Eisenhower had allocated the capture of the Saarland or Palatinate region south of the Moselle river and east of the Saar river to Sixth Army Group's Seventh Army led by General Alexander Patch. When the Germans blunted Seventh Army's attacks, Patton sought that mission for Third Army. He wrote to Bradley on 19 February 1945, requesting reinforcements and permission to launch an offensive toward the Rhine river through the Saar-Moselle pocket. When he received no reply, Patton tried telephoning Bradley but was told he was out. Finally, Patton met Bradley to make his case, and found him 'very tired … and not at all sure of himself. I asked definitively if there was any objection to my making a run for Coblenz ahead of time and of taking Cologne if opportunity suddenly developed.'[579] Bradley wearily agreed and transferred 10th Armored to Third Army.

Patton recalled that

> one of the luckiest things that ever happened to me was the failure of the Sixth Army Group to do this because through the retention of the Moselle-Saar Triangle, the Third Army was able to capture Trier and start the attack through the Palatinate. At the time, however, I was very bitter. This is another example of the many times I have encountered in life where great disappointments have proved to be the road to future success.[580]

At times, Patton's subconscious bolstered his reason in determining his war plans. When an attack by 11th Armored and 4th Infantry divisions stalled before Prum, he stewed over what to do before wearily falling asleep then:

> I awoke at 0300 [am] on the morning of the sixth [of February 1945] with the complete plan for a breakthrough by the VIII and XII Corps in my head … Whether these tactical thoughts of mine are the result of inspiration or insomnia, I have never been able to determine, but nearly every tactical idea I have ever had has come into my head full-born, much after the manner of Minerva from the head of Jupiter.[581]

All along Patton's troops endured enemy fire, heavily defended fortified positions, and miserable cold rainy weather. Patton marveled that:

> crossing ... over these rivers was a magnificent feat of arms. The rivers were in flood to such an extent that the barbed wire along the Siegfried Line, which abutted the rivers, was under water, and when the men disembarked from the boats, they were caught in it. The whole hillside was covered with German pillboxes and barbed wire. A civilian observer told me afterward that he did not see how human beings could be brave enough to succeed in such an attack. Actually the audacity of the attack and the strength of the position materially aided in our successes.[582]

Combat teams of troops with varied skills became adept at systematically destroying Siegfried Line defenses and their defenders. Patton explained how

> the 90th Division alone put out one hundred and twenty pillboxes in about forty-eight hours, with the loss of less than one hundred and twenty men. This feat was accomplished by careful reconnaissance, then smothering the embrasures with machine-gun and rifle fire, and using dynamite charges against the back door, or else by using self-propelled 155mm guns at short range. At three hundred yards the 155mm shell will remove a pillbox for every round fired.[583]

Patton launched Walker's XX Corps, spearheaded by borrowed 10th Armored Division, toward Trier. By 27 February 1945, 10th Armored Division had fought its way within half a dozen miles of Trier. Patton phoned Bradley and begged him to retain 10th Armored Division for a few more days even though he was supposed to return it to Seventh Army at midnight. Bradley agreed. The following day, 10th Armored Division barged into the city with two columns, each aimed a bridge over the Moselle. The Germans blew up one bridge but the Americans captured the other. On the morning of 1 March 1945, Patton arrived to oversee 10th Armored Division as it cleared the far bank of enemy troops. As he did so he received a message from Eisenhower's headquarters ordering him to bypass Trier if he needed four divisions to capture it. Patton replied, 'Have taken Trier with two divisions. What do you want me to do, give it back?'[584]

Third Army's 4th Armored Division reached the Rhine river a few miles north of Coblenz on 7 March 1945. Learning of that event, Seventh Army commander General 'Sandy' Patch telephoned Patton with these opening words: 'Georgie, This is Sandy. Let me be the first to congratulate you on being the last to reach the Rhine!' Patton shot back: 'Sandy, let me be the last to congratulate you on being the first to be driven from the Rhine.'[585]

By 13 March 1945, Third Army had overrun a wedge of Saarland down the Moselle river to Coblentz on the Rhine river and along the Rhine as far north as Andernach. Patton then pivoted most of Third Army south-east to cross the Moselle river at half a dozen points and dash through the Siegfried Line's rear. He sent 4th Armored Division toward Mainz, 11th Armored Division toward Worms and 10th Armored Division toward Kaiserslautern. On 20 March 1945, 4th Armored Division captured Worms while 11th Armored Division and 90th Infantry Division captured Mainz on the Rhine river. Other divisions along with truck borne landing craft and pontoon bridges swelled Third Army's riverside ranks. Patton issued this celebratory proclamation to his troops: 'In the period from 29 January to 23 March [1945], you have wrested 6,484 square miles of territory from the enemy' and

> have captured 140,122 enemy soldiers and have killed or wounded an additional 99,000, thereby eliminating practically all the German Seventh and First Armies. History records no greater achievement in so limited a time.[586]

10.1 Comparison of Third Army Casualties Suffered and Inflicted, 30 January 1945 – 21 March 1945[587]

	Third Army	German Army
Killed	4,570	30,300
Wounded	21,193	75,000
Missing/Captured	3,181	69,900
Non-Battle	23,979	
Total	52,923	175,200

10.2 Comparison of Third Army and German Force Armor and Artillery Losses, 30 January 1945 – 12 March 1945[588]

Third Army		German Army	
Light Tanks	14	Medium Tanks	87
Medium Tanks	66	Panther or Tiger	335
Artillery	14	Artillery	284

To Patton's chagrin, Third Army was not first across the Rhine. On 7 March 1945, First Army's Ninth Armored Division captured the Ludendorff Bridge at Remagen, the last bridge standing. As they had at all other bridges over the Rhine river, the Germans had rigged explosives to detonate when the enemy approached. However, this time, although the explosives ignited they were not strong enough to destroy the bridge. Hodges rushed divisions to reinforce troops already across the Rhine river and expand the bridgehead and construct eight pontoon bridges up and down river from Ludendorff Bridge.

The question for Patton was where to cross the Rhine river. He chose the town of Oppenheim, 8 miles upstream from Mainz. The opposite shore was open, flat and lightly defended. He assigned that operation to General Safford Irwin's 5th Infantry Division. On the night of 22 March 1945, Irwin sent across 6 battalions in 500 assault boats to secure a 1-mile-long stretch of river bank and push 1 mile inland. The operation cost 5th Division only twenty-eight dead and wounded.

Patton telephoned Bradley and excitedly told him the news. Bradley recalled their exchange:

> 'Brad, don't tell anyone but I am across.' I gulped and replied, 'Well, I'll be damned. You mean across the Rhine?' He went on: 'Sure am. I sneaked a division over last night. But there are so few Krauts around they don't know yet. So don't make any announcement. We'll keep it a secret until we see how it goes.'… I authorized Patton to put ten divisions in the Oppenheim bridgehead. Later that evening, when Patton was absolutely certain that his foothold across the Rhine was firm, he telephoned again. 'Brad,' he shouted, his high pitched voice full of triumph, 'for God's sake tell the world we're across … I want the world to know that Third Army made it before Monty starts across.'[589]

Patton had his liaison officer at Bradley's headquarters ensure that the press release announcing that Third Army had crossed the Rhine river include this line: 'Without benefit of aerial bombardment, ground smoke, artillery preparation, or airborne assistance.'[590] That was a clear jab at Montgomery's pending massive assault nearly two months in planning.

Patton beat Montgomery across the Rhine by one day. Montgomery naturally gave Demsey's British Second Army the glory of crossing the Rhine river, while Crerar's First Canadian and Simpson's American Ninth solely played supporting roles. He minutely planned his latest massive offensive designed to steamroll the enemy. From 11 to 21 March 1945, heavy bombers dropped 50,000 tons of bombs and fight-bombers flew 7,311 stories. Two Airborne divisions – the British 6th and the American 17th – dropped behind enemy lines. Montgomery's 24 March 1945 crossing involved 1,034 cannons each firing 600 rounds over 5.5 hours as 250,000 troops in 6 infantry divisions, 3 armored divisions, 6 independent brigades reached the Rhine's eastern bank. The airborne troops suffered 2,700 casualties and 79 shot down planes but took 3,500 prisoners. Over the next two days, Crerar's First Canadian and Simpson's Ninth armies also crossed the Rhine river. Twenty-First Army Group troops inflicted around 16,000 casualties, mostly prisoners while the British and Americans respectively suffered around 3,900 and 2,800 casualties.[591]

Meanwhile, Third Army's 7,500-man engineer corps built the first of 6 pontoon bridges across that stretch of Rhine river. Over the next days, the rest of 5th Division rumbled across followed by 90th Division. As some brigades pushed inland others raced up or down the east river bank to secure other landing and pontoon bridge sites for other divisions impatiently waiting on the west bank. Ever more Third Army divisions rumbled across those bridges and arched toward the next river barrier, the Main, with Frankfurt 20 miles from its confluence with the Rhine river. Spearheading the advance, 4th Armored Division captured three bridges across the Main river on 25 March 1945. Patton and Bradley secured Eisenhower's approval for a plan whereby First and Third armies met in a pincher at Kassel, 140 miles from Dusseldorf on the Rhine river to trap and capture 317,000 Germans in that pocket by 18 April 1945.

***

Patton learned about a German prisoner-of-war camp with 800 or 900 inmates 60 miles east of Frankfort at Hammelburg, where his son-in-law Lieutenant Colonel John Waters was likely held; the actual number was 1,291 prisoners. He conferred with with generals Manton Eddy and William Hoge, who respectively commanded XII Corps and 4th Armored Division, about diverting troops to liberate that camp. Patton initially wanted to send a combat command of around 4,000 troops and 150 tanks to liberate the prisoners, 'but, unfortunately, was talked out of it by Eddy and Hoge ... so I compromised by sending one armored company and one company of armored infantry.'[592] That task force, commanded by Captain Abraham Baum, included just 307 troops in ten Sherman tanks, 6 light tanks, 27 halftracks, 7 jeeps, 3 motorized assault guns and a cargo carrier. That turned out to be a fatal military decision. A political problem was that Hammelburg was not in Third Army's zone, but in Seventh Army's.

Patton's gamble troubled him. He wrote to Beatrice that:

> Last night I sent an armored column to a place 40 miles east of Frankfort where John and some 900 prisoners are said to be. I have been nervous as a cat all day as every one [*sic*] but me thought it too great a risk … If I lose that column it will possibility be a new incident, but I won't lose it.[593]

The task force fought a series of skirmishes with scattered German forces all the way to the camp and there Baum tried to negotiate with the camp's commander its surrender. Waters was among three American officers who approached their liberators. A nervous German guard fired at Waters and a bullet sliced through his leg into his backside and clipped his spine. Then overwhelming numbers of German troops and tanks converged on the task force, and devastated it, killing 32 and wounding and capturing 256 others, while just a dozen or so escaped.

Patton learned the raid's fate on 30 March 1945, when German radio reported that the entire column had been killed or captured. Patton confided to his diary that:

> So far I have only made one mistake, and that was when I lost two companies of the 4th Armored Division in making the attack on Hammelburg. I made it with only two companies on account of the strenuous objections … to making any [effort] at all. Had I sent a combat command as I first intended to do, this mistake would not have occurred.[594]

He did not learn Water's fate until 4 April 1945, when three prisoners who escaped reached American lines. With mingled relief, guilt and fear, he wrote in his diary that:

> Johnny Waters … had been badly wounded and recaptured. Apparently the wound is serious but not dangerous … Seventh Army will probably relieve [capture] the camp today or tomorrow. I felt very gloomy … that I may have caused Waters' death, but I believe that I did the right thing, and I certainly could never have lived with myself had I known that I was within 40 miles of 900 Americans and not made an attempt to rescue them.[595]

Patch's 14th Armored Division liberated the camp on 5 April 1945.

Eisenhower wearily informed Marshall of Patton's latest 'incident':

> He sent a little expedition on a wild goose chase in an effort to liberate some American prisoners. The upshot was that he got 25 prisoners back and lost a full company of medium tanks. Foolishly, he then imposed censorship on the movement, meaning to lift it later which he forgot to do ... One bad, though Patton says accidental, feature of the affair was that his own son-in-law was one of the 25 released. Patton is a problem child, but he is a great fighting leader in pursuit and exploitation.[596]

Patton, Eisenhower and Bradley spent their most emotionally wrenching day of the war together on 12 April 1945. Patton had invited them to join him to tour Germany's gold reserve hidden in a vast underground potassium mine near Merkers that Third Army troops had discovered on 6 April 1945. As the elevator carried them down nearly 2,000 feet of cable to the floor, Patton quipped,

> If that clothesline should part, promotions in the United States army would be considerably stimulated.' Eisenhower replied, 'O.K. George, that's enough. No more cracks until we are above ground again.'[597]

The elation they felt at seeing all those gold bars piled to the ceiling transformed into revulsion and hatred for Nazi Germany during their next stop, the Ohrdruf Nord concentration camp. Patton vomited at the sight of skeleton like bodies of the dead and dying, and the stench. He later wrote Beatrice that:

> Yesterday I saw the most horrible sight I have ever seen. It was a German slave camp. We took all the soldiers we could to see it, as I believe it is one of the best arguments against fraternization that I know.[598]

They retired to Patton's headquarters. Eisenhower recalled that

> the day ... ended on a note of dramatic climax. Bradley, Patton, and I sat up late talking of future plans ... We went to bed just before twelve o'clock, Bradley and I in a small house at Patton's headquarters, and he in his trailer. His watch had stopped, and he turned on the radio to get the time signals from the British Broadcasting Corporation. While doing so he heard the news of President Roosevelt's death. He stepped back into the house ... We pondered ... the effect the president's death might have upon the future peace ... [W]e were doubtful that there was any other individual in America as experienced as he in the business of dealing with the other Allied political leaders. [I]t seemed to us, from

> the international viewpoint, to be a most critical time to be forced to change national leaders. We went to bed depressed and sad.[599]

President Harry S. Truman did not impress Patton who lamented 'that in order to secure political preference, people are made Vice Presidents who were never intended, neither by Party nor by the Lord to be Presidents.'[600] Patton's view of Truman soon changed. The new president promoted him to lieutenant general on 14 April 1945, two days after taking the oath of office. Truman further impressed Pattons as he upheld Roosevelt's global war strategy, stood up to Soviet tyrant Stalin during the Potsdam summit, and ordered the atomic bombings of Hiroshima and Nagasaki that forced Japan's government to surrender.

A few days later, Patton accompanied Eisenhower to Buchenwald concentration camp but could not complete the visit. Eisenhower described what he witnessed:

> The visual evidence and the verbal testimony of starvation, cruelty, and bestiality were so overpowering as to leave me a bit sick. In one room where there were piled twenty or thirty naked men, killed by starvation. General Patton would not even enter. He said he would get sick if he did.[601]

As victory increasingly appeared just a matter of weeks, Patton was determined not to rest on his brilliant laurels but win ever more. He wrote to Army Chief of Staff George Marshall that:

> When the operations in Germany are brought to a successful conclusion, I should like to be considered for any type of combat command from division up against the Japanese. I am sure my method of fighting would be successful. I also am of such an age that this is my last war, and I would like to see it through to the end.[602]

Patton's exhilaration at his army's rapid advance swelled as each day they racked up more captured enemy soldiers, equipment, supplies, towns and cities. In his exuberance, he tried talking Eisenhower into letting him race Third Army to Berlin via Leipzig and taking it before the Soviets did. Patton's chief of staff, General Hobart Gay, recorded this exchange between them over Berlin. Eisenhower explained that:

> From a tactical point of view, it is highly inadvisable for the American army to take Berlin, and he hoped political influence would not cause him to take the city. It had no tactical or strategical value, and would

> place upon American forces the burden of caring for thousands and thousands of Germans, displaced persons, [and] Allied prisoners of war.

To that, Patton retorted: 'Ike, I don't see how you figure that one. We had better take Berlin quick, and [then go eastward] on to the Oder [river].' Eisenhower replied, 'Well, who wants it.' Patton placed his hands on Eisenhower's shoulders, looked into his eyes, and stated, 'I think history will answer that for you.'[603]

Until early 1945, Eisenhower had agreed that Berlin was the ultimate objective. In doing so, he followed guidelines issued by his commander-in-chief and the Combined Chiefs of Staff. In November 1943, President Roosevelt let his subordinate commanders know that he anticipated and welcomed 'a race for Berlin' in which '[w]e may have to put United States divisions into Berlin as soon as possible.' The Combined Chiefs of Staff issued that goal as a directive in February 1944. Eisenhower wrote to Montgomery in September 1944, that:

> Clearly, Berlin is the main prize and the prize in defense of which the enemy is likely to concentrate the bulk of his forces. There is no doubt whatsoever, in my mind, that we should concentrate all our energies and resources on a rapid thrust to Berlin.[604]

But recently Eisenhower had abandoned that view because he now had stronger reasons for avoiding Berlin. Roosevelt, Churchill and Stalin had agreed to split Germany into occupation zones with Berlin in the Soviet zone. The Soviets were on the Oder river 40 miles from Berlin while the closest American troops were 200 miles away on the Rhine river. A strong enough American task force would somehow have to fight its way through German resistance then into Berlin's less guarded western defenses. But what would be the point? Doing so would enrage the Soviets by denying them the glory of capturing their allocated prize and, anyway, the task force would soon have to withdraw to the American zone. When queried by Patton and others eager to take Hitler's capital, Eisenhower ended his schpeel with a rhetorical question: 'Why should we endanger the life of a single American or Briton to capture areas we soon will be handing back to the Russians?'[605]

Eisenhower made those arguments official on 7 April 1945, with this directive:

> I regard it as militarily unsound to make Berlin a major objective particularly in view of the fact that it is only 35 miles from the Russian

> lines. I am the first to admit that a war is waged in pursuance of political aims and if the Combined Chiefs of Staff should decide that the Allied effort to take Berlin outweighs purely military considerations in this theater, I would cheerfully readjust my planes and my thinking so as to carry out such an operation.

Yet, the following day, when Montgomery asked him to elaborate his views, he replied that: 'Naturally, if I get an opportunity to capture Berlin cheaply, I will take it.'[606]

That opportunity soon appeared. Eisenhower could have two American armies converge on Berlin, Ninth via Magdeburg and First via Leipzig. An advanced unit of William Simpson's Ninth Army crossed the Elbe river near Magdeburg on 14 April 1945. Simpson told Bradley that with no known enemy troops before him his army could reach Berlin within twenty-four hours. Bradley took him to sit tight and wait for the Russians.

Instead, Eisenhower became obsessed with a rumor collected by Berne station of the Office of Strategic Service (OSS) from a Swiss newspaper that the Germans had constructed a vast National Redoubt in the mountains of southern Bavaria where Hitler intended to concentrate his forces' remnants for a last stand. He assigned General Lattre de Tassigny's 1st French Army and General Alexander Patch's Seventh Army to search for that fortress, instructing each army commander to have prisoners interrogated about the National Redoubt. Progress reports from the armies increasingly concluded that the mission was a likely chimera with absolutely no evidence that the fortress existed. Like Eisenhower, Bradley initially accepted that OSS report and the diversion of those armies to find the fortress only later ruefully to admit: 'I am astonished we could have believed it as innocently as we did.'[607]

Meanwhile, the Soviets launched a massive offensive from the Oder river on 17 April 1945 that routed the Germans and within days they were fighting in Berlin's suburbs. Reports of that forced Eisenhower to turn his eyes again eastward, now concerned about Soviet advances, intentions and behaviors. Hamlet-like, he shifted his view:

> You know the Russians have been arrogant, and I just don't know what our future is going to be with them. I've got to send Patton down into Austria to take as much of Austria as possible. But I sure wish I had more of my divisions concentrated up here on the First Army front, ready to meet these people when they come in on the Elbe and the Mulde Rivers.[608]

He could have had that by authorizing his commanders to do so a few weeks earlier.

***

Meanwhile, Patton got Bradley's hesitant permission to curl his army south-east on parallel routes into Austria as far as possible. He excitedly told Eisenhower that one of his columns had advanced into Czechoslovakia on 18 April 1945 and could liberate Prague. Eisenhower angered him by ordering him to halt at Pilsen and let the Soviets march into Prague. Patton received permission to resume Third Army's advance on 4 May 1945 to a line that included Karlsbad, Pilsen and Ceske Budejovic 55 to 95 miles short of Prague. He learned from a radio report on 5 May 1945 that the Czechs had revolted against the Germans in Prague. He recalled that

> I was eager to go on and assist them, and asked Bradley for authority to do so, but this was denied. As a matter of fact ... reconnaissance elements of the Third Army were in the vicinity of Prague ... I was very much chagrined because I felt and still feel that we should have gone on to the Moldau River and, if the Russians did not like it, let them go to hell. I did not find out until weeks afterwards the reasons, which were sound, which implemented General Eisenhower's decision to order us to stop where he did.[609]

The Red Army captured Prague on 9 May 1945, and swiftly imposed the same reign of communist terror there as they had in their other conquests across eastern and central Europe.

Third Army's last offensive lasted just twenty-four days and reaped enormous results. Between the Rhine river and eastern Czechoslovakia, those successes included

> four assault crossings of the Rhine [river], the capture of twenty-two major cities with a total population of more than 3 million, the liberation of 12,400 square miles of territory, the liberation of Ohrdruf and Buchenwald and 40,000 Allied prisoners; seizure of the great gold bullion cache at Merkers; and the 280,661 German POWs, with 14,300 more killed and 31,200 wounded. Weyland's airmen damaged or destroyed 10,774 motor vehicles, 663 armored vehicles and tanks, 446 locomotives, 5,685 railway cars, and 786 planes both in the air and on the ground.

That cost Third Army 1,757 killed, 5,885 wounded and 782 wounded along with 49 XIX Tactical pilots.[610]

10.3 Final Tally: Comparison of Third Army Casualties Suffered and Inflicted, 28 July 1944 – 8 May 1945[611]

	Third Army	German Army
Killed	21,441	144,500
Wounded	99,224	386,200
Missing/Captured	16,200	956,000
Total	136,865	1,486,700
Non-battle	111,562	N/A
Total	248,427	N/A

10.4 Final Tally: Comparison of Third Army and German Army Armor and Artillery Losses, 28 July 1944 – 8 May 1945[612]

Third Army		German Army	
Light Tanks	308	Medium Tanks	1,529
Medium Tanks	949	Panther or Tiger	858
Artillery	175	Artillery	3,454

First Army and Soviet Red Army troops joyfully greeted each other at the Elbe river on 25 April 1945. The Soviets completed their encirclement of Berlin and fought their way shattered block by block toward the center. On 30 April, Hitler turned over his regime's command to Admiral Karl Dönitz, married his girlfriend Eva Braun then had her swallow a cyanide pill while he thrust a Lugar pistol against his temple and pulled the trigger. On 2 May 1945, General Heinrich von Vietinghoff unconditionally surrendered all German forces in Italy. Dönitz sent General Hans-Georg von Friedburg to Eisenhower's headquarters at Rheims to negotiate a surrender of all German forces fighting the Western Allies. Eisenhower demanded the surrender of all German forces to representatives of all the Allies. Dönitz then sent General Alfred Jodl to accept that condition. Jodl signed the 'Act of Military Surrender' on 7 May 1945, to take effect on 8 May.

Victory in Europe came at an enormous cost. From 6 June 1944 to 9 May 1945, Allied armies in northern Europe expanded steadily to peak at 5,412,219 troops, 970,044 vehicles and 18,292,310 tons of supplies. American troops numbered 1,703,613 in 61 divisions. American warplanes numbered 14,845 of 28,000 Allied aircraft. The IX XIX, and XXIX Tactical Air Commands attached respectively to the First, Third, and Ninth armies were critical to the Allied victory on the Western Front. From D-Day to VE Day, their fighter-bombers flew 212,731 sorties of which 69,326 were close air support. For Third Army, XIX Tactical Command fighter-bombers fired an average 500 .50 caliber rounds each sortie and dropped 120 bombs for every 100 sorties.[613]

The Americans suffered 586,628 casualties, including 80,211 killed, 325,969 wounded, 40,271 prisoners and 10,328 missing. Frontline infantry composed just 14 per cent of the army but suffered 70 per cent of the casualties. There were around 91,000 cold weather casualties mostly from trench foot and frost bite. There were also 151,920 neuropsychiatric cases better known as combat exhaustion then; most men returned to their units after hospital therapy. The British, French, Canadians and other Allies suffered 179,666 casualties.[614] Meanwhile, the Soviet Army numbered over 4 million troops while over 27 million Soviet soldiers and civilians died during World War II.

Of American infantry in northern Europe, half had fought for at least 150 days, and 40 per cent for at least 200 days. Overall, less than 3 per cent of American soldiers and 4 per cent of marines were killed in action, ratios far below the other belligerents. Only 16 per cent of American troops fought on foot at that the front. German infantry was the most adept at tactics. Overall, Germans killed one and a half American or British troops for every man they lost against them. American troops suffered ten times more combat fatigue than Germans. About one of nine American troops received varying psychiatric diagnoses. One reason is that the Germans more frequently rotated frontline units that suffered heavy losses and replenished them far in the rear. Another reason for that stunning difference may be that the Germans executed over 25,000 troops for 'cowardice' that was likely a psychosis that could have been treated by doctors in hospitals.[615]

Patton's Third Army played a critical role in determining when and how the Allies crushed the Third Reich. Third Army's strength peaked at 437,860 troops on 8 May 1945. During its 281 days fighting in Europe, Third Army inflicted 1,486,700 casualties on the Germans, including 144,500 killed, 386,200 wounded, and 956,000 captured, and destroyed 1,529 medium tanks, 858 Panther or Tiger tanks, and 3,454 cannons, while suffering 248,427 casualties, including 221,441 dead, 99,224 wounded, 16,200 captured and 111,562 noncombat losses, and lost 308 light tanks, 949 medium tanks and 175 cannons. Third Army suffered 19,536 combat exhaustion casualties, of whom 70 per cent returned to their units. The artillery fired 5,870,843 rounds. Tank destroyers knocked out 648 German tanks and 211 self-propelled guns, 175 artillery pieces. XIX Tactical Air Command flew 7,326 missions with 74,447 sorties, dropped 17,486 tons of bombs, 3,205 tons of napalm, launched 4,599 rockets, shot down 1,640 airplanes, lost 582 airplanes, destroyed 3,833 tanks and armored vehicles, 35,541 motor vehicles, 4,337 locomotives, 3,664 factories and 285 bridges.[616]

Patton assembled his staff on 10 May 1945 and wistfully told them:

> This is our last briefing in Europe. The war is over for us here. I think that I have had to do less work than any army commander in history, because each one of you on the staff has performed so well. I thank you very much and I congratulate you on what you have accomplished.[617]

Chapter 11

BEING

> 'They could probably maintain themselves in the type of fighting I could give them for five days. After that it would make no difference how many million men they have, and if you wanted Moscow I could give it to you.'
>
> '[W]ith the exception of my immediate family the whole attitude of the people in America is quite inimical to that which exists in Europe. None of them realize that one cannot fight two and a half years and be the same. Yet you are expected to get back into the identical groove. From which you departed and from which your non-warlike compatriots have never moved.'
>
> George S. Patton

Patton spent the last seven months of his life struggling to adjust to peace and sorrow that his fighting days were likely over.[618] He increasingly longed for the adrenalin rush of commanding hundreds of thousands of troops, making critical strategic and tactical decisions, and dodging death. In his diary, he wrote:

> Another war has ended and with it my usefulness to the world. It is personally for me a very sad thought. Now all that is left to do is to sit around and await the arrival of the undertaker and posthumous immortality.[619]

For now, the respective roles for Patton and Third Army were to be Bavaria's military governor and occupation force. Third Army's ranks steadily thinned as units were sent back to the United States. Patton knew well that those who fight in or are engulfed by war can never truly convey its horrors to those for whom war is an abstraction. He worried that he and other returning veterans would have trouble readjusting to a society spared mass destruction. For Patton a critical element of leadership was preparing young men for the stress and horrors of combat. With the guns silents, he had a different but still crucial duty. In a farewell address to departing troops in July 1945, he tried to prepare them for what lay ahead:

> Now that all or nearly all of you are returning to civil life, I believe that I should continue to do my best to instruct you how to save your lives and the lives of your children ... You have found out that discipline, self-reliance, and mutual responsibility and faith are necessary in the Army. These traits are just as necessary in civil life.

He then spoke about national attitudes and policies that might spare future generations:

> In closing, let me say it is my profound hope that we shall never again be engaged in war, but also let me remind you of the words attributed to George Washington: 'In time of peace, prepare for war.'[620]

General Maxwell Taylor, who brilliantly and valiantly commanded 101st Airborne Division during World War II, was appointed West Point's superintendent. He wrote to Patton requesting advice for how to reform the curriculum. Patton replied that the program should teach practical soldering and tactics more and academic subjects less, with one exception:

> I am convinced that much more emphasis should be placed on history ... The purpose of history ... is to learn how human beings react when exposed to the danger of wounds or death, and how high ranking individuals react when submitted to the onerous responsibility of conducting war or the preparation for war ... I believe that gallantry and a desire to attain military prestige can be cultivated.[621]

Patton flew back to America with air force General Jimmy Doolittle for four weeks' leave on 7 June 1945. They arrived in Boston for a triumphal parade from the airport to downtown with 750,000 cheering spectators packing the roadsides. He reunited with Beatrice and his children at the Copley Plaza Hotel. That night he was honored with a tribute dinner packed with dignitaries, including Governor Maurice Tobin, at the hotel. He wept during his speech when he struggled to speak about Third Army, especially all those killed and maimed. Two days later Patton with Beatrice and Doolittle with his wife flew to Los

Angeles for a victory parade that 130,000 joyous people attended. Patton and Beatrice then flew alone back to Washington for meetings with Secretary of War Stimson and Chief of Staff Marshall. Only then was he free to join his family at the Pride's Crossing estate. Throughout his leave, he made a series of controversial statements about the war, the Germans and the Russians that the press covered.

Patton flew to Paris on 4 July 1945, and then on to his Third Army headquarters at Munich. He was relieved to get away from all the exuberant crowds and politicians. In his diary, he wrote that

> with the exception of my immediate family the whole attitude of the people in America is quite inimical to that which exists in Europe. None of them realize that one cannot fight two and a half years and be the same. Yet you are expected to get back into the identical groove from which you departed and from which your non-warlike compatriots have never moved.[622]

Patton feared that Russia's conquest of eastern Europe would likely be the prelude to World War III. On 7 May 1945, the day Germany surrendered, he tried to talk visiting Undersecretary of War Robert Patterson to prepare for war against the Soviet Union and let him lead it after it erupted. His aide Major Alexander Stiller recorded their exchange. When Patterson argued that the Soviets were too strong to fight, Patton replied:

> Their supply system is inadequate to maintain them in a serious action I could put to them ... They could probably maintain themselves in the type of fighting I could give them for five days. After that it would make no difference how many million men they have, and if you wanted Moscow I could give it to you ... Let's not give them time to build up their supplies. If we do, then I repeat, we have had a victory over the Germans and disarmed them; we have failed in the liberation of Europe; we have lost the war! ... We the Armed Forces of the U.S.A. have put our government in the position to dictate the peace ... We came to give them back the right to govern themselves. We must either finish the job now – while we are here and ready – or later under less favorable circumstances.[623]

Yet, Patton was cordial when he met Russian military delegations. On 13 May 1945, he invited General Nikanor Zakhvatayez, who commanded 4th Guards Army, to Linz, where he presented him and a dozen of his officers with an honor guard and the Legion of Merit.

> [Then] we went to the officers [*sic*] club ... and had lunch, which consisted mostly of whiskey. The Russians tried to drink American whiskey without water with very bad results. I unquestionably drank the Russia commander under the table and walked out under my own steam.

In his first toast, Patton raised a glass to Stalin and the 4th Guards Army, then smashed the glass on the floor. That prompted the general joyfully to give Patton a bear hug. Patton pretended to be just as exuberant but dismissed the Russians as 'a scurvy race and simply savage. We could beat [the] hell out of them.'[624]

Two days later, Patton accepted an invitation to meet Marshal Fydor Tolbukhin, who commanded the Third Ukrainian Front at Austrian Emperor Joseph's former château. The marshal presented Patton with the First Degree Order of Kutusov, the fifty-eighth ever awarded. Patton dismissed Tolbukhin as 'a very inferior man' who 'sweated profusely'. During lunch, Patton and his staff enjoyed a 'splendid show' by a Russian dance group while their hosts 'did their best to get us drunk, but we had taken the precaution of drinking two ounces of mineral oil before starting on the expedition. We were also very careful of what we drank.' Patton had

> never seen in any army at any time ... as severe discipline as exists in the Russian army. The officers with few exceptions give the appearance of recently civilized Mongolian bandits. The men passed in review with a very good imitation of the goose step. They give me the impression of something that is to be feared in future world political reorganization.[625]

Patton got a chance to meet Marshall Georgy Zhukov, the only Soviet general who rivaled him in military prowess, during a parade of American, British and Russian troops in Berlin on 11 September 1945. Patton was not impressed:

> He was in full dress uniform much like a comic opera and covered with medals. He is short, rather fat and a prehensile chin like an ape but good blue eyes. He was in the cavalry. Our troops looked the best, the Russians next. The R[ussian]'s had a lot of new heavy tanks of which they are very proud. The Marshall asked me how I liked them. I said I did not, and we had quite an argument. Apparently I was the first person to disagree with him.[626]

Patton visited Berlin during the Potsdam summit among Truman, Stalin and Churchill.[627] He did not meet any of the Big Three but did confer with Secretary of War Henry Stimson and Chief of Staff George Marshall. In his diary, he wrote that:

> Berlin gave me the blues. We have destroyed a good race and we [are] about to replace them with Mongolian savages. And all Europe will be communist. It's said that for the first week after they took it, all women who ran were shot and those who did not were raped. I could have taken it had I been allowed.[628]

Patton did not meet Stalin. The tyrant might have summoned Patton had he known he was present. Patton had taken cold comfort in November 1944, to learn that Stalin was among his legion of fans. During his visit to the Allied front, Averell Harriman, America's ambassador to Moscow, told Patton that

> Stalin had praised the Third Army in the highest terms ... He said ... in the presence of the Chief of Staff of the Red Army, 'Red Army could not have conceived and certainly could not have executed the advance of the Third Army across France.

Harriman added that 'Stalin is a strong, ruthless revolutionist and therefore a very potential threat to future world conditions.'[629] Patton could not agree more with that reality.

The Potsdam summit's most critical event was top secret at the time. On 16 July 1945, Truman learned that the Manhattan Project had successfully tested an atomic bomb in New Mexico's desert. America now had the power to end the Pacific War without an invasion of Japan that lasted years and cost millions of lives.[630] That also meant that the United States no longer needed the Soviet Union to join the war against Japan, which would expand Moscow's power in north-east Asia But not knowing whether the bomb would work if dropped from a B-29, Truman and his advisors agreed that they had better keep the Soviets committed to war. Truman told Stalin about the test of a bomb of unprecedented destructive power to wield against Japan. Stalin approved. The news did not surprise him. Spies within the Manhattan Project kept the Kremlin informed of its progress.

Truman, Churchill and an envoy of Chiang Kai-shek's regime in China issued the Potsdam Declaration on 26 July 1945, a demand that Tokyo unconditionally surrender or else face 'prompt and utter destruction.' Japan's government replied with one word – *Mokusatsu* – which means to view something with contempt and loathing. Truman ordered the military to drop the two existing bombs where and when they would have the most impact. An atomic bomb destroyed Hiroshima on 6 August 1945 and another Nagasaki on 9 August 1945; the Soviet Union declared war against Japan, on 8 August 1945, and launched a massive offensive the next day against Japanese forces in China and Korea. Even then Japan's Supreme War Council split evenly over what to do, with three members adamant that the Japanese must fight to the death while the other three wanted to surrender. After days of debate, Emperor Hirohito agreed that Japan must give up. Tokyo sent word to the Allied powers on 14 August 1945 that it accepted the Potsdam Declaration and Hirohito announced that decision in a radio broadcast to the Japanese people on 15 August 1945. On 2 September 1945, the surrender ceremony took place aboard the battleship USS *Missouri,* anchored in Tokyo Bay along with around 250 other Allied warships. World War II finally ended.

Sixty million people died during World War II, four times more than World War I's dead; three of four dead were civilians, killed by bombing, crossfires, execution, starvation or disease. The United States suffered 405,399 total military deaths, including 291,557 from combat and 113,842 from other causes like accidents, disease and mortal wounds, and 670,826 non-mortal wounded along with 12,100 civilian deaths. Among the other major belligerents, the Soviet Union suffered as many as 27 million dead, China 20 million, Germany 7 million, Japan 3.1 million, France 2.2 million, Italy 540,000 and Britain 540,000. Among minor countries invaded by Japanese, German or Italian forces, Poland suffered as many as 6 million dead, Indonesia 4 million, Yugoslavia 1.7 million and the Philippines 1.4 million.[631]

***

During a private dinner with Dwight Eisenhower, on 1 August 1945, Patton was appalled to learn that his longstanding suspicions about Germany's post-war fate were true. During their Tehran summit in November 1943, Roosevelt and Churchill with Stalin had ceded Berlin and Vienna to the Soviets. At the time, neither Roosevelt nor Churchill could imagine their armies getting to the Rhine river before the Soviets overran most of Germany and Austria, and perhaps as far as the Rhine. Hence, they agreed to a Soviet zone running 100 miles west of Berlin and half of Austria including Vienna. Churchill always regretted that decision and with the American and British advances beyond the Rhine river in March 1945, saw an opportunity to redraft those lines with boots on the ground. Eisenhower confided to Patton that

> when we were going along well and could easily have taken Berlin, Churchill asked Ike to do it, and Ike replied by stating that it was Churchill's fault that the line had been established where it was. I believe this was a great mistake on his part, because had we taken the country to the Moldau River and Berlin, we would have prevented what I believe historians will consider a horrid crime and great loss of prestige in letting the Russians take the two leading capitals of Europe.[632]

Germany would be a vital Western ally in a war with the Soviet Union. For that, Patton advocated a conciliatory policy toward Germany that included tolerating rank and file Nazi Party members to remain working in public positions. On several occasions, he explained that to reporters with remarks that were supposed to be off the record. On 8 May 1945, the day Germany's surrender took effect, he insisted that

> SS means no more in Germany than being a Democrat in America –that is not to be quoted. I means [*sic*] by that that initially the SS people were special sons-of-bitches, but as the war progressed they ran out of sons-of-bitches and put anyone in there. Some of the top SS men will be treated as criminals, but there is no reason for trying someone who was drafted into this outfit.[633]

The Joint Chiefs of Staff issued, on 21 May 1945, a directive to the army commanders to purge Nazis from government posts in their respective sectors. Patton explained to General Lucius Clay, Eisenhower's deputy and later military governor of America's occupation zone, why the purge was wrong and his reluctance to implement it. When Eisenhower learned that Patton was disobeying his directive, on 11 September 1945, he wrote to him this explanation of the policy:

> As you know, I have announced a firm policy of uprooting the whole Nazi organization regardless of the fact that we may at times suffer from local administrative inefficiency. Reduced to its fundamentals, the United States entered this war as a foe of Nazism; victory is not complete until we have eliminated from positions of responsibility, and in appropriate cases properly punished, every active adherent to the Nazi party ... I expect just as loyal in execution of this and other policies applying to the German occupation as I received during the war.[634]

Patton paid lip service to Eisenhower's policy while continuing to drag his feet in implementing it. He lost a key supporter when Secretary of War Stimson retired on 19 September 1945 and President Truman replaced him with Undersecretary of War Robert Patterson.

Patton's most controversial remarks came on 11 September 1945, when he declared that:

> It is no more possible for a man to be a civil servant in Germany and not have paid lip service to Nazism than it is for a man to be a postmaster in America and not have paid lip service to the Democratic Party or the Republican Party.[635]

Reporters eager for a story distorted Patton's analogy to equate Nazis with Democrats and Republicans. That provoked the latest political storm. During a press conference on 25 September 1945, Patton tried to explain away his comparison but just gave reporters more grist for their mill against him. The following day, reporters pestered General Bedell Smith, Eisenhower's chief of staff, with questions of what he thought of Patton's analogy and what should be done about it. Smith tried to cover for Patton but eventually agreed that Eisenhower should meet with him for an explanation.[636]

Eisenhower summoned Patton to his Frankfurt headquarters on 29 September 1945. Patton recalled that:

> Ike was quite friendly and gave me a long oration on my inability to keep my mouth shut. I told him that in this particular case the words I was said to have said had been deliberately altered. One curious thing came up in the course of the conversation. I was thinking yesterday was that perhaps my greatest virtue and my greatest fault was my honesty and lack of ulterior motive. Ike said my greatest virtue and my greatest fault was my audacity.[637]

Then Eisenhower told Patton that he was transferring him from command of Third Army, that governed Bavaria, to head Fifteenth Army, a paper organization charged with writing the history of America European military operations and key lessons to be learned. On 1 October 1945, Patton assumed command of Fifteenth Army at its headquarters in Bad Nauheim, Germany.

Patton turned 60 years old on 11 November 1945. He was still lean and fit, but his receded, close-cropped hair was white. He had a bittersweet birthday party with his staff in the Grand Hotel's ballroom in Bad Nauheim.

***

Patton and General Hobart Gay, his chief of staff, went pheasant hunting on the morning of 9 December 1945. Patton was scheduled to fly back to the United States the following morning. Private Horace Wooding, Patton's driver for four months, conveyed them in a Cadillac limousine from Bad Nauheim to a nearby woods and then back to headquarters. As they returned at 11.45 am, an oncoming army truck made a sharp turn that crashed into the automobile's right side where Patton was sitting in the back with Gay beside him. Wooding explained that Patton

> was thrown forward and hit his head on the railing above the rear of the driver's seat. The partition glass at the time was in a lowered position. It took all the skin from the General's forehead for approximately three inches above his eyebrow and three inches across, scalping him and completely separating the spinal column. The car was knocked back approximately ten feet … The General was conscious at the time and swore a little. Within five minutes MPs were there.[638]

Only Patton was injured. An ambulance appeared and raced him to the hospital where he was placed in emergency care at 12.45 pm. Although paralyzed, he was conscious and his first words to the doctors were, 'Relax gentlemen, I am in no condition to be a terror later.' As they stripped and examined him, he quipped, 'Jesus Christ, what a way to start a leave.' When the chaplain appeared, he remarked, 'Well let him get started. I guess I need it.'[639] Soon two outstanding doctors worked on him, General Albert Kenner, the European theater's chief American surgeon, and Colonel Earl Lowry, the chief surgeon consultant. Upon learning of her husband's severe injury, Beatrice flew over to be with him.

The surgeons told him the heartbreaking news that his spinal cord was completely severed and even with surgery to reattach it his chance of walking again was slight and riding a horse was nil. Eisenhower wrote to

> assure you that you will always have a job and not to worry about this accident closing out any of them for your selection. It is always difficult for me to express my true sentiments when I am deeply moved … You are never out of my thoughts and … my hopes and prayers are tied up in your speedy recovery.[640]

A pulmonary edema and massive heart congestion killed Patton on 21 December 1945.

His daughters separately experienced paranormal visits by Patton when he died. Ruth Ellen awakened to see her bedroom filled with light and her father laying on a seat near a bay window:

> He had his head propped on his hand. He was in full uniform and looking at me fixedly. I sat up in my bed – I could see him plainly. When he saw me looking at him, he gave me the sweetest smile I have ever seen. It was loving and very reassuring … Then he was gone … I felt as if some burden had been lifted.

Beatrice was also asleep when the telephone rang: 'She picked it up and then there was a lot of static … and she heard George's voice say: "Little Bee, are you all right?" Then it was cut off.' She later learned from the telephone company no one from Germany called her house that night.[641]

Beatrice agreed that he should be interned near his troops. Of three main cemeteries holding Third Army soldiers, she chose the largest at Hamm, a few miles east of Luxembourg City. There General George S. Patton is buried at the head of 5,017 graves of his fellow soldiers, of whom most died during the Battle of the Bulge.

Chapter 12

LEGACY

> 'The purpose of history … is to learn how human beings react when exposed to the danger of wounds or death, and how high ranking individuals react when submitted to the onerous responsibility of conducting war or the preparation for war.'
>
> George S. Patton

> 'General Patton is the most feared general on all fronts. The successes of the Third Army are still overshadowing all other events of the war, including the campaigns in Russia …
>
> He is the most modern general and the best commander of armored and infantry troops combined.'
>
> Lieutenant Colonel Freiherr von Wangenheim

So, what is General George S. Patton's place in history? In America's four centuries of warfare, only three generals have decisively shaped it, and Patton was not among them.[642] Two were crucial in determining America's existence, George Washington for the nation winning independence and Ulysses S. Grant for crushing the Confederate rebellion and reuniting the nation. Winfield Scott's campaign captured Mexico City in September 1847 and held it until Mexico's government finally ceded Texas and the south-west to the United States. As such, all three generals were irreplaceable. It is unlikely that any of their deputies could have duplicated their feats.

Each of the hundreds of other generals and countless lesser ranked leaders had varying impacts in how brilliant, mediocre or inept he was at war, but no general came close to having as decisive an existential impact as Washington and Grant or as territorial an impact as Scott. Nonetheless, for each of those other leaders, alternatives who might have replaced them, facing similar tough command decisions, might have chosen differently with different results. Victories might have been decisive rather than limited or transformed into defeats, or defeats transformed into victories. The trouble is that we can only speculate and never truly know what might have happened.

Patton's record as a general is clear. The larger, more armored and better supplied his armies, and the freer he was to decide what to do with them, the more rapid and further they advanced to inflict more defeats on the enemy. In that no other American army commander matched him during World War II. Patton's greatest regret was that he never had a chance to square off with General Erin Rommel and defeat him in battle. Among his wartime joys was continually outperforming rival Bernard Montgomery as a general, made more challenging because Army Group commander Harold Alexander in Sicily and Supreme Commander Dwight D. Eisenhower in France and Germany favored Montgomery by approving his planned offensives and feeding him scarce supplies.

Then there are Patton's 'What ifs?' – the plans he submitted that his superiors prevented him from doing. Quite likely, Seventh Army could have ended the Sicilian campaign sooner with fewer Allied and more Axis casualties had Alexander not transferred that key road west of Mount Etna to Montgomery's army. Quite likely Third Army would have bagged tens of thousands more German troops had Montgomery permitted it to advance to Falaise and cut off their retreat. Quite likely, Third Army would have inflicted devastating defeats on the Germans had Eisenhower and Bradley approved his plan after he crossed the Seine to punch north and cut off the enemy's retreat. Quite likely Third Army would have breached the Siegfried Line and possibly fought its way to the Rhine had Eisenhower given him the gasoline, other key supplies and reinforcements in early September 1944 that he instead gave Montgomery for his Market Garden plan. Quite likely, Third Army would have trapped far more German troops and tanks in the Bulge had Eisenhower let him attack its base rather than mid-section. Had high command greenlighted any of these plans, the grand strategic results might well have been decisive, with the war shortened, far fewer casaulties, and American and British armies overrunning all of Germany and Austria to raise the Stars and Stripes and the Union Jack over Berlin and Vienna rather than ceding much of each to the Red Army.

Patton was the toughest critic of his generalship and character. Although his command style was to exude confidence and decisiveness around his subordinates, he confided to his diary his doubts and mistakes. Yet in evaluating himself, the only serious mistake he found was sending a 307-man combat team rather than a regiment to liberate the prisoners at Hammelburg; the Germans killed or captured most of that team. There may have been other attacks he ordered over the objections of his subordinates that failed, as well as others that succeeded.

Like any commander, Patton relied on the army hierarchy below him to implement his plans. Among Patton's attributes was generously giving subordinates credit for successes they shared through teamwork. Among the outstanding leaders that served under him were generals Matthew Ridgway of 82nd Airborne Division, John Wood of 4th Armored Division, Lucian Truscott of 3rd Infantry Division, and Colonel William Darby of 1st Ranger Regiment. As for his Third Army corps commanders, Patton noted these distinctions:

> General [Walton] Walker [XX] is always the most willing and cooperative. He will fight any time, any place, with anything that the Army commander desires to give him. General [Troy] Middleton [VIII] is the most methodical, probably the best tactician, very firm in his relations with the other corps commanders ... General [Manton] Eddy [XII] is very nervous, very much inclined to grasping, and always worried that some other corps commander is getting a better deal than he is, but when the decision is made, he always does what he is told.[643]

Patton was a genuine American hero who somehow survived countless bullets, bombs, and mines designed to kill or maim him in the Punitive Expedition, World War I, and World War II. He was an expert horsemen, pistol shot and swordsman, and stayed in top physical shape until his life's end. He won an extraordinary array of medals for combat courage and leadership including two Silver Stars, two Distinguished Service Crosses, the Bronze Star, the French Croix de Guerre, and the Purple Heart along with three Distinguished Service Medals for outstanding administrative work.

Leading from the front involves more than giving commands and epitomizing courage. Patton instructed his officers to:

> Take time to talk with the troops. They know more about the war than anybody. Far more than we do! Let them know we are doing everything we can to help them ... Tell them the truth that they are the most important part of the army. They will not trust you if you do not trust them.[644]

By not just appearing at the front, but speaking with the soldiers, Patton gathered vital information while boosting morale for those who saw or heard about his visit. Also, that was the best antidote to the unfair quip by some troops that 'Blood and Guts Patton' was 'his guts and our blood.'

Yet Patton harbored plenty of flaws. He was a narcissist who constantly strove to be center-stage and outshine his rivals. He contrived an idealized version of himself as the epitome of the brilliant general and fearless soldier, immaculately dressed, and spent his life playing that role. He was a braggart who regaled listeners with at times exaggerated tales of his past deeds and those yet to come. His boasting did have one positive element. He sought to surpass his past glories with greater future victories. He was a social iconoclast who loved disturbing those around him with explicit descriptions of combat, sports and sex spiced with vulgar words and images. Of course, behind that cartoon hero was a complex psyche tormented with insecurities and self-doubts.

Military leaders can be sorted among five character types, although most can fit more or less in two or more categories. For instance, Patton was above all a relentless warrior but also a showboat and a bulldog. Each type is about one's dominant characteristics, not war record. Leaders, of course, vary greatly in how well, poorly or averagely they fulfill their duties. Even the best make mistakes. The disastrous assaults that Ulysses S. Grant and Robert Lee respectively ordered at Cold Harbor and Cemetery Ridge haunted them the rest of their lives. Although the examples for each type below are generally first rate generals, plenty of mediocre or worse leaders can replace them.

12.1. Military Leader Types

Warriors	George S. Patton, Dan Morgan, George Rogers Clark, Andrew Jackson and Nathan Forrest
Demi-Gods	George Washington, Robert Lee, Thomas Jackson and John Pershing
Showboats	Winfield Scott, George McClellan and Douglas MacArthur
Bulldogs	Nathaniel Greene, Zachery Taylor, Ulysses S. Grant, Wiliam Sherman and Omar Bradley
Methodicals	Henry Halleck, Dwight D. Eisenhower and George Marshall

'Warriors' are naturally fierce competitors, adventurers and fighters determined to defeat any foe. They lead from the front and by example. Patton was a warrior along with generals Dan Morgan, George Rogers Clark, Andrew Jackson and Nathan Forest. Each was brilliant at strategy and tactics, but even more brilliant at inspiring his men to extraordinary efforts by his decisiveness, prowess, ruthlessness and exuberance. They reveled in the comradeship of war, of being first among a band of brothers sharing epic quests, who between campaigns feasted, imbibed, bantered, and reflected. Of course, being a warrior and a good general are not inseparable. A warrior might be brilliant at leading 100 men in battle but not 1,000 let alone 100,000. For instance, John Hood was both a warrior and an awful general whose frontal attacks decimated his army at Atlanta, Franklin and Nashville.

'Demi-gods' can be just as bold and creative at war as warriors but exude gravitas rather than machismo and are aloof introverts rather than extroverts. They command obedience with a few pointed words or even a sharp glance. George Washington, Robert E. Lee, Thomas 'Stonewall' Jackson, and John Pershing were demi-gods.

'Showboats' are narcissists who love being the center of attention as they play the role of 'great commander'. Winfield Scott, George McClellan and Douglass MacArthur dressed immaculately and tended to pontificate rather than speak with others. Each had a dress quirk – Scott a plumed hat, McClellan a kepi and MacArthur at times sunglasses and a corncob pipe. Of the three, Scott was actually a great general who never lost a battle. McClellan was popular with his troops largely because he avoided combat as much as possible and failed ruthlessly to pursue defeated foes. MacArthur was a controversial general who ineptly lost the Philippines but ingeniously conceived the Inchon landing that routed the communist army during the Korean War. Although primarily a warrior, Patton was also constantly on stage as a showboat with his 'war face' and ivory-handled revolvers. For their attention to detail, showboats can also be methodicals, although not Patton who issued orders and let his subordinates decide how to realize them.

'Bulldogs' are low-key, plain-dressed, and plain-speaking but decisive generals who constantly seek to outmaneuver and defeat the enemy. Nathaniel Greene, Zachery Taylor, Ulysses S. Grant, William Sherman and Omar Bradley were bulldogs. Patton was also a bulldog who sought relentlessly to destroy the enemy through a series of rapid movements and ruthless attacks.

'Methodicals' emphasize war's collegiality, administration, training and logistics while leaving combat to others. They prefer devising and implementing war's grand military strategies as they mobilize all needed personnel, supplies, facilities, transport and organizations. As such, they make excellent staff officers. Henry Halleck, George Marshall, and Dwight D. Eisenhower were methodicals. McClellan was also a methodical who would have been a first-rate chief of staff for a commander who could contain his narcissism.

Charisma is a key form of soft or psychological power. Charismatic leaders exude a commanding presence in appearance and demeanor. They are extraordinarily confident, decisive, tough and skilled, and assert those attributes to inspire others to follow them by manipulating their needs, desires, hopes, and fears. Of the five military types, three exude very different versions of charisma, warriors, demi-gods and showboats.

Not all charismatic generals are successful – MacArthur and McCellan both won and lost vital battles and campaigns. Nor are all successful generals charismatic. Bulldogs like Greene, Taylor, Grant, Sherman and Bradley were low key professionals that decisively won battles and campaigns.

No one in the military understood Patton better than Eisenhower. Their friendship began in the tank corps in 1920. During World War II, Eisenhower was Patton's guardian agent, repeatedly saving him from being cashiered for a series of controversial acts. In his memoirs, he provided copious insights into the strengths and weaknesses of Patton's complex psychology and military leadership. As for his personality flaws,

> I knew well that Patton delighted to startle his hearers with fantastic statements; many men who believe they knew him well never penetrated past the shell of showmanship in which he constantly and carefully clothed himself ... All the mannerisms and idiosyncrasies he developed were of his own deliberate adoption. One of his poses ... was that of the most hard-boiled individual in the Army. Actually he was so soft-hearted, particularly where a personal friend was concerned, that it was possibly his greatest fault.[645]

As a military leader, Patton

> was essentially a shrewd battle leader who invariably gained the devotion of his subordinates. From early life his one ambition was to be a successful battlefield commander. Because of this he was an inveterate reader of military history and his heroes were the great captains of past ages.

Of Patton's generalship, Eisenhower most lauded this element:

> Patton was a shrewd student of warfare who always clearly appreciated the value of speed in operations. Speed ... makes possible the full exploitation of every favorable opportunity and prevents the enemy from readjusting his forces to meet successive attacks. Thus through speed and determination each successive advantage is more easily and economically gained that the previous one. Continuation of the process finally results in the demoralization of the enemy. Thereupon speed must be redoubled – relentless and speedy pursuit is the most profitable action in war.[646]

Eisenhower paid Patton the highest tribute in March 1945 when he expressed, 'You have made your Army a fighting force that is not excelled ... by any army of equal size in history.'[647] He explained the emotional roots of Patton's leadership:

> His emotional tenseness and his impulsiveness were the very qualities that made him, in open situations, such a remarkable leader of an army. In pursuit and exploitation there is need for a commander who sees nothing but the necessity of getting ahead; the more he drives his men the more he will save their lives. He must be indifferent to fatigue and ruthless in demanding the last atom of physical energy.[648]

Yet another vital perspective on Patton as a leader comes from his harshest critic. Omar Bradley vented his loathing of Patton dozens of times in his two autobiographies. He called Patton 'the most fiercely ambitious man and the strangest duck I have ever known.' Bradley was genuinely appalled by his crude, boastful behavior, and especially the massacres of German prisoners that he inspired and his slapping two soldiers in Sicily. He dismissed Patton's generalship:

> To George, tactics was simply a process of bulling ahead. He never seemed to think out a campaign. Seldom made a careful estimate of the situation. I thought him a shallow commander ... On the battlefield there is a great difference between recklessness and aggressiveness, but the distinction was blurred in Patton's mind.

As a leader, he 'was unmercifully hard on his men, demanding the utmost in military efficiency and bearing. Most of them respected but despised him.' As for Patton's personality and the psychology behind it, although

> he could be the epitome of grace and charm at social or official functions, he was at the same time the most profane man I ever knew. I sometimes wondered if this macho profanity was unconscious overcompensation for his most serious personal flaw: a voice that was almost comically squeaky and high-pitched, altogether lacking in command authority.[649]

At best, Bradley harbored very mixed feelings about Patton. He at once despised Patton's profane personality yet recognized his military brilliance, rating him number one as a combat commander and number five of ten for his overall generalship.[650] In comparing the staffs of the First, Third, and Ninth armies he commanded in Twelfth Army Group, Bradley thought

> Simpson was another very thorough and a well trained infantryman. He had one of the best staffs over there...Patton's staff was not as efficient as the First or Ninth Armies, and divisions would notice this when they would be transferred from Patton's Army, say, to First Army – where they would get better supplies, and quicker replacements, and so forth.[651]

Bradley had his own insecurities, including his humble face and childhood, and appeared to be as jealous as he was scornful of Patton's flamboyance and ambition. That jealousy may have exaggerated his criticism. In a more reflective moment, he offered this balanced assessment:

> Patton was a superb field general and leader – perhaps our very best – but a man with many human and professional flaws. Those flaws had the potential for danger, even disaster, so much that Marshall and Ike felt Patton had to be continuously watched and tethered.[652]

Bradley did not mourn Patton's death but thought it was a disguised blessing:

> I believe it was better for George Patton and his professional reputation that he died when he did ... He would have gone into retirement hungering for the old limelight, beyond doubt indiscreetly sounding off on any subject any time, any place. In time, he probably would have become a boring parody of himself –a decrepit, bitter, pitiful figure, unwittingly debasing the legend.[653]

The two presidents that Patton served during World War II had opposed views of him. For Franklin D. Roosevelt: 'He is our greatest fighting general, and sheer joy.' For Harry S. Truman: 'Don't see how a country can produce such men as Robert E. Lee, John J. Pershing, Eisenhower, and Bradley, and at the same time Custers, Pattons, and MacArthurs.'[654]

The ultimate evaluation of Patton's generalship is with those who most feared him. No enemy leader worried Germans more than Patton. Under interrogation, captured Lieutenant Colonel Freiherr von Wangenheim admitted that:

> The greatest threat ... was the whereabouts of the feared U.S. Third Army. General Patton is always the main topic of military discussion. Where is he? When will he attack? Where How? With what? Those are the questions that raced through the head of every German general ... General Patton is the most feared general on all fronts. The successes of the Third Army are still overshadowing all other events of the war, including the campaigns in Russia ... He is the most modern general and the best commander of armored and infantry troops combined.[655]

ACKNOWLEDGEMENTS

As always, I am so grateful for Frontline's team of John Grehan, Martin Mace, Lisa Hoosan, and Lori Jones to produce my book. Lori's proofreading of my book was wonderful. They are all as kind as they are professional.

BIBLIOGRAPHY

Primary

Alexander, Field Marshal Earl of Tunis, *The Alexander Memoirs, 1940–1945*, New York: McGraw-Hill, 1962.

Blumenson, Martin, *The Patton Papers, 1885–1940*, New York: Da Capo, 1996.

Blumenson, Martin, *The Patton Papers, 1940–1945*, New York: Da Capo, 1996.

Bradley, Omar, *A Soldier's Story*, New York: Henry Holt, 1951.

Bradley, Omar, with Clay Blair, *A General's Life: An Autobiography of General of the Army*, New York: Simon and Schuster, 1983.

Brooks, Stephen, *Montgomery and the Eighth Army: A Selection From the Diaries, Correspondence, and Other Papers of Field Mashall the Viscount Montgomery of Alamein*, London: Bodley Head, 1991.

Butcher, Harry, *My Three Years with Eisenhower*, New York: Simon and Schuster, 1946.

Churchill, Winston, *Memoirs of the Second World War* (abridged version), Boston: Houghton Mifflin, 1987.

Clark, Mark, *Calculated Risk*, New York: Harper and Row, 1951.

Collins, General J. Lawton, *Fighting Joe: An Autobiography*, New York: Presidio Press, 1994.

Danchev, Alex and Todman, Daniel (eds.), *War Diaries, 1939–1945, Alan Brooke*, Berkeley: University of California Press, 2001.

Eisenhower, Dwight, *Crusade in Europe*, Garden City, New York, Doubleday, 1948.

Eisenhower, Dwight, *At Ease: Stories I Tell My Friends*, Garden City, New York, Doubleday, 1967.

Ferrell, Robert (ed.), *The Eisenhower Diaries*, New York: W.W. Norton, 1981.

Gavin, James, *On to Berlin: A Fighting General's True Story of Airborne Combat in World War II*, New York: Bantam Books, 1979.

Harmon, Ernest, *Combat Commander, Autobiography of a Soldier*, New York: Prentice Hall, 1970.

Hart, Basil Liddel (ed.), *The Rommel Papers*, New York: Harcourt Brace, 1953.

Hobbs, Joseph, *Dear General: Eisenhower's Wartime Letters to Marshall*, Baltimore: Johns Hopkins University Press, 1971.

Langworth, Richard (ed.), *Churchill by Himself*, New York: Public Affairs, 2009.

Lerner, William (ed.), *Historical Statistics of the United States: Colonial Times to 1970*, 2 volumes, Washington DC: US Government Bureau of the Census, 1975.

Marshall, George, *Memoirs of My Service in World War I, 1917–1918*, Boston: Houghton Mifflin, 1976.
Montgomery, Bernard, *The Memoirs of Field Marshall Montgomery*, New York: Da Capo Press, 1958.
Mulligan, William (ed.), *Neuropsychiatry in World War II*, 2 vols., Washington: Department of the Army, Office of the Surgeon General, 1973.
Murphy, Robert, *Diplomat Among Warriors*, Garden City, New York: Doubleday, 1964.
Patton, General George S., *War as I Knew It*, New York: Houghton Mifflin, 1995.
Pershing, John J., *My Life Before the Great War, 1860–1917*, Lexington: University of Kentucky Press, 2013.
Pershing, John J., *My Experiences in the World War*, vols. 1–2, New York: Arcadia Press, 2019.
Prioli, Carmine (ed.), *The Poems of General George S. Patton*, New York: Edwin Mellen Press, 1991.
Semmes, Harry, *Portrait of Patton*, New York: Appleton-Century-Crofts, 1955.
Smith, Walter Bedell Smith, *Eisenhower's Six Great Decisions: Europe, 1944–1945*, New York: Longmans, Green, 1956.
Taylor, Maxwell, *The Uncertain Trumpet*, New York: Harper, 1959.
Totten, Ruth Ellen Patton, *The Button Box: A Daughter's Loving Memory of Beatrice Ayer Patton*, Columbia: University of Missouri Press, 2005.
Truscott, Lucian, *Command Missions: A Personal Story*, New York: E.P. Dutton, 1954.
US Department of the Army, Office of the Adjutant General, Statistical and Accounting Branch, *Army Battle Casualties and Nonbattle Deaths in World War II, Final Report, 7 December 1941 – 31 December 1946* (1 June 1952).
Williamson, Porter (ed.), *General Patton's Principles for Life and Leadership*, Tucson: Management and Systems Consultants, 2009.

Secondary

Acquilla, John, *Why the Axis Lost: An Analysis of Strategic Errors*, Jefferson, North Carolina: McFarland, 2020.
Ambrose, Stephen, *Eisenhower and Berlin, 1945: The Decision to Halt at the Elbe*, New York: W.W. Norton, 1967.
Ambrose, Stephen, *Eisenhower: Soldier and President*, New York: Touchstone, 1991.
Atkinson, Rick, *An Army at Dawn: The War in North Africa, 1942–1943*, New York: Henry Holt, 2002.
Atkinson, Rick, *The Day of Battle: The War in Sicily and Italy, 1943–1944*, New York: Henry Holt, 2007.
Atkinson, Rick, *The Guns at Last Light: The War in Western Europe, 1944–1945*, New York: Henry Holt, 2013.
Axelrod, Alan, *How America Won World War I: The US Military Victory in the Great War: The Causes, the Course, and the Consequences* (Guilford, Connecticut: Globe Pequot, 2018.
Ayer, Fred, *George S. Patton Jr: Before the Colors Fade, Portrait of a Soldier*, London: Cassell, 1964.
Baigent, Michael, *Secret Germany: Stauffenberg and the True Story of Operation Valkyrie*, New York: Skyhorse, 2009.

Barron, Leo, *Patton's First Victory: How General George Patton Turned the Tide in North Africa and Defeated the Africa Korps at El Guettar*, New York: Stackpole Books, 2018.

Baum, Richard, and Major Abe Baum, *Raid!: The Untold Story of Patton's Secret Mission*, New York: G.P. Putnam's Sons, 1981.

Bennett, David, *A Magnificent Disaster: The Failure of Market Garden, The Arnhem Operation, September 1944*, New York: Casemate, 2011.

Bennett, Ralph, *Ultra and the Mediterranean Strategy*, New York: William Morrow, 1989.

Bergstrom, Christer, *The Ardennes: Hitler's Winter Offensive, 1944–45*, New York: Casemate, 2014.

Bishop, Patrick, *Operation Jubilee: Dieppe, 1942, The Folly and the Sacrifice*, New York: Signal, 2021.

Black, Conrad, *Flight of the Eagle: The Grand Strategies that Brought America from Colonial Dependence to World Leadership*, New York: Encounter Books, 2013.

Blumenson, Martin, *Patton: The Man Behind the Legend*, New York: William Morrow, 1985.

Blumenson, Martin, *The Battle of the Generals: The Untold Story of the Falaise Pocket that Should Have Won World War II*, New York: William Morrow, 1994.

Blumenson, Martin, *Kasserine Pass: Rommel's Bloody, Climatic Battle for Tunisia*, New York: Cooper Square Press, 2000.

Brewer, William, *Operation Torch: The Allied Gamble to Invade North Africa*, New York: St Martin's, 1988.

Brower, Charles (ed.), *World War II in Europe: The Final Year*, New York: St Martin's Press, 1998.

Buckingham, William, *Arnhem: The Complete Story of Operation Market Garden, 17–25 September 1944*, New York: Amberley Publishing, 2020.

Caddick-Adams, Peter, *Snow and Steel: The Battle of the Bulge, 1944–45*, New York: Oxford University Press, 2014.

Carafano, James, *After D-Day: Operation Cobra and the Normandy Breakout*, Boulder, Colo.: Lynne Rienner, 2000.

Carroll, Andrew, *My Fellow Soldiers: General John J. Pershing and the Americans Who Helped Win World War I*, New York: Penguin, 2017.

Cole, Wayne, *Roosevelt and the Isolationists, 1932–45*, Lincoln: University of Nebraska Press, 1983.

Colley, David, *The Road to Victory: The Untold Story of World War II's Red Ball Express*, Washington DC: Potomac Books, 2000.

Cooksley, Peter, *Flying Bomb: The Story of Hitler's V-Weapons in World War II*, New York: Charles Scribners' Sons, 1979.

Cooper, Bryan, *Tank Battles of World War I*, Barnsley: Pen & Sword, 2023.

Cooper, Steven, *French Tanks of World War I*, London: Osprey, 2010.

Cray, Ed, *General of the Army: George C. Marshall, Soldier and Statesman*, New York: Touchstone, 1990.

Cross, Robin, *Operation Dragoon: The Allied Liberation of the South of France, 1944*, New York: Pegasus, 2019.

Crosswell, D.K.R., *The Chief of Staff: The Military Career of General Walter Bedell Smith*, Westport, Connecticut: Greenwood Press, 1991.

Dallek, Robert, *Franklin D. Roosevelt and American Foreign Policy, 1932–1945*, New York: Oxford University Press, 1979.

Davis, Franklin, *Across the Rhine*, New York: Time-Life, 1980.

Davis, Richard, *Carl A. Spaatz and the Air War in Europe*, Washington DC: Center for Air Force History, 1993.

DeFelice, Jim, *Omar Bradley: General at War*, New York: Regnery, 2014.

D'Este, Carlo, *Bitter Victory: The Battle for Sicily, 1943*, New York: E.P. Dutton, 1988.

D'Este, Carlo, *Decision in Normandy: The Real Story of Montgomery and the Allied Campaign*, New York: Penguin, 1994.

D'Este, Carlo, *Patton: A Genius for War*, New York: Harper Perennial, 1996.

D'Este, Carlo, *Eisenhower: A Soldier's Life*, New York: Henry Holt, 2002.

Dimbleby, Jonathan, *Destiny in the Desert: The Road to El Alamein – The Battle that Turned the Tide*, New York: Profile Books, 2012.

Doubler, Michael, *Closing with the Enemy: How GIs Fought the War in Europe*, Lawrence: University Press of Kansas, 1994.

Dupuy, Trevor, *Hitler's Last Gamble: The Battle of the Bulge, December 1944 to January 1945*, New York: Harper Collins, 1994.

Eisenhower, John, *Intervention! The United States and the Mexican Revolution, 1913–1917*, New York: W.W. Norton, 1993.

Eisenhower, John, *Yanks: The Epic Story of the American Army in World War I*, New York: Free Press, 2001.

Elphick, Peter, *Liberty: The Ships that Won the War*, Annapolis, Maryland: Naval Institute Press, 2006.

Farwell, Byron, *The United States in the Great War, 1917–1918*, New York: W.W. Norton, 1999.

Fargo, Ladislas, *The Last Days of Patton*, New York: McGraw-Hill, 1981.

Fargo, Ladislas, *Patton: Ordeal and Triumph*, New York: Westholme Publishing, 2005.

Ferguson, Neil, *The Pity of War: Explaining World War I*, New York: Basic Books, 1999.

Ferrell, Robert, *America's Deadliest Battle: Meuse-Argonne, 1918*, Lawrence: University Press of Kansas, 2007.

Fletcher, David, *British Battle Tanks: World War I to 1939*, London: Osprey, 2016.

Forty, George, *Patton's Third Army at War*, New York: Charles Scribner's, 1978.

Forty, Simon, *Across the Rhine, January – May 1945*, New York: Casemate, 2020.

Frank, Richard, *Downfall: The End of the Imperial Japanese Empire*, New York: Penguin, 2001.

Frankel, Nat, *Patton's Best: An Informal History of the Fourth Armored Division*, New York: Hawthorn Books, 1978.

Gabel, Christopher, *The US Army GHQ Maneuvers of 1941*, Washington DC: Center for Military History, 1991.

Galante, Pierre, *Operation Valkyrie: The German Generals Plot against Hitler*, New York: Cooper Square Press, 2002.

Gelb, Norman, *Desperate Venture: The Story of Operation Torch: The Allied Invasion of North Africa*, New York: W.W. Norton, 1992.

Gelb, Norman, *Ike and Monty: Generals at War*, New York: William Morrow, 1994.

Gilbert, Charles, *American Financing of World War I*, New York: Praeger, 1970.

Gilbert, Martin, *The Second World War: A Complete History*, New York: Henry Holt, 2004.

Graham, Dominick, and Shelford Bidwell, *Tug of War: The Battle for Italy, 1943–1945*, New York: St Martin's Press, 1986.

Guinn, Jeff, *War on the Border: Villa, Pershing, and the Texas Rangers, and an American Invasion*, New York: Simon and Schuster, 2021.

Hallas, James, *Squandered Victory: The American First Army at St Mihiel*, New York: Praeger, 1995.

Hallas, James, *Doughboy War: The American Expeditionary Force in World War I*, Boulder, Colorado: Lynne Rienner, 2000.

Hamilton, Nigel, *Alex, The Life of Field Marshal Earl Alexander of Tunis*, London: Atheneum, 1975.

Hamilton, Nigel, *Monty: Master of the Battlefield*, London: Hamish Hamilton, 1983.

Hamilton, Nigel, *Monty, The Field Marshal*, London: Hamish Hamilton, 1986.

Hamilton, Nigel, *Monty, The Battles of Field Marshal Bernard Montgomery*, New York: Random House, 1994.

Hammond, Byrn, *Cambrai 1917: The Myth of the First Great Tank Battle*, London: Weidenfeld and Nicolson, 2008.

Hanson, Victor, *The Second World Wars: The First Globa Conflict Was Fought and Won*, New York: Basic Books, 2020.

Harkins, Paul, *When the Third Cracked Europe: The Story of Patton's Incredible Army* Harrisburg, Pennsylvania: Stackpole Books, 1969.

Hart, Basil Liddel, *History of the Second World War*, London: Cassell, 1970.

Hastings, Max, *Overlord: D-Day and the Battle for Normandy, 1944*, New York: Simon and Schuster, 1984.

Hirshson, Stanley, *General Patton: A Solder's Life*, New York: Harper Perennial, 2003.

Houston, Donald, *Hell on Wheels: The Second Armored Division*, San Rafael, California: Presidio Press, 1977.

Hunt, John, *Empire and Revolution: The Americans in Mexico since the Civil War*, Berkeley: University of California Press, 2002.

Hurst, James, *Pancho Villa and Black Jack Pershing: The Punitive Expedition in Mexico*, New York: Praeger, 2008.

Irons, Roy, *Hitler's Terror Weapons: The Price of Vengeance*, New York: Harper Collins, 2003.

Irving, David, *The War between the Generals: Inside the Allied High Command*, New York: Congdon and Lattes, 1986.

Johnson, Hubert, *Breakthrough: Tactics, Technology, and the Search for Victory in World War I*, Novato, California: Presidio Press, 1994.

Jordan, Jonathan, *Brothers, Rivals, Victors: Eisenhower, Patton, Bradley and the Partnership that Drove the Allied Conquest in Europe*, New York: Dutton Caliber, 2018.

Kaplan, Lawrence (ed.), *Pershing's Tankers: Personal Accounts of the AEF Tank Corps in World War I*, Lexington: University of Kentucky Press, 2018.

Katz, Friedrich, *The Secret War in Mexico: Europe, the United States, and the Mexican Revolution*, Chicago: University of Chicago Press, 1981.

Keegan, John, *Six Armies in Normandy: From D-Day to the Liberation of Paris*, New York: Viking, 1982.

Kelly, Orr, *Meeting the Fox: The Allied Invasion of Africa from Operation Torch to Kasserine Pass to Victory in Tunisia*, New York: Wiley, 2002.

Kemp, Anthony, *The Unknown Battle: Metz, 1944*, New York: Stein and Day, 1985.

Kennett, Lee, *G.I.: The American Soldier in World War II*, New York: Charles Scribner's Sons, 1986.

Kimball, Warren, *The Most Unsordid Act: Lease-Lease, 1939–1945*, New York: Routledge, 2019.

Koch, Oscar, *G-2 Intelligence for Patton*, Philadelphia: Army Times / Whitmore, 1971.

Jordan, Jonathan, *Brothers-Rivals-Victors: Eisenhower, Patton, Bradley, and the Partnership that Drove the Allied Conquest in Europe*, New York: Nal Caliber, 2011.

Lengel, Edward, *To Conquer Hell: The Meuse-Argonne, 1918, The Epic Battle That Ended the First World War*, New York: Henry Holt, 2008.

Liddel Hart, Basil, *History of the Second World War*, London: Cassell, 1970.

Linenthal, Edward, *Changing Images of the Warrior Hero in America: A History of Popular Symbolism*, New York: Edwin Mellen Press, 1982.

Malkin, Craig, *Rethinking Narcissism: The Secret to Recognizing and Coping with Narcissists*, New York; Harper Perennial, 2016.

MacDonald, Charles, *The Siegfried Line Campaign*, Washington DC: Office of the Chief of Military History, 1963.

MacDonald, *A Time for Trumpets: The Untold Story of the Battle of the Bulge*, New York: William Morrow, 1997.

Marshall, S.L.A., *Men Against Fire: The Problem of Battle Command*, Norman: University of Oklahoma Press, 2000.

Mawdsley, Evan, *World War II: A New History*, New York: Cambridge University Press, 2020.

Meacham, Jon, *Franklin and Winston: An Intimate Portrait of an Epic Friendship*, New York: Random House, 2003.

Mellor, William, *Patton: The Last Cavalier*, New York: Putnam, 1971.

Merriam, Robert, *The Battle of the Bulge*, New York: Ballantine Books, 1978.

Meyer, G.J., *A World Undone: The Story of the Great War, 1914–1918*, New York: Bantam, 2015.

Miller, Merle, *Ike the Soldier: As They Knew Him*, New York: Putnam, 1986.

Mitchell, Ralph, *The 101st Airborne Division's Defense of Bastogne*, Fort Leavenworth, Kansas: Combat Studies Institute, 1986.

Mitcham, Samuel, and von Stauffenberg, Friedrich, *The Battle of Sicily: How the Allies Lost Their Chance for Total Victory*, New York: Orion Books, 1991.

Morelock, J.D., *Generals of the Ardennes; American Leadership in the Battle of the Bulge*, Washington DC: National Defense University Press, 1994.

Mroz, Albert, *American Military Vehicles of World War I*, Jefferson, North Carolina: McFarland, 2009.

Murray, G.E., *Eisenhower versus Montgomery: The Continuing Debate*, Westport, Connecticut: Praeger, 1996.

Neiberg, Michael, *Potsdam: The End of World War II and the Remaking of Europe*, New York: Basic Books, 2015.

Nester, William, *Winston Churchill and the Art of Leadership*, Barnsley: Pen & Sword / Frontline Books, 2020.

Nester, William, *Franklin D. Roosevelt and the Art of Leadership*, Barnsley: Pen & Sword / Frontline Books, 2024.

Nester, William, *Land of War: A History of European Warfare from Achilles to Putin*, New York: Stackpole Books, 2023.

Nester, William, *World of War: A History of American Warfare from Jamestown to the War on Terror*, New York: Stackpole Books, 2024.

Odom, Charles, *General George S. Patton and Eisenhower*, New Orleans: Word Picture Productions, 1985.

Osgood, Steven, *Omar Nelson Bradley: America's GI General*, Columbia: University of Missouri Press, 2017.

Otte, Maarten, *The St Mihiel Offensive, 12 to 16 September 1918*, Barnsley: Pen & Sword, 2020.

Parrish, Thomas, *Roosevelt and Marshall: Partners in Politics and War*, New York: William Morrow, 1989.

Parwell, Byron, *The United States in the Great War, 1917–1918*, New York: W.W. Norton, 1999.

Passingham, Ian, *The German Offensives of 1918: The Last Desperate Gamble*, Barnsley: Pen & Sword, 2008.

Patton, Robert, *The Pattons: The Personal History of an American Family*, New York: Crown, 1994.

Payne, Stanley, *A History of Fascism, 1914–1945*, Madison: University of Wisconsin Press, 1995.

Paxton, Robert, *The Anatomy of Fascism*, New York: Vintage, 2004.

Perry, John, *Pershing: General of the Great War*, New York: Thomas Nelson, 2011.

Persico, Joseph, *Eleventh Month, Eleventh Day, Eleventh Hour: Armistice Day, 1918, World War I and Its Violent Climax*, New York: Random House, 2005.

Phillips, Robert, *To Save Bastogne*, New York: Stein and Day, 1983.

Pogue, Forrest, *George C. Marshall: Ordeal and Hope, 1939–1942*, New York: Viking, 1966.

Pogue, Forrest, *George C. Marshall: Organizer of Victory, 1943–1945*, New York: Viking, 1973.

Prioli, Carmine (ed.), *Lines of Fire: The Poems of General George S. Patton,Jr*, Lewiston, New York: Edwin Mellen Press, 1991.

Province, Charles, *The Unknown Patton*, New York: Bonanza Books, 1983.

Quick, Robert, *An Affair of Honor: Woodrow Wilson and the Occupation of Veracruz*, Lexington: University of Kentucky Press, 1962.

Reardon, Mark, *Victory at Mortain: Stopping Hitler's Panzer Counteroffensive*, Lawrence: University Press of Kansas, 2002.

Reynolds, David, *The Creation of the Anglo-American Alliance, 1937–1941*, Chapel Hill: University of North Carolina Press, 1981.

Reynolds, David, *From Munich to Pearl Harbor: Roosevelt's America and the Origins of the Second World War*, Chicago: Ivan Dee, 2001.

Rohmer, Richard, *Patton's Gap: An Account of the Battle of Normandy*, London: Arms and Armor Press, 1981.

Ruppenthal, Roland, *Logistical Support for the Armies: May 1941 to September 1944*, Vol. 1, Washington DC: Office of the Chief of Military History, 1953.

Ruppenthal, Roland, *Logistical Support for the Armies: September 1944 to May 1945*, Vol. 2, Washington DC: Office of the Chief of Military History, 1953.
Ryan, Cornelius, *The Longest Day*, New York: Touchstone, 1994.
Ryan, Cornelius, *A Bridge Too Far*, New York: Simon and Schuster, 1995.
Sainsbury, Keith, *The North African Landings, 1942*, Newark: University of Delaware Press, 1979.
Sainsbury, Keith, *The Turning Point: Roosevelt, Stalin, Churchill, and Chiang Kai-shek, 1943: The Moscow, Cairo, and Tehran Conferences*, New York: Oxford University Press, 1985.
Sainsbury, Keith, *Churchill and Roosevelt at War: The War They Fought and the Peace They Hoped to Make*, New York: New York University Press, 1994.
Saunders, Tim, *Operation Plunder: The British and Canadian Operations*, Barnsley: Pen & Sword, 2007.
Schultz, Duane, *Patton's Last Gamble: The Disastrous Raid on POW Camp Hammelburg in World War II*, New York: Stackpole Books, 2018.
Shapiro, Milton, *Tank Command: Patton's 4th Armored Division*, New York: David McKay, 1979.
Smith, Francis, *History of the Third Army*, Washington DC: Historical Section, Army Ground Press, 1946.
Smith, Jean, *Lucius D. Clay: An American Life*, New York: Henry Holt, 1990.
Smith, Jean, *Eisenhower in War and Peace*, New York: Random House, 2013.
Smith, Gene, *Until the Last Trumpet Sounds: The Life of General of the Armies John J. Pershing*, New York: John Wiley, 2001.
Smythe, Donald, *Pershing: General of the Armies*, Bloomington: University of Indiana Press, 1986.
Striner, Richard, *Woodrow Wilson and World War I: A Burden Too Great to Bear*, New York: Rowman and Littlefield, 2016.
Taylor, A.J.P., *The First World War*, London: Harmondsworth, 1966.
Taylor, A.J.P., *War by Timetable: How the First World War Began*, New York: American Heritage Press, 1969.
Toland, John, *Battle: The Story of the Bulge*, New York: Random House, 1959.
Toland, John, *The Last 100 Days: The Tumultuous and Controversial Story of the Final Days of World War II in Europe*, New York: Modern Library, 2003.
Tucker-Jones, Anthony, *Operation Dragoon: The Liberation of Southern France, 1944*, Barnsley: Pen & Sword, 2010.
Van Creveld, Martin, *Fighting Power: German and US Army Performances, 1939–1845*, Westport, Connecticut: Greenwood, 1982.
Weeks, Albert, *Russia's Life Saver: Lend Lease Aid to the USSR in World War II*, New York: Lexington Books, 2004.
Weighley, Russell, *History of the United States Army*, New York: Macmillan, 1967.
Weigley, Russell, *Eisenhower's Lieutenants: The Campaigns of France and Germany, 1944–1945*, Bloomington: University of Indiana Press, 1981.
Welsome, Eileen, *The General and the Jaguar: Pershing's Hunt for Pancho Villa: A True Tale of Revolution and Revenge*, New York: Little, Brown, 2009.
Whiting, Charles, *Patton*, New York: Ballantine, 1970.
Whiting, Charles, *48 Hours to Hammelburg: Patton's Secret Mission*, New York: PJB Books, 1982.

Whiting, Charles, *Bounce the Rhine*, New York: Stein and Day, 1986.
Whiting, Charles, *Patton's Last Battle*, New York: Stein and Day, 1987.
Whiting, Charles, *The Battle of Hurtgen Forest*, New York: Da Capo, 2000.
Williams, Vernon, *Lieutenant. Patton and the American Army in the Mexican Punitive Expedition, 1915–1916*, Austin: Presidial Press, 1983.
Williamson, Porter, *Patton's Principles for Life and Leadership*, Tucson: Management and Systems Consultants, 2009.
Wilson, Dale, *Treat 'Em Rough: The Birth of American Armor, 1917–1920*, Novato, California: Presidio Press, 1990.
Wishnevsky, Stephen, *Courtney Hicks Hodges: From Private to Four Star General in the United States Army*, Jefferson, North Carolina: McFarland, 2006.
Zabecki, David, *The German 1918 Offensives: A Case Study of the Operational Level of War*, New York: Routledge, 2006.

Articles

Dietrich, Steven, 'The Professional Reading of General George S. Patton, Jr', *Journal of Military History*, Vol. 53 (October 1989), 387–418.
Weingartner, James, 'Massacre at Biscari: Patton and an American War Crime', *Historian*, Vol. 52 (November 1989), 27–39.

ENDNOTES

Patton Papers

Martin Blumenson, *The Patton Papers, 1885–1940*, Vol. 1 (New York: Da Capo, 1996).
Martin Blumenson, Martin, *The Patton Papers, 1940–1945*, Vol 2. (New York: Da Capo, 1996).

Patton, War As I Knew It

General George S. Patton, *War As I Knew It* (New York: Houghton Mifflin, 1995).

1 For the best biographies, see Fred Ayer, *George S. Patton Jr: Before the Colors Fade, Portrait of a Soldier* (London: Cassell, 1964); Charles Whiting, *Patton* (New York: Ballantine, 1970); William Mellor, *Patton: The Last Cavalier* (New York: Putnam, 1971); Charles Province, *The Unknown Patton* (New York: Bonanza Books, 1983); Martin Blumenson, *Patton: The Man Behind the Legend* (New York: William Morrow, 1985); Carlo D'Este, *Patton: A Genius for War* (New York: Harper Perennial, 1996); Stanley Hirshson, *General Patton: A Solder's Life* (New York: Harper Perennial, 2003); Ladislas Fargo, *Patton: Ordeal and Triumph* (New York: Westholme Publishing, 2005). For published primary sources of Patton's words see George Patton, *War as I Knew It* (New York: Houghton Mifflin, 1995); Martin Blumenson, *The Patton Papers, 1885–1940* (New York: Da Capo, 1996); Martin Blumenson, *The Patton Papers, 1940–1945* (New York: Da Capo, 1996); Porter Williamson (ed.), *General Patton's Principles for Life and Leadership* (Tucson: Management and Systems Consultants, 2009).

2 William Nester, *World of War: A History of American Warfare from Jamestown to the War on Terror* (New York: Stackpole Books, 2024); William Nester, *Land of War: A History of European Warfare from Achilles to Putin* (New York: Stackpole Books, 2023).

3 Patton Papers, 2:625.

4 Patton Papers, 1:163.

5 D'Este, *Patton*, 104–05; *Patton Papers*, 1:119, 137.

6 *Patton Papers*, 1:132; 2:647; Patton, *War As I Knew It*, 248, 335, 340, 354.

7 Patton, *War As I Knew It*, 357.

8 Patton Papers, 1:676.

9 Patton, *War As I Knew It*, 366.

10 Patton Papers, 1:463.
11 Patton, *War As I Knew It*, 342.
12 *Patton Papers*, 2:296–97.
13 *Patton Papers*, 2:148–49.
14 *Patton Papers*, 1:792, 818.
15 Patton Papers, 1:463.
16 *Patton Papers*, 2:259–60.
17 Patton, *War As I Knew It*, 336.
18 Patton Papers, 2:317.
19 *Patton Papers*, 2:339–40.
20 Patton Papers,1:104.
21 Patton Papers, 1:167.
22 Patton Papers, 2:320.
23 Patton Papers, 2:636.
24 Patton Papers, 1:133.
25 Patton Papers, 2:247.
26 *Patton Papers*, 2:736–37.
27 Patton Papers, 1:686.
28 Both quotes from Stanley Hirshon, *General Patton: A Soldier's Life* (New York: Harper Perennial, 2003), 4.
29 His autobiography is replete with criticisms: Omar Bradley and Clay Blair, *A General's Life: An Autobiography by General of the Army* (New York: Simon and Shuster, 1983).
30 *Patton Papers*, 1:102.
31 Carmine Prioli (ed.), *The Poems of General George S. Patton* (New York: Edwin Mellen Press, 1991), 159,
32 *Patton Papers*, 1:675.
33 *Patton Papers*, 2:316.
34 *Patton Papers*, 1:783.
35 *Patton Papers*, 1:8, 2:843.
36 Craig Malkin, *Rethinking Narcissism: The Secret to Recognizing and Coping with Narcissists* (New York; Harper Perennial, 2016).
37 *Patton Papers*, 2:717.
38 Patton, *War As I Knew It*, 8.
39 *Patton Papers*, 1:173.
40 D'Este, *Patton*, 260–61.
41 D'Este, *Patton*, 326.
42 *Patton Papers*, 1:146–47.
43 Harry Semmes, *Portrait of Patton* (New York: Appleton-Century-Crofts, 1955), 44–45.
44 Prioli, *The Poems of Patton*, 128–29.
45 *Patton Papers*, 1:160.
46 *Patton Papers*, 1:344.
47 *Patton Papers*, 1:550, 347; 470.
48 *Patton Papers*, 1:428.
49 *Patton Papers*, 2:6.
50 *Patton Papers*, 2:259.
51 D'Este, *Patton*, 799.
52 *Patton Papers*, 2:463–64.
53 *Patton Papers*, 2:852–53.
54 *Patton Papers*, 1:30–31.
55 *Patton Papers*, 1:34.

56 D'Este, *Patton*, 46, 47.
57 *Patton Papers*, 1:52.
58 Patton Papers, 1:78.
59 Hirshon, *Patton*, 31.
60 *Patton Papers*, 1:89.
61 *Patton Papers*, 1:97–98.
62 *Patton Papers*, 1:90.
63 *Patton Papers*, 1:96–97.
64 *Patton Papers*, 1:176–77.
65 *Patton Papers*, 1:106.
66 *Patton Papers*, 2;259.
67 Patton, *War As I Knew It*, 368.
68 *Patton Papers*, 1:112, 137, 157, 191.
69 *Patton Papers*, 1:157.
70 *Patton Papers*, 1:158.
71 *Patton Papers*, 1:160.
72 Russell Weighley, *History of the United States Army* (New York: Macmillan, 1967), 334.
73 *Patton Papers*, 1:193.
74 *Patton Papers*, 1:195–96.
75 D'Este, *Patton*, 114.
76 *Patton Papers*, 1:200–01.
77 D'Este, *Patton*, 116.
78 D'Este, *Patton*, 122.
79 *Patton Papers*, 1:226.
80 *Patton Papers*, 1:232.
81 Patton, *War As I Knew It*, 368.
82 *Patton Papers*, 1:283.
83 For overviews of World War I see A.J.P. Taylor, The First World War (London: Harmondsworth, 1966); John Keegan, The First World War (New York: Alfred Knopf, 1999); Neil Ferguson, The Pity of War: Explaining World War I (New York: Basic Books, 1999); G.J. Meyer, A World Undone: The Story of the Great War, 1914–1918 (New York: Bantam, 2015).

For World War I's origins see A.J.P. Taylor, War by Timetable: How the First World War Began (New York: American Heritage Press, 1969); Edward McCullough, How the First World War Began: The Triple Entente and the Coming of the Great War, 1914–1918 (New York: Black Rose Books, 1999).

For World War I tactics see Hubert Johnson, *Breakthrough: Tactics, Technology, and the Search for Victory in World War I* (Novato, California: Presidio Press, 1994).
84 Taylor, *First World War;* Taylor, *War by Timetable.*
85 Ferguson, *Pity of War*, 152.
86 Richard Striner, *Woodrow Wilson and World War I: A Burden Too Great to Bear* (New York: Rowman and Littlefield, 2016).
87 *Patton Papers*, 1:280–81.
88 John Hunt, *Empire and Revolution: The Americans in Mexico since the Civil War* (Berkeley: University of California Press, 2002).
89 For America and Mexico's revolution, see Friedrich Katz, *The Secret War in Mexico: Europe, the United States, and the Mexican Revolution* (Chicago: University of Chicago Press, 1981); John Eisenhower, *Intervention! The United States and the Mexican Revolution, 1913–1917* (New York: W.W. Norton, 1993); James Hurst, *Pancho Villa and Black Jack Pershing: The Punitive Expedition in Mexico* (New York: Praeger, 2008); Jeff Guinn, *War on the Border: Villa, Pershing, and the Texas Rangers, and an American Invasion* (New York: Simon and Schuster, 2021).

90 Robert Quick, *An Affair of Honor: Woodrow Wilson and the Occupation of Veracruz* (Lexington: University of Kentucky Press, 1962).
91 Williams, *Patton*, 7.
92 Guinn, *War on the Border*, 76.
93 Guinn, *War on the Border*, 93.
94 *Patton Papers*, 1:295, 299.
95 *Patton Papers*, 1:298.
96 Donald Smythe, *Pershing: General of the Armies* (Bloomington: University of Indiana Press, 1986); Gene Smith, *Until the Last Trumpet Sounds: The Life of General of the Armies John J. Pershing* (New York: John Wiley, 2001); John J. Pershing, *My Life Before the Great War, 1860–1917* (Lexington: University of Kentucky Press, 2013).
97 *Patton Papers*, 1:431.
98 Guinn, *War on the Border*, 107.
99 *Patton Papers*, 1:303.
100 *Patton Papers*, 1:303, 304.
101 *Patton Papers*, 1:306.
102 *Patton Papers*, 1:307–08.
103 Guinn, *War on the Border*, 124.
104 Eileen Welsome, *The General and the Jaguar: Pershing's Hunt for Pancho Villa: A True Tale of Revolution and Revenge* (New York: Little, Brown, 2009).
105 Vernon Williams, Lieutenant Patton and the American Army in the Mexican Punitive Expedition, 1915–1916 (Austin: Presidial Press, 1983).
106 *Patton Papers*, 1:320.
107 Patton, *War As I Knew It*, 369–71.
108 *Patton Papers*, 1:325–25.
109 *Patton Papers*, 1:330–35.
110 *Patton Papers*, 1:336.
111 *Patton Papers*, 1:341.
112 *Patton Papers*, 1:362.
113 *Patton Papers*, 1:363–64.
114 *Patton Papers*, 1:352.
115 *Patton Papers*, 1:354.
116 *Patton Papers*, 1:367.
117 Guinn, *War on the Border*, 235–36.
118 For the best overviews on America's participation see Byron Farwell, The United States in the Great War, 1917–1918 (New York: W.W. Norton, 1999); James Hallas, Doughboy War: The American Expeditionary Force in World War I (Boulder, Colo.: Lynne Rienner, 2000); John Eisenhower, Yanks: The Epic Story of the American Army in World War I (New York: Free Press, 2001); Alan Axelrod, How America Won World War I: The US Military Victory in the Great War, the Causes, the Course, and the Consequences (Guilford, Connecticut: Globe Pequot, 2018).
119 Eisenhower, *Yanks*, 7.
120 Axelrod, *How America Won World War*, 39.
121 Eisenhower, *Yanks*, 9.
122 Eisenhower, *Yanks*, 10.
123 William Lerner (ed.), *Historical Statistics of the United States: Colonial Times to 1970*, 2 vols. (Washington DC: US Government Bureau of the Census 1975), 2:1104, 1114.
124 Charles Gilbert, *American Financing of World War I* (New York: Praeger, 1970).
125 Eisenhower, *Yanks*, 50–53.

126 William Lerner (ed.), *Historical Statistics of the United States: Colonial Times to 1970*, 2 vols. (Washington DC: US Government Bureau of the Census 1975), 2:1142.
127 William Lerner (ed.), *Historical Statistics of the United States: Colonial Times to 1970*, 2 vols. (Washington DC: US Government Bureau of the Census 1975), 2:1142.
128 Farwell, *Over There*, 149–51.
129 William Lerner (ed.), *Historical Statistics of the United States: Colonial Times to 1970*, 2 vols. (Washington DC: US Government Bureau of the Census 1975), 2:1142.
130 Eisenhower, *Yanks*, 46.
131 Eisenhower, *Yanks*, 91.
132 John Perry, *Pershing: General of the Great War* (New York: Thomas Nelson, 2011). Andrew Carroll, My Fellow Soldiers: General John J. Pershing and the Americans Who Helped Win World War I (New York: Penguin, 2017); John J. Pershing, My Experiences in the World War, vols. 1–2 (New York: Arcadia Press, 2019).
133 Pershing, *World War*, 30–31.
134 Pershing, *World War*, 14.
135 *Patton Papers*, 1:422.
136 *Patton Papers*, 1:426.
137 *Patton Papers*, 1:474, 431.
138 *Patton Papers*, 2:256.
139 *Patton Papers*, 1:431, 425.
140 *Patton Papers*, 1:400.
141 *Patton Papers*, 1:428.
142 *Patton Papers*, 2:856.
143 *Patton Papers*, 1:410.
144 *Patton Papers*, 1:408, 420.
145 Eisenhower, *Yanks*, 78, 80.
146 Pershing, *World War*, 57.
147 Pershing, *World War*, 158.
148 Pershing, *World War*, 87.
149 Eisenhower, *Yanks*, 57–58.
150 Lucian Thayer, America's First Eagles: The Official History of the US Air Service, 1917–1918 (Mesa, Arizona: James Bender Publishing and Champlin Fighter Museum Press, 1983).
151 Pershing, *World War*, 75.
152 Pershing, *World War*, 77
153 Farwell, *Over There*, 141, 145.
154 George Marshall, *Memoirs of My Service in World War I, 1917–1918* (Boston: Houghton Mifflin, 1976).
155 *Patton Papers*, 1:403.
156 *Patton Papers*, 1:423.
157 *Patton Papers*, 1:427.
158 Dale Wilson, Treat 'Em Rough: The Birth of American Armor, 1917–1920 (Novato, California: Presidio Press, 1990); Albert Mroz, American Military Vehicles of World War I (Jefferson, North Carolina: McFarland, 2009); Lawrence Kaplan (ed.), Pershing's Tankers: Personal Accounts of the AEF Tank Corps in World War I (Lexington: University of Kentucky Press, 2018); Bryan Cooper, Tank Battles of World War I (Barnsley: Pen & Sword, 2023).
159 David Fletcher, *British Battle Tanks: World War I to 1939* (London: Osprey, 2016).
160 Steven Cooper, *French Tanks of World War I* (London: Osprey, 2010).

161 *Patton Papers*, 1: 479.
162 *Patton Papers*, 1:474.
163 Hirshson, *Patton*, 102.
164 Byrn Hammond, *Cambrai 1917: The Myth of the First Great Tank Battle* (London: Weidenfeld and Nicolson, 2008).
165 *Patton Papers*, 1:450.
166 *Patton Papers*, 1:454–55.
167 *Patton Papers*, 1:455.
168 *Patton Papers*, 1:456.
169 *Patton Papers*, 1:446.
170 *Patton Papers*, 1:493.
171 *Patton Papers*, 1:535.
172 *Patton Papers*, 1:562.
173 Eisenhower, *Yanks*, 47.
174 *Patton Papers*, 1:509.
175 Patton, *War As I Knew It*, 372.
176 David Zabecki, *The German 1918 Offensives: A Case Study of the Operational Level of War* (New York: Routledge, 2006); Ian Passingham, *The German Offensives of 1918: The Last Desperate Gamble* (Barnsley: Pen & Sword, 2008).
177 Pershing, *World War*, 83.
178 Pershing, *World War*, 232–34.
179 James Hallas, *Squandered Victory: The American First Army at St Mihiel* (New York: Praeger, 1995); Maarten Otte, *The St Mihiel Offensive, 12 to 16 September 1918* (Barnsley: Pen & Sword, 2020).
180 Pershing, *World War*, 342.
181 *Patton Papers*, 1:568.
182 *Patton Papers*, 1:581–82.
183 *Patton Papers*, 1:585.
184 *Patton Papers*, 1:587.
185 *Patton Papers*, 1:589–90.
186 *Patton Papers*, 1:590–92, 596.
187 Robert Ferrell, *America's Deadliest Battle: Meuse-Argonne, 1918* (Lawrence: University Press of Kansas, 2007); Edward Lengel, *To Conquer Hell: The Meuse-Argonne, 1918, The Epic Battle That Ended the First World War* (New York: Henry Holt, 2008).
188 *Patton Papers*, 1:602.
189 *Patton Papers*, 1:616–17.
190 *Patton Papers*, 1:613.
191 *Patton Papers*, 1:616–17.
192 Hirshson, *Patton*, 134.
193 *Patton Papers*, 1:629, 622, 631.
194 *Patton Papers*, 1: 623.
195 Joseph Persico, *Eleventh Month, Eleventh Day, Eleventh Hour: Armistice Day, 1918, World War I and Its Violent Climax* (New York: Random House, 2005).
196 Pershing, *World War*, 406, 402.
197 Farwell, *Over There*, 19, 189–205, 265; Ferguson, *Pity of War*, 316; Hirshson, *Patton*, 131.
198 Ferguson, *Pity of War*, 295, 299.
199 Ferguson, *Pity of War*, 295.
200 Ferguson, *Pity of War*, 336, 445.
201 Ferguson, *Pity of War*, 325.
202 *Patton Papers*, 1:665.

203 Hirshon, *Patton*, 136.
204 *Patton Papers*, 1:642, 661.
205 *Patton Papers*, 1:680, 687, 688.
206 *Patton Papers*, 1:721.
207 Charles Odom, *General George S. Patton and Eisenhower* (New Orleans: Word Picture Productions, 1985).
208 For the best military biography of Eisenhower see Carlo D'Este, *Eisenhower: A Soldier's Life* (New York: Henry Holt, 2002). See also Merle Miller, *Ike the Soldier: As They Knew Him* (New York: Putnam, 1986); Stephen Ambrose, *Eisenhower: Soldier and President* (New York: Touchstone, 1991); Jean Smith, *Eisenhower in War and Peace* (New York: Random House, 2013).
209 Robert Patton, *The Pattons: The Personal History of an American Family* (New York: Crown, 1994), 128–29.
210 Dwight Eisenhower, *At Ease: Stories I Tell My Friends* (Garden City, New York: Doubleday, 1967), 169.
211 Eisenhower, *At Ease*, 173.
212 Eisenhower, *At Ease*, 171, 173.
213 Eisenhower, *At Ease*, 173.
214 Ruth Ellen Patton Totten, *The Button Box: A Daughter's Loving Memory of Beatrice Ayer Patton* (Columbia: University of Missouri Press, 2005), 122.
215 *Patton Papers*, 1:937-38.
216 *Patton Papers*, 1:806, 809–10.
217 *Patton Papers*, 1:889.
218 *Patton Papers*, 1:722.
219 *Patton Papers*, 1:751, 760, 764.
220 *Patton Papers*, 1:778.
221 *Patton Papers*, 1:784.
222 *Patton Papers*, 1:787–88.
223 *Patton Papers*, 1:793.
224 *Patton Papers*, 1:801.
225 Patton Papers, 1:896–97.
226 Stanley Payne, *A History of Fascism, 1914–1945* (Madison: University of Wisconsin Press, 1995); Robert Paxton, *The Anatomy of Fascism* (New York: Vintage, 2004).
227 Wayne Cole, *Roosevelt and the Isolationists, 1932–45* (Lincoln: University of Nebraska Press, 1983).
228 Totten, *Button Box*, 258.
229 Totten, *Button Box*, 261.
230 Forrest Pogue, *George C. Marshall: Ordeal and Hope, 1939–1942* (New York: Viking, 1966); Forrest Pogue, *George C. Marshall: Organizer of Victory, 1943–1945* (New York: Viking, 1973); Ed Cray, *General of the Army: George C. Marshall Soldier and Statesman* (New York: Touchstone Books, 1990).
231 Cray, *General of the Army*, 374.
232 *Patton Papers*, 1:939.
233 *Patton Papers*, 1:939; 944.
234 Warren Kimball, The Most Unsordid Act: Lease-Lease, 1939–1945 (New York: Routledge, 2019); Albert Weeks, Russia's Life Saver: Lend Lease Aid to the USSR in World War II (New York: Lexington Books, 2004).
235 For overviews of Roosevelt's foreign policy and the Anglo-American alliance see Robert Dallek, *Franklin D. Roosevelt and American Foreign Policy, 1932–1945* (New York: Oxford University Press, 1979); David Reynolds, *The Creation of the Anglo-American Alliance, 1937–1941* (Chapel Hill: University of North Carolina Press,

1981); David Reynolds, *From Munich to Pearl Harbor: Roosevelt's America and the Origins of the Second World War* (Chicago: Ivan Dee, 2001).

For relations between Roosevelt and Churchill see Keith Sainsbury, *Churchill and Roosevelt at War: The War They Fought and the Peace They Hoped to Make* (New York: New York University Press, 1994); Jon Meacham, *Franklin and Winston: An Intimate Portrait of an Epic Friendship* (New York: Random House, 2003).

For biographies of each see William Nester, *Winston Churchill and the Art of Leadership* (Barnsley: Pen & Sword / Frontline Books, 2020); William Nester, *Franklin D. Roosevelt and the Art of Leadership* (Barnsley: Pen & Sword / Frontline Books, 2024).

236 William Lerner (ed.), *Historical Statistics of the United States: Colonial Times to 1970*, 2 vols. (Washington DC: US Government Bureau of the Census 1975), 2:1141.

237 William Lerner (ed.), *Historical Statistics of the United States: Colonial Times to 1970*, 2 vols. (Washington DC: US Government Bureau of the Census 1975), 2:1141.

238 William Lerner (ed.), *Historical Statistics of the United States: Colonial Times to 1970*, 2 vols. (Washington DC: US Government Bureau of the Census 1975), 2:1141.

239 Doubler, *Closing with the Enemy*, 266.

240 Atkinson, *Guns at Last Light*, 19, 240.

241 William Lerner (ed.), *Historical Statistics of the United States: Colonial Times to 1970*, 2 vols. (Washington DC: US Government Bureau of the Census 1975), 2:1141.

242 Lerner, *Historical Statistics*, 1:224,135.

243 For a good overview of the American army's development in organization and doctrine during World War II, see Russell Weighley, *Eisenhower's Lieutenants: The Campaign of France and Germany, 1944–1945* (Bloomington: Indiana University Press, 1981), 1–76.

244 Weighley, *Eisenhower's Lieutenants*, 19.

245 For the best comparison of weapons and tactics see Victor Hanson, *The Second World Wars: The First Global Conflict Was Fought and Won* (New York: Basic Books, 2020).

246 *Patton Papers*, 2:310.

247 Patton, *War As I Knew It*, 220.

248 Hanson, *Second World Wars*, 141, 160–62, 165–66,

249 Peter Elphick, *Liberty: The Ships that Won the War* (Annapolis, Maryland: Naval Institute Press, 2006).

250 Hanson, *Second World Wars*, 222.

251 Hanson, *Second World Wars*, 75.

252 Doubler, *Closing with the Enemy*, 67–69, 77–78, 86.

253 Atkinson, *Guns at Last Light*, 350–51; Hanson, *Second World Wars*, 101.

254 *Patton Papers*, 2:681.

255 Martin Van Creveld, *Fighting Power: German and US Army Performances, 1939-1845* (Westport, Connecticut: Greenwood, 1982); Lee Kennett, *G.I.: The American Soldier in World War II* (New York: Charles Scribner's Sons, 1986); Michael Doubler, *Closing with the Enemy: How GIs Fought the War in Europe, 1944–1945* (Lawrence: University Press of Kansas, 1994); S.L.A. Marshall, *Men Against Fire: The Problem of Battle Command* (Norman: University of Oklahoma Press, 2000).

256 Weighley, *Eisenhower's Lieutenants*, 4, 7.

257 D'Este, *Patton*, 380.

258 *Patton Papers*, 1:956.

259 *Patton Papers*, 1:956.
260 *Patton Papers*, 2:14–15.
261 Donald Houston, *Hell on Wheels: The 2nd Armored Division* (Novato, California: Presidio, 1977), 43.
262 Hirshon, *Patton*, 236.
263 Houston, *Hell on Wheels*, 46–47.
264 Christopher Gabel, *The US Army GHQ Manuevers of 1941* (Washington DC: Center of Military History, 1991).
265 *Patton Papers*, 2:36.
266 *Patton Papers*, 2:36.
267 Pogue, *Marshall: Ordeal and Hope*, 89.
268 Bradley, *A General's Life*, 99–100.
269 Both quotes from *Patton Papers*, 2;42, 43.
270 *Patton Papers*, 2:44–45.
271 D'Este, *Patton*, 378.
272 Basil Liddel Hart, *History of the Second World War* (London: Cassell, 1970); Martin Gilbert, *The Second World War: A Complete History* (New York: Henry Holt, 2004); Evan Mawdsley *World War II: A New History* (New York: Cambridge University Press, 2020).
273 Winston Churchill, *Memoirs of the Second World War* (abridged version) (Boston: Houghton Mifflin, 1987), 506–08.
274 *Patton Papers*, 2:46.
275 *Patton Papers*, 2:67.
276 Jonathan Jordan, *Brothers-Rivals-Victors: Eisenhower, Patton, Bradley, and the Partnership that Drove the Allied Conquest in Europe* (New York: Nal Caliber, 2011), 46.
277 Dwight Eisenhower, *Crusade in Europe* (Garden City, New York: Doubleday, 1948), 41.
278 Keith Sainsbury, *The North African Landings, 1942* (Newark: University of Delaware Press, 1979); William Brewer, *Operation Torch: The Allied Gamble to Invade North Africa* (New York: St Martin's, 1988); Norman Gelb, *Desperate Venture: The Story of Operation Torch, the Allied Invasion of North Africa* (New York: W.W. Norton, 1992); Rick Atkinson, *An Army at Dawn: The War in North Africa, 1942–1943* (New York: Henry Holt, 2002); Orr Kelly, *Meeting the Fox: The Allied Invasion of Africa from Operation Torch to Kasserine Pass to Victory in Tunisia* (New York: Wiley, 2002).
279 Eisenhower, *Crusade in Europe*, 78.
280 *Patton Papers*, 2:83.
281 *Patton Papers*, 2:93.
282 Oscar Koch, *G-2 Intelligence for Patton* (Philadelphia: Army Times / Whitmore, 1971).
283 Patrick Bishop, *Operation Jubilee: Dieppe, 1942, The Folly and the Sacrifice* (New York: Signal, 2021).
284 Eisenhower, *Crusade in Europe*, 82.
285 *Patton Papers*, 2:93.
286 *Patton Papers*, 2:94.
287 D'Este, *Patton*, 425.
288 *Patton Papers*, 2:103.
289 *Patton Papers*, 2:9597.
290 Jonathan Dimbleby, *Destiny in the Desert: The Road to El Alamein – The Battle that Turned the Tide* (New York: Profile Books, 2012).
291 Norman Gelb, *Ike and Monty: Generals at War* (New York: William Morrow, 1994); G.E. Murray, *Eisenhower versus Montgomery: The Continuing Debate* (Westport, Connecticut: Praeger, 1996).

292 Jonathan Jordan, *Brothers, Rivals, Victors: Eisenhower, Patton, Bradley and the Partnership that Drove the Allied Conquest in Europe* (New York: Dutton Caliber, 2018), 175.
293 Harry Butcher, *Three Years with Eisenhower* (New York: Simon and Schuster, 1946), 568.
294 Bernard Montgomery, *The Memoirs of Field Marshall Montgomery* (New York: Da Capo Press, 1958); Nigel Hamilton, *Monty: Master of the Battlefield* (London: Hamish Hamilton, 1983); Nigel Hamilton, *Monty, The Field Marshal*, (London: Hamish Hamilton, 1986); Nigel Hamilton, *Monty, The Battles of Field Marshal Bernard Montgomery* (New York: Random House, 1994).
295 Hamilton, *Monty: Master of the Battlefield, 1942–1944*, xxv.
296 Atkinson, *Army at Dawn*, 107.
297 Atkinson, *Army at Dawn*, 76.
298 *Patton Papers*, 2:100.
299 *Patton Papers*, 2:102.
300 *Patton Papers*, 2:97.
301 *Patton Papers*, 2:114.
302 Atkinson, *Army at Dawn*, 144.
303 Patton, *War As I Knew It*, 8.
304 *Patton Papers*, 2:108.
305 *Patton Papers*, 2:109.
306 D'Este, *Eisenhower*, 355.
307 *Patton Papers*, 2:111.
308 Atkinson, *Army at Dawn*, 150, 159.
309 Atkinson, *Army at Dawn*, 159–60.
310 Jordan, *Brothers-Rivals-Victors*, 102.
311 Mark Clark, *Calculated Risk* (New York: Harper and Row, 1951), 127.
312 Richard Langworth (ed.), *Churchill by Himself* (New York: Public Affairs, 2009), 8.
313 *Patton Papers*, 2:143–44.
314 *Patton Papers*, 2:125.
315 *Patton Papers*, 2:146.
316 *Patton Papers*, 2;119.
317 D'Este, *Patton*, 452; Patton Papers, 2:171.
318 Jordan, *Brothers-Rivals-Victors*, 197.
319 *Patton Papers*, 2:122–23.
320 *Patton Papers*, 2:172.
321 Atkinson, *Army at Dawn*, 288.
322 Carlo D'Este, *Eisenhower: A Soldier's Story* (New York: Henry Holt, 2002), 382.
323 Eisenhower, *Crusade in Europe*, 160.
324 *Patton Papers*, 2:162.
325 *Patton Papers*, 2:169.
326 *Patton Papers*, 2:156.
327 Alex Danchev and Daniel Todman (eds.), *War Diaries, 1939–1945, Alan Brooke* (Berkely: University of California Press, 2001), 362.
328 *Patton Papers*, 2:171.
329 Martin Blumenson, *Kasserine Pass: Rommel's Bloody, Climatic Battle for Tunisia* (New York: Cooper Square Press, 2000).
330 Atkinson, *Army at Dawn*, 377.
331 D'Este, *Bitter Victory*, 59.
332 Leo Barron, *Patton's First Victory: How General George Patton Turned the Tide in North Africa and Defeated Afrika Korps at El Guettar* (New York: Stackpole, 2017).

333 Jonathan Jordan, *Brothers, Rivals, Victors: Eisenhower, Patton, Bradley and the Partnership that Drove the Allied Conquest in Europe* (New York: Dutton Caliber, 2018).
334 Jim DeFelice, *Omar Bradley: General at War* (New York: Regnery, 2014); Steven Osgood, *Omar Nelson Bradley: America's GI General* (Columbia: University of Missouri Press, 2017).
335 Bradley, *A General's Life*, 63.
336 *Patton Papers*, 2:232.
337 Omar Bradley, *A Soldier's Story* (New York: Henry Holt, 1951); Omar Bradley, with Clay Blair, *A General's Life* (New York: Simon and Schuster, 1983).
338 *Patton Papers*, 2:252.
339 *Patton Papers*, 2:187.
340 Omar Bradley, *A Soldier's Story* (New York: Henry Holt, 1951), 44–45.
341 Bradley, *A General's Story*, 140.
342 Eisenhower, *Crusade in Europe*, 150.
343 *Patton Papers*, 2:55.
344 *Patton Papers*, 2;195.
345 *Patton Papers*, 2:218.
346 Leo Barron, *Patton's First Victory: How General George Patton Turned the Tide in North Africa and Defeated the Afrika Korps at El Guettar* (New York: Stackpole Books, 2018).
347 Barron, *Patton's First Victory*, 188.
348 *Patton Papers*, 2:197–98.
349 *Patton Papers*, 2:199.
350 *Patton Papers*, 2:200.
351 *Patton Papers*, 2:196, 198.
352 *Patton Papers*, 2:207.
353 *Patton Papers*, 2:208–09.
354 Jordan, *Brothers-Rivals-Victors*, 157.
355 *Patton Papers*, 2:213.
356 D'Este, *Eisenhower*, 370.
357 *Patton Papers*, 2:231.
358 *Patton Papers*, 2:223.
359 Bradley, *A General's Story*, 151.
360 Bradley, *A General's Life*, 146.
361 *Patton Papers*, 2:232.
362 Bradley, *A General's Life*, 159; Atkinson, *Army at Dawn*, 536–37.
363 Samuel Mitcham and Friedrich von Stauffenberg, *The Battle of Sicily: How the Allies Lost Their Chance for Total Victory* (New York: Orion Books, 1991); Carlo D'Este, *Bitter Victory: The Battle for Sicily, 1943* (New York: E.P. Dutton, 1988); Rick Atkinson, *The Day of Battle: The War in Sicily and Italy, 1943–1944* (New York: Henry Holt, 2007).
364 For an overview of the conference and the quotations see *Patton Papers*, 2:234–37.
365 *Patton Papers*, 2:236.
366 D'Este, *Eisenhower*, 424.
367 *Patton Papers*, 2:235–38.
368 *Patton Papers*, 2:240.
369 Ladislas Fargo, *Patton: Ordeal and Triumph* (New York: Westholme Publishing, 2005), 273.
370 *Patton Papers*, 2:229.
371 *Patton Papers*, 2:247, 276.
372 Bradley, *A General's Life*, 170.

373 *Patton Papers*, 2:250, 255.
374 *Patton Papers*, 257, 268.
375 *Patton Papers*, 2:244.
376 *Patton Papers*, 2:244.
377 *Patton Papers*, 2:245.
378 *Patton Papers*, 2:272.
379 D'Este, *Bitter Victory*, 606.
380 D'Este, *Bitter Victory*, 596.
381 Patton, *War As I Knew It*, 54–55.
382 Patton, *War As I Knew It*, 55.
383 *Patton Papers*, 2:278-79.
384 *Patton Papers*, 2:279.
385 *Patton Papers*, 2:280.
386 D'Este, *Bitter Victory*, 305-08.
387 *Patton Papers*, 2:283–84. For more details of the meeting see Bradley, *A General's Story*, 184–86.
388 *Patton Papers*, 2:283.
389 *Patton Papers*, 2:289–90.
390 Bradley, *A General's Life*, 188.
391 Bradley, *A General's Life*, 189.
392 Bradley, *A General's Life*, 188–89.
393 D'Este, *Bitter Victory*, 333.
394 *Patton Papers*, 2:290.
395 Patton, *War As I Knew It*, 57–58.
396 *Patton Papers*, 2:293–94.
397 *Patton Papers*, 2:288–89.
398 Patton, *War As I Knew It*, 63; D'Este, *Bitter Victory*, 424.
399 Bradley, *A General's Story*, 193.
400 *Patton Papers*, 2:302–03.
401 *Patton Papers*, 2:302.
402 *Patton Papers*, 2:306.
403 Bradley, *A General's Life*, 136, 195.
404 *Patton Papers*, 2:314.
405 *Patton Papers*, 2: 322.
406 D'Este, *Bitter Victory*, 514–15, 523.
407 D'Este, *Bitter Victory*, 609.
408 D'Este, *Bitter Victory*, 552, 560, 597; Bradley, *A General's Story*, 200.
409 Bradley, *A General's Story*, 194.
410 D'Este, *Bitter Victory*, 524–25, 526.
411 D'Este, *Bitter Victory*, 532.
412 Eisenhower, *Crusade in Europe*, 167.
413 Dominick Graham and Shelford Bidwell, *Tug of War: The Battle for Italy, 1943-1945* (New York: St Martin's Press, 1986).
414 D'Este, *Bitter Victory*, 430.
415 Eisenhower, *Crusade in Europe*, 186.
416 *Patton Papers*, 2:344.
417 Atkinson, *Day of Battle*, 581.
418 John Acquilla, *Why the Axis Lost: An Analysis of Strategic Errors* (Jefferson, North Carolina: McFarland, 2020), 116.
419 *Patton Papers*, 2:334–35.
420 *Patton Papers*, 2:318.
421 *Patton Papers*, 2:325.

422 Hirshon, *Patton*, 2.
423 Hirshon, *Patton*, 1.
424 Carlo D'Este, *Bitter Victory: The Battle for Sicily, 1943* (New York: E.P. Dutton, 1988), 317.
425 James Weingartner, 'Massacre at Biscari: Patton and an American War Crime' *Historian*, Vol. 52 (November 1989), 27–39; Hirshon, *Patton*, 2–3.
426 *Patton Papers*, 2:288.
427 D'Este, *Bitter Victory*, 318–19.
428 *Patton Papers*, 2: 219, 312–13; Jordan, *Brothers-Rivals-Victors*, 235.
429 *Patton Papers*, 2:330.
430 *Patton Papers*, 2:333.
431 *Patton Papers*, 2:331–32.
432 *Patton Papers*, 2:329.
433 Jordan, *Brothers-Rivals-Victors*, 240.
434 Eisenhower, *Crusade in Europe*, 181.
435 *Patton Papers*, 2:340–41.
436 Dwight Eisenhower, *Crusade in Europe* (Garden City, New York: Doubleday, 1948), 180–81.
437 *Patton Papers*, 2:337–38.
438 *Patton Papers*, 2:360.
439 Hirshon, *Patton*, 418.
440 Keith Sainsbury, *The Turning Point: Roosevelt, Stalin, Churchill, and Chiang Kai-shek, 1943: The Moscow, Cairo, and Tehran Conferences* (New York: Oxford University Press, 1985).
441 Conrad Black, *Flight of the Eagle: The Grand Strategies that Brought America from Colonial Dependence to World Leadership* (New York: Encounter Books, 2013), 421.
442 Eisenhower, *Crusade in Europe*, 207; Forrest Pogue, *George C. Marshall: Organizer of Victory, 1943–1945* (New York: Viking, 1973), 321.
443 *Patton Papers*, 2:374–84; Jordan, *Brothers-Rivals-Victors*, 270.
444 *Patton Papers*, 2:393.
445 *Patton Papers*, 2:349.
446 Eisenhower, *Crusade in Europe*, 215–16.
447 Bradley, *A General's Life*, 218–19.
448 *Patton Papers*, 2:369.
449 *Patton Papers*, 2:407.
450 D'Este, *Patton*, 567–68.
451 *Patton Papers*, 2:457–58.
452 Atkinson, *Guns at Last Light*, 125.
453 *Patton Papers*, 2:43.
454 *Patton Papers*, 2: 435.
455 Eisenhower, *Crusade in Europe*, 224.
456 *Patton Papers*, 2:440–41.
457 D'Este, *Eisenhower*, 506.
458 *Patton Papers*, 2:444–45.
459 *Patton Papers*, 2:452.
460 Eisenhower, *Crusade in Europe*, 225.
461 *Patton Papers*, 2:469–70.
462 *Patton Papers*, 2:451.
463 Jean Smith, *Eisenhower in War and Peace* (New York: Random House, 2013), 345.
464 For D-Day, the classic is: Cornelius Ryan, *The Longest Day* (New York: Touchstone, 1994).

For the Normandy campaign see John Keegan, *Six Armies in Normandy: From D-Day to the Liberation of Paris* (New York: Viking, 1982); Max Hastings, *Overlord: D-Day and the Battle for Normandy, 1944* (New York: Simon and Schuster, 1984); Carlo D'Este, Carlo, *Decision in Normandy: The Real Story of Montgomery and the Allied Campaign* (New York: Penguin, 1994).

For overviews of the northern European campaigns from Normandy to Germany see Russell Weigley, *Eisenhower's Lieutenants: The Campaigns of France and Germany, 1944–1945* (Bloomington: University of Indiana Press, 1981); Charles Brower (ed.) *World War II in Europe: The Final Year* (New York: St Martin's Press, 1998); Rick Atkinson, *The Guns at Last Light: The War in Western Europe, 1944–1945* (New York: Henry Holt, 2013).

465 Atkinson, *Guns at Last Light*, 3.
466 Weighley, *Eisenhower's Lieutenants*, 31; Atkinson, *Guns at Last Light*, 81.
467 Atkinson, *Guns at Last Light*, 23.
468 Weighley, *Eisenhower's Lieutenants*, 94.
469 Weighley, *Eisenhower's Lieutenants*, 106–07.
470 Weighley, *Eisenhower's Lieutenants*, 106.
471 Doubler, *Closing with the Enemy*, 46.
472 Reardon, *Victory at Mortain*, 10; Weighley, *Eisenhower's Lieutenants*, 170.
473 *Patton Papers*, 2:468–69.
474 *Patton Papers*, 2:472.
475 *Patton Papers*, 2:480, 482, 481.
476 Francis Smith, *History of the Third Army* (Washington DC: Historical Section, Army Ground Press, 1946); Paul Harkins, *When the Third Cracked Europe: The Story of Patton's Incredible Army* (Harrisburg, Pa.: Stackpole Books, 1969); George Forty, *Patton's Third Army at War* (New York: Charles Scribner's, 1978).
477 Pierre Galante, *Operation Valkyrie: The German Generals Plot against Hitler* (New York: Cooper Square Press, 2002); Michael Baigent, *Secret Germany: Stauffenberg and the True Story of Operation Valkyrie* (New York: Skyhorse, 2009).
478 Stephen Wishnevsky, *Courtney Hicks Hodges: From Private to Four Star General in the United States Army* (Jefferson, North Carolina: McFarland, 2006).
479 *Patton Papers*, 2:479.
480 *Patton Papers*, 2:479.
481 *Patton Papers*, 2:481.
482 James Carafano, *After D-Day: Operation Cobra and the Normandy Breakout* (Boulder, Colo.: Lynne Rienner, 2000).
483 *Patton Papers*, 2:482.
484 Doubler, *Closing with the Enemy*, 79–80.
485 *Patton Papers*, 2: 490.
486 Patton, *War As I Knew It*, 95.
487 Patton, *War As I Knew It*, 98, 383–84.
488 Weigley, *Eisenhower's Lieutenants*, 174.
489 Patton, *War As I Knew It*, 97–97.
490 *Patton Papers*, 2:491; Patton, *War As I Knew It*, 382.
491 Nat Frankel, *Patton's Best: An Informal History of the Fourth Armored Division* (New York: Hawthorn Books, 1978); Milton Shapiro, *Tank Command: Patton's 4th Armored Division* (New York: David McKay, 1979).
492 Patton, *War As I Knew It*, 101.
493 Province, *Patton's Third Army*, 22, 25–26.
494 Mark Reardon, *Victory at Mortain: Stopping Hitler's Panzer Counteroffensive* (Lawrence: University Press of Kentucky, 2002).
495 *Patton Papers*, 2:503.

496 Richard Rohmer, *Patton's Gap: An Account of the Battle of Normandy* (London: Arms and Armor Press, 1981); Martin Blumenson, *The Battle of the Generals: The Untold Story of the Falaise Pocket that Should Have Won World War II* (New York: William Morrow, 1994).
497 Bradley, *A General's Life*, 295.
498 *Patton Papers*, 2:524.
499 Bradley, *A General's Life*, 298–99.
500 Weighley, *Eisenhower's Lieutenants*, 206.
501 *Patton Papers*, 2:508–09.
502 Weighley, *Eisenhower's Lieutenants*, 209–10.
503 Weighley, *Eisenhower's Lieutenant*, 214; Blumenson, *Battle of the Generals*, 21.
504 *Patton Papers*, 2:510–11.
505 *Patton Papers*, 2:518.
506 Hirshon, *Patton*, 504.
507 *Patton Papers*, 2:520–21.
508 Patton, *War As I Knew It*, 116; *Patton Papers*, 2:526.
509 Anthony Tucker-Jones, *Operation Dragoon: The Liberation of Southern France, 1944* (Barnsley: Pen & Sword, 2010); Robin Cross, *Operation Dragoon: The Allied Liberation of the South of France, 1944* (New York: Pegasus, 2019).
510 Weighley, *Eisenhower's Lieutenants*, 356, 370–71.
511 Patton, *War As I Knew It*, 113.
512 Patton, *War As I Knew It*, 114.
513 Peter Cooksley, *Flying Bomb: The Story of Hitler's V-Weapons in World War II* (New York: Charles Scribners' Sons, 1979); Roy Irons, *Hitler's Terror Weapons: The Price of Vengeance* (New York: Harper Collins, 2003).
514 Roland Ruppenthal, *Logistical Support for the Armies: May 1941 to September 1944*, Vol. 1 (Washington DC: Office of the Chief of Military History, 1953); Roland Ruppenthal, *Logistical Support for the Armies: September 1944 to May 1945*, Vol. 2 (Washington DC: Office of the Chief of1Military History, 1953); D'Este, *Eisenhower*, 585, 589; Atkinson, *Guns at Last Light*, 242, 244–45
515 Atkinson, *Guns at Last Light*, 242.
516 Weighley, *Eisenhower's Lieutenants*, 266.
517 Weighley, *Eisenhower's Lieutenants*, 270–71.
518 D'Este, *Eisenhower*, 588.
519 *Patton Papers*, 2:537.
520 Charles MacDonald, *The Siegfried Line Campaign* (Washington DC: Office of the Chief of Military History, 1963).
521 Weighley, *Eisenhower's Lieutenants*, 266–67.
522 Patton, *War As I Knew It*, 120.
523 *Patton Papers*, 2:537.
524 Cornelius, Ryan, *A Bridge Too Far* (New York: Simon and Schuster, 1995); David Bennett, *A Magnificent Disaster: The Failure of Market Garden, The Arnhem Operation, September 1944* (New York: Casemate, 2011); William Buckingham, *Arnhem: The Complete Story of Operation Market Garden, 17 –25 September 1944* (New York: Amberley Publishing, 2020).
525 Bradley, *A General's Story*, 328.
526 Bradley, *A General's Life*, 311.
527 Weighley, *Eisenhower's Lieutenants*, 293.
528 Atkinson, *Guns at Last Light*, 286.
529 Bradley, *A General's Story*, 332–33.
530 Carlo D'Este, *Eisenhower: A Soldier's Life* (New York: Henry Holt, 2002), 621.
531 Weighley, *Eisenhower's Lieutenants*, 377.

532 Charles Whiting, *The Battle of Hurtgen Forest* (New York: Da Capo, 2000).
533 Jordan, *Brothers-Rivals-Victors*, 412.
534 Doubler, *Closing with the Enemy*, 241.
535 Hirshon, *Patton*, 608; Weighley, *Eisenhower's Lieutenants*, 438.
536 Calculated by subtracting Chart 8.1's calculations from this one, Patton, *War As I Knew It*, 126.
537 Calculated by subtracting Chart 8.2's calculations from this one, Patton, *War As I Knew It*, 126.
538 Calculated by subtracting Chart 8.1's and Chart 8.3's calculations from this one, Patton, *War As I Knew It*, 192.
539 Calculated by subtracting Chart 8.2's and Char 8.4's calculations from this one, Patton, *War As I Knew It*, 192.
540 Anthony Kemp, *The Unknown Battle: Metz, 1944* (New York: Stein and Day, 1985).
541 For a good account of Patton's last year the battle of the Bulge to his death see Charles Whiting, *Patton's Last Battle* (New York: Stein and Day, 1987).
542 *Patton Papers*, 2:582.
543 Province, *Patton's Third Army*, 109, 113–14,
544 John Toland, *Battle: The Story of the Bulge* (New York: Random House, 1959); Robert Merriam, *The Battle of the Bulge* (New York: Ballantine Books, 1978); Trevor Dupuy, *Hitler's Last Gamble: The Battle of the Bulge, December 1944 to January 1945* (New York: Harper Collins, 1994); J.D. Morelock, *Generals of the Ardennes; American Leadership in the Battle of the Bulge* (Washington DC: National Defense University Press, 1994); Charles MacDonald, *A Time for Trumpets: The Untold Story of the Battle of the Bulge* (New York: William Morrow, 1997); Peter Caddick-Adams, *Snow and Steel: The Battle of the Bulge, 1944–45* (New York: Oxford University Press, 2014); Christer Bergstrom, *The Ardennes: Hitler's Winter Offensive, 1944–45* (New York: Casemate, 2014).
545 *Patton Papers*, 2:595.
546 Bradley, *A General's Life*, 357–58.
547 Eisenhower, *Crusade in Europe*, 350.
548 D'Este, *Eisenhower*, 644–46.
549 Jonathan Jordan, *Brothers-Rivals-Victors: Eisenhower, Patton, Bradley, and the Partnership that Drove the Allied Conquest in Europe*, (New York: Nal Caliber, 2011), 5.
550 *Patton Papers*, 2:601.
551 Bradley, *A General's Life*, 368.
552 *Patton Papers*, 2:606.
553 *Patton Papers*, 2:608.
554 Patton, *War As I Knew It*, 197-98.
555 Bradley, *A General's Life*, 367.
556 Omar Bradley, *A Soldier's Story* (New York: Henry Hot, 1951), 473.
557 Robert Phillips, *To Save Bastogne* (New York: Stein and Day, 1983); Ralph Mitchell, *The 101st Airborne Division's Defense of Bastogne* (Fort Leavenworth, Kansas: Combat Studies Institute, 1986).
558 *Patton Papers*, 2:608.
559 Doubler, *Closing with the Enemy*, 222.
560 Charles Province, *Patton's Third Army: A Chronology of the Third Army Advance, August 1944 to May 1945* (New York: Hippocrene Books, 1992), 131.
561 Province, *Patton's Third Army*, 139.
562 *Patton Papers*, 2:610.
563 *Patton Papers*, 2:611.

564 *Patton Papers*, 2:612
565 *Patton Papers*, 2:627.
566 *Patton Papers*, 2:615.
567 D'Este, *Patton*, 701; D'Este, *Eisenhower*, 662; Weighley, *Eisenhower's Lieutenants*, 574; Province, *Patton's Third Army*, 154.
568 Calculated by subtracting the figures from the previous charts, *Patton, War As I Knew* It, 201, 229.
569 Calculated by subtracting the figures from the previous charts, *Patton, War As I Knew* It, 201, 229.
570 Jordan, *Brothers-Rivals-Victors*, 466.
571 Bradley, *A General's Life*, 382–83.
572 Bradley, *A General's Life*, 382, 384.
573 *Patton Papers*, 2:724.
574 Russell Weighley, *Eisenhower's Lieutenants: The Campaign of France and Germany, 1944–1945* (Bloomington: Indiana University Press, 1981), 571, 572.
575 Carlo D'Este, *Eisenhower: A Soldier's Life* (New York: Henry Holt, 2002), 674.
576 Atkinson, *Guns at Last Light*, 512.
577 Franklin Davis, *Across the Rhine* (New York: Time-Life, 1980); Charles Whiting, *Bounce the Rhine* (New York: Stein and Day, 1986); John Toland, *The Last 100 Days: The Tumultuous and Controversial Story of the Final Days of World War II in Europe* (New York: Modern Library, 2003).
578 *Patton Papers*, 2:653.
579 *Patton Papers*, 2:644.
580 Patton, *War As I Knew It*, 235–36.
581 Patton, *War As I Knew It*, 238.
582 Patton, *War As I Knew It*, 238–39.
583 Patton, *War As I Knew It*, 243.
584 Patton, *War As I Knew It*, xx–xxi.
585 Hirshon, *Patton*, 610.
586 *Patton Papers*, 2:660.
587 Calculated by subtracting the figures from the previous charts, *Patton, War As I Knew* It, 201, 229, 256.
588 Calculated by subtracting the figures from the previous charts, *Patton, War As I Knew* It, 201, 229, 256.
589 Omar Bradley, with Clay Blair *A General's Life* (New York: Simon and Schuster, 1983), 412.
590 D'Este, *Patton*, 712.
591 Tim Saunders, *Operation Plunder: The British and Canadian Operations* (Barnsley: Pen & Sword, 2007); Simon Forty, *Across the Rhine, January-May 1945* (New York: Casemate, 2020).
592 Patton, *War As I Knew It*, 275.
593 *Patton Papers*, 2:666.
594 *Patton Papers*, 2:668.
595 *Patton Papers*, 2:671.
596 *Patton Papers*, 2:675-76.
597 Jordan, *Brothers-Rivals-Victors*, 506.
598 *Patton Papers*, 2:685.
599 Dwight Eisenhower, *Crusade in Europe* (Garden City, New York: Doubleday, 1948), 409.
600 *Paper Papers*, 2:685.
601 *Patton Papers*, 2:688.
602 *Patton Papers*, 2:654.

603 *Patton Papers*, 2:685; Toland, *Last Hundred Days*, 371.
604 Quotes from D'Este, *Eisenhower*, 691.
605 Robert Murphy, *Diplomat Among Warriors* (Garden City, New York: Doubleday, 1964), 254.
606 Quotes from D'Este, *Eisenhower*, 692.
607 Bradley, *A Soldier's Story* (New York: Henry Holt, 1951), 536.
608 D'Este, *Eisenhower*, 694.
609 Patton, *War As I Knew It*, 326–27.
610 D'Este, *Patton*, 724, 923 footnote 75.
611 Patton, *War As I Knew It*, 331.
612 Patton, *War As I Knew It*, 331.
613 Doubler, *Closing with the Enemy*, 75.
614 US Department of the Army, Office of the Adjutant General, Statistical and Accounting Branch, *Army Battle Casualties and Nonbattle Deaths in World War II, Final Report, 7 December 1941–31 December 1946* (1 June 1952), 84–85; William Mulligan (ed.), *Neuropsychiatry in World War II*, 2 vols. (Washington: Department of the Army, Office of the Surgeon General, 1973), 2:286.
615 Hanson, *Second World Wars*, 214–15, 217, 222–24.
616 Patton, *War As I Knew It*, 331; Province, *Patton's Third Army*, 280–82; Mullins, *Neuropsychiatry in World War II*, 286–88.
617 Hirshon, *Patton*, 635.
618 Ladislas Fargo, *The Last Days of Patton* (New York: McGraw-Hill, 1981).
619 *Patton Papers*, 2:736.
620 *Patton Papers*, 2:727.
621 *Patton Papers*, 2:750.
622 *Patton Papers*, 2:722–23.
623 *Patton Papers*, 2:698-99.
624 *Patton Papers*, 2:711–12.
625 *Patton Papers*, 2:712.
626 *Patton Papers*, 2:748.
627 Michael Neiberg, *Potsdam: The End of World War II and the Remaking of Europe* (New York: Basic Books, 2015).
628 *Patton Papers*, 2:731.
629 *Patton Papers*, 2:583.
630 Richard Frank, *Downfall: The End of the Imperial Japanese Empire* (New York: Penguin, 2001).
631 John Ellis, *World War II: A Statistical Survey for All the Combatants* (New York: Facts On File, 1993), 253–54.
632 *Patton Papers*, 2:732-33.
633 *Patton Papers*, 2:700-01.
634 *Patton Papers*, 2:749.
635 *Patton Papers*, 2:738.
636 *Patton Papers*, 2:770-72, 774–78, 778–79.
637 *Patton Papers*, 2:782–83.
638 *Patton Papers*, 2:818–19.
639 *Patton Papers*, 2:820.
640 *Patton Papers*, 2:826.
641 D'Este, *Patton*, 796.
642 William Nester, *World of War: A History of American Warfare from Jamestown to the War on Terror* (New York: Stackpole Books, 2024).
643 *Patton Papers*, 2:680.

644 Porter Williamson, *General Patton's Principles for Life & Leadership* (Tucson: Management and Systems Consultants, 2009), 30–31.
645 Eisenhower, *Crusade in Europe*, 82.
646 Eisenhower, *Crusade in Europe*, 82, 176.
647 *Patton Papers*, 1:4.
648 Dwight Eisenhower, *Crusade in Europe* (Garden City, New York: Doubleday, 148), 181.
649 Bradley, *A General's Life*, 98, 183; D'Este, *Patton*, 525.
650 *Patton Papers*, 2:723.
651 Hirshon, *Patton*, 701.
652 Bradley, *A General's Life*, 139.
653 Bradley, *A General's Life*, 464.
654 Both quotes from D'Este, *Patton*, 755.
655 *Patton Papers*, 2:654.

INDEX